Risk-Based Investment Management in Practice

Global Financial Markets series

Global Financial Markets is a series of practical guides to the latest financial market tools, techniques and strategies. Written for practitioners across a range of disciplines it provides comprehensive but practical coverage of key topics in finance covering strategy, markets, financial products, tools and techniques and their implementation. This series will appeal to a broad readership, from new entrants to experienced practitioners across the financial services industry, including areas such as institutional investment; financial derivatives; investment strategy; private banking; risk management; corporate finance and M&A, financial accounting and governance, and many more.

Titles include:

Daniel Capocci
THE COMPLETE GUIDE TO HEDGE FUNDS AND HEDGE FUND STRATEGIES

Frances Cowell
RISK-BASED INVESTMENT MANAGEMENT IN PRACTICE 2nd Edition

Guy Fraser-Sampson
INTELLIGENT INVESTING
A Guide to the Practical and Behavioural Aspects of Investment Strategy

Michael Hünseler
CREDIT PORTFOLIO MANAGEMENT
A Practitioner's Guide to the Active Management of Credit Risks

Ross K. McGill
US WITHHOLDING TAX
Practical Implications of QI and FATCA

David Murphy
OTC DERIVATIVES, BILATERAL TRADING AND CENTRAL CLEARING
An Introduction to Regulatory Policy, Trading Impact and Systemic Risk

Gianluca Oricchio
PRIVATE COMPANY VALUATION
How Credit Risk Reshaped Equity Markets and Corporate Finance Valuation Tools

Andrew Sutherland and Jason Court
THE FRONT OFFICE MANUAL
The Definitive Guide to Trading, Structuring and Sales

Michael C. S. Wong and Wilson F. C. Chan (*editors*)
INVESTING IN ASIAN OFFSHORE CURRENCY MARKETS
The Shift from Dollars to Renminbi

Global Financial Markets series
Series Standing Order ISBN: 978–1137–32734–5

You can receive future titles in this series as they are published by placing a standing order. Please contact your bookseller or, in case of difficulty, write to us at the address below with your name and address, the title of the series and the ISBN quoted above.

Customer Services Department, Macmillan Distribution Ltd, Houndmills, Basingstoke, Hampshire RG21 6XS, England

---

Risk-Based Investment Management in Practice

2nd Edition

Frances Cowell

palgrave
macmillan

First published 2013 by
PALGRAVE MACMILLAN

Palgrave Macmillan in the UK is an imprint of Macmillan Publishers Limited, registered in England, company number 785998, of Houndmills, Basingstoke, Hampshire RG21 6XS.

Palgrave Macmillan in the US is a division of St Martin's Press LLC, 175 Fifth Avenue, New York, NY 10010.

Palgrave Macmillan is the global academic imprint of the above companies and has companies and representatives throughout the world.

Palgrave® and Macmillan® are registered trademarks in the United States, the United Kingdom, Europe and other countries.

ISBN: 978–1–137–34639–1

This book is printed on paper suitable for recycling and made from fully managed and sustained forest sources. Logging, pulping and manufacturing processes are expected to conform to the environmental regulations of the country of origin.

A catalogue record for this book is available from the British Library.

A catalog record for this book is available from the Library of Congress.

Contents

List of Tables, Figures and Examples

Tables

Figures

Examples

Preface

As an investment manager in Australia before the days of risk models, it often intrigued me that stock prices often did not behave as expected, for example gold stock prices seemed disconnected from the price of gold itself, so holding them in the portfolio did not necessarily give the exposure that might have been expected.

The explanation of course is that gold stocks include prospectors as well as producers, many of which hedge their future production in order to protect themselves from volatility in the price of gold. They thereby dampen or even cancel the relationship with the price of the underlying metal. Many commodities producers are similarly unresponsive to the price of their respective commodities because they sell their produce through long term, fixed price contracts, and so are insensitive to fluctuations in the spot price.

Before the days of risk models, the relationship between commodity stocks and their commodities could be estimated only through laborious and error prone analysis of company reports and broker research. A good risk model can tell you in a few seconds.

This meant in effect that, as an investment manager I often misunderstood the risk exposures in my own portfolio. How therefore, could I hope to achieve my target returns, except mainly by chance?

Before the days of reliable risk measurement, this problem was of course very common. What is surprising is how frequently it still happens that investment managers understand their portfolios less well than they think they do.

In a dealing room I once visited was a poster shouting: 'No pain, no gain!' Clearly the aim was to encourage aggressive risk taking. But it intrigued me that it seemed to equate risk with losses – of other people's money, of course. Nowhere was there evidence of any value placed on objective evaluation of exactly how the risk/losses were to result in gains.

Until relatively recently, risk management was typically regarded as a supporting act to investment managers, largely confined to generating risk analyses and reports (it sometimes still is). Yet of the two, the risk manager's job, if done well, is the more intrinsically interesting and intellectually demanding. While the investment manager seeks out sources of return hidden in valuations of individual securities, the risk manager seeks ways to harness the investment managers' insights so they are not swamped by unintentional risk and in doing so, ensures that the whole is worth at least as much as the sum of its parts.

While simple risk management is mostly invisible, effective risk based investment management, which distinguishes calculated from incidental risks, adds value continuously and visibly.

In writing this book I have sought to expand on the difference between the two, and show how the value added by effective risk management can be crystalized.

The aim is to help investors ask the right questions of investment managers and to make sense of the answers. As well as investors, this will benefit any non-financial professional who is interested in a serious explanation of how risk management works, how it sometimes fails and how it can add value in the form of materially enhanced investment performance.

Any book about risk-based investment management can hardly avoid going into some detail about how risk is modelled and measured and the assumptions and work-arounds that are necessary for any practical application. Conscious that the details can seem daunting to a non-financial reader, I have sought to avoid jargon as much as possible. Where it cannot be avoided, I have tried to make the explanation intuitive.

Inevitably this brings the reader face-to-face with CAPM, the Nobel Prize winning insight of Harry Markowitz, who is widely regarded as the father of Modern Portfolio Theory (MPT). There are many criticisms of CAPM, many of them justified but, as Winston Churchill observed in the House of Commons in 1947: 'Democracy is the worst form of government, except for all those others that have been tried from time to time'[1], even tenacious adherents to MPT (of which I am one), might say something similar about CAPM.

At the very least there is a benefit in working with the devil you know. The longevity and sheer tractability of CAPM means it has been tested continuously for several decades in academia and by practitioners, so its limitations are well understood.

Many, if not most alternatives to CAPM revert to pre-1952 methodologies. This prompts the question: 'If we did not have CAPM, would we have to invent it?' and the answer: 'Yes, because we didn't and so we did.' The relationship between commodity stocks and commodities illustrates that.

Most people with no investment experience will tell you that you can't achieve investment returns without taking risks – preferably calculated risks – and ask if managing calculated risk isn't what investment management is about. I agree, but would add that that it is about not only managing calculated risks, but also eliminating unnecessary risks and knowing how to tell the difference. This book aims to confirm this common sense observation and elaborate on how it works in practice.

---

1 http://wais.stanford.edu/Democracy/democracy_DemocracyAndChurchill(090503).html

Acknowledgements

The biggest thank you is to my colleagues at R-Squared Risk Management, with whom I have worked both as colleague and as their client for more than two decades, and from whom I have learned – and continue to learn – so much.

My other teachers are my clients, who continue to challenge me with new investment problems and new perspectives on old problems.

The other big contributors to this book are my past colleagues, who, over the decades have corrected me, encouraged me and prodded me; and who provided the material in the case studies.

One feels spoiled by the abiding readiness of Wikipedia to help with fact-checking and supplementary research, making possible in minutes or hours what would, only a few years ago, have taken days. 'If we didn't have Wikipedia, would we have to invent it?'

FactSet and R-Squared Risk Management have been more than generous with supporting data and analyses, and have been a source of both practical help and encouragement.

Part 1

Introduction

1
Introduction

Investment management is one of the few highly paid professions for which no formal qualification is universally recognized. Yet few people would dismiss the responsibilities of investment managers as simple or trivial. Even evaluating the quality of their work is complex and inexact.

Professional investment management is relatively recent and for the first half of the twentieth century was confined to a limited range of investment techniques and instruments. That started to change in the second half of the century: financial instruments have proliferated and become more complex and markets have become more volatile, for example.

Yet derivatives were used in the Middle East in ancient times, in the markets in Rotterdam in the sixteenth and seventeenth centuries and in the USA during the 1930s. With inferior information and non-existent supervision and regulation, many of these early investments carried risks that would be unthinkable today.

Markets appear more volatile now than they used to be – but there has never been a time when investments did not sometimes go wrong, because there was never a time when people were infallible. Soundness of judgement has always been subject to compromise; alchemy was once regarded as a trusted mainstream science. Before the invention of the telegraph, markets would swing violently on rumours during wars. Investors from time to time seemed to behave irrationally, giving rise to investment 'bubbles', which burst – 'inevitably'. One need only be reminded of Tulipmania to realize that this is by no means a modern phenomenon. Many people today know somebody who became rich or poor, or both, as a result of the Poseidon boom in 1966.[1]

Markets are perceived to be more global nowadays, with large capital flows to and from emerging markets such as South America and South East Asia. In this trading environment, currencies can appear to be growing ever more volatile. Certainly international capital flows are greater nowadays than they were in the twentieth century, when most countries were subject to controls on international capital movements and very high transactions costs, but currencies were not necessarily less volatile. Prior to World War I, international investment was a major source of wealth to the economies of the Old World. The South Sea Bubble, the Dutch East India Company and the British venture that followed it are some examples. The very purpose of Columbus' voyage was to seek access to new markets and investment opportunities in East Asia. The Romans accumulated vast investments outside their home country, trading in places as far away as Africa and South East Asia. It is true that money moves about the globe much faster now than it used to, but so do goods – and people.

Some major changes have occurred however. One is that investments are much more widely held than even a few decades ago. In most western countries, investors now come from all backgrounds. People who grew up in developed countries after World War II, rich and poor alike, have collectively accumulated vast sums of personal savings, either privately or in company or government sponsored pension funds, mutual and trust funds and elsewhere. Investments are no longer the preserve of the very wealthy. Since these investments will, for the majority of investors, one day be their primary source of income, risk control and accountability are more important than ever before. The average investor has a fairly low tolerance for losing money and, because there are now large numbers of 'average' investors who vote, governments take an increasingly active interest in seeing that things do not go too horribly wrong. This 'democratization' of investment management is driving the imperative for greater accountability and risk control.

Another important difference between these and earlier decades is the way in which advances in technology have increased the amount of available information and transformed the way it is used and transmitted. The communications revolution speeds up funds flow around the world, sometimes even challenging governments and monetary authorities to keep up with appropriate policy responses.

The ability to analyse data in bulk encouraged the development of new ways of applying it to gain insights into the behaviour of investments. Thus we see an increasing number of investment modelling techniques, based on advanced mathematics, which are not immediately comprehensible to many investors.

The purpose of this book is to examine how investment theory developed since the middle of the twentieth century has improved understanding of the relationship between risk and investment outcomes, and how this understanding is used to select investment portfolios. This chapter gives an overview of some of the issues that usually determine investment management objectives and precede the investment selection process.

Table 1.1 Typical investment management process

Define fund structure	Pension, mutual, trust, other Defined benefit or defined contribution Open or closed pooled funds Domicile and tax status The investment consultant
Define investment strategy	Risk and return The strategy benchmark Risk tolerance How many investment managers? Specialist or balanced? Investment universe Permitted investments Currency management
Design mandates	Define mandate specific benchmarks Define risk tolerance
Select investment managers	Qualifications and experience Service level Sensible processes Fees
Evaluate investment managers	Scrutinize both good and bad performance

A typical investment management process might look something like Table 1.1

Defining the investment fund structure

Individual investors may choose to do their own investing, by purchasing stocks and bonds or investing in specialist funds, trusts or investment companies on their own behalf, or they may follow the advice of their stockbroker. To accommodate tax or other legal considerations they may choose to engage a financial planner or tax expert. At the other end of the spectrum are investors entrusting their savings to professional investors, usually large institutional investors, such as mutual funds, pension funds or insurance companies, who typically provide a package of research, investment strategy, structure and administration.

Many investors invest in small and medium-sized pension funds and other pooled funds. These funds make use of a mixture of external and in-house advice for tax and economic analysis. Because different kinds of investment funds can cater to different fiduciary and tax requirements and constraints, the investor is usually faced with enough choice of investment funds to ensure a reasonable fit with his or her investment requirements.

For pension funds, mutual funds, trust funds, investment companies and other pooled funds, how investments are structured depends on the objectives and constraints of the majority of investors. Issues that are usually taken into account when devising investment structure for a fund are:

- The expected investment horizon.
- Cash flow and other liquidity requirements.
- Domicile and tax status.
- Minimum investment required.
- Any special ethical or legal constraints?

The investment horizon can range from a few months to many years. For example, pension funds tend to have long investment horizons, reflecting the expected length of the working and retirement lives of their members, while mutual and trust funds generally have short horizons, reflecting investors' preference to trade in and out of them regularly.

Liquidity requirements can be driven by the membership profile, as in the case of mature pension funds, perceived market demand or tax status. The question of income versus capital growth tends to be closely aligned with the tax status of the fund, and this in turn affects the choice of domicile.

Many funds stipulate minimum investment amounts, both for initial investment in the fund, and for subsequent investment and withdrawal. The purpose of these limitations is usually to contain the manager's administration costs: the cost of administering a \$1000 investment is the same as a \$1 000 000 investment. But, because administration is usually charged to the investor as a percentage of the sum invested, minimum investment amounts are set to ensure that administration fees cover their cost to the investment manager.

Ethical funds have enjoyed increasing popularity in recent decades. Investors have the choice of avoiding financing arms manufacturers, tobacco companies and organizations engaging in environmentally contentious businesses. Sometimes legal limitations are imposed on the fund; for example, many corporate pension funds are prohibited from owning large interests in the company itself.

Fund structures

The main fund structure types are:

- Defined benefit or defined contribution.
- Open or closed.

Defined benefit, or final salary, funds assure the investor a fixed payment at the end of the investment period, that will be paid either as a lump sum or an annuity. The investor's contribution to the fund may vary over time as the fund's total value fluctuates according to varying returns on its investments. Managers of defined benefit funds usually maintain a reserve as part of the fund to smooth the impact of withdrawals and disappointing investment returns.

When reserves do get too high relative to the estimated future obligations of the fund, the fund manager may declare a 'contribution holiday' – a period during which investors pay lower contributions than normal, or none at all, until the reserves again reach an acceptable level. This practice runs the obvious risk of being unfair to some investors while providing a windfall to others. It can also give the impression that the fund is unacceptably volatile, and reduce fund member confidence in the fund's manager and administration. To reassure investors, some defined benefit funds build into in the investment strategy guarantees, either of capital or minimum returns.

The fund's future obligations, also known as its liabilities, are valued using a Discounted Cash Flow procedure (an example of which is given in Chapter 3). This means that the value of the fund depends not only on the nominal amount held in the fund and its reserves but also on its future obligations and the discount factor used to value them. Funds with long-dated liabilities can be very sensitive to changes in the discount factor. Many corporate pension funds use the company's borrowing rate as the discount factor, which can be much higher than the prevailing government bond rate. Many believe that this can be misleading, arguing that, as fund members believe their pension will be paid no matter what, such discount rates are too high; understating the liabilities of the fund and therefore over-stating the value of the fund. They maintain that the interest rates earned by government bonds would better reflect members' belief that their pension is a low-risk asset.

Defined contribution funds require the investor to pay in a fixed sum each week, month or year; although many defined contribution funds in fact allow members to contribute additional funds as the opportunity arises. Upon withdrawal from the fund, the investor receives both the principal paid in and the investment returns to the fund less fees and costs.

Defined contribution funds do not need to maintain reserves: each member's account grows according to his or her contributions plus or minus net investment returns. Of course it is not really that simple because each member's differing appetite for risk depends on such factors as his or her age and whether or not he or she has other assets and liabilities. When designing the investment strategy for a defined contribution fund, the fund's managers try to accommodate the majority of members' risk preferences, so members whose risk tolerance is very different from the majority may suffer from an inappropriate balance of risk and return. To accommodate different risk preferences, many plan sponsors offer target funds, whereby the investment mix adjusts automatically as the member's investment horizon shortens.

Defined contribution funds shift the risk of investment shortfall from the fund's manager to the investor/member. Because each member's account is in effect an individual account, similar to a holding in a mutual fund, investors tend to compare the returns of their fund with those of other funds, and can hold the management accountable for any disappointing results. This comparison is often unfair since apparently comparable funds may be managed to different specifications, and so have a correspondingly different balance of risk and return. Many investors make the mistake of comparing their multi-asset class, balanced fund with the local share price index without fully appreciating that the inevitable difference in returns merely reflects the differences in risk profiles.

An **open fund** allows the investor to put money in and take it out at any time, simply by applying to the fund manager for new units or advising the manager of the intention to redeem units. Units are thus issued or redeemed at the fund's current market valuation, which is the sum of the market values of the fund's holdings.

A **closed fund** creates and issues its units at the inception of the fund, after which investors buy and sell them at prices determined by supply and demand. Closed funds are often listed on stock exchanges and traded in the same way as any other equity. Theoretically their market values should always be very close to the sum of the market value of the fund's holdings, but closed funds can exhibit surprising divergences between their theoretical unit price and their market price. This divergence can be driven by perceived scarcity of units in the fund, or anticipation of a sharp downturn in the market for the assets held by the fund. More often, the observed price divergence can reflect the cost of transacting the fund's underlying assets.

The role of the investment consultant

Consultants provide investment advice and a number of other services. For individual investors, they can help coordinate decisions regarding retirement savings, insurance and tax. For pension funds and other pooled funds, the consultant can provide the expertise necessary to administer and manage asset and liability structures, as well as legal and regulatory issues. An important function for defined benefit schemes is to provide estimates of the likely timing of contributions and withdrawals, thus forecasting the overall growth of the fund, ensuring a prudent balance of assets and liabilities and the most appropriate reserving policy. Many investment consultants also help choose the broad mix of assets for the fund, draw up investment management mandates, help select investment managers and monitor their on-going performance.

By providing a source of independent analysis and specialist advice, investment consultants can help pension plan managers and trustees manage the risks and responsibilities inherent in group funds. By following the advice of experts in the field of pension fund liabilities and assets, sponsors and trustees can demonstrate that they have sought the best solutions to these potentially difficult problems, and that they have taken all reasonable steps to ensure the success of the fund.

The consultant's contribution draws on strong analytic capabilities combined with often impressive research resources spanning extensive economic data about individual investment managers and funds, including past performance data, favoured investment processes, the quality and breadth of the skills of its investment personnel and the quality of its risk management.

The investment consultant should ideally be independent of both fund and managers, so how he or she is paid is important. Investment consultant fee bases vary of course, but many consultants are paid, as are lawyers and management consultants, by the hour; whereas some have fixed fees for services, rather like a doctor. Both have their advantages and disadvantages. Fixed fees for service may encourage the consultant to recommend services that are only marginally required. The benefit is that the consultant has the incentive to enhance his or her earnings capacity by continuously upgrading the range and quality of services on offer, encouraging innovation. Consultants who are paid by the hour generally perform services according to the investor's requirements, leaving the consultant little time and incentive to explore and research new ideas and approaches, which would be of ultimate benefit to the investor. The result, sometimes, is that the investor is directed toward investment options with which the consultant is familiar while other, perhaps more appropriate, investments may be overlooked.

The relationship between the investment consultant and the investor depends on confidence and trust. But although both confidence and trust are necessary to the success of the relationship, they may not by themselves be sufficient. The questions the investor might pose are:

- Does the consultant give the advice most suitable in view of the specific objectives and requirements of the investment fund?
- To what extent is the consultant adding value in terms of investment returns and risk control?
- To what extent is the consultant accountable for disappointing results?

The answers to the first two questions can be difficult to answer because it is impossible to say what the outcome would have been if another course of action had been followed. One solution is to examine the performance of other funds that use the same consultant. This can be a good idea, but the insights it can deliver are limited:

- Compared funds may not share the same investment objectives and limitations, and therefore provide little or no validity.
- The other funds may be reluctant to divulge what they consider to be confidential information.
- The results obtained by compared funds may have been due to luck rather than management.

Given the importance of the consultant's role in the fund's management, many fund managers would like some means of holding the consultant in some way accountable for the success of the fund. To this end, some funds have tried to evaluate the performance of consultants by hiring further independent advice: consultants to evaluate the consultants. This might highlight some particular strengths and weaknesses on the part of the consultant, but any quantification of the consultant's contribution is bound to be inexact.

The investment strategy

The investment objective of a fund is to meet its current and future liabilities given current and projected contributions. This is combined with economic projections to define the investment strategy, which is the single most important determinant of the success of the fund. The most important component of the strategy is how much risk it should take, where that risk should lie and how it should be defined.

Risk and return

Investment risk is probably the most misunderstood aspect of investment. Although tempting to think of risk as something to be minimized or eliminated, this ignores the primary objective of investment funds, which is to generate returns, often to meet anticipated liabilities. Eliminate the risk and you eliminate the possibility of returns.

The mix of risky and riskless assets determines the risk of the fund. In the simplest terms, the higher the ratio of risky to riskless assets in the fund, the riskier the fund will be. Risky assets are typically equities, long-term bonds and property, while short-term interest rate securities backed by a government or a government-backed issuer are usually thought of as riskless assets.

The fund's risk level should take account of the expected liabilities of the fund. In practice this means setting the fund's risk at a level that is consistent with the timing of projected demands. Investors with short investment horizons are generally more averse to risk than those able to weather periods of poor returns in order to achieve superior long-term gains. For example, a couple nearing retirement seeking a safe return for their life savings have clearly different requirements to, say, a single person in his or her late twenties investing a large sum from an unexpected inheritance for a long-term return.

The strategy benchmark

The output of the investment strategy is some long-term asset allocation, also known as strategy allocation, to be used as a benchmark for the purpose of constructing portfolios and evaluating the fund's performance. The long-term benchmark forms the backbone of the fund's structure. If it is not well specified, the fund will be in danger of earning insufficient returns to meet its liabilities or objectives, or of undertaking too much risk and thereby subjecting the fund to undue volatility for the welfare of its members. For defined benefits schemes the long-term benchmark is crucial to maintain the appropriate level of reserves.

Ideally the benchmark, or strategy allocation, should have the following characteristics:

- Efficiency: the benchmark should have an attractive balance of risk and return.
- Investability: the benchmark should include only assets that are available for purchase by the fund.
- Measurability: the total return of the benchmark should be readily available.
- Low cost: turnover and liquidity characteristics should be such that the cost of management is reasonable.
- Adequate breadth: the benchmark should have broad exposure to industries, sectors and countries to facilitate prudent diversification.

Defined contribution funds are often compared to the best performing fund and the median fund. This is more human than rational, as the best performers and the median funds are rarely the same funds, or even the same investment management firms, from one year to the next.

Some funds choose peer group funds as formal benchmarks. This has obvious appeal, in that it formalizes what happens anyway and ensures that the benchmark is both investable and achievable. Peer group benchmarks minimize the risk to the fund managers of delivering poor performance relative to competitors. This does not necessarily help the investor, because it also minimizes the chances of superior returns by building in popular investment biases. It can also build in a performance bias by adopting the consensus asset allocation from the last period, which may not be suitable for the investment horizon. It also takes no account of the fund's membership profile – and therefore its most suitable investment strategy.

Many funds augment their long-term, strategic asset allocation with short-term, tactical asset allocation. The short-term asset allocation is usually designed to exploit short-term return expectations that are different from the long-term expected outcome.

Risk tolerance

Probably the most important aspect of the short-term asset allocation is how far it is allowed to differ from the long-term benchmark. In general, the broader the tolerance for divergence from benchmark, the greater will be the range of return variation around that of the benchmark, and therefore the more likely the fund is to out-perform. If the differences are big enough and in the wrong direction, the fund may fail to meet its objectives. On the other hand, too tight a constraint prevents the fund from benefiting from short-term asset return forecasts that can deliver superior returns.

If the fund already has diminished reserves, a strategy imposing a minimum return may need to be applied until reserves are built up again. Such a strategy may use derivative instruments to deliver the desired result or it may be achieved with cleverly designed sequences of decision rules. Both approaches can allow participation in asset growth, with allowable minimum returns that may be slightly negative. Guaranteed minimum return portfolios always earn less than similar portfolios without the guarantee, with the difference reflecting the cost of the guarantee.

For investors who cannot tolerate any capital depletion, a capital guarantee may be needed. In effect this is simply a special case of a guaranteed minimum return strategy, where the minimum return is set to zero either in nominal or real (inflation adjusted) terms.

How many investment managers?

The number of investment managers to be employed depends mostly on how big the fund is in terms of assets. The advantage of having several investment managers is that it diversifies manager risk. Manager risk is the risk that a manager will fail to perform to specification, the fund breach a mandate, go bust, lose its most talented staff or in some other way seriously fail to meet the expectations of the investor. If the fund has employed ten managers, for example, and one disappoints, the overall damage is limited. If the fund has invested with only one manager, and something untoward happens, then it can suffer materially. To avoid this, many large pension funds employ dozens – even hundreds – of investment managers, which can be hard to manage. Too many managers can also have the effect of diluting the fund's carefully thought-out strategy, resulting in a bland, costly mix of investments that fails to meet its objectives.

Even relatively small funds often divide investment management between at least two or three managers, who may have common or very similar mandates. This method facilitates a meaningful comparison of performance, by which the fund managers can pose uniform questions to each manager, thus learning as much about why the funds perform as they do by observing the differences between responses as from the responses themselves. For example, two portfolio managers sharing the same mandate may consistently miss their target by a similar amount. This could indicate that the target return cannot be obtained without assuming unacceptable risk or breaching mandate restrictions. Another useful comparison is the level of transactions costs incurred by different portfolio managers for similar portfolios, which can highlight unnecessary turnover that benefits the investment manager but is costly to the investor.

But, as investment management fees are usually inversely related to the size of the mandate, a fund that is split between fewer managers is, other things being equal, less costly than if the same mandate is split between a larger number of managers.

Specialist versus balanced

Small to medium funds often specify balanced mandates as opposed to specialist ones. A balanced mandate is where the same investment manager both decides short-term asset allocation and manages individual asset class portfolios. Specialist managers, by contrast, manage individual asset classes, such as equities, domestic bonds, domestic property, international bonds and international equities.

The balanced investment management mandate is in some ways the simplest, because there is only one result to evaluate: either the manager is doing better than the benchmark or not. Cash flow management is relatively simple: advice of the funds flow is remitted to the manager who then invests the sum according to the current asset allocation of the fund. The managers need only ensure that the terms of the investment management mandate are respected. This simplicity can sometimes be a bit illusory however, because it is often hard to determine exactly where the investment manager is doing well, and where he or she may be under performing. Only rigorous analysis of performance can add insight into whether or not the investment manager has added value and can inform ways of improving future performance.

Another advantage of balanced mandates is that they can have lower management fees than a series of specialist mandates for a fund of the same size. For small to medium funds, the fee differential can be significant.

Even greater economies are achievable if the investor is willing to pool the fund's investment with others. This will work only if the benchmark asset allocation and risk profile of the pooled vehicle is the same as, or very similar to, that of the fund. If the asset allocation does not precisely match the fund's requirements, the 'gap' can often be filled using a derivatives overlay.

Most medium to large funds engage separate investment managers for asset allocation and the management of individual asset classes. The advantages of this are that:

- The fund manager can choose investment managers who have particular expertise in asset allocation and management of individual asset classes such as equities, bonds and so on, thus increasing the likelihood of superior overall returns.
- The level of manager risk is greatly reduced, as no single manager exerts a dominant effect on the outcome of the fund.
- Because each mandate is different, the value added by each manger is unlikely to cancel out that of any other manager.
- Attribution analysis is made simpler by separating asset allocation and each specialist asset class manager.
- The fund can fine-tune the mixture of active and passive management, and quantitative and traditional management, of physical assets.

For funds engaging specialist asset class managers, the choice for the fund managers becomes whether to conduct their own short-term asset allocation, probably with the help of their consultant, or to define an asset allocation mandate and hire a specialist manager with particular expertise in asset allocation.

The asset allocation manager usually does not manage physical assets for the fund, but simply determines the amount to be invested in each asset class. Once the mix of asset classes has been identified, individual asset class managers are informed of the amount they need to invest or divest in order to implement the short-term asset allocation.

Table 1.2 Investment structures: advantages and disadvantages

Investment structure	Advantages	Disadvantages
Balanced – one investment manager	Can minimize management fees Simplifies administration	Maximizes manager risk Evaluation and attribution of return are difficult Limited choice of asset classes
Balanced – multiple investment managers	Controls manager risk Allows comparison of manager performance	Potential that manager styles will cancel each other out Evaluation and attribution of return are difficult
Specialist investment mandates	Allows separation of asset allocation and security selection Asset allocation can be conducted by fund managers or specialist asset allocation managers Facilitates performance evaluation and attribution Investment manager styles less likely to cancel each other out Maximum choice and flexibility of asset classes	High cost, especially for small amounts under management More administrative complexity

Another way of doing this is to leave the sum invested with each asset class manager unchanged, typically at the level of the long-term benchmark asset allocation, and use derivative instruments to implement short-term, tactical asset allocation decisions. Such mandates are usually called asset allocation, tactical asset allocation (TAA) or derivatives overlay mandates. This approach has the benefit of greatly reducing the amount of physical assets being bought and sold, consequently reducing the regular transactions costs of the fund and improving the fund's performance. The advantages and disadvantages of each investment structure are summarized in Table 1.2.

The investment universe

The investment strategy should also specify what investments are permitted. The range of allowable investments is sometimes referred to as the investment universe. At its simplest, this could comprise a basic list of asset classes by name. The limitation is that, as new asset classes develop – for example, private equity and commodities trading funds – the list becomes out of date, consequently imposing unintentional constraints on the portfolios.

The investment universe often specifies some instrument criteria, such as listing on a recognized exchange or membership of a defined index. There may also be constraints such as minimum asset size or maximum size of ownership for a fund that invests in small companies.

The investment universe also usually specifies which investment instruments are allowed, including what kind of derivative instruments can be included, and for what purpose, such as risk control or liquidity management.

Currency management

If the fund is investing outside its home country, then the investment strategy should address how currency is to be treated. The main choices are:

- To assume foreign currency exposures equal the respective holdings of assets denominated in each currency.
- To hedge all foreign currency exposure back to base currency.
- To manage foreign currency as a separate asset class.

The investment management mandate

Having set the broad strategy of the fund so that asset appreciation and yield will meet likely calls on the fund and the level of risk is acceptable, the fund managers, usually with the help of the consultant, design the investment management mandate or mandates.

The investment management mandate describes the investment objectives and constraints of the investment manager. It specifies the investment universe, the benchmark, risk limits and return objectives, preferred investment processes and fees. It forms the basis of the contract between the fund and the investment manager.

Defining mandate specific benchmarks

Whether the investment mandate is for a balanced portfolio or a specialist asset class, defining the benchmark is an early step.

For balanced mandates and pure asset allocation mandates, the benchmark is usually the fund's long-term, or strategy, benchmark. For specialist asset class mandates, it is some representation of the asset class in question, such as a recognized share price index, for example the S&P500 of the FT Allshare, although the benchmark can be anything that delivers a rate of return. A benchmark for specialist asset class mandates should ideally have the following characteristics:

- It should meet the investment objectives of the fund. Sometimes this necessitates designing a customized benchmark.
- It should be investable. In other words the securities that make up the benchmark should be freely traded on a recognized exchange.
- Ideally it should permit the use of derivatives, at least for the purposes of liquidity management and periodic asset class reweighting, as they can reduce the cost of managing the fund and help target risk.
- Public quotation of the benchmark reduces ambiguity. While it is preferable to identify a benchmark that is quoted publicly, customized or less widely recognized benchmarks can work well provided their components are publicly quoted. This allows independent computation of benchmark performance by investor, investment manager and custodian; so avoiding confusion about the relative performance of the portfolio.

Defining risk targets and tolerances

Both return and risk are usually described in relative terms, that is, the target return is x per cent above the return to the benchmark; or the target risk is y per cent relative to the benchmark. The mandate may also set maximum acceptable levels of relative risk and minimum acceptable returns over a given period. For example, the maximum relative risk may be 3 per cent per annum, with a minimum allowed performance of 6 per cent per annum below benchmark for any rolling three-year period.

Investment managers naturally compare their own performance with that of their rivals. This is an understandable reaction when one considers how investment managers are rewarded. To illustrate, suppose a manager has a strong view regarding the prospects for a particular asset or group of assets. To exploit this view he or she needs to implement a portfolio that is quite different from both the benchmark position and those of other funds. Should this view prove to be correct, the happy investor – at least in theory – lauds him or her, and, if the performance continues, the investment manager should be rewarded with new clients.

But first it is necessary to convince the client and the market that this was good judgement, not just good luck, and that the high returns were not achieved at the cost of unacceptably high risk. The more unconventional the portfolio the more difficult it is to communicate its rationale and prospective benefits. On the other hand, if this unconventional looking portfolio suffers under-performance, even for a relatively short while, the costs to the investment manager can be enormous because he or she is alone in delivering poor returns. The prudent manager therefore shuns such portfolios and sticks to portfolio allocations that, although different from the benchmark, are not radically dissimilar from other managers. That way, everybody either gets it right together, or they get it wrong together; and the consequences for the investment manager of being wrong are significantly reduced.

Alternatively, if the investment manager is not confident of delivering superior returns, he or she will 'benchmark hug', that is to say keep the portfolio holdings close to those of the benchmark in order to avoid delivering disappointing returns. To avoid this, many fund managers stipulate both minimum and maximum risk tolerances in the investment mandate.

This is not new. J.M. Keynes observed the same phenomenon in *The General Theory*. Writing of the long-term investor:

> it is in the essence of his behaviour that he should be eccentric, unconventional and rash in the eyes of average opinion. If he is successful, that will only confirm the general belief in his rashness; and if in the short run he is unsuccessful, which is very likely, he will not receive much mercy. Worldly wisdom teaches us it is better for reputation to fail conventionally than to succeed unconventionally.[2]

When specifying specialist asset class mandates, there is an advantage in ensuring that each mandate differs significantly from each of the others. The best way to ensure this is by engaging only one manager per asset class, although this can increase manager risk. Where the fund has a number of managers devoted to the same asset class, it should take care to ensure that the mandates are distinct and do not overlap; for example, by specifying distinct sub-sectors within the asset class or different sources of risk and return. Similar mandates in parallel run the risk that the sources of superior returns being exploited by one manager are diluted or even cancelled out by the portfolio compositions of the others, resulting in an expensive index fund. Alternatively risks can compound, resulting in unmanaged risk.

Should portfolio protection or a guaranteed return be required, there are two ways in which it can be effected:

- The first is a pooled, balanced investment product, whereby the same manager is responsible for protection as well as management of individual asset classes.

- The second is by means of a specialist mandate that complements the rest of the fund.

The arguments that apply for balanced versus specialist also apply here, for example:

- Do the available pooled vehicles suit the objectives of the fund?
- Do the economies of specialist mandates suit those of the fund?
- Does the issue of manager risk warrant having separate mandates?
- How long is the portfolio protection required and, when it is no longer needed, can the same investment manager continue with a regular balanced mandate or will a new balanced manager be sought?

Most mandates impose a limit on how much of the fund can remain uninvested. The uninvested portion of a fund is the portion held in liquid, low risk assets, as new cash is allocated to the fund, dividends are earned by it and so on. The lower this limit, the better to ensure that the fund's asset allocation strategy is not compromised by too large a holding in low-yielding money market instruments.

Manager selection

To select and engage investment managers, the consultant usually prepares, from his or her manager research database, a list of investment managers that have already been screened for suitability for the job.

Some questions usually asked of each investment manager are:

- How many other, similar mandates does the investment manager currently manage?
- What has been the performance of these portfolios?
- What range of service can the investment manager provide?
- What are the investment manager's fees and charges?

The fund manager is usually also interested to know something about the people employed by the investment manager, such as their general level of qualification and experience, how long they have worked for that investment manager and what backup is provided in the event that they leave or become ill.

The investment manager's previous performance usually gives much less information than many people realize, because past performance by investment managers rarely provides any indication of future performance. Much academic research has been devoted to this, with some studies showing that there can be persistence in relative performance, others showing no relationship and yet others showing that the relationship is often negative; in other words tomorrow's best performers can be today's worst performers, and vice-versa. Indeed, there are intuitive explanations for all three results.

There are plenty of reasons why investment managers' performance may not persist, including:

- As skilled personnel leave and are replaced with people with even slightly different skill sets the relative strengths and weaknesses of the investment management company change. When this happens, the investment manager's approach can change to exploit the new talent.
- When members of senior investment staff leave the company, their replacements nearly always seek to impose some modification of the investment management process. Even if this is only a change of emphasis, it can impact on investment returns.
- Investment managers adapt their approaches to asset selection, either in response to changed market or economic conditions, or because the old strategy was no longer working.
- The investment manager may simply decide that the existing approach, although delivering acceptable results, can benefit from modernization or improvement.
- Many investment styles deliver diminishing returns to scale, either because they depend on an asset type that is characterized by limited supply, such as small stocks, or because successful strategies attract more investment, raising prices of the assets they favour and thereby lowering the subsequent returns. Successful strategies also attract imitators, with the same effect on prices and returns.

What the investor would also like to know is: 'to what extent is the investment manager's performance due to chance, and how much is management?' There is no way to answer this definitively, since it is as easy to be wrong for the right reasons as right for the wrong reasons; it is important that the investment manager's account of his or her approach to asset selection makes sense and the reasoning behind it is consistent and clear. Possibly one of the best ways to judge the likely competence of an investment manager is to look for evidence of clarity, consistency and commonsense in their explanation of how they select and manage investments, and why they do it that way.

A disciplined approach to aligning sources of risk to sources of expected return and a clear exit policy – for realizing gains and containing relative losses – is usually a good indication of a robust and consistent investment process.

Portfolio evaluation

A primary aim is to find out how much the portfolio result was due to management and how much due to luck.

Many investors make the mistake of scrutinizing poor performance and paying little attention to good performance. Superior overall returns very often camouflage potential problems. For example, the investment returns may be due to exceptional results in one asset class, while the contribution from other asset classes and the asset allocation are negligible or negative. Concentrations in returns are due to concentration of risk, which can render the portfolio vulnerable to extreme losses should market conditions change suddenly. Asking the question 'why has the fund done well?' therefore is as important as asking 'why has it not done well?'

Example 1.1 is a simplified illustration of portfolio evaluation, showing the contribution to return from short-term asset allocation compared to what would have been earned from the long-term asset allocation. For the purpose of simplification, we assume that the asset class actually returned is the same as the asset class benchmark return in each case. In practice this would happen only if all the asset classes were managed as index funds. Actual return allocation reports give much more detail, as we will see in Chapter 18.

In Example 1.1 the manager has successfully foreseen strong performance in domestic and international equities markets and relatively weak returns in domestic and international bonds, to add 2.37 per cent (12.35–9.98) to the fund's return. Asset class contributions to return are

Example 1.1 Assessing the value of tactical asset allocation

Asset class	Asset class return %	Long-term allocation %	Short-term allocation %	Contribution to return %
Domestic equities	13.00	30.00	50.00	0.61
Domestic bonds	6.00	25.00	15.00	0.40
International equities	18.00	20.00	25.00	0.40
International bonds	3.50	20.00	5.00	0.97
Domestic cash	5.50	5.00	5.00	0.00
		100.00	100.00	
Total return achieved		9.98	12.35	2.37

calculated here as the difference between the short-term allocation and the long-term allocation multiplied by the difference between the asset class return and the return to the benchmark overall. For example:

$$0.61\% = (50.00\% - 30.00\%) \times (13.00\% - 9.98\%)$$

The role of the custodian

Custodians are usually subsidiaries of very large banks because of the very high barriers to entry, mostly in the form of the cost of establishing and managing the necessary infrastructure. Custodians perform a number of functions. They:

- Authorize payments and receipts for purchases and sales of assets, and the subsequent transfer of funds from and to the right bank accounts.
- Receive dividends, coupons and other distributions.
- Provide monthly, quarterly and annual statements of portfolio holdings, transactions reports, currency exposures, derivatives exposures and tax reports as required by the fund's managers.
- Provide portfolio valuations as required by the fund's managers.
- Retain custody of all documentation supporting ownership of the assets held by the fund. The custodian takes physical possession of share certificates, for example.
- Provide return reporting for each portfolio as required. Some custodians also provide return attribution analysis.

Custodian fee schedules are often based on the number of transactions, with some transactions commanding much higher fees than others. Differential custodian fees between securities and instruments can affect the outcome of an investment strategy, by favouring particular investment strategies, instruments and investment destinations over others.

Many large custodians also provide stock lending services. Stock lending is where funds expecting to hold assets for a long period, seek to augment their investment returns by renting out their share certificates or other evidence of ownership of physical assets; for example, to investors who need to borrow share certificates in order to provide collateral for derivatives positions, or to meet settlement conditions for securities sold in order to profit from a subsequent fall in price. The returns earned by lending share certificates vary according to supply and demand as well as the prevailing short-term interest rates. In return for accepting the 'rent', the lender accepts the risk that the borrower may not be able to return the stock when required, so there is also an element of counterparty risk.

The custodian as stock lending intermediary has the advantage of knowing exactly where to find large quantities of long-term holdings of stocks, and so will be a natural first call for would-be borrowers.

Fund administration

The administrator takes care of fund accounting. This can include independent valuation of the fund, but is mainly concerned with who owns how much of it. This entails keeping records of contributions and withdrawals by members, and purchases and sales of units by investors, as well as fund distributions. Like custodians, fund administrators rely on heavy investment in systems to process transactions by investors and members as speedily as possible.

Governance

An independent oversight board, of trustees or directors, takes responsibility for the smooth functioning of investment management, custodian and administrator as well as appointing auditors and independent trustees as necessary. The board of trustees or the board of directors is responsible to the investors or members of the fund as well as to the regulatory authority if the fund is regulated.

Boards typically comprise five to eight individuals, some chosen by the investment manager, although boards increasingly seek independent members. Ideally, board members are multi-disciplinary, covering a range of investment, risk, marketing, legal and accounting skills in order to ensure the most effective scrutiny of the fund's performance and compliance with all terms of its trust deed or prospectus.

The fund structure, the strategy benchmark, target return and risk tolerances, together with the investment universe and treatment of foreign currency exposures provide the framework within which the portfolio selection is carried out.

Endnotes

1. A fairly comprehensive account is given in *Extraordinary Popular Delusions and the Madness of Crowds*, 1841. Also see Ferdinand Braudel, *Civilisation and Capitalism 15th–18th Centuries*. 1981–1984.
2. Keynes, J.M., *The General Theory of Employment Interest and Money*, N.Y.: Harcourt, Brace and Company, 1936. pp. 157–158.

2
Risk-Based Portfolio Selection – An Overview

We hire investment managers to earn active returns that we cannot achieve ourselves. The investment manager does this by taking risks. You do not pay your investment manager simply not to lose your money: that is what banks are for.

Anyone can take risks, but only calculated risks are likely to earn active returns. Calculating and targeting risk requires skill. Investment selection skill is how investment managers differentiate themselves from their competitors. Risk-based investment management is the process by which the skill of the investment manager is harnessed to maximize its potential to give active returns.

Specialist portfolio selection skill can reside in asset allocation or security selection within asset classes. Within asset classes skill can be concentrated in particular niches, such as small stocks or high-yield assets.

Risk-based investment management seeks to align risk with sources of expected return, by allocating risk where the likelihood of it resulting in positive return is greatest, which means aligning portfolio risk with the available portfolio selection skills.

Modern portfolio theory provides the framework by which sources of portfolio risk can be quantified so that they can be aligned with the available portfolio selection skill.

This chapter gives an overview of why and how risk-based portfolio selection improves on the outcome that results from simply buying the stocks you like. It discusses:

- The implications of stock by stock portfolio selection.
- Risk-based portfolio selection.
- Asset allocation.
- Scenario analysis.

Stock by stock portfolio selection

Until about the turn of the twentieth century, most investors tended to select their portfolios from the opportunities presented to them through word-of-mouth or local media. Often this 'universe' was limited to local share and bond issues augmented by sometimes high-profile 'new world' projects. Investors often sought to diversify risks where possible and to offset their risks using derivatives, but for many investors the scope for diversification and hedging was limited.

With a relatively limited range of choices, investors selected their portfolios 'bottom-up', meaning that they added investments to their portfolios as they became available. This methodology persists, where managers have particular familiarity with individual companies that can deliver extra return from early purchase and sale of rising and falling stocks respectively.

Bottom-up security selection (which in principle can apply to any asset class but in practice is most often found in domestic equity portfolios and portfolios of non-traded assets, such as direct property and direct equity) selects only assets that the investment manager is very familiar with. Sector, industry and country exposures are simply the resulting sum of the exposures of the assets in the portfolio. They can be allowed to vary substantially from a benchmark index or comparator portfolio, if one is used, although in practice most bottom-up portfolios do have some exposure constraints.

Bottom-up selection is, in a sense, the purest form of stock-picking, with a great deal of intuitive appeal, being driven by the fundamental prospects for each investment.

Detailed understanding of individual assets ensures that the investment is held only while superior returns are known to be likely. Should some event threaten future returns, the bottom-up manager can be expected to be among the first to spot it and reduce the portfolio's exposure accordingly.

Despite its intuitive appeal, there are a number of potential limitations with stock by stock portfolio selection: These include:

- Even with a large team of analysts, an investment management firm can maintain research in only a relatively small number of assets compared with the available universe of investments. Being confined to a small range of stocks, many investment opportunities are inevitably missed.
- If the portfolio is benchmarked to an asset class index and has overweight positions in some stocks compared to that benchmark, it

follows that it must have underweight positions in other securities compared to that benchmark. In economic terms, this is the same as being sold short[1] those securities, relative to the benchmark. Since those securities are mostly those that the investment manager is not familiar with, they represent economic exposures, or risks, that are not well understood by the manager, and therefore risks that are not being managed.
- The investment management firm can be dangerously dependent on a few good analysts or investment managers, who might leave the firm and even set up in competition.
- The manager's expertise can be very concentrated in a few industries or regions, which can result in systematic biases in the portfolio that are unrelated to any views of the investment manager.

Limiting the range of investment opportunities limits the scope of the portfolio to earn active returns. From the risk manager's perspective, another limitation of pure bottom-up selection is that risk management is necessarily exogenous: in effect an add-on to, rather than integrated into, the investment selection process. When risk controls are applied separately to the portfolio selection process they often damp down the investment manager's preferred positions, thereby imposing a drag on performance.

Risk-based portfolio selection

More robust risk control is achieved by selecting the portfolio from the risk perspective. Rather than ask the question: how risky is this portfolio? Or even: how risky is the portfolio if x were to happen? Risk-based investment selection:

- Distinguishes between the weight of assets in the portfolio and the portfolio's exposure to them, which are usually not the same thing.
- Quantifies how much assets and common factors contribute to portfolio return variation, taking into account the interactions between them.
- Allows the investment manager to judge if the risks in the portfolio are justified by the expected returns they will bring.

Exposures then can be allocated to assets and factors that the investment manager is confident will result in positive returns and away from assets and factors where he or she is less confident of a positive contribution.

Example 2.1 shows a portfolio's exposure to asset classes and how each contributes to portfolio level risk.

Example 2.1 Exposure and contribution to risk

Asset	Portfolio weight %	Asset class portfolio exposure to its sector %	Exposure to sector %	Contribution to portfolio variance	Contribution to portfolio variance %
Domestic equities	35.00	1.05	36.75	34.86	29.07
Domestic bonds	20.00	0.95	19.00	0.80	0.67
International equities	25.00	1.07	26.75	59.80	49.86
International bonds	15.00	0.91	13.65	24.48	20.41
Domestic cash	5.00	0.00	0.00	0.00	0.00
Total	100.00			10.95	100.00

Example 2.1 shows that the portfolio has an exposure of 36.75 per cent to domestic equities and that this 36.75 per cent exposure contributes 29.07 per cent to the portfolio's most likely return variation of 10.95 per cent per year. Its exposure to international equities is lower, at 26.75 per cent, but this represents nearly half of the likely return variation of the portfolio. To deliver a positive overall outcome, both asset classes must perform well over the investment horizon.

Note that the portfolio's exposure to each asset class differs from its weighting, or monetary allocation. This reflects the fact that individual asset class portfolios are actively managed, so the assets in them are different from the composition of the asset class itself. It also reflects the interactions due to correlations between asset class returns.

Within this framework, the volatility of individual asset class portfolios is, by itself, relatively unimportant, as volatility in individual portfolios can be smoothed substantially with calculated diversification. Unnecessary sources of risk can be diversified or hedged so that they no longer represent a source of vulnerability.

Asset allocation

With a wide range of investment opportunities the investor needs some way to order and categorize them so as to give a coherent structure to the portfolio selection process and ensure effective diversification. Most multi-asset class portfolios are selected using a two-stage process whereby investments are first allocated by type of investment (equity versus bond, for example) and geography; with individual assets within asset classes selected separately.

By separating selection between asset classes and selection within them, the investor can allocate risk according to the available portfolio selection skill.[2] For example, if the investment manager is confident that he or she has identified a talented asset allocation manager, then a relatively aggressive mandate can be awarded to that manager. If, on the other hand, a suitably skilled manager of international equities cannot be found, then that asset class can be managed in an indexed portfolio. The eventual mix of asset class mandates can include:

- Smoothed return, protected and structured funds.
- Passively-managed, including indexed, asset class portfolios.
- Conventional, actively-managed asset class portfolios.
- Absolute return, 'pure alpha' portfolios and hedge funds.
- Smoothed return, protected and structured funds.

In other words, within asset classes there is a range of portfolio types giving the investor scope to allocate the amount of risk that is merited by the available skill in each asset class, which is the aim of risk-based portfolio selection at the asset allocation level.

It improves outcomes in at least two ways:

1. By providing the framework to select from very large universes of investments, risk-based investment selection can effectively expand the investment opportunity set, thereby increasing potential sources of positive return. By providing a tractable framework for thinking about sources of risk, investors can take calculated risk in, or achieve more effective diversification with, for example, alternative asset classes, such as venture capital, private equity, private debt, securitized assets like credit card receivables, mortgages, an artist's future music royalties, commodities funds, emerging country infrastructure projects and hedge funds.
2. By helping to match risk with sources of return, unwanted risk can be eliminated without necessarily compromising the investment manager's preferred positioning. This effect is to reduce overall volatility and allow more risk to be assumed where it will add to return.

Scenario analysis

Scenario analysis is widely used to help allocate to different asset classes. It works by defining a number of 'scenarios' and then assigning a probability to each, with the sum of the probabilities equal to 100 per cent. Each scenario represents a set of events that could occur together, such as high returns to equities, low interest rates or a depreciating currency. There might, for example, be five scenarios, ranging from very high growth to economic meltdown. A simplified example set of scenarios is set out in Example 2.2.

The analysis in Example 2.2 shows that the most likely outcome for this portfolio weighting is a return of 11.05 per cent, while the scenario weighted outcome is a 10.85 per cent return. In this case, the most likely outcome can be significantly improved by increasing the weighting to international equities at the expense of domestic equities, but this would in turn reduce the returns to be gained if scenarios one or two turn out to be more accurate predictions.

Scenario analyses typically have many more rows than are shown here, because portfolios usually comprise more asset classes and the scenario analysis usually allows several assumptions with respect to currency pairs, inflation, commodity prices and short-term and long-term interest rates. There may be more than one table, too, to accommodate short-term, medium-term and long-term forecasts.

Scenario analyses are often regarded as a good way of integrating asset class risk into the asset allocation decision. While superficially intuitive,

Example 2.2 Scenario analysis

	Probability	**10%**	**15%**	**50%**	**20%**	**5%**	**100%**
Asset	**Portfolio weight**	**Scenario 1**	**Scenario 2**	**Scenario 3**	**Scenario 4**	**Scenario 5**	**Average**
	%	%	%	%	%	%	%
Domestic equities	35.00	45.00	22.00	13.00	5.00	–20.00	14.30
Domestic bonds	20.00	4.00	8.00	6.00	–2.00	–12.00	3.60
International equities	25.00	12.00	20.00	18.00	25.00	–10.00	17.70
International bonds	15.00	–3.00	4.00	3.50	4.50	–4.00	2.75
Domestic cash	5.00	3.00	5.00	5.50	6.50	12.00	5.70
Total	100.00	19.25	15.15	11.05	8.60	–11.90	10.85

scenario analysis in practice can be error-prone because it embeds a number of assumptions which may not be realistic; for example:

- It frequently equates portfolio weight with exposure to an asset class, which is usually not the same thing.
- It assumes that the scenarios presented represent all feasible outcomes.
- It assumes that the possible outcomes presented are themselves realistic. For example, can we know that if domestic equities return 13 per cent, then domestic bonds will return 6 per cent and international equities 18 per cent?
- Each of these three outcomes may indeed have a probability of 50 per cent of occurring, but is there really a 50 per cent chance that they'll all happen together?

In practice, defining realistic scenarios is surprisingly tricky to do, while poorly defined scenarios give misleading results. To see why scenario analysis can be difficult in practice, consider a simple, eight-asset portfolio to which five scenarios are applied. The investment manager must forecast returns for each asset and each scenario, in other words 40 forecasts. But these return forecasts must be consistent within each scenario, which entails forecasting correlations between each pair of assets. For eight assets there are 28 pairs, so 140 correlations for all five scenarios. The magnitude and direction of each correlation is driven by the precise conditions of the scenario, such as the scope for currency, interest rate and fiscal policy manoeuvre of governments and central banks, and size and distribution of outstanding derivatives positions and margin lending, together with multiple other considerations each requiring a set of forecasts or assumptions.

To complete the analysis four probability forecasts for the five scenarios are needed. This amounts to 184 forecasts. Since most balanced funds have many more than eight asset classes, the total is usually much more. As the scope for error increases with the number of forecasts, scenario analysis leaves plenty of opportunity for mistakes.

The other disadvantage is that it is impossible to ensure that all possible scenarios are included. Omitting even one scenario can pose problems. For example, the risk system built for Long Term Capital Management (LTCM) included the capability for scenario analysis, so it is likely that this was part of its suite of risk measures. Presumably the possibility of a Russian debt crisis, which lead to the demise of the fund, was not included. Widespread use of scenario analyses in the early 2000s excluded a US sub-prime meltdown scenario.

The composition of the asset class portfolios themselves can change the outcome. For example, the domestic equities portfolios may together deliver more or less than the 13 per cent return to the UK equity market in the central scenario in Example 2.2. After all, active investment managers are paid to assume risk in order to exceed the asset class return. So the investor is expecting that the portfolio return to the asset class will be greater than the return to the asset class itself. Will they all add value in this particular 50 per cent scenario or will some underperform?

Summary

Risk-based investment management effectively goes much further than even the most detailed scenario analysis or stress test by effectively covering all realistic scenarios, taking account of the interactions between portfolio selection decisions. By showing where the potential for extra returns are greatest, risk-based portfolio selection allows the investor to make the most of the available investment selection skill.

Modern investment theory was developed in the second half of the twentieth century to shed light on what interactions between assets and common factors mean in practice to the likelihood of a portfolio achieving its investment objectives. It provides a simple framework by which portfolio selection can benefit from the full scope of the investable universe.

Risk-based portfolio selection builds on modern investment theory to enhance portfolio return by targeting risk where it harnesses investment selection skill to deliver the best returns with acceptable risk and eliminates unnecessary portfolio return volatility.

Endnotes

1. Short selling is the sale of an asset or contract that has not previously been purchased.
2. Many investment professionals and academics believe that allocation to asset classes has a much bigger impact on overall portfolio outcome than security selection within asset classes. For example, the decision to overweight UK equities has more impact than the choice between buying shares in Tesco or Sainsbury. For most portfolios this is probably true, depending on how active asset allocation and security selection within asset classes are managed.

   The counter-argument says that security selection, because it entails a much larger number of individual choices, offers more scope to add value overall.

3
Investment Management Theory

> Well that's all very well in practice, but how does it work in theory?
>
> Anon

This chapter introduces the basic principles of investment theory, including:

- The efficient markets hypothesis.
- Risky assets and the risk free asset.
- The capital asset pricing model
- Normal distributions of asset returns.
- Discounted cash flow.
- Interest rates.
- Options.

The efficient markets hypothesis (EMH)

Efficient market theory says that the price of an asset incorporates all information currently known about its prospects for delivering returns in the future and the risks associated with it. If the price of an asset is too low, implying a high return for its level of risk, then investors will bid the price up until it reaches its 'efficient' return. If the price is too high, then it will be bid down, until the relationship between its risk and return is consistent with other assets. Thus, efficient market theory says, assets will always trade at or about their equilibrium or 'fair price', where investors are indifferent between holding the asset and not holding it.

According to EMH, changes in an asset's price are due to the emergence of new reports concerning the asset or the market in which it trades, or a reassessment of the riskiness of the asset, including changes in the economic environment that affect the return investors demand for risk.

If markets are efficient, then the relationship between the risk and return of all assets is quantifiable. As risk increases so should return, in a roughly predictable if not linear fashion, as described in Example 3.1.

The curved line is called the efficient frontier and shows the relationship between risk and return for efficiently priced assets. The y-axis shows return and the x-axis shows risk. The efficient frontier is always positively sloped, meaning that it goes up from left to right as increased return is associated with increased risk, but the actual shape depends on the market or universe of assets in question. The line is nearly always quite steep at the low-return, low-risk end. This shows that, for very low-risk assets, even a small increase in risk yields a relatively large increase in return. While in the high-risk, high-return zone, the marginal increase of return to risk diminishes.

In an 'efficient' world an overpriced asset is found below the efficient frontier because its expected return is too low for its level of risk, in other words, its risk is underpriced. If an asset appears above the line, it is in theory underpriced. That not all assets sit exactly on the efficient frontier suggests that markets are not always efficient in the strictest sense.

There are three versions of market efficiency, which are strong, semi-strong and weak.

The strong version says that current security prices reflect all information relevant to the firm, including information available only to insiders. This says that even using insider information, investors cannot gain above equilibrium profits from trading in a security because other people

Example 3.1 The efficient frontier

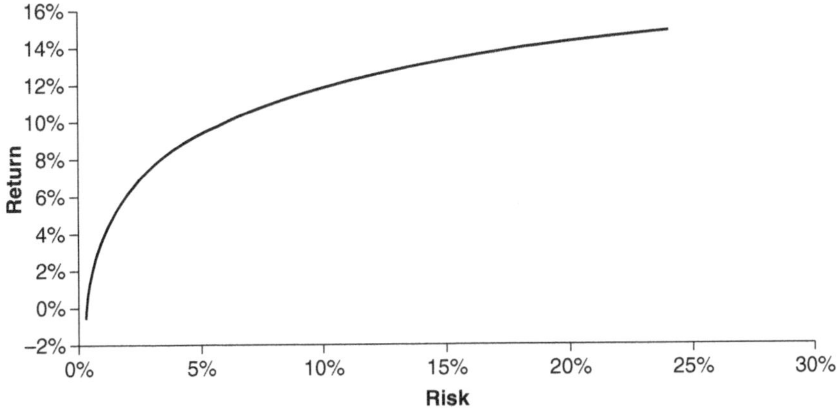

privy to the information will already have traded on it and the price will already have adjusted accordingly.

The semi-strong version says that all publicly available information about a security is reflected in its current price. Fundamental analyses using company accounts and statements have already been analysed by professional investors and prices adjusted accordingly. Less well-informed investors will follow the 'smart money' and the weight of their buying or selling will soon cause the asset's price to converge to its fair price. According to this version, above equilibrium returns can be generated only using insider information.

The weak version says that security prices reflect all information that can be derived from examining market trading data such as the history of prices, trading volume or the amount sold short (by investors having sold more than they own). This says that trend analysis is fruitless, because these data are freely available and virtually costless to analyse, but that fundamental analysis and insider trading can yield above equilibrium rewards.

Markets may never be efficient from the point of view of every investor, even according to the weak definition of efficiency. One reason is that different investors have different tax profiles and are subject to different regulatory regimes, and so, even if they happen to agree about the prospects for a particular asset, they will place different values on it according to their own perspectives.

Example 3.2 shows how differential tax treatment of domestic and institutional investors affects the value they will place on an individual security. The domestic investor is entitled to a tax credit equal to the domestic corporate rate of taxation, while the international investor is entitled to a rebate equal to the rate of withholding tax payable. Both are adjusted by the percentage of the dividend to which the tax credit applies. In some jurisdictions this is less than 100 per cent, depending on the amount of tax paid by the company issuing the dividends. The value of the dividend tax credit, and therefore the security, is higher for the domestic investor,

Example 3.2 Value of dividend tax credits for domestic and international investors

Share price	$50.00	
Dividend per share	$1.75	
Dividend yield	3.5%	
Corporate tax rate for domestic investor	35%	
Withholding tax for international investor	15%	
Rate of tax credit	100%	
	Domestic	International
Value of Dividend Tax Credit	$0.61	$0.26
Value of Cum-dividend Share	$52.36	$52.01

who is entitled to the tax rebate at 35 per cent, than for the international investor with a tax rebate entitlement of only 15 per cent.

If markets are not efficient, then what is the point of EMH? One answer is that it provides the framework for estimating how mispriced an asset is and therefore how much is to be gained if and when it converges to, or at least toward, its fair price.

Markets are often inefficient, but when they correct the inefficiency, they can overshoot their fair price. The inefficiency can thus be in either direction. There is so far no consistent evidence of systematic departures from efficiency in either direction.

Risky assets and the risk-free asset

Investment theory demands that there exist both risky assets and at least one risk-free asset. The return to the risk-free asset isolates and quantifies the time value of money. In practice no asset is entirely risk free; even call deposits can lose their value through inflation, for example. Short-term government instruments are usually used as the risk-free point of reference when pricing risky assets.

There are two main types of risky assets: bonds and equities, corresponding to financial and real assets respectively. Bonds are in effect loans: the investor lends money to (buys a bond from) a borrower, who undertakes to repay the principal of the loan and interest, either at the end of the loan period or at intervals during the loan period. The bond may be secured, or collateralized, by an asset, or it may be unsecured. Either way, the best outcome for the investor is that he or she is repaid the loan principal with interest. The bond holder has no claim on any growth in the assets to which the bond may be linked. The borrower benefits from any growth in the asset's value, which is levered by the amount of the loan. By the same token he or she stands to lose more than the value of his or her investment should the asset fall in value, as he or she is still obliged to repay the loan plus outstanding interest.

Equity is any investment that is not a bond, therefore including shares in companies as well as property.[1] Equity is ownership or part ownership of an asset and all equity holders participate in both growth and falls in the value of the asset.

The capital asset pricing model (CAPM)

Developed by Harry Markowitz in 1952, for which he won a Nobel Prize, CAPM provides a simple framework that allows the investor to estimate the risk and return to an asset or portfolio of assets, given what is known, or thought to be known, about the asset or portfolio, the market in which it invests and the relationship between them.

Since its conception CAPM has survived extensive efforts to demonstrate its limitations and even to prove it wrong: as a result its limitations are now well understood. That it is still widely used suggests that its strengths outweigh its limitations.

It has long been understood that, in general, investments earning high returns usually also have high risks. 'Safe' investments are those that earn modest but steady rewards. The important insight added by CAPM is that these extra returns accrue only to risk that cannot be diversified away. Taking on unnecessary (diversifiable) risk does not lead to higher returns.

CAPM can be applied either to a single asset relative to another, a group of assets within a portfolio or a portfolio of assets relative to a nominated benchmark. A benchmark can in theory be any asset or group of assets, including a risk-free asset.

It is most often applied to equities portfolios, in which case the benchmark is usually some market proxy or index, or an alternative or comparator portfolio.

CAPM says that the return to an asset over a given period is the sum of:

- The expected return due to perceived mis-pricing of the asset. This can be the return implied by the difference between the current price of the asset and its estimated fair price in the EMH framework. It is specific to the asset and assumed to have a fixed value.
- The expected return of the market in which the asset trades minus the return to the risk-free asset, or cash.
- The sensitivity of the asset to its benchmark or the market in which it invests minus the return to cash, expressed as its beta to the market or benchmark.
- Return variation due to random fluctuations in the price of the stock.

In more detail, the return to asset or portfolio *i* (r_i) is expressed as follows:

$$r_i = \alpha_i + \beta_i \, . \, (r_m + r_f) + \varepsilon_i \qquad (3.1)$$

Where:

r_m = the return to the market

r_f = the risk-free rate of return

α_i = alpha: intentional or active risk to the asset or portfolio due to perceived mis-pricing of the asset

β_i = beta: the relationship of the asset or portfolio to its benchmark or the market

ε_i = residual or error, corresponding to random fluctuations in the value of the asset or portfolio

- Alpha is the amount by which the market has mis-priced the asset or portfolio *i*. This is what active managers seek in order to gain their return advantage. An asset with a positive alpha is underpriced (above the efficient frontier) and can be expected to deliver high returns relative to its risk. Over-priced assets lie below the efficient frontier. Increasing the expected alpha of a portfolio by adding high-alpha assets increases its expected return without increasing its risk. If the asset or portfolio is priced efficiently, alpha is zero.
- Beta is the sensitivity of asset or portfolio *i* to moves in the benchmark or the market. An asset or portfolio that moves exactly in line with the market has a beta of 1.0. An asset or portfolio with a beta of 1.2, for example, overshoots market rises and falls by 20 per cent, while an asset or portfolio with a beta of 0.9 matches only 90 per cent of moves in both directions. A portfolio consisting entirely of cash has a beta of zero relative to the equity market. The beta of a portfolio to a market is the weighted sum of the betas to that market of the portfolio's component assets.

  Because beta is related to the market, it cannot be eliminated by diversification or hedging without also eliminating the portfolio's market return. Increasing the beta of a portfolio will increase both its risk and return, other things being equal.
- The market return is the return to the market in which the portfolio is invested, such as the equity market. The objective of a portfolio is usually to earn the market return plus some alpha. In practice the 'market' is usually some proxy for the overall market, such as the S&P500 for US equities or the FT Allshare for UK equities, although it can also be a comparator asset or portfolio of assets.
- The interest rate is the 'risk-free' interest rate, a theoretical rate, since truly risk-free rates rarely if ever occur in practice. For the purposes of CAPM, the interest rate for a very short-term government or bank-backed bond is substituted.
- The residual is that part of an asset's return that is not explained by either alpha or beta and fluctuates randomly. Because it is random it adds volatility of returns without necessarily adding to return itself. Adding residual risk to a portfolio will do nothing to increase its expected return, so investment managers have every incentive to eliminate this risk through diversification. The residual is the part of the portfolio's risk that is diversifiable. The sum of the residuals of all the assets within a market is zero, so the more assets in a portfolio, the lower its residual risk will be, other things being equal.

Alpha and residual risk are unique to that asset or portfolio, while market risk, together with the beta, is referred to as systematic risk because it is common to all assets in the market.

The active manager seeks a positive alpha, while a passive or indexed portfolio assumes an alpha of zero. Both seek a residual as close as possible to zero.

CAPM says that the return to an asset or a portfolio is its benchmark adjusted return, plus any non-zero alpha, plus or minus its random, residual variation. The benchmark related return is given by the return to the benchmark times the portfolio or asset beta to benchmark.

Example 3.3 shows the performance over time of a portfolio, together with its benchmark related return and the benchmark return. The dotted lines represent the band around the benchmark related return due to random residual variation that is predicted by CAPM. By convention, this 'tracking error' describes the variation bands within which the portfolio will perform 68 per cent of the time.

The figures in Example 3.3 show that the outperformance of 2.63 per cent came at the expense of 4.56 per cent risk or tracking error. Moreover, of the 2.63 per cent, 0.41 per cent was attributable to the portfolio having an average beta to its benchmark of 1.05, so is due to the market's appreciation. Had the market fallen instead, this 0.41 per cent would have worked against it and the outperformance correspondingly less for the same level of risk.

Example 3.3 Active portfolio and market returns

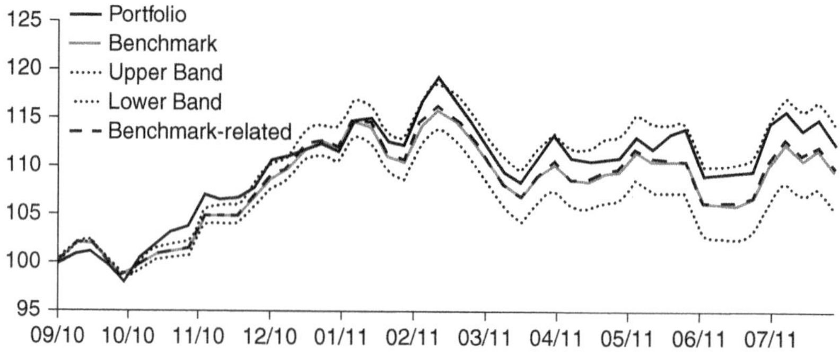

Beta	1.05
Tracking Error	0.63%
Tracking Error annualized	**4.56%**
Portfolio Return	11.47%
Benchmark Return	8.84%
Relative Return	**2.63%**
Benchmark-related Return	0.41%
Alpha	2.22%

Fama–French expansion

Of course asset prices are sensitive to things other than the market in which they trade. In the early 1990s Eugene Fama and Kenneth French noticed that by adding two further factors, more return variation could be explained. The two factors are size, which they defined as small (market capitalization) minus big (SMB) and high minus low (book to market) or (HML). Stocks with high betas to these factors are referred to as value stocks, while stocks with low betas to these factors are called growth stocks. Fama–French factors are often referred to as Style factors. This is known as the Fama–French three factor model. It has the same structure as CAPM, but with three factors instead of the single market factor.

CAPM assumes:

- The future returns to an asset do not depend on its returns in the past.
- There are no transactions costs, taxes or other market frictions.
- All investors are price takers, meaning that they cannot affect the price of an asset.
- All investors have access to the same information about an asset.
- Investors prefer lower volatility for a given expected return and higher expected return for a given volatility.
- Returns are normally distributed.

Normal distributions of asset returns

Probably the most contentious of CAPM's assumptions is that asset price returns are normally distributed. In a normal distribution, variations above the average, or mean, are as likely as variations below it. The distribution of returns, in other words, is symmetric about the mean. Normal distributions can be seen in approximations of many things in nature, such as people's heights, weights, shoe sizes and other characteristics. The normal distribution does not describe the world precisely, but is a good practical approximation with some very useful mathematical properties.

It can be defined by just two statistics: the mean and the standard deviation.

The standard deviation is a measure of the dispersion of the data, in this case asset or portfolio return variation. The normal distribution says that 68 per cent of outcomes will occur within the range given by the standard deviation. In investments context, the standard deviation is known as the tracking error, if talking about variations of a portfolio from a benchmark return. It is called volatility if talking about nominal or absolute variation. It is illustrated in Example 3.4.

Example 3.4 The normal distribution

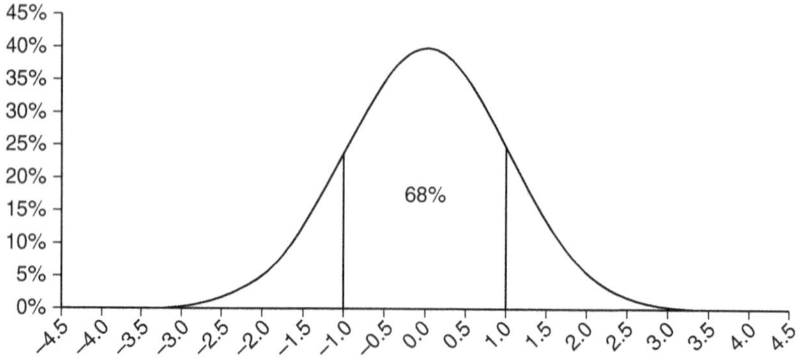

Example 3.4 is a generic representation of a normal distribution. The height of the curve represents the frequency of a particular result, while the x-axis gives the range of possible results, here expressed as the number of standard deviations. The highest point on the curve corresponds with 0.0 on the x-axis. This is the average, or mean, of the distribution. It is also the median, or mid-point. The mean is equal to the median because the distribution is symmetrical, an important property of the normal distribution. The area between the vertical lines, at –1.0 and 1.0 standard deviations respectively, represents 68 per cent (2 x 34 per cent) of the 100 per cent probability of the distribution. This standardized measurement of the dispersion is another of the most important properties of the normal distribution. If the returns of two assets are both normally distributed, then the extent to which they co-vary can be computed precisely, even if they have different mean returns and different standard deviations. This covariance is assumed to be stable whatever the returns to the two assets are. In this sense, the relationship between them is said to be linear.

To see how well it represents reality, look at the chart in Example 3.5, which depicts S&P500 monthly returns from November 2003 to December 2012 and S&P500 daily returns from August 2007 to December 2012. The fit is good in neither case, with more clustering of returns near the middle of the distribution and very high and very low returns happening more often than the normal distribution would predict. But note also that in each case they occur at different points along the range of possible outcomes, so neither would be a good predictor of the other. And the fit is clearly better for daily returns than for monthly, suggesting that the more numerous the observations, the better the fit with normal distribution. This is not simply because daily returns behave better, but is due more to the fact that there are a larger number of daily observations

Example 3.5 Observed and theoretical normal distributions

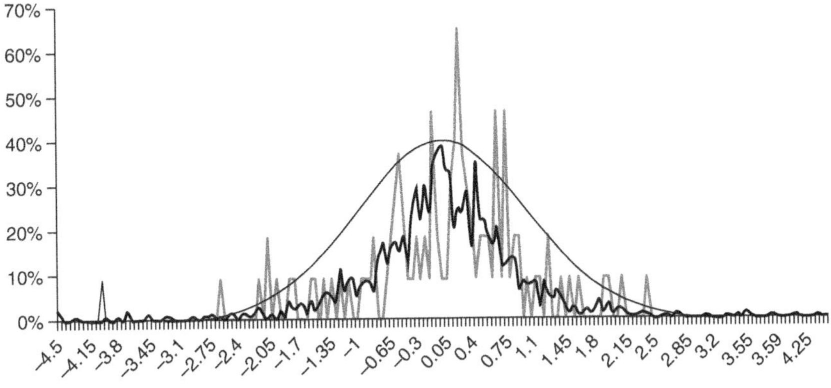

Source: FactSet

than monthly. Notice also that actual returns cluster quite close to the centre of the distribution, as predicted by the normal assumption, rather than to one side or another.

Normal distribution is not perfect, but it can be a workable and relatively unbiased approximation for many, if not most, purposes.

Discounted cash flows (DCF)

This is a simple method for estimating the present value of a payment, or stream of payments, to be received some time in the future. It is the core principle of bond pricing and is sometimes used to help value equities. In fact it has many applications because of its simplicity.

Inputs to the DCF computation are:

- The sums to be received in the future.
- The dates on which they are to be received.
- The interest rate or discount factor by which they are to be discounted.

The formula for computing DCF is:

$$PV = \frac{CF_1}{(1+i)} + \frac{CF_2}{(1+i)^2} + \dots\dots\dots + \frac{CF_n}{(1+i)^n} \qquad (3.2)$$

Where:
PV = the present value of the future cash flows
CF = the nominal amount of each cash flow

i = the discount factor for each period
n = the number of periods

The sums to be received and the dates on which they are to be received are both fairly straightforward, if they are known. They correspond to the coupons and principle receivable from a bond, for example. Cash flows need not be uniform for the length of the DCF computation and can be negative as well as positive. A payment in the future is discounted in the same way as a receipt.

The lengths of the periods are usually assumed to be uniform, say monthly, semi-annually or annually; although they can vary, in which case the discount rate is adjusted to reflect the length of each period. So an annual rate of 5 per cent is given as 2.47 per cent if paid semi-annually, since 2.47 per cent at six-monthly intervals compounds to 5 per cent.

The discount rate should reflect the following considerations:

- The time value of money.
- Expected inflation.
- The risk associated with the cash flows.

Note that for each cash flow the discount rate is raised to the power of the number of periods in the future at which it occurs. For example, it is squared for the second cash flow, cubed for the third and so on. This says that the further in the future a payment is, the less valuable it is in today's money.

The longer the DCF horizon, the more sensitive it is to changes in the discount factor, as shown in Example 3.6.

Example 3.6 Discounted cash flow

Annual cash flows	\$10.00	\$10.00
Assumed time horizon in years	10	30
Discount rate = 3.50%		
Present value of last cash flow in horizon	\$7.09	\$3.56
Present value of future cash flows	\$93.15	\$193.92
Discount rate = 3.51%		
Present value of last cash flow in horizon	\$7.08	\$3.55
Present value of future cash flows	\$93.12	\$193.69

As the discount factor in Example 3.6 is increased from 3.50 per cent to 3.51 per cent the present value of the ten-year income stream decreases from $93.15 to $93.12. The same increase in the discount factor reduces the present value of the 30-year income stream from $193.92 to $193.69. The reduction is seven times as large.

Interest rates

Accepted economic theory says that interest rates are determined by:

- The time value of money.
- Current expected inflation risk.
- Currency risk, if the bond is denominated in a currency other than that of the investor.
- Credit risk, including sovereign risk.

The time value of money reflects the fact that most people prefer to consume today rather than some time in the future, other things being equal, and possibly the opportunity cost, which is driven by the yield on alternative uses of the money. The other three expressions: inflation, currency and credit risk, reflect uncertainty about recovering the full value of the bond. Inflation and currency risk are the risk that the bond will depreciate. Credit risk is the risk that the borrower will unable to honour his or her obligations.

Options

An option is the right but not the obligation to buy or sell an asset at a specified price at some time in the future. The holder of the option has potentially unlimited gains, with losses limited to the amount paid for the option.

Modern options pricing theory was developed in the 1970s and is widely used to help understand fair prices for smoothed return funds, guaranteed minimum return funds and capital guaranteed funds, as well as credit risk inherent in corporate and sovereign bonds and options themselves.

The underlying theory is simple, flexible and easy to apply. It says simply that the price of an option is the current intrinsic value (the current asset price less the option exercise price for a call option) plus the future value of exercise adjusted for the probability that the option will be exercised.

$$pc = s \times N(d1) - pe \times N(d2) / e^{iy} \tag{3.3}$$

Where:

$N(d1) = [\ln (s / pe) + vol^2 / 2 \times y] / vol \times \sqrt{y}$

$N(d2) = N(d1) - vol \times \sqrt{y}$

And:

pc = the price of the call option
s = the current price of the underlying asset
pe = the exercise price of the option
i = the risk-free interest rate
vol = the volatility of the underlying asset
y = the time to expiry in years
e^{iy} = the interest rate continuously compounded

Importantly the price of the option is indifferent to the expected return to the underlying asset, because it assumes the asset price is itself efficient and therefore reflects all known information about its future return prospects.

The probability of the option being exercised in the future is determined by the expected volatility of returns to the underlying asset, which are assumed to conform to a normal distribution. The more volatile the returns to the underlying asset, the more likely the option is to be exercised, so the more valuable the option is.

More detail about option theory is given in the Appendices.

Endnote

1. Property investment is an equity because the investor participates in both growth and decline in the value of the asset. The holder of a mortgage on a property holds a bond, of course, but the owner of the property holds the equity. This asset class sometimes seems to behave like a bond, but that is mainly because it can be more sensitive to interest rate fluctuations than other equity investments.

Part II

Risk Management

4
Risk Management

A group of novice skiers in their early twenties were coming to the end of a three-week skiing tour in the Tyrol. Most of them had progressed from the green to blue slopes, but on the afternoon of the last day a small group rose to the challenge of the red slope.

Descending the chairlift and gasping at the near-sheer fall of the three-kilometre run, horror and panic infused the obligatory bravado. The chairlift was not equipped to take downward passengers, except in stretchers, and in any case had now stopped and the operators were preparing to ski back to the village. Dusk wasn't far off. There was no alternative to skiing down, and skiing down meant dozens of hop-turns without mistakes.

Self-inflicted, to be sure (depending on how much judgement you think young twenty-somethings actually have in practice), the only way to survive was to take an enormous risk – or dozens if you count each hop-turn.

There is a parallel for investment funds, and that is that doing nothing is not an option. Investment objectives can be reached only by taking risks. The trick is to ensure that, as far as possible, the risks are calculated and well-managed. Unlike skiing, there are no green slopes to practise on.

Investment risk is one of the most misunderstood subjects of investment management, which is a shame because it is what drives investment returns. Unlike other types of risk, investment risk is actually sought by the investment manager. As well as investment risk, investment management firms are subject to:

- Business risk, which is the risk that their business loses money or fails to make a profit. It is borne by the investment management company, which seeks to eliminate it, either with systems to guard against it or through insurance.

- Compliance risk, which is the risk of a breach of a client mandate, a fund trust deed or of prevailing regulations. It is also borne by the investment manager, who seeks to eliminate it.

Investment risk – the risk that investment performance falls short of expectations:

- Borne by the investor.
- Managed, not eliminated.
- Penalty is lower investment returns on funds under management.
- Responsibility of the chief investment officer (CIO), chief operations officer (COO), chief financial officer (CFO) or chief risk officer (CRO).
- Equity market risk.
- Interest rate risk.
- Currency risk.
- Credit risk.
- Market timing risk.
- Allocation risk.
- Counterparty risk.
- Liquidity risk.
- Gearing/leverage.

Business risk – the risks to business profitability:

- Borne by the investment manager.
- Ideally eliminated.
- Penalties are usually financial, affecting the firm's profitability.
- Responsibility of the CIO, COO, CFO or CRO.
- Business continuity risk.
- Reputational risk.
- Financial risk.
- Operational risk: settlements, errors and omissions.
- Key person risk.
- Counterparty risk.

Compliance risk – the risk of a breach of regulation or contract:

- Borne by the investment manager.
- Ideally eliminated.
- Penalties can include restriction or withdrawal of authorization.
- Responsibility of the COO, CFO or CRO.
- Failure to comply with investment mandates, trust deeds or prospectuses and prevailing regulations.

- Company-wide regulation.
- Fund-specific regulation.
- Breach of investment mandate or trust deed.

There are some areas of potential overlap. For example, a significant or persistent failure of investment risk becomes a source of reputational risk if it leads to lack of confidence in the manager to deliver target returns. A significant drop in asset prices, and therefore funds under management, becomes a business risk, as management fees are levied as a percentage of funds under management. Counterparty risk can be treated as a type of operational or investment risk, depending on how it arises. In the context of risk management, it is treated as a type of credit risk.

This chapter is about investment risk management. It addresses:

- Objectives – what investment risk management can achieve and what it cannot.
- Necessary conditions – what is needed.
- Risk management tools.
- Distinguishing characteristics of effective investment risk management.
- The risk management and review process.
- Risk management versus risk reporting.
- Investment risk management policy.
- Investment risk management versus compliance.
- Risk targets and limits.
- Risk management for extreme markets.

More detail about methodologies used for modelling risk, ways of measuring it and derivatives risk is given in Chapters 5, 6 and 7.

Objectives

Investment risk is the risk that the investor pays the investment manager to assume on behalf of the investor in order to deliver returns above what can be earned in low-risk assets such as a bank deposit.

The job of the investment manager is therefore to ensure that the risk of investment portfolios gives the best chance possible of the portfolio achieving its return objectives:

- The level of risk should be sufficient to enable target returns – either in absolute terms or relative to a specified benchmark – to be met while remaining within the investor's range of risk tolerance.

- This risk should be targeted where the investment manager believes it can contribute most to active returns. The portfolio's risk profile should reflect the investment manager's views.

So the risk manager's job is to manage risk, not eliminate it. To manage risk effectively, it must first be measured accurately.

By quantifying not only the overall risk of a portfolio but also the exposures that contribute to risk, the investment manager can distinguish between those risks that will contribute to expected return and incidental risks that merely add to portfolio volatility without contributing to positive returns. These unwanted risks can be eliminated by means of diversification or hedging. The portfolio benefits in the following ways:

- Portfolio volatility is reduced by the elimination of unwanted risk, which improves the investment manager's information ratio (the ratio of active return to active risk).
- Fewer negative returns from unwanted exposures benefits portfolio returns over time.
- This allows more risk to be targeted to promising sources of return, thus improving the prospects of meeting return targets.
- It helps to focus research effort on material sources of risk.
- The vulnerability of the portfolio to extreme events is reduced by the elimination of unwanted and unnecessary sources of risk.
- Hedging against extreme outcomes can be achieved more cost-effectively where sources of portfolio risk are accurately quantified.

Effective risk management can significantly enhance returns. What risk management cannot do is forecast crashes and crises. A crash is, after all, a large negative return or a series of negative returns. Predicting returns is the domain of investment managers, their strategists and analysts. It follows that predicting a crash is, like predicting any asset returns, the job of investment managers, their strategists and analysts. Good risk measurement can quantify the portfolio's vulnerability to a crash should it happen, and give enough detail to enable the investment manager to protect against the worst outcomes. But it cannot forecast returns, including sharply negative ones.

Effective risk management also adds value by signalling to clients and potential clients that the stock selection, portfolio construction and management process is a disciplined exercise subject to independent review.

Necessary conditions

Risk management is most effective when integrated in the portfolio selection and review process. At the same time, risk reviews that are independent of the investment manager are increasingly valued by investors. There are at least two ways of resolving the apparent contradiction of integration with independence:

- The ideal is where the investment manager approaches portfolio selection from a risk perspective, matching expected asset returns with their respective contributions to portfolio risk in order to achieve the best risk-adjusted expected return. In this case, the risk manager reviews the portfolio composition regularly to see that its risk profile conforms to the objectives of the portfolio and that there are no errors or hidden risk concentrations that the investment manager might have overlooked.
- The risk manager provides risk analyses as an arm's length resource for the benefit of the investment manager, in the same way that research analysts provide asset forecasts as a resource for use by the investment manager.

Either way, it is important that the risk manager and the investment manager have equal standing in the organization so that neither can overrule the other.

The risk manager needs to be at least as skilled as the investment manager, because he or she must be comfortable with the investment manager's techniques and strategies, and able to spot potential areas of weakness, as well as recommend remedial or pre-emptive actions.

A sufficiently skilled risk manager can quickly gain the confidence of the investment manager so that the investment management and review process becomes collaborative, whereby the risk manager contributes a valued second opinion to harness and enhance the investment manager's portfolio selection skill. Without the confidence of the investment manager, the job of the risk manager can deteriorate into a game of cat-and-mouse, benefiting nobody.

Many investment management firms position the risk management team outside the investment management function, often grouping it with compliance and reporting to the COO, the CFO or the CRO. This of course ensures independence from investment decisions, but impedes integration. Proximity to the compliance and business risk teams can foster a 'policing' approach to risk management, further limiting the scope for collaboration with investment managers. Distance from the investment management teams can also deter some talented potential risk managers, who otherwise might have seen it as a step toward a career in investment management. Risk management that is too removed from the investment process has less scope to add value or enhance returns.

Risk management tools

Even the most skilled risk manager can retain the confidence of the investment manager only when supported by credible risk analyses that are relevant to the way the investment manager selects his or her portfolio. Credible and relevant risk analyses can come only from the right risk analysis resources, including:

- Risk model.
- Appropriate data.
- Risk measures.
- Thoughtful interpretation.

To be useful, the risk model must be chosen for the portfolio. The best results are achieved with a purpose-built model, but this is often not practicable. Whether customized or off-the-shelf, the model methodology must be based on sound economic theory that is appropriate to the objectives of the portfolio, the instruments in it and what factors the investment manager takes into account when selecting the portfolio. The model's risk decomposition capability should reflect these selection factors and attribute risk to them realistically and reliably.

Choosing the tools to match the objective may seem obvious, but it can be less simple than it appears. While many risk systems have obvious similarities, some are better suited to some tasks than to others. There is no 'best' solution to all risk requirements and it may be useful to use more than one risk tool. Since there is no perfect risk model – all have their limitations – using more than one can add insight in a smiliar way to looking at a three-dimensional object from different angles.

Input data should be selected from representative periods of history that are believed to be relevant to likely future market conditions. Data periodicity, whether daily, weekly or monthly, can materially affect the magnitude of the annualized risk forecast. Because risk statistics are annualized by extrapolation, which can give a misleading estimation of likely future risk, any covariance matrix should be validated and tested for robustness.

Risk measures are in effect summaries of risk, which, although derived from a single risk analysis, should be chosen carefully to serve to their intended purpose.

Results must be interpreted carefully, taking into account the modelling methodology used and its potential limitations and weaknesses, the data sample used, periodicity and the validity of any extrapolation. The risk manager and the investment manager must be alert to any sources of error or ambiguity.

Distinguishing features of effective risk management

- The risk model must be well constructed and based on sound economic theory.
- Computational methodology must be sound in order to give accurate and valid results.
- The risk analysis and risk decomposition must be designed according to the way the portfolio is constructed.
- The relationship between investment manager and risk manager must be collaborative.
- The risk management process must be accountable.
- The process must be credible to all parties.

Both the portfolio construction and the risk management processes should be subject to constant review. As well as evaluating portfolio outcomes, it is a good idea to regularly review the performance of the risk model to see how well it explains observed portfolio risk. Markets change, as do portfolio selection processes, so even the best model can become out of date and need to be revised to keep up. Ways of evaluating the risk model are described in Chapter 5 on risk modelling.

The risk management and review process

The process by which risk management decisions are taken reinforces the efficiency and credibility of risk management itself. It should include the following stages:

- Agree the investment objectives and risk parameters with the investor.
- Ensure that the standing of the risk management function within the organization is sufficiently senior.
- Undertake mandate-level risk analysis.
- Perform regular risk reviews.

The primary stage of the risk management process is to agree with the investor the return objectives and risk targets and tolerances needed to achieve them. This happens when a new product or mandate is specified.

The investment manager and the risk manager seek to answer the following questions:

- Are the stated return and risk targets consistent with each other?
- Are the benchmarks and reference portfolios appropriate to the investment objectives?

- Do limits and constraints serve the purpose intended for them, or do they leave portfolios vulnerable to unintended consequences?
- Are the right investment instruments allowed and are the allowed instruments right for the portfolio?
- Can appropriate risk analysis and profiling be carried out with existing resources? If not, what extra resources are needed?

The investment risk manager ideally should report directly to the CIO and have equal standing with asset class managers, portfolio strategists and other senior investment managers to ensure the independence and credibility of the risk management process. This avoids the situation where one party is overruled by another and in this way reinforces the credibility of the process and encourages accountability.

The alternative, which is to group investment risk management with compliance or sometimes business risk management, can ensure the independence of the risk manager, but often at the expense of risk being viewed as a policing rather than a collaborative function. In this situation, the investment risk manager can find it difficult to win the confidence of the investment manager. It can also encourage a box-ticking approach to risk management, thus forfeiting the potential of investment risk management to add value to the investment management process.

There is another benefit to keeping risk management work close to investment management: it attracts talented professionals who see proximity to investment decisions as a promising stage in their career progression.

Investment risk analysis is most effective when being undertaken at the level of the mandate, for example at the total fund level for balanced mandates and at the applicable asset class or regional level for specialist mandates. Mandate-level risk analysis can be complemented by single asset-class sub-portfolio risk analyses as required.

The investment manager and the risk manager typically review the portfolio risk profile regularly. The objective of the review cycle is to link explicitly sources of risk with sources of return. These can be things like global themes or risk factors devised to capture returns from relative asset mispricing. Each source of risk is usually associated with an expected return or range of expected returns, maximum tolerable loss, preferably some timeframe and, crucially, an exit strategy. The risk manager confirms that the portfolio risk level and profile are appropriate to the portfolio objectives and the investment outlook, while the investment manager confirms that the main sources of risk accord with his or her expectations of return. A record of the decisions and their rationale reinforces accountability and therefore the credibility of the process and at the same time facilitates risk-based performance analysis.

Reviewing portfolio risk profiles can help distinguish the effects of good management from those of chance. A disappointing outcome in one period can be evaluated in the context of the reasoning behind the decision that gave rise to it; so a position can be preserved if it is expected that the longer-term payoff will compensate short-term underperformance. Alternatively, if conditions have changed, then an informed decision to reposition the portfolios can be taken. Credit can be given for being wrong for the right reasons, and outcomes that are right for the wrong reasons can be dealt with.

The risk review process shows if any portfolio limits or constraints are either failing or are having unanticipated secondary effects on the risk profile. If they are, they may need to be revisited. Risk limits are discussed in more detail later in this chapter.

Reporting versus management

Risk reporting and risk management are often confounded and sometimes even equated with each other. This is a bit like equating the purchase of a recipe book with preparing a meal. Risk management is about using risk profile information to align sources of risk and return in a portfolio in order to achieve the best investment outcome. By contrast, risk reporting in effect checks that the risk management is working. Typically, risk reports are distributed to the following interested parties:

- CIO.
- Portfolio managers.
- Middle and back office.
- Performance reporting.
- Client services.
- Marketing.
- Compliance.
- Governance oversight bodies.
- Regulators.

While each recipient uses risk reports differently, a single risk analysis usually generates the necessary information for all of them, either directly or indirectly, by providing basic information from which the measures demanded by each report can be calculated and the requirements of each recipient met.

Investment risk management policy

Most large investment management organizations maintain an investment risk management policy. Often this is to comply with prevailing regulations, but just as often it is for internal governance. Its purpose is to ensure that what should happen does indeed happen.

It achieves this by describing the organization's orientation to risk management, who is ultimately responsible for it and what internal reviews take place, how often and by whom. It also describes the relationship between risk management and other parts of the organization such as:

- Routine investment management operations.
- Marketing and client services.
- Legal and compliance.
- Internal audit.
- Governance bodies.
- Regulators.

It also forms the basis for any procedures manuals.

Investment risk management versus compliance

Risk management teams and compliance teams typically work closely together. While sometimes they are in the same team, the two functions are distinct.

Compliance risk is a form of business risk, borne by the investment management company, whereas investment risk, in the main, is not. If there is a failure of compliance, the investment manager must make good any damage; or even pay penalties if there is a breach of a regulation. By contrast investment risk management is management of the risk that is borne by the investor and is managed rather than minimized or eliminated.

While investment risk management relies on judgement, for example about whether or not a particular concentration of risk could render the portfolio unacceptably vulnerable; compliance is a binary decision. Investment mandates, trust deeds and relations stipulate fixed limits that typically allow no room for judgement. A portfolio either complies with its mandate and regulatory provisions or it doesn't.

Compliance risk, being mostly binary, is often controlled by means of automated checks built into front office and portfolio management systems, for example pre-deal checking software, and spot checks on dealing, portfolio composition and other procedures. Compliance risk management combines:

- Procedures and checking mechanisms.
- Monitoring compliance with the provisions in investment mandates and trust deeds.
- Legal expertise.
- A good working knowledge of the regulatory environment.

Compliance with the relevant legal and regulatory conditions is not the same as risk management.

Risk targets and limits

Containing a fund's exposure to risky assets, risky asset groups such as regions, countries, currencies, industries, counterparties or other risk factors is often assumed to be an effective way to limit the damage incurred when the prices of those risky assets fall. But limits are often ineffective and in some circumstances can have precisely the opposite effect.

This is partly because limits often confound economic exposure with money allocation. Equating the two supposes, for example, that the assets in the portfolio and any associated benchmark all have gearing ratios equal to 100 per cent, which is clearly unrealistic. This method also assumes that what are often arbitrary categories assigned to each asset describe its price sensitivities precisely and comprehensively. By this reckoning, Samsung would be sensitive to the South Korean market and the South Korean won, but not to any other market or currency, which casual observation tells us is not the case.

In the days before modern risk measurement technology, limiting monetary allocation to asset categories was the only way to control risk. This was better than nothing, but it was at best only a crude approximation of risk control. We now have the tools, data, computing power and understanding to address directly the risks that determine performance, so it makes sense to do so.

Targets and limits in terms of risk, or economic exposure, can avoid these inconsistencies. The ability to measure exposure to risk factors, as opposed to the simple measures of monetary allocations that preceded it, brings a powerful extra advantage because it can target not only the sensitivity of the portfolio to a risk factor but also to what extent over or under exposure to the factor affects the risk of the portfolio.

For example, a portfolio exposure, or beta, of 1.15 to the USD (meaning that if the USD/GBP falls by 1 per cent, other things being equal, the portfolio will fall by 1.15 per cent) is less perilous if this mismatch represents only 5 per cent of the portfolio's risk than if it represents 25 per cent. In other words you can measure and control the vulnerability of portfolio return to each active exposure as well as the exposure itself. But this solution is not free of contradictions either.

Limiting risk or economic exposure can come at the cost of returns foregone; and limits that are imposed without reference to how the investment manager selects his or her portfolio can increase, rather than reduce, risk by forcing him or her to seek returns where he or she is less confident of achieving them.

The essence of active investment management is to allocate risk to exposures that are expected to make a positive contribution to active return and eliminate those that will only contribute to random volatility. Limiting risks that will drive positive returns necessarily limits those returns. Unintended risk, on the other hand, should be eliminated rather than limited.

Exposure limits can introduce other problems too. One is that hard limits introduce the boundary problem: a small change in exposure tips the portfolio from being within tolerance to being outside it. This problem is compounded by the fact that all limits are necessarily arbitrary, and so can oblige the investment manager to carry out trades that serve only to ensure compliance, do nothing to benefit the portfolio and may in fact impede performance by departing from the manager's preferred positioning and increasing transactions costs – without actually reducing risk.

Yet many investors are uncomfortable with a mandate that imposes no limits or controls at all. So now the question becomes how tightly limits should be set. Setting limits too narrowly means that they will bite too frequently and so give rise to return-destroying transactions; while setting them too widely renders them meaningless.

Moreover, markets evolve and conditions change, and limits set in one environment can soon begin to have perverse effects in another.

The challenge is to find a stable solution that neither impedes the manager's ability to allocate risk efficiently nor gives rise to transactions that add no value to the portfolio. One way is to target risk directly.

Because targets can be matched to return objectives and forecasts, they are both more powerful and more robust than limits. Unlike limits, targets are neither arbitrary nor do they suffer from boundary error.

Even with impeccable management of risk exposures and concentrations, mishaps can occur. Managers' forecasting ability is not perfect and some safety mechanism may be desirable to contain the consequences of their fallibility. The investor understandably would prefer to protect the portfolio against the manager getting it horribly wrong.

A practical solution that mitigates both boundary error and arbitrariness is to complement risk targets with dual limits, in effect a combination of:

- Narrow, soft, internal limits that serve as a warning and oblige the investment manager to formally explain or, within a defined time interval, take action such as re-evaluate the portfolio's positioning.
- Hard, wide, external limits that oblige him or her to modify the position.

These limits too are arbitrary and suffer from boundary error, but are less likely to lead to artificial transactions. The internal limits can, indeed should, be breached regularly without automatically leading to counter-productive transactions. This way the external limits are breached only in extreme circumstances. The result is more efficient risk management, less vulnerability to shocks, lower portfolio turnover and more robust performance.

Risk management in extreme markets

For a long time it was widely believed that a sound enough risk tool would give valid and reliable risk forecasts in all market conditions. The observation that 'one-in-one-hundred' events seemed to occur suspiciously frequently was thought by some to be due to quirks in the input data sample, which would correct over time; while risk measurement sceptics cited it as evidence that risk forecasting is a hopeless task.

The crisis of 2007/08 seemed to give more ammunition to the sceptics. A closer look at how risk forecasting tools work however, suggests that the sceptics are in danger of throwing the baby out with the bathwater. Yet it is clear that risk measurement needs a rethink if it is to help manage risks in unusually volatile market conditions. This is because extreme markets behave in ways that violate some core assumptions of the EMH and the CAPM.

Normal or stable markets are characterized by relatively small asset price movements, consistent with approximate market efficiency. A defining feature is stable – or progressively evolving – relationships, or covariances, between assets. This relative stability in key covariances is what allows normal risk diversification techniques, based on mean-variance technology, to work most of the time.

Normal risk estimation falls short when applied to extreme markets for two main reasons:

- It underestimates the likelihood of an extreme event.
- It underestimates the scale of an extreme event when it happens.

Extreme events are more likely than is usually predicted by normal risk analysis because data samples rarely include a shock. Nearly all risk analyses draw on historical return information to compute the covariances that drive risk measurement. If this sample data include no extreme event, then the risk model will assign a very low probability of one happening. Include a shock and any risk tool will accord some reasonable likelihood of it happening again. Add to this the fact that many crises are preceded by a period of abnormal calm, and the underestimation is greater still. The most intuitive solution – include longer return histories in the sample data – introduces other, often less tractable problems, such as structural changes in the composition of markets (think of how the wave of privatizations in the early 1990s and the dotcom boom of the late 1990s changed the shape of investment opportunities) and stock survivorship bias,[1] which render much data irrelevant and confound risk forecasts.

The tendency of normal risk models to understate the severity of shocks is because the EMH assumes that correlations between assets and risk factors are more or less stable, and that the returns to an asset or risk factor from one period to the next are unrelated to each other, meaning that you cannot predict an asset's return for tomorrow from its return today.

In a crisis these core assumptions are violated:

- Correlations between assets change, sometimes dramatically: 'diversification fails just when you need it', as investors sell even cheap assets to raise cash in order to meet redemptions.
- Sequential returns can become correlated: extreme markets can trend sharply down, as margin lending and dynamic hedging provisions are triggered. They can also reverse sharply as investors perceive they have overshot their fair price.
- Liquidity dries up unpredictably.

While recent history has directed attention to extreme events and their costs, the greater threat to portfolio well-being derives from excess day-to-day volatility – death by a thousand cuts, if you like. Too much emphasis on extreme risk can compromise the task of aligning risk with expected returns, with the result that portfolio performance suffers.

More can be achieved by aiming for a target return over a given investment horizon with as little volatility as possible. While unanticipated extreme markets can cause enormous damage to returns when they occur; and these happen more often than one would like, it is normal, or stable, markets that prevail most of the time. To earn active returns over time, the investment manager must act on the balance of probabilities, which is usually the normal or stable market.

Guarding against extreme losses is a necessary complement, but it is not the main objective of investment management. It makes no sense to manage day-to-day risk from the perspective of a relatively unlikely event. This would be like dousing the inside of your house with water each morning as you leave for work in case there is a fire while you are away.

In practice the investment manager might hedge against some extreme events by buying out-of-the-money options when he or she judges that the danger of a shock warrants the costs, which can help contain the impact on his or her day-to-day performance. Even out-of-the-money hedging is not cheap, so the more accurate and relevant the analysis, the more targeted, and therefore cost-effective, the hedge.

It therefore makes sense to manage sources of vulnerability to shocks as a complement to normal risk management rather than as a substitute for it. Accurately quantifying sources of extreme vulnerability can allow effective protection against extreme losses with minimum cost to the portfolio and without altering the investment manager's preferred exposures.

Summary

Investment risk is one source of risk to which investment management firms are exposed. Unlike other risks, investment risk is the risk that they are paid to take on their clients' behalves in order to achieve active returns. Effective investment risk management aims to ensure that the overall level of risk in the portfolio is high enough to achieve target returns but not so high that it exposes the portfolio to unnecessary volatility. More importantly, it ensures that the factors contributing to portfolio risk are consistent with the investment manager's views on which factors will contribute to active return.

Effective investment risk management depends on relevant and credible risk analysis and an independent and accountable risk management function, ideally in collaboration with investment managers and subject to constant review, so as to ensure its responsiveness to portfolios and markets. It also benefits from a good working relationship with, while being distinct from, the compliance function.

Recent developments in investment risk modelling have drawn attention to the difference between risk in extreme markets and risk in stable markets. To be effective, the investment risk process should address them as distinct and complementary, rather than as substitutes for each other.

Case Study

This is a large institutional investment manager charged with managing several hundred funds and individual mandates spanning asset allocation overlay mandates, balanced funds and a dozen asset classes including equities, bonds and hedge funds. Some portfolios are managed by regional subsidiaries in Japan, South-East Asia and Australia, but most are managed at its headquarters. There were 17 teams of investment managers altogether.

The CIO believed that effective risk management could add value, not only to the investment management process, both directly, by enforcing discipline on an otherwise sprawling team, and indirectly, by enhancing portfolio performance as well. With a large investment management team – 20 people reported directly to him – he had scope to justify a team of specialized, professional risk analysts, with the head of investment risk reporting directly to him. The team grew to include five risk managers and eight risk analysts. Already being part of the investment management team, they found it natural to work together, although the roles they carried out within the team were distinct.

Central to the investment management process were monthly risk meetings – one for each team of investment managers. They were attended by the investment managers themselves, the relevant risk manager and risk analyst and, from time to time, the CIO. All meetings were minuted and any outstanding actions brought to the attention of the CIO and other desk heads at the monthly investment review meeting.

Each meeting entailed detailed scrutiny of risk profiles for each portfolio, with each risk profile including analyses using two or three risk models. Divergences from target risk levels and any unanticipated concentrations of risk were highlighted and the investment manager invited either to detail any planned corrective action or justify maintaining the position in terms of his conviction regarding the exposure.

Any disagreement between the risk manager and the investment manager was escalated, first to the head of investment risk and the investment management desk head, who both reported directly to the CIO and therefore were on equal footing with each other. If no resolution was reached, each would put his or her case to the CIO, who would determine a course of action. All decisions were minuted, together with the reasoning behind them.

The process was thus accountable and transparent. Risk analyses retained credibility with the investment managers only through continuous cooperation between the two teams, which also ensured that the analyses were both relevant and responsive to the portfolios and issues that arose in their day-to-day management.

This type of risk management structure generally served its purpose well, but in addition to anticipated effects, there were some surprising ones.

Newly-recruited investment managers often bristled at being subjected to review by risk analysts, who they considered, at least at first, of a lower rank to themselves. Typically they would come to see the value in an informed second opinion – and the advantage of being able to share responsibility when something went wrong. In particular, many investment managers were very good at identifying assets that would deliver high returns, but were less skilled at combining these in a portfolio that reflected their stock-picking skill. The risk analyses they were forced to take notice of often showed how unwanted risk had crept into the portfolio and pointed to actions that could neutralize it.

A necessary feature of risk management is that it is visible usually only when it fails: successful risk management is mostly invisible. Exceptions to this rule do exist, however. One was where risk models were pointing to a growing concentration of risk in a small number of risk factors that were not associated with any deliberate portfolio selection: it resulted only from asset price trending in a specific segment of the market. As risk concentrations grew to uncomfortable levels, the decision was taken to reduce holdings in assets where it was most concentrated. The result was that the portfolios avoided the bursting of a minor asset price bubble and greatly out-performed their competitors. Investment managers thus came to see risk management as a means of enhancing their performance.

The risk management process that developed was, unsurprisingly, costly and labour-intensive. The cost of multiple risk systems, data sources and analysts was frequently questioned by the finance director, who, like many non-investment professionals, did not appreciate that the diversity of portfolios under management demanded sometimes-specialized risk tools. He considered a single risk tool sufficient for all purposes. The head of investment risk therefore spent considerable time and attention defending the costs involved. Being able to cite isolated performance boosts helped of course, but the tendency to regard risk management as a dead-weight cost rather than a source of value-added is widespread. The much greater cost of multiple teams of security analysts was not questioned in the same way because their contribution to portfolio outcomes is more visible.

Other boosts came from the marketing and client services teams, who found that a strong risk management capability was a great help in attracting and retaining clients – especially during inevitable periods of lacklustre performance. Client presentations gave prominence to the risk management capability as a competitive strength.

The positioning of the investment risk team enhanced the effectiveness of the compliance team. As with many large organizations, the compliance team reported to the finance director, so was separate from the investment management teams. While the aims of compliance and investment risk management are distinct, the investment risk team provided a kind of bridge between compliance and investment managers because it was at least partially independent from them, yet in a good position to spot any looming breaches before they happened and keep the compliance team abreast of corrective action. While far from a policing function, the investment management teams were able to keep the police at bay, further endearing them to the investment managers.

Compliance found them a useful resource in understanding the positioning of portfolios vis-à-vis their objectives and mandatory and regulatory limits.

One of the more important features of this risk management process was its ability to attract and retain talented risk analysts. This was despite remuneration that was at the low end of market ranges. Highly qualified analysts were attracted to the prospect of working closely with and perhaps migrating to the investment management teams – which many did, although others preferred to pursue a career as a risk specialist. This brought another advantage as members of the investment teams, having experience in risk management, leant toward a risk-based portfolio construction process, fostering further co-operation.

The head of investment risk attributed the success of the investment risk management process to it being:

- Accurate and relevant.
- Credible and responsive.
- Integrated and collaborative.
- Transparent and accountable.

Endnote

1. Survivorship bias stems from the omission by many time-series analyses of stocks that failed at some time between the start of the data sample and the time of the analysis. It biases results because the errors thus introduced cannot be assumed to average out over large sample sizes.

5
Risk Modelling

> He (Ludwig Wittgenstein) once asked me: 'Why do people say it is more logical to think that the sun turns around the Earth than Earth rotating around its own axis?' I answered: 'I think because it seems as if the sun turns around the Earth.' 'Good,' he said, 'but how would it have been if it had seemed as if the Earth rotates around its own axis then?[1]

Much investment theory is gratifyingly intuitive. But occasionally, the superficially obvious explanation turns out to be very complicated when you think about it and try to explain it through analysis. And the more you think about it, or try to explain it mathematically, the more impossible it gets. Copernicus showed that an apparently more complex model was actually simpler when you thought about it.

In order to manage risk you must be able to measure it. To be able to measure it accurately you must have the right risk model.

The aim of a risk model is to quantify portfolio-level risk and, just as important, the sources of its risk. This is distinct from the job of modelling individual assets. To model individual assets you would use a different model for each one, as described in Chapters 10, 12 and 13 on security selection.

Portfolio risk models work because pairs of assets covary. They covary because they are exposed to the same common factors, which covary with each other. Risk modelling methodologies differ in how they account for the ways in which assets and common factors covary with each other and how these effects compound and offset to give portfolio-wide risk estimates.

There are two broad 'families' of risk estimation methodology: mean variance models derived from the CAPM framework and systems that work by simulating outcomes. Within each are a number of different techniques, as described in Figure 5.1. This chapter examines each

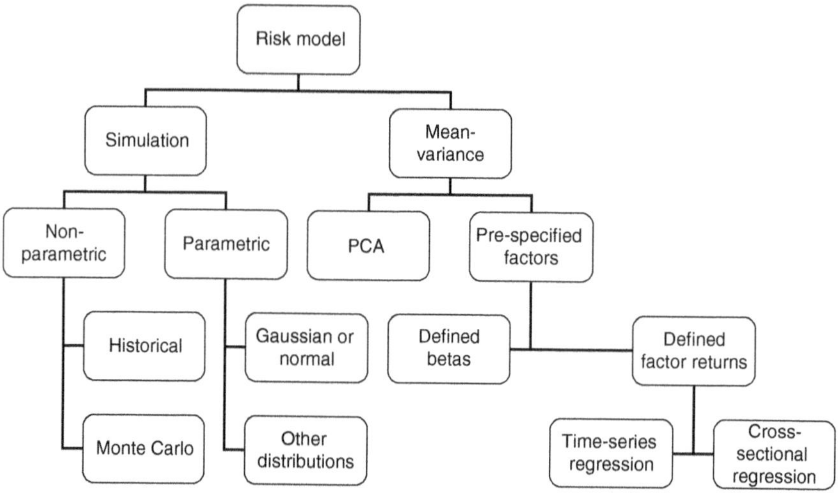

Figure 5.1 Risk modelling methodologies

methodology in turn before discussing how the results of risk models can be affected by data sampling and concluding with ways of testing to see how effective a risk model is. It does so by describing:

- The main variants of mean-variance risk modelling.
- The main variants of mean simulation.
- Mean-variance modelling versus simulation.
- Data.
- Adapting mean-variance to extreme markets.
- Risk model testing.

Mean-variance[2]

Mean-variance models are derived from CAPM, which was developed in the 1950s, initially for equities portfolios in the US. The first equity risk models estimated stock covariances in terms of their exposures, or betas, to a single risk factor, assumed to be the market factor and usually approximated by the S&P500 index. This was convenient because, for most portfolios at the time, the S&P500 was also the benchmark.

But stocks covary with things other than the market, such as industry groups and whether they are large-capitalization or small-capitalization stocks. Risk models with more than one factor showed they did a better job of estimating portfolio risk than the single factor model.

Having more than one factor of course introduced the slight complication of measuring how the different factors covary with each other. This necessitated an expansion of the CAPM formula to include more than one factor, stock betas for each factor and a factor covariance matrix. Nearly all modern equity risk models are multi-factor. For any multi-factor risk model, the factor covariance matrix is the main determinant of how well it models risk.

Providers of equity risk models differentiate themselves from each other by their choice of risk factors and by how the risk factors are constructed.[3] Together these dictate how well the factor covariance matrix – and therefore the model – works.

The two main ways of defining risk factors are to derive them directly from the data using a statistical technique known as principal components analysis (PCA) or to pre-specify the factors.

Principal component analysis – this type of statistical factor model will by construction have the best possible fit with the in-sample data. While this can be useful to compare headline risk for two portfolios, its usefulness in quantifying contributions to risk is limited because it is often hard to give economic meaning to the resulting factors, which emerge from the analysis as Factor 1, Factor 2 and so on. To complicate matters further, Factor 1 is usually assumed to be the market in which the portfolio is invested, but it could be a hybrid of the market and something else altogether, such as a domestic industry group or a currency effect. Factor 1 this period also may not be the same factor as Factor 1 next period, so comparison of a portfolio risk profile from one period to the next is difficult. This limits the usefulness of this type of factor model for most investment management applications. However, because it can give a very good estimate of portfolio-level risk, PCA is often used for trading desks needing to construct short-term tracking baskets.

Pre-specified factor models: the advantage of pre-specifying factors is that the factors can be chosen to reflect the way investment managers think about their portfolios. They are also the same factors from one period to the next: an energy factor this month will be the same as the energy factor next month, so a change in the portfolio's exposure to the energy factor and its contribution to portfolio risk tell you something about the composition of the portfolio and the market.

All pre-specified factor models have some estimation error, which can derive from, among other things, a mismatch between the model factors and the risks in the portfolio. The effect of estimation error is that some systematic, or factor related, risk is not explained by the model factors and wrongly attributed to residual, or stock-specific, risk. Or it can be missed altogether, resulting in under-estimation of risk. But the choice of model factors is not the only possible source of estimation error.

Models that use pre-specified factors can derive factor returns in one of two ways, each with advantages and disadvantages:

Time-series method – measure the factor returns (and hence the factor covariances) directly from empirical data, and then estimate the factor sensitivities, or betas, by time-series regressions. For example, to estimate the sensitivity of HSBC to the banking sector, the returns to HSBC are compared, using statistical regression, to the returns to a known index of banking stocks.

Cross-sectional method –apply the factor betas directly from empirical data and then estimate the factor returns by cross-sectional regressions and so derive the factor covariances. For example, the exposure of HSBC to a dividend factor would be derived from what is currently known about HSBC, such as its dividend payout ratio.[4] The return to the factor is computed from the aggregate of stocks with betas to it.

In either case, there will be an inevitable loss of information and the introduction of some estimation error into the model. In the time series method:

- The estimation error will be in the stock betas. In the cross-sectional method, the estimation error will be in the factor returns, and hence in the factor covariances. Note also that both methods presume that the variables to be derived from empirical data are actually observable. The observability issue is discussed further.
- The factor covariances should correspond directly with the observed behaviour of the factors – the bank factor will behave like the publicly-quoted index of bank stocks; while the stock betas will have estimation errors. In the cross-sectional method the factor covariances will have estimation error from the cross-sectional regressions and from sampling, while the stock betas are given.
- The estimation error in the stock betas will be diversified away at the portfolio level. In the cross-sectional method, the estimation error in the factor covariances is not diversified away, but remains the same for a portfolio as it was at the stock level. Estimation errors in the stock residual risks – exposures of individual stocks that are not attributable to common factors – will also tend to diversify away at the portfolio level.

For portfolio risk analysis, it is clearly better for the estimation error to be in the stock betas than for it to be in the factor covariance matrix.

The limitation of the time-series method is that it can be used only when the estimated stock betas are stable over time. However there are some factors, such as the Fama–French factors, value and growth, which are interesting precisely because the betas are not stable over time. For example, we like high book-to-price ratio stocks because we don't expect them to stay that way for long. In these cases, cross-sectional beta estimations are more appropriate.

Size is an often used factor in risk models. Investment managers buy small stocks because they believe that one day they will be medium or large stocks. So for medium to long investment horizons, size is a factor whose beta must be observed rather than estimated from time series. Over short investment horizons, say less than a year, it can make sense to estimate stock betas to size using time-series regression as the progression from small to medium is unlikely to happen in that time.

So in many circumstances, it makes sense for a risk model to have both kinds of factor beta estimation. But there will still be some estimation error whereby risk that is actually factor-related can be wrongly attributed to stock-specific effects. One way to capture this risk is to supplement pre-specified factors with statistical factors, effectively borrowing from the PCA methodology.

In combination with pre-specified factors, statistical factors can capture things like:

- Transient factors, which are systematic effects that occur only in particular market conditions and then disappear. A good example of a transient factor is a short-lived interest rate shock that affects capital-intensive stocks more than others. Another example, observed in the mid-2000s, was the brief appearance of a common factor affecting stocks with celebrity CEOs, who featured in the press at the time.
- Emerging factors, which may herald new market trends, such as new industry groups or markets that are not specified in the model but which endure. The emergence of new markets in Africa is a recent example.

Statistical factors share the difficulties of interpretation of PCA, but as they usually account for only a small portion of the portfolio-level risk, they do not significantly impede overall interpretation of the risk model's results. On the contrary, they can add important insight and ensure that the risk that is attributed to stock-specific effects really is stock-specific.

Risk models can therefore be hybrid in two different senses:

- Combine pre-defined factors with statistical factors to ensure that 'stock risk' really is 'stock risk', and does not contain any residual common factor effects.
- Include both time-series factors (with estimated betas) and cross-sectional factors (derived from observed betas), as appropriate for the various factors.

Observable factor betas

Investment managers and investors find risk analyses most helpful if risk is attributed according to recognizable risk factors. Apart from being intuitive, observable risk factors add to the transparency of a risk model, which aids interpretation and helps spot any errors.

The time-series method usually allows us to find reasonably good proxies for the returns to the chosen factors. Thus the returns to a 'US market' factor can be proxied by the S&P500, the Russell 3000 or the Wilshire 5000.

However in the cross-sectional method it is necessary to observe the exposures of all the stocks to all the factors directly, which increases the scope for errors. For example, for a global risk model with 50 factors covering 20000 stocks, we would need to observe 1000000 betas each time the model is updated.

The commonly used short cut is to use binary, or dummy, variables as stock betas for currency, industry and country exposures. This means, for example, that Société Générale is given a beta of 1.0 on the Euro, 1.0 on France, and 1.0 on banking, and 0.0 for all other factors. While this is very easy to do (and has to be done only once), it is unrealistic. Clearly, not all banks have a beta of 1.00 on banking. This error is systematic, cannot be diversified away and will compound at the portfolio level: it will also affect the usefulness of the model for portfolio optimization. An optimizer fed with binary betas will (incorrectly) think that all banks are equally risky. If a more risky bank is given a higher expected return, the optimizer will probably overweight it while under-estimating its risk. One work-around is to split the binary betas between industries or countries. But this necessitates an arbitrary allocation of exposure and supposes that the stock's industry exposures sum to 1.0, which is hardly more realistic. Using binary variables for betas gives portfolio betas that correspond directly to the weight of the respective holdings in the portfolio. Thus, if 15 per cent of the portfolio's holdings are banks, the portfolio beta to banks will appear to be 0.15. However this is to confound weight with exposure, which are not the same thing. For example, being 100 per cent invested does not always mean you have a market beta of one.

Despite the differences in estimation methods, mean-variance risk models share some features:

- They are transparent, being based on well-tested economic theory and well-understood intermediate computations.
- They can be easy to interpret, as they incorporate stable and mostly intuitive relationships between stocks and common factors and between common factors.

- They give an intuitive and relatively stable risk attribution, and distinguish between the exposure of assets to risk factors and how much they contribute to portfolio risk.
- They can be used to forecast risk over most investment horizons that are relevant to investment managers, including daily, weekly and monthly.

Their disadvantages are:

- They can be used only for equities and some asset allocation and multifund purposes.
- They do not easily accommodate instability in asset and factor covariances that can characterize extreme markets.

Simulation

With a wide range of non-financial applications, the adaptation of simulation to financial markets became popular in the mid-1990s. It was used by global banks (JP Morgan was the first) who sought to estimate the risk of severe losses over very short time intervals for global portfolios comprising bonds, short-term interest rate instruments, loans, foreign currencies and complex derivatives.

Simulation works by computing, from a given portfolio composition, information about each instrument held and a sample of historical returns, a large number of possible outcomes for each of the portfolio's holdings. From these outcomes it derives aggregate measures such as mean (expected return), standard deviation (tracking error), Value at Risk (VaR), Conditional Value at Risk (CVaR) and other estimates of extreme loss.

Each holding is modelled according to the characteristics of the instrument, such as bond call provisions and option exercise price and dates. This means that simulation can accommodate any investment instrument that itself can be modelled. One of the ways that providers of simulation systems differentiate themselves is by the sophistication of their instrument-level modelling and the range of instruments they cover. Instrument-level models are used to calculate changes in the price of each asset that result from each simulation. The change in the portfolio value is the weighted sum of the changes in the values of the component holdings of the portfolio.

Importantly, the change in the price of any given asset is particular to the 'event' simulated. For example, the price change for a bond that is caused by interest rates increasing from 2 per cent to 2.05 per cent is less than the price change caused by interest rates increasing from 6 per cent to 6.05 per cent. This 'non-linearity' is a feature of bonds, options and structured products, but is not shared by equities, which are said to be 'linear': the change in the value of an equity resulting from an increase in the share price from \$100 to \$105 is the same as the change in value that results in the share price increasing from \$500 to \$505.

The ability of simulation to capture differential responsiveness in instrument values is of course powerful, but simulation is less good at capturing the interactions between changes in asset prices; and less good still at identifying common factors in a way that can help quantify sources of portfolio risk.

Simulation is nearly always carried out over very short time horizons, typically one day. This means that it reflects daily portfolio fluctuations, which do not necessarily extrapolate to longer horizons such as monthly or yearly.

Most portfolio simulations are either parametric or non-parametric. Parametric simulation is where the manager imposes a pre-defined distribution. In a non-parametric distribution the data are left to yield their results in whatever distribution results.

Non-parametric simulations

Historic simulation – as its name would imply, this is a matter of feeding in historical returns to see how a given portfolio would have behaved over the period from which the historical returns were extracted. The output is a large number of possible outcomes that is taken to describe how the portfolio would behave should similar conditions re-occur.

Monte Carlo simulation – Monte Carlo derives its name from the town in Monaco, where the outcomes at the famous casino are said to be in some sense random. Instead of applying historical returns, the simulation applies random returns to the holdings in the portfolio to generate a large number of possible outcomes. It is therefore not tied to a particular data sample in the way that historical simulation is. The limitation is that true randomness can be surprisingly difficult to achieve in practice: systematic biases can creep in, and can be difficult to spot and correct for.

Parametric simulations

Gaussian simulation imposes a symmetrical Gaussian or normal return distribution on the simulation.

Non-Gaussian simulation imposes some other, known distribution on the simulation. There are a number of reasons to use non-normal distributions. For example, some distributions are good for deriving results from relatively small samples of data, while others can accommodate asymmetrical (skewed) return distributions or a relatively high probability of extreme outcomes (kurtosis or 'fat tails').

Risk decomposition

To estimate how groups of holdings contribute to each portfolio outcome, simulation systems usually aggregate holdings into 'buckets' according to defined characteristics such as industry group or currency of denomination. This is necessarily arbitrary and may not provide for membership of multiple buckets.

The bucket method computes, for each bucket, a VaR, CVaR and so on, as if each bucket were a self-contained portfolio. Buckets are sometimes wrongly interpreted as exposures to common factors, when this is not the case. Unlike factor decomposition of risk, the buckets method says nothing about how the risk of each bucket compounds or offsets the risk of the other buckets, and therefore gives no information about how much they contribute to portfolio level VaR, CVaR and so on.

Some simulation systems identify 'volatility clusters' that can show which groups of assets have covaried over the sample period. The limitation is that it can be difficult to derive economic meaning from the information and the clusters that are identified do not necessarily persist from one period to the next.

To compensate for its relative weakness in estimating interactions between instruments and common factors, some simulation methodologies incorporate copula analyses to help model co-dependencies. A potentially serious drawback of this is that the complexity of the embedded processes can mean that they are poorly understood by the analysts who use them, with the result that errors can go unchecked.[5] Complexity combined with the difficulty of scrutinizing the results can encourage unquestioning acceptance of the output, which is dangerous if the results are to be used to support investment decisions.

Simulation techniques can differ substantially in detail, although some features they share are:

- Their instrument coverage is usually very broad, virtually comprehensive for some systems.
- Simulation can do a good job of estimating skew and fat tails in portfolio-level outcomes. Apart from being able to analyse options and optionality, it can also take account of how asset sensitivities change with market conditions. The ability to accommodate non-linear asset sensitivities is widely considered helpful in modelling the behaviour of

stressed markets, which are characterized by sharp changes in the way assets covary with each other.

- Simulation is usually poor at attributing risk to its sources.
- It is typically confined to very short simulation horizons, which do not necessarily extrapolate to longer horizons. While this is suitable for the complex and ever-changing portfolio of assets held by a bank, it is less relevant to investment funds with horizons calibrated in months or years.
- The process often embeds very complex modelling of instruments and interactions, which can lack transparency and hinder interpretation of the results.

Mean-variance versus simulation

The most visible difference between simulation and mean-variance is the range of investments they can accommodate. As a rule, investments with some kind of contingent claim or liability, such as options or corporate bonds, are outside the range of mean-variance but within scope of simulation, as summarized in Table 5.1.

Table 5.1 Simulation and mean-variance: instrument coverage

Instrument	Exposure	Simulation	Mean-variance
Physical equity	Linear	Yes	Yes
Equity index future	Linear	Yes	Yes
Single-equity future	Linear	Yes	Yes
Equity swap	Linear	Yes	Yes
Equity index option	Non-linear	Yes	No
Single-equity option	Non-linear	Yes	No
Physical currency	Linear	Yes	Yes
Currency forward	Linear	Yes	Yes
Currency swap	Linear	Yes	Yes
Physical government bond	Non-linear	Yes	No
Government bond index future	Linear	Yes	Yes
Government bond index option	Non-linear	Yes	No
Government bond swap	Non-linear	Yes	No
Physical corporate bond	Non-linear	Yes	No
Credit Default Swap (CDS)	Non-linear	Yes	No
Asset Backed Security (ABS)	Non-linear	Yes	No
Commodity future	Linear	Yes	Yes
Commodity option	Non-linear	Yes	No

Table 5.2 Simulation and mean-variance: advantages and disadvantages

	Mean-variance	Simulation
Portfolio-level risk	Yes	Yes
Valid decomposition of risk	Potentially good	Poor
Instrument coverage	Linear only	Comprehensive
Best in market conditions that are:	Stable	Extreme
Forecast horizon	Short or long	Short only
Transparency of intermediate computations	Potentially good	Poor
Ease of interpretation	Potentially good	Poor
Ease of spotting errors	Potentially good	Poor

Instruments with no material option-like characteristics, such as equities, are here described as linear because their factor exposures are stable in most conditions. In practice they are also known as 'fixed-delta' or 'delta-one'. Instruments with option-like characteristics or contingent exposures are described as non-linear. They are also known as 'variable-delta' instruments.

Table 5.2 gives a summary of the practical strengths and weaknesses of simulation and mean-variance methodologies.

Data

All risk modelling methodologies rely to some extent on samples of historical return data.[6] How the data sample is selected is an important determinant of the results of any risk model, as illustrated by the apparent 'failure' of many risk models in 2007 and 2008. This section discusses issues that arise when selecting data samples for input to a risk model, including:

- The period of history.
- The length of history.
- Weighting of observations.
- Periodicity of observations.
- Timing of observations.

Risk models generally sample their data from between two and eight years of asset return history, so in mid-2008 their samples dated from about 2000 at the earliest. This period was characterized by unusually calm markets: volatility in the largest stock markets tended to range from 18 to

20 per cent, compared with a norm of 23 to 28 per cent before the mid-1990s. With only low volatility returns to work with, any risk model will give a very low or even a zero probability of an extreme event. Add some volatility to the sample data and the model will accord a higher probability. It is not unusual for markets to exhibit uncharacteristic calm in the lead up to a shock, so the bias introduced by unrepresentative data can be greatest just when it is most damaging.

The length of history is important: too short and the sample risks being unrepresentative of the forecast period; too long and even less tractable problems can arise. For example, it may capture structural changes in the market that are no longer relevant: think of how the wave of privatizations in the 1990s and the advent of dot-com stocks permanently altered the investment universe. Long histories also embed survivorship bias, as the omission of companies that failed during the period distorts the sample.

Historical returns can be weighted equally or in a way that gives more importance to recent observations. Equal weighting can give odd results as an extreme event suddenly drops out of the rolling sample, resulting in a discrete jolt in risk numbers. Differential weighting is therefore preferred for most risk modelling.

Being able to control the period from which historical data are drawn, how frequent the observations are and how they are weighted has the obvious advantage that the manager can ensure that appropriate extreme events are included and weighted appropriately. The danger is in choosing data to support a pre-conceived outcome, although this can be managed by establishing appropriate policy guidelines. Some risk systems come with fixed data histories, which the provider has found to give the most valid and stable results for most purposes, while others allow the user considerable control over how the data are treated.

The importance of the periodicity of the data sample is often underappreciated. Whether the data are sampled monthly, weekly or daily affects what kind of volatility is captured by the model and determines the horizon of the estimate. Daily observations give forecast volatilities for a day, weekly for a week and monthly for a month. Daily, weekly and monthly volatilities are typically multiplied by the square root of 250, 52 or 12 to give annualized volatility forecasts.

The frequency of return observations can say different things about the likely volatility of an investment – independently of the period in history from which they were collected. Example 5.1 shows annualized volatility estimates for the same market over the same period of time, but with different sample frequencies.

For an intuitive explanation of these results, consider how price movements can sometimes over-react to news and then correct, resulting in more 'noise' at the level of daily returns than weekly or monthly. The opposite can be true if markets are trending: consecutive daily price movements in the same direction appear more volatile when observed from one month to the next – or in the case of the FTSE World in Example 5.1 from one week to the next – than would be implied by relatively small daily variations.

Example 5.1 Data periodicity

	FTSE World	S&P500	FTSE UK
Daily volatility	1.18%	1.60%	1.50%
Annualized	18.69%	25.27%	23.75%
Weekly volatility	2.73%	3.04%	3.19%
Annualized	19.69%	21.89%	23.02%
Monthly volatility	4.46%	4.69%	4.88%
Annualized	15.45%	16.26%	16.91%

Source: FactSet

It is easy to assume that more frequent data are somehow more thorough than less frequent data sampling. But this is often an illusion: too frequent sampling can confound the results with noise that is not relevant to the investment decision.

Not only does it matter how often you sample return data, it can also matter when you choose to do it. Most risk models sample their weekly and monthly data at the end of the week or month, which seems the obvious thing to do. But end-of-period trading can differ from mid-period activity as some market participants rebalance their portfolios ready for reporting – often reversing the transactions at the start of the following period. So biases can creep into end-of-period prices and the returns that are calculated from them.[7] To see how big this effect can be, consider the comparison between end-of-month and mid-month returns for two large equity markets shown in Example 5.2.

Example 5.2 Timing of observations

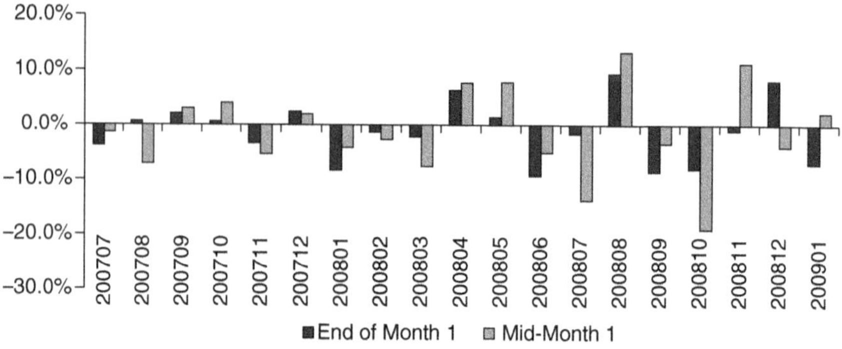

Source: FactSet

	End of month	Mid-month
Mean	0.1%	0.1%
Volatilty	4.5%	5.6%
Annualized	15.4%	19.4%

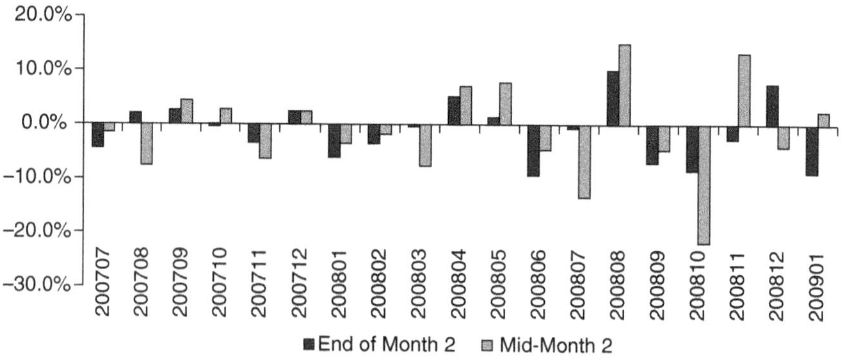

Source: FactSet

	End of month	Mid-month
Mean	0.4%	0.4%
Volatilty	4.7%	5.9%
Annualized	16.3%	20.5%

Although not widely recognized, the end-of-period effect, as shown in Example 5.2, can introduce bias into estimations of portfolio risk, as the differences in annualized volatilities show. While techniques exist to correct for this source of bias, only advanced providers apply them to their risk models.

Adapting mean-variance models to extreme markets

A common criticism of mean-variance models is that they capture the effects of extreme market conditions poorly. There is clearly substance to this charge, but a number of providers have adapted their methodology to overcome at least some of the short-comings while retaining the power of mean-variance to attribute risk efficiently.

The most popular approaches to modelling extreme risk are to tweak a normal mean-variance model and to simulate defined events. To tweak a normal model, you can either simply scale up systematic volatilities to reflect the underestimation of market volatility inherent in standard mean-variance risk measurements, or take sample data only from periods of turmoil. The first ignores the problem of changed correlations between factors, and is unsatisfactory for portfolios with high stock-specific component of risk as it also ignores correlations in these sources of risk. It also ignores serial correlations between factors and assets due to the effects of margin-lending and portfolio protection induced selling as well as the drying up of liquidity in extreme markets. The second can suffer from a shortage of data, at least in most markets.

Risk model testing

If you are using the output of your risk model to support investment decisions, you will be interested to know how well it forecasts risk. Not only can this help validate the model you are using, it can also be very a useful way of comparing the power of two or more similar models.

An obvious way of testing a risk model is to compare its forecasts of risk with the risk that is subsequently observed in the portfolio, its benchmark and the variation between them. In practice, this exercise is often confounded by changes in the composition of the portfolio and the benchmark over time, which can render the risk model test invalid.

Useable results can sometimes be derived from portfolios with very low turnover, but few portfolios retain substantially the same percentage holdings in them over extended time intervals. Even relatively low turnover can confound the results and it is not possible to tell how much of the apparent forecasting error is actually due to changes in the composition of the portfolio and benchmark.

This can be controlled by testing the model over an extended period using constant-holding portfolios and benchmarks. This entails keeping the portfolio and benchmark percentage weights constant throughout the exercise.

Example 5.3 Risk model testing

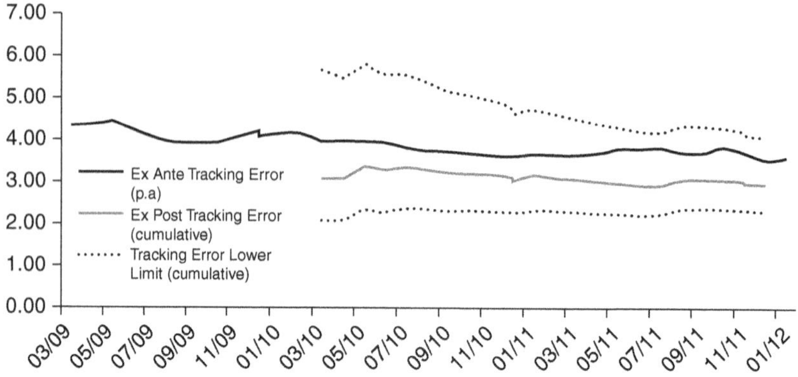

Source: R-Squared Risk Management

Example 5.3 shows a successful risk model. Note that, the forecast tracking error is slightly higher than the observed measure, but well within the 95 per cent confidence bands. It is more common for risk forecasts to underestimate risk; the over-estimation in this example is almost certainly due to the fact that the model was sampling from data that included the volatile market conditions of 2009. The model in question is double-hybrid and corrects for end-of-period biases.

Summary

No single risk methodology is unambiguously better than the others for all types of portfolio. Each of the two 'families' of risk modelling is better for some risk modelling applications than for others. Within each family, a range of methodological variations serve different risk modelling purposes.

All risk modelling techniques are sensitive to the data with which they model portfolio risk, though some techniques are more sensitive than others. The validity of any risk analysis depends on using the appropriate data sample.

A good way to see how well a risk model performs, or to compare the validity of two risk models for a particular portfolio type, is to test them, by comparing, for a low turnover or a constant weights portfolio, the risk forecasts given with observed return variations.

Case Study

A mid-sized investment management company specializing in the management of portfolios for small and mid-sized organizations sought to distinguish itself with leading risk management.

The majority of the firm's clients sought portfolios with higher than average income. Many also wanted to avoid investment in assets that breached various ethical guidelines. Investment mandates included global equities and UK equities. It decided to support its claim to superior risk management by engaging to have an equity risk model built to mirror its investment process and strategies. Despite is commitment to superior risk management the investment manager's budget constraints obliged it to make do with a single customized model rather than separate models for UK and global equities, and it was decided that a global model would be built for use with both types of portfolio.

The investment selection process focussed on choosing regions, for global mandates, and within them economic sectors and industry groups that were expected to perform well over the investment horizon. Subsequent stages of the selection process screened stocks for sustainable dividend-paying capacity and by economic activity in order to eliminate firms that did not meet ethical, environmental and social responsibility criteria. All portfolios were hedged to their base currency.

The first step in this process was to define the parameters for a customized risk model that would best harness the manager's investment selection skills and reflect the process of selection by region and economic sector within regions. The most visible aspect of an equity risk model is the risk factors it includes. Ideally risk factors should be as independent of each other as possible. This helps ensure that the risk that is captured by each factor is indeed attributable to that factor and not to another, highly-correlated factor. In practice it is not always possible to choose perfectly uncorrelated factors as some markets are dominated by a few economic sectors – as the UK is with banks and Taiwan is with electronics, resulting in correlations between industry and country factors. Risk can appear to migrate between highly-correlated factors from one period to the next, making the model appear unstable. This can be circumvented by the use of factor blocs, where each risk factor is assigned to a bloc and each of the blocs is accorded a priority relative to the others. Risk is then attributed sequentially to factor blocs according to their place in the hierarchy. Factors in subsequent blocs are estimated from the residuals of the preceding blocs, reducing correlations between the factors.

The risk manager was keen that all risk factors should be visible and transparent, which in practice meant favouring factors that derive their returns, and therefore the factor covariance matrix from publicly-available index return series, rather than cross-sectional factors, which tend to be less visible.

At first it was thought that the factor hierarchy should include income factors and a selection of ethical, environmental-sustainability or social responsibility factors. But when no suitable global income factor could be identified, it was decided to dispense with the income factor. This decision was supported by the observation that income can be highly correlated with country and industry; with high income a characteristic of utilities and finance sectors and low income a feature of markets such as Japan and Taiwan.

When the question of ethical bias was discussed in detail, it became evident that there were in fact three aspects to this:

- Social responsibility, including questions of corporate governance.
- Environmental sustainability.
- Ethical investment, such as avoiding pornography, tobacco, gambling and so on.

Thus not one but three publicly-quoted global ethical factors would need to be identified, which turned out to be impossible. Again eschewing cross-sectional factors, it was decided that at least the second two of these would be accounted for in sector factors. The first would be partially accounted for by regional factors. The risk manager was surprised to learn that pornography was found to be impossible to avoid in practice without depriving the portfolios of the opportunity to invest in the Telecoms sector.

The model thus comprised the following risk factors:

Currency:

- US Dollar,
- Canadian Dollar,
- Australian Dollar,
- Japanese Yen,
- Swiss Franc,
- Euro.

Country and region:

- USA,
- Canada,
- South Africa,
- Australia,
- New Zealand,
- Japan,
- Asia Pacific ex Japan,
- Switzerland,
- Nordic Region,
- Euroland,
- UK.

Industry and sector:

- oil and gas,
- basic materials,
- industrials,

- consumer goods,
- tobacco,
- health care,
- consumer services,
- telecommunications,
- utilities,
- financials,
- real estate,
- technology.

Statistical:

- statistical factor 1,
- statistical factor 2,
- statistical factor 3,
- statistical factor 4,
- statistical factor 5.

Currencies were given priority because of their importance in calculating the appropriate currency hedge, which was estimated from the portfolio's betas to currency factors. A typical attribution of risk for the two portfolios relative to their benchmark indices is shown in Example 5.4. The risk manager was unsurprised to see that the domestic equities portfolio demonstrated non-trivial exposures to currencies other than sterling. The large UK banks are known for their global reach, so one would expect them to have non-sterling exposures. Similarly, entities such as Unilever, Rolls Royce and GlaxoSmithKline, to mention a few well-known examples, have significant exposure to foreign currencies.

Note that the model is single hybrid in the sense that it includes both time-series and statistical factors. The latter were included to capture any income or ethical effects not captured by region and industry factors, as well as any transient factor effects, although in practice these were captured by sector and country factors as expected, and the contribution from the statistical factors turned out to be minor. Statistical factors are by construction independent from each other, so risk captured by them cannot overlap with other factors.

Example 5.4 Portfolio contribution to risk

	UK Equities	Global Equities
Currency	6.9%	24.3%
Country & Region	37.1%	36.3%
Industry & Sector	25.1%	22.7%
Statistical	9.1%	3.7%
Factor-related risk	78.3%	87.1%
Stock-specific risk	21.7%	12.9%
Total	100%	100%

Comparison with other, off-the-shelf risk models vindicated the decision to deploy a customized model: it consistently gave more valid risk estimates than even the best of the off-the-shelf alternatives.

This was a potent marketing advantage. Also important was the ability to relate the risk profile of the portfolio to visible economic sectors: clients and prospective investors found comfort in seeing a risk attributed to things they recognized readily.

Endnotes

1. Translated from the Dutch translated version of 'Egotunnel' by Thomas Metzinger, the original quote can be found on p. 151 of Elizabeth Anscombe's *An Introduction to Wittgenstein's Tractatus'* (London, 1959). Source: www.goodreads.com; available at http://tpdr.wordpress.com/2010/04/07/wittgenstein-quoted/.
2. For the following description of mean-variance risk models I have benefitted enormously from the knowledge and insights (and his generosity with both) of Jason MacQueen of R-Squared Risk Management, whose understanding of the subject is unrivalled. I am therefore very grateful for the help he has given me. The material in this chapter is adapted from his talk 'The Structure of Risk Models', given at a meeting of the London Quant Group in January 2012.
3. They also differentiate themselves by how they select and treat the data sample used to support the model, but its impact on overall model performance is minor compared to that of the factor covariance matrix.
4. A light-hearted example of a factor exposure derived in this way is the observation that, in 1968, the best performing US stocks were those with 'x' in their name, led by Exxon and Xerox. It was dubbed 'the X Factor'.
5. An excellent account of how this can happen is given by Donald MacKenzie and Taylor Spears (2012) in *The Formula that Killed Wall Street? The Gaussian Copula and the Material Cultures of Modelling.*
6. Even Monte Carlo simulation, which usually calibrates the mean and dispersion of its 'random values' from what is known to have happened in the past.
7. This effect was first documented in an excellent paper by Daniella Acker and Nigel Duck (2006), 'Reference day risk and the use of monthly returns: A warning note'.

6
Risk Measurement

A man is strolling in the street just after dusk when he comes across a stranger crouching beneath a lamp-post, evidently looking for something on the ground.

- Good evening, have you lost something?
- Yes, I've lost a cufflink.
- Let me help you look for it. Where did you lose it?
- Over there.
- But if you lost it over there, why are you looking for it here?
- Because the light is better.

If you look in the wrong place, you are unlikely to find what you're looking for. That is obvious. To get the answer you want or need, you must ask the right question. To understand the risk in an investment, you must take the right measurements.

To get the information you need, you must ask the right question. The right question depends on what you will do with the answer when you get it. This chapter discusses:

- The purpose of risk measurement.
- Frequently used risk measures.
- Some useful tips to derive more insight from risk measurement.
- Measuring risk for extreme markets.
- How the choice of data sample can affect risk measures.
- Ways of meeting the particular challenges of multi-strategy portfolios, funds of funds and funds of hedge funds.

The purposes of risk measurement

The two main reasons to measure risk are:

- To manage it, including to support investment decisions.
- To report and monitor it.

Risk management

Risk management entails portfolio construction, rebalancing and hedging that can change the composition of the portfolio, with the aim of aligning risk with expected return. It must:

- Ensure that the overall level of risk is consistent with the return objectives and risk tolerances of the investment mandate.
- Ensure that exposure to the market is appropriate to the portfolio objectives.
- Align all sources of risk with the investment manager's expected sources of return.
- Eliminate incidental exposure to factors and assets with negative (or unknown) expected return.
- Quantify sources of vulnerability to extreme events and shocks.
- Hedge the most dangerous sources of extreme risk – for example, using deep out-of-the-money options – ideally without materially changing the portfolio's risk profile and therefore its ability to meet investment objectives.

Within the limits set by the investment mandate, risk management demands that the investment manager and the risk manager use their judgement to decide whether or not a portfolio's risk profile is appropriate. To support this judgement, risk measures must be:

- Relevant.
- Accurate.
- Immediate.

The investment manager must be confident that he or she is acting only on sound information about his or her portfolio.

Risk reporting

Measures for reporting risk do not support any changes to the composition of the portfolio itself. They aim to:

- Ensure that the overall level of risk is consistent with the return objectives and risk tolerances of the investment mandate.
- Ensure that exposure to the market is appropriate to the portfolio objectives.
- Quantify the main causes of the portfolio's vulnerability to shocks.
- Facilitate comparison with the range of tolerances given by the investment mandate or prospectus.
- Facilitate comparison with peer portfolios.

They are prepared for:

- Investors.
- Senior management.
- Governance bodies.
- Regulators.
- Creditors.
- Prospective investors.
- Marketing.

Risk analyses that are prepared for investors, governance bodies and regulators should of course be accurate, but drill-down is frequently not needed. The reporting timetable tends to be fixed, with longer lead times than demanded by risk management. While they should be as relevant as possible, this ideal is sometimes compromised by the need to standardize reports to facilitate comparison with peer-group funds.

Risk monitoring often results in some healthy questioning of the profile, for example when one or more measures is very different from the previous period. The primary purpose is to reassure its readers, for whom it may be the main source of information about the fund, that the portfolio complies with the terms of its mandate and will meet its objectives. Risk reporting and monitoring is in effect a check that risk management is working.

Risk measures

In order to manage risk you must first measure it meaningfully and accurately. This means not only using the right risk tools but also deriving from them the right risk measures. While a number of well-known risk measures have become accepted as 'standard', they may not give the information you need to do so.

This section describes some frequently used risk measures, including:

- Volatility.
- Tracking error.

- VaR.
- CVaR.
- Maximum drawdown.
- Beta to benchmark.
- Beta to market.
- Portfolio value per basis point (PVBP).
- Maturity.
- Duration.
- Slope.
- Convexity.
- Credit quality.
- Risk decomposition.
- Scenario analysis.
- Stress testing.
- Sensitivity analysis.
- Liquidity.
- Leverage.
- Currency exposure.

Portfolio volatility

Volatility measures by how much the portfolio's returns will vary in absolute terms, in other words relative to the risk-free interest rate, most of the time in stable markets.

It is the primary risk measure for funds with investment targets expressed as absolute returns, such as strategy benchmarks for multi-asset class funds and single asset class, absolute return funds. Observed portfolio volatility is measured as the standard deviation of the portfolio returns, so it assumes that those returns are symmetrically distributed and that returns that exceed the target are just as likely as those that fall short. This means that it is less satisfactory for portfolios with significant optionality, such as a corporate bond portfolio and some hedge funds, but it works well for equities, including long-short portfolios, and TAA portfolios.

Risk is often confounded with portfolio volatility, when in fact the two are distinct. While volatility is a measure of how much returns can vary, risk is better thought of as the likelihood of failing to meet investment objectives. Most investment portfolios aim to deliver a return above some benchmark or comparator portfolio, so a low-volatility portfolio can prove more risky if it impedes the chances of achieving the target return.

Example 6.1 Risk versus volatility

Summary statistics	Portfolio 1	Portfolio 2	Target
Return	45.12%	5.75%	36.45%
Annualized return	14.65%	2.07%	12.00%
Annualized volatility	19.86%	6.26%	0.00%

Example 6.1 illustrates a target return of 12 per cent per annum, which is better met by portfolio 1, with annual volatility of 20 per cent, than by portfolio 2, with annual volatility of 6 per cent. Portfolio 2 has almost no chance of achieving the target return, so from the point of view of its investors it is the more risky portfolio.

Investment risk is also often thought of as the possibility of extreme loss resulting from a market-wide shock or an event that affects the portfolio more than its peers. Monitoring the portfolio's vulnerability to extreme outcomes is a necessary complement to monitoring its positioning for day-to-day management, but by itself does not add information about how likely the portfolio is to achieve its target return, so cannot satisfy the aim of risk measurement.

Volatility is forecast from the volatility of the historical returns of the assets in the portfolio and the covariances between them. For a portfolio with a large number of assets in it, a risk model is used to reduce the size of the covariance matrix and volatility is thus forecast from stock betas to common factors, the volatility of the historical returns of the common factors and the factor covariance matrix, rather than the covariances of the asset returns themselves. Volatility is often used in conjunction with return to give the Sharpe ratio to compare the balance of return and risk between peer-group portfolios.

$$\text{Sharpe ratio} = \frac{(r_p - r_f)}{\sigma_p} \tag{6.1}$$

Where:

R_p = the return to the portfolio
r_f = the risk free rate of return
σ_p = portfolio volatility

Tracking error

Tracking error is similar to portfolio volatility, but instead of measuring the absolute returns to the portfolio, it measures the difference between the portfolio's returns and those of its benchmark. For a portfolio with an investment objective expressed as a margin over some benchmark, this is the primary estimate of the likelihood of its succeeding. Tracking error was originally devised for equities portfolios, but can be used more widely.

Observed tracking error is measured as the standard deviation of the difference between portfolio and benchmark returns, so it assumes that those differences are symmetrically distributed and that out-performance is just as likely as under-performance. This means that it is less satisfactory for a portfolio with significant optionality, such as a corporate bond portfolio and some hedge funds, but works well for equities and TAA funds.

Tracking error is forecast using the volatilities of the historical returns of the assets in the portfolio and benchmark and the covariances between them. If the portfolio or the benchmark has a large number of assets in it, a risk model is used. Tracking error is thus forecast from stock betas to common factors, the historical returns of the common factors and the factor covariance matrix. Tracking error is often combined with return above benchmark to give the information ratio, which is used to compare the balance of relative return and relative risk between peer-group portfolios.

Example 6.2 Volatility and tracking error

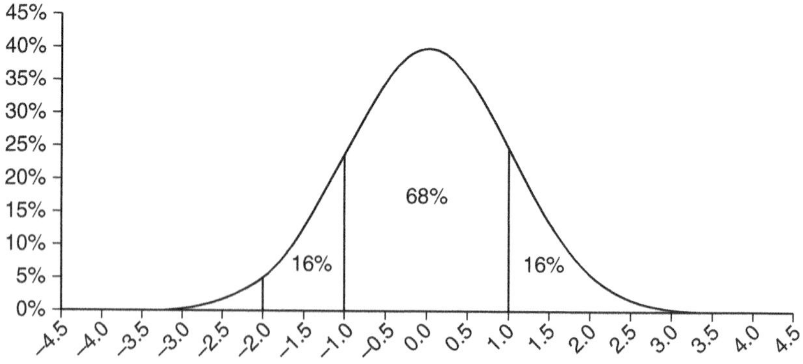

In Example 6.2, volatility and tracking error are the ranges of returns marked by the vertical lines, which represent 68 per cent of outcomes in each case. Volatility refers to absolute return ranges while tracking error refers to ranges of returns relative to a benchmark.

Value at Risk (VaR)

Value at Risk (VaR) is a measure of extreme loss. For example, it gives the outcome that is predicted with a probability of 5 per cent or 1 per cent, expressed as 95 per cent VaR and 99 per cent VaR respectively. It is conceptually similar to volatility and tracking error in that it quantifies a return that corresponds to a given probability; although VaR can also be expressed as the amount of nominal loss in monetary terms. The differences between VaR and tracking error and volatility are:

- Tracking error measures the amount of likely return variation between a portfolio and its benchmark or comparator portfolio, while VaR refers to absolute returns.
- Whereas volatility and tracking error measure the range of return variation that is most likely in stable market conditions, VaR focuses on the risk of very negative returns.
- Both volatility and tracking error demand that returns be symmetrical, while VaR makes no assumptions about the distribution of returns.
- Volatility and tracking error, being intended for TAA and equity portfolios, have limited applications in bond and structured portfolios or wherever there are very asymmetrical returns. VaR can be used with any type of portfolio.
- Volatility and tracking error measure the 68 per cent or outcomes that are most likely to occur, while the range of outcomes captured by VaR is set by the investment manager, typically at 95 per cent or 99 per cent (but in principle can be at any level or probability).
- Because it concentrates on downside risk, VaR ignores the link between risk and positive returns. It does not say anything about how portfolio risk will contribute to investment objectives.
- Because VaR is a point value, it doesn't necessarily say anything about 'how much worse it could get'. If returns are assumed to be symmetrically distributed or conform to some other known distribution, then this question is answered by the distribution parameters (mean, standard deviation, skew and kurtosis). If the return distribution is not known, perhaps because it is derived from a non-parametric simulation, then VaR must be augmented with some other measure of extreme risk to complete the analysis.

VaR is usually complemented by other risk measures, such as CVaR, maximum drawdown and stress testing.

Conditional Value at Risk (CVaR) – also known as expected shortfall (ES) and expected tail loss (ETL) is designed to show how much worse the outcome can be than indicated by VaR. It describes the shape of the loss distribution in the tail, to the left of VaR, thus indicating how long the tail could be, rather than simply a point outcome.

VaR describes the return at which the vertical line occurs – in the case of Example 6.3 it is 95 per cent VaR. CVaR is the shape, in particular the length of the tail to the left of VaR. The dotted line at –1.0 is the volatility, which can also be expressed at an 84 per cent VaR, as the area to its left represents 16 per cent of possible outcomes.

Maximum drawdown – strictly-speaking this is not a risk measure as it measures a single event in the past, defined as the magnitude of the decline from an historical peak to a trough in the value of the fund. It adds no information about how representative it is of the portfolio's volatility or what might have contributed to the fall in value.

Beta to benchmark – measures how sensitive the portfolio is to the benchmark return. A beta of 1 means that the value of portfolio will, on average, go up and down in line with the benchmark. A beta of 1.1 means that it will overshoot by 10 per cent in both directions, while a beta of 0.9 is a portfolio that will, on average, be only 90 per cent responsive to benchmark returns in both directions.

Beta assumes symmetrically distributed returns. It is equal to the weighted sum of the betas of the component assets, each of which in turn is computed from the correlation between portfolio and benchmark returns and the volatility of the returns to each. Beta to benchmark is usually given as a complement to portfolio tracking error.

Example 6.3 95 per cent VaR

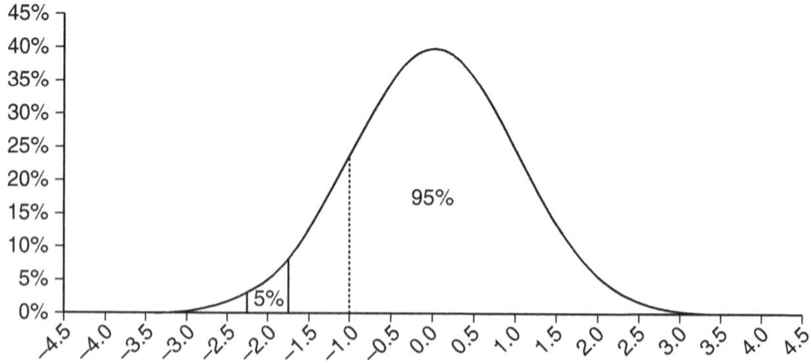

Beta to market – computed in the same way as the beta to benchmark and, as with beta to benchmark, this should be read in conjunction with portfolio tracking error, beta to benchmark, where there is one, and a risk factor decomposition of the portfolio.

Portfolio value per basis point (PVBP) – this applies only to bonds and is the simplest measure of the portfolio's sensitivity to interest rate fluctuations. It is the weighted sum of the Dollar value of 0.01 per cent (DV01) of each bond in the portfolio. As the name suggests, it measures the change in the portfolio's value if the interest rate changes by one basis point (0.01 per cent).

Although this measure is useful for very small fluctuations in the interest rate, it is less so for larger fluctuations because it changes according to the level of the interest rate.

Maturity – the maturity of a bond is simply the time until it matures and the principal and any outstanding interest become due. The maturity of a portfolio is the weighted average of the maturity of the bonds in it. This of course tells you something about the portfolio because, other things being equal, long-maturity bonds are more sensitive to interest rate fluctuations than short bonds. But other things are usually not equal. Bond sensitivity to interest rate fluctuations is also affected by how much interest is outstanding and maturity says nothing about that: a five-year bond paying an annual coupon of 6 per cent is less sensitive to interest rate fluctuations than a five-year zero-coupon bond (which pays all interest at the end of its life), yet both have the same maturity.

Duration – this measures the weighted-average time until bond cash flows are paid. Because it gives information about both the maturity and the cash flow of a bond, it is the most commonly used bond descriptor. The duration of the portfolio is the weighted average of the duration of the bonds in it.

Slope – this measures the sensitivity of the bond or portfolio to a change in the slope of the yield curve. The slope describes the difference in yields between bonds of increasing maturity.

Convexity – this measures the sensitivity of duration to fluctuations in the interest rate. The more convex the bond or portfolio, the more its value changes with bigger yield fluctuations.

Credit quality – the credit quality of a bond is a measure of the current risk of default by the borrower and the risk of 're-rating' the bond. Credit quality is expressed either in terms of its credit rating or as a market-based measure, typically given by the interest rate margin or spread over a government issued bond of similar duration.

The credit quality of a bond indicates whether it can be held in some types of portfolio or posted as collateral against derivatives positions.

Credit ratings have the advantage of being widely recognized and to a degree standardized across markets, facilitating international comparisons. Many investment mandates and regulations use them as investment criteria. Their limitations stem from their being discrete measures and because they are dependent on the expertise of rating agencies, rather than derived directly from market prices.

Market-sourced alternatives are:

- Average credit yield spread over a comparable credit-risk-free bond, such as a domestic government bond.
- Option-adjusted spread, which uses option modelling to estimate the yield spread that explains the difference in price between a corporate bond and a comparable credit-risk-free bond.

A limitation of market-sourced measures of credit risk is that they depend on a transparent and liquid market in securities linked to the bond in question, so cannot be easily applied to all bonds.

Portfolio-level credit risk is usually modelled using simulation in order to capture the optionality inherent in corporate bonds and interactions between bonds that may offset or compound the exposures of each other.

Risk decomposition

While headline risk estimates can tell you whether a portfolio is likely to meet its return target, risk decomposition tells you whether the risks that drive returns are coming from sources of risk that fit with the portfolio's objectives. The investment manager will want to know that his or her portfolio properly reflects his or her views so that risk is directed to where he or she believes it will contribute to returns, and that no unintended risk has crept in that could be a drag on performance or a source of vulnerability to shocks. Investors, senior management and governance bodies want reassurance that risk is well calculated and consistent with the stated objectives of the portfolio and that the possibility of unpleasant surprises has been eliminated as far as possible.

Risk can be broken down by exposure to individual assets to show which positions are contributing most to portfolio risk. For portfolios with large numbers of holdings, asset level risk profiles can miss important concentrations of risk from clusters of assets that, individually may contribute little, but together can have a much bigger effect. There are three ways of doing this.

The first is to cluster like assets in 'buckets' and sum their risk contributions. This works for bonds, where the main risk metric is duration, which is additive. The bucket approach ignores any interactions between the returns to individual bonds. While it can measure betas of groups of equities to the market, a benchmark or other risk factors, it cannot measure how exposures given by the stock betas contribute to the overall risk of the portfolio. For this, interactions between the assets within each bucket need to be taken into account, usually by means of decomposition by common factor, as described further.

The second is corporate and sovereign bonds, and other assets with asymmetrical return distributions, for which simulation methodologies usually approximate factor exposures by measuring the VaR of the buckets of assets within the portfolio. This approximation should be treated with caution, because the VaR of the 'buckets' do not sum to the VaR of the portfolio, as interactions effects cause the VaR of some buckets to offset or compound others. More advanced simulation systems use copulas and other complex modelling techniques to address this limitation.

A more sophisticated method is given by CAPM for assets with normal distributions, which allows the contribution to portfolio volatility and tracking error by common factors.

Risk decomposition by common factor – a good equity risk model will be able to answer two questions:

- What is the directional exposure of the portfolio to factor returns?
- How much does each of these factor exposures contribute to headline portfolio risk?

For equities portfolios, the first question is answered by the portfolio beta to each factor. It is measured in the same way as portfolio beta to benchmark and local market.

The percentage contribution to equity portfolio risk from each factor answers the second question. In a mean-variance model it is a function of the beta of the portfolio to the factor, the volatility of the portfolio and the covariance of the portfolio to the factor. It should be a direct reflection of the investment manager's view on the factor's potential contribution to portfolio return and be consistent with the stated objectives of the portfolio.

Risk decomposition by asset – this is analogous to percentage contribution of factors to portfolio risk but shows instead how much risk is concentrated in individual stock exposures. Most risk analyses highlight the largest contributors to risk from individual assets.

Example 6.4 Equity portfolio risk profile

Global equity portfolio versus quoted benchmark			
Beta			1.00
Tracking error			1.90%
Portfolio volatility			19.07%
Benchmark volatility			18.95%
95% VaR			-7.00%
Dividend yield			2.64%
Number of stocks			50
% of Portfolio tradable in 5 days or less			82.73%
Factor-related risk			59.30%
Stock-specific risk			40.70%
Factor risk ranked by contribution to risk	**Relative holding**	**Relative beta**	**Contribution to risk**
Swiss Franc		0.11	17.10%
Sweden large		–0.04	6.69%
Japanese Yen		–0.34	3.98%
France small		–0.02	3.40%
Building and construction		–0.01	3.06%
Ranked by relative beta			
Swiss Franc		0.11	17.10%
Biotechnology and pharmaceuticals		0.04	2.43%
Germany large		0.04	-1.43%
Consumer staples		0.04	-0.22%
Quality		0.03	0.54%
Japanese Yen		–0.03	3.98%
Sweden large		–0.04	6.90%
Growth trend		–0.04	0.45%
Growth momentum		–0.06	-0.15%
Leverage		–0.13	0.30%

Stock level			
Novartis	6.20%	0.74	13.04%
Nestlé	8.13%	0.73	11.73%
Sanofi	4.73%	0.70	3.99%
UBS	2.35%	1.34	3.98%
Zurich Insurance	1.47%	1.32	2.66%

Source: R-Squared Risk Management

Example 6.4 shows a European equity portfolio benchmarked to a quoted European equity index. It breaks down the difference in return between the portfolio and its benchmark. The portfolio is relatively concentrated, with 50 holdings compared to 328 in the benchmark.

With a portfolio beta to benchmark of 1.00, the portfolio matches benchmark fluctuations, so despite its relative concentration appears quite conservative overall. With a tracking error of only 1.90 per cent, the range of likely outcomes is relatively small. If an information ratio of 0.5 is assumed, which is typical for this type of portfolio, then the portfolio can be expected to outperform its benchmark on average by less than 0.95 per cent

In absolute terms it is slightly more volatile than the benchmark. Note that, while volatility is positive as it represents a range of returns that can be above or below the expected return, VaR measures only downside risk.

The portfolio risk profile shows that beneath the bland summary are some surprisingly concentrated risks, in particular the portfolio's exposure to Swiss Francs, which makes up over 17 per cent of overall risk. Tracking error could be reduced by decreasing this exposure unless the investment manager is confident that the Swiss Franc will appreciate against the Euro.

Notice the discrepancy between holding size of individual assets, their beta to the market and their contributions to risk. Nestlé has the largest relative holding but the portfolio has more exposure to three of the four other stocks. The smaller holding in Novartis contributes more to risk, while the much smaller holding in UBS, at 2.35 per cent, gives more exposure to the benchmark, with a beta of 1.34, than either of the larger holdings. This illustrates the distinction between exposure and weight.

Marginal contribution to risk measures the increase or decrease in portfolio-level risk that would result from a very small increase in the exposure to the common factor or the asset in question, other things being equal. Many risk systems include marginal contribution to risk to help investors understand the contribution to portfolio risk due to factor and asset exposures. However it can be misleading because, by construction, other things cannot be equal: an increase in the percentage exposure to one asset necessarily reduces the percentage exposure to all other assets in the portfolio, each of which will have a different impact on the risk of the portfolio overall. Similarly for common factors: to increase the exposure to a common factor, you must alter the portfolio holdings in some way, which will change the exposures to all other common factors as well as the portfolio overall. The measure is at best hypothetical and not necessarily helpful in informing investment decisions.

Scenario analysis

Scenario analysis is where a portfolio is tested against predefined scenarios in order to estimate its return under each. It is most often used to help determine asset allocations for multi-asset-class portfolios. The advantage of scenario analysis is that it accommodates all instruments and strategies and does not necessarily impose any direct assumptions about the distribution of returns, either for individual assets or for the portfolio overall. It also shows how much each asset class contributes to return in each scenario, and therefore how much each might affect return variation.

One disadvantage is that defining realistic scenarios is surprisingly tricky to do, while poorly defined scenarios give misleading results. To see why scenario analysis can be difficult in practice, consider a simple, eight-asset portfolio to which five scenarios are applied. The investment manager must forecast returns for each asset and each scenario, in other words 40 forecasts. But these return forecasts must be consistent within each scenario, which entails forecasting correlations between each pair of assets. For eight assets there are 28 pairs, so 140 correlations for all five scenarios. The magnitude and direction of each correlation is driven by the precise conditions of the scenario, such as the scope for currency, interest rate and fiscal policy manoeuvre of governments and central banks, and size and distribution of outstanding derivatives positions and margin lending together with multiple other considerations. To complete the analysis four probability forecasts for the five scenarios are needed. This amounts to 184 forecasts. Since most portfolios have many more than eight asset classes, the total is usually much more. As the scope for error increases with the number of forecasts, scenario analysis leaves plenty of opportunity for mistakes.

Another disadvantage is that it is impossible to ensure that all possible scenarios are included. Omitting even one scenario can mislead.

The risk system built for LTCM included the capability for scenario analysis, so it is likely that this was part of its suite of risk measures. Presumably the possibility of a Russian debt crisis, which lead to the demise of the fund, was not included. Widespread use of scenario analyses in the early 2000s excluded a US sub-prime meltdown scenario.

Historical scenarios

Historical scenarios are used to overcome some of the complexities of user defined scenarios and are often used to gauge the portfolio's susceptibility to a crisis or a shock. The limitation is that crises never repeat because central banks and other market participants learn from earlier ones: the oil shock of the 2000s, for example, did not result in stagflation, partly because of what was learned from previous oil shocks. The 2008 market collapse resembles no other in history, partly because of what had been learned from earlier shocks.

While crises never repeat exactly, the symptoms they give rise to can. Sharp asset price falls, changes in yield curve slope and currency shocks can be modelled. Thoughtful use of the information contained in previous crises coupled with consideration of current conditions and robustness testing can inform sensible selection of shock factors and design of stress tests.

Stress testing

Stress testing entails defining an economic shock such as a change in the oil price or the yield to government bonds and working out what impact it would have on the portfolio. There are two main types of stress test.

Deterministic or uncorrelated single stress tests – these quantify the effect on portfolio return of an isolated economic shock, such as a 20 per cent drop in the domestic currency. But shocks do not occur in isolation; for example, a currency shock is always accompanied by shifts in interest rates and equity markets.

Conditional or correlated multiple stress tests – these take into account the relationships between the shock factor and other components of the portfolio. These tests therefore entail modelling dozens or even hundreds of relationships between shock factors and asset prices and flow-on effects to other stock indices, interest rates and currencies.

The effect of a shock is very sensitive to its scale; for example, a 10 per cent shock cannot be extrapolated to a 50 per cent shock – think of the difference in investor reactions to a 1 per cent and a 5 per cent fall in equity prices. The relationship between the scale of a shock and its consequences is usually non-linear and therefore can be complex to model.

Similarly shocks can be instantaneous or sequential, reflecting the effect of market fluctuations on subsequent observations. For example, a sequential shock test takes account of asset sales resulting from previous price falls as the provisions of margin trading and dynamic hedging are triggered. Modelling the relationships between shock factors and other portfolio components is further complicated when various time lags between related events are taken into account.

Sensitivity analysis

Sensitivity analysis computes the impact on a portfolio of small changes from one period to the next in the values of assets and factors to which it is exposed. For example, a portfolio comprising equities and bonds will be subject to various combinations of small changes in equity prices and interest rates, yield curve shifts, exchange rates and so on. The main advantage of this measure is its conceptual simplicity: there is no need to define complex scenarios or shocks and it doesn't depend on any particular return distribution, so can accommodate all investment instruments. Its limitation is that, as it measures only small changes over very short time intervals, it does not measure risks that affect medium and long-term returns that can endure over larger market price movements. It also ignores interaction effects.

Table 6.1 summarizes which risk measures are most applicable to each type of portfolio.

Liquidity

Liquidity measures indicate how tradable the portfolio is. They are typically expressed as the percentage of the portfolio by value that can be liquidated in a given time period, although more than one measure of liquidity is normally used. The aim is to provide comfort that the portfolio will not be subject to undue costs if a partial liquidation becomes necessary at short notice.

Liquidity is usually estimated from recent average trading in each of the portfolio's holdings, typically the most recent one to three months. This is an imperfect measure of course, as many assets trade fitfully and can exhibit quite high turnover for several weeks followed by very sparse turnover. It usually does not reflect the difference between the price at which the assets can be sold, usually the bid price, and the price at which they are currently valued, which is given by the last trade price or, if the

Table 6.1 Risk measures and their applications

	Asset allocation	Bonds	Equities	Structured products
Volatility	✓		✓	
Tracking error	✓		✓	
VaR	✓	✓	✓	✓
CVaR	✓	✓	✓	✓
Beta	✓		✓	
PVBP		✓		
Maturity		✓		
Duration		✓		
Slope		✓		
Twist		✓		
Convexity		✓		
Credit quality		✓		
Contribution to risk	✓		✓	
Scenario analysis	✓			✓
Stress tests	✓	✓	✓	✓
Sensitivity analysis	✓			✓

asset did not trade recently, by the mid-point between the latest buy and sell quotes in the market.

Most liquidity measures are derived from stable market conditions, so do not reflect the 'drying up' that characterizes extreme markets.

Leverage

Leverage is, economically speaking, the same thing as gearing: a means of gaining economic exposure that is greater than the amount originally invested. There are a number of ways of achieving leverage:

- Borrow and invest the borrowed funds in your chosen asset or fund.
- Buy geared investments; for example, a fund or a stock that is itself leveraged.
- Buy assets with higher than average exposure to the market, such as high-beta equities or high-duration bonds.
- Buy uncovered derivatives, where the face value of the contract exceeds the amount paid up front.
- Any combination of these.

All have the same effects on return and risk. The only material difference between them is how they affect the portfolio's exposure to counterparties and whether they are subject to margin calls.

A popular measure of leverage is to compare the face value of the investments with the underlying amount invested. This captures leverage due to borrowing, but ignores the effects of uncovered derivatives positions and investments in geared and high beta or high duration assets. Its measure is often used to compare the portfolio's leverage to the limits defined by the investment mandate or applicable regulation. Limits expressed this way have the big disadvantage that they are easy to circumvent.

Borrowing is relatively easy to measure, but derivative exposure often isn't, especially if long and short positions offset only approximately (for example a five-year bond future versus a shorter two-year bond future); call versus put options, and so on. Capturing the underlying gearing in individual assets can be even trickier.

A robust measure is to take direct account of the portfolio's exposure to its market by measuring its beta to the risky asset in question, such as the equity market, for an equity portfolio; or duration relative to some comparator bond, such as a ten-year government issue, for a bond portfolio. This approach can capture all sources of leverage and can be measured using publicly available information such as past asset prices and bond terms and conditions. It cannot easily be circumvented.

While beta to the market is the most robust means of gauging the leverage of an equity portfolio, it is not fool-proof. Betas are estimates that depend on the sample data from which they are computed. Yet, while an error is almost inevitable, it is usually small compared to the systematic error that often biases the face-value measure of leverage.

Currency exposure

Estimates of portfolio exposure to currency fluctuations are used to calculate the amount needed to hedge the portfolio back to its base currency. Currency exposure is usually given by the sum of the face value of assets denominated in each currency. But this confounds the sum of portfolio weights in assets denominated in a particular currency with the portfolio's exposure to the currency. To see why, consider Toyota, a Japanese carmaker. The face value method tells us that Toyota has exposure to the Japanese Yen and to no other currency. Yet casual observation contradicts this, as the vast majority of its sales and a large proportion of its manufacturing takes place outside Japan. Nestlé, which is exposed to fluctuations in currencies other than the Swiss Franc, is a similar example, as are many other firms.

A more robust and meaningful way is to measure the beta of the stock to the currency factor. This of course is subject to the same beta estimation error that affects its use as a measure of leverage, but the error is likely to be small compared to the systematic bias in the face value method, so will inform more robust currency hedges.

Data

As discussed in Chapter 5 on risk modelling, how the data sample is selected is an important determinant of the results of any risk model. Attention must be given to:

- The length of history: too short and the sample risks being unrepresentative of the forecast period; too long and even less tractable problems, such as survivorship bias and structured changes in the market, can arise.
- Historical returns can be weighted equally or in a way that gives more importance to recent observations.
- The frequency of return observations can say different things about the likely volatility of an investment – independently of the period in history from which they were collected. Extrapolating from daily to monthly or annual results gives invalid and potentially misleading results.

Useful tips

Extra insight can be gained from:

Snapshot versus representative risk measures – a question that often arises for portfolios with very high turnover is whether the snapshot risk profile at period end is representative of the portfolio's risk at other times. An effective way to gauge this is to view the detailed snapshot at the end of the period together with an ad-hoc snapshot at a random mid-period date and daily risk summaries, such as volatility or VaR, throughout the period.

Multi-dimensional risk analysis – even for low-turnover portfolios, a single snapshot may not always give a comprehensive view of the portfolio's risk. Extra insight can often be gained by comparing the profiles given by two different risk models. Of course, the two models may be so different that this results in the 'apples versus pears' problem, so an even better solution is to supplement a monthly model with a daily or weekly model built using the same factor hierarchy and computational methodology.

Risk Measurement in Extreme markets

Until recently, most investment managers assumed that normal risk measurement would cover both normal risk and extreme events. The observation that 'one-in-one-hundred' events seemed to occur suspiciously frequently was thought to be due to quirks in the input data sample, which would correct over time. The latest crisis showed how complacent that assumption was. But if it was naïve to believe that extreme risk could be measured using normal estimation techniques, it is at least as illogical to believe that normal risk can be extrapolated from methods aimed at estimating extreme risk. It is becoming clear to academics and practitioners alike that stable and extreme markets differ in more ways than in the amount of volatility they exhibit. Risk estimation intended to measure risk exposures in stable market conditions falls short when applied to extreme markets for two main reasons:

- It underestimates the likelihood of an extreme event.
- It underestimates the consequences of an extreme event when it happens.

Extreme events are more likely than is usually predicted by normal risk analysis because data samples rarely include an extreme event. Include a shock in the sample and most risk models will accord some likelihood of an extreme outcome within the forecast horizon.

The tendency of normal risk models to understate the severity of shocks is because normal risk models assume that markets are more or less efficient and correlations between assets and risk factors are fairly stable, which they are most of the time. In a crisis, correlations between assets change, sometimes sharply, and assets become difficult to trade as liquidity dries up. This means that the exposures that contribute to vulnerability in extreme market conditions may not be the same as those that contribute most to risk and return in stable markets.

Because extreme markets behave differently to normal or stable markets, they demand purpose built modelling methodologies and measures that capture the effects of extreme market characteristics, such as serial correlations, which are correlations between return in consecutive periods. The measures so far adapted for extreme markets include VaR, CVaR and stress tests.

Risk measurement for multi-asset class funds, multi-strategy and funds-of-hedge funds

Unlike single-asset class funds, balanced funds, multi-strategy and funds-of-hedge funds all combine sub-portfolios of different asset classes. To be effective, risk measurement, and therefore risk management, must be suitable for the master portfolio as well as each of its sub-portfolios. This task is complicated by two considerations:

- The composition of the sub-portfolios may not be known, as in the case of many hedge funds; or cannot be collated within a reasonable time frame to give a relevant risk decomposition, as in the case of many multi-strategy funds-of-funds.
- Because different asset classes demand different risk modelling techniques, combining portfolios within a fund or a mandate can present a challenge for modelling and methodology.

As with any risk analysis, risk measurement for multi-asset class portfolios should seek to relate sources of risk with sources of expected return and the decisions that comprise the portfolio selection process. In practice, this means attributing risk to:

- The asset allocation decision: how much risk is implicit in the allocation to each sub-portfolio?
- Selection within sub-portfolios: how much risk is due to the composition of the sub-portfolios themselves?
- Interaction effects: where exposures in the sub-portfolios offset or compound the effects of allocation between funds.

Because the risk in the master portfolio comprises interaction effects as well as the risks in the sub-portfolios themselves, it cannot be measured as the simple sum of the sub-portfolio risks.

No single risk methodology is likely to be ideal for all parts of the portfolio, although some of the more sophisticated simulation systems can give usable profiles for each. Systems that can accommodate multi-asset class portfolios in a single analysis are necessarily complex, so tend to be expensive and demand considerable resources to keep them functioning properly and of course depend on current information about sub-portfolio composition. In the absence of timely data and a suitable risk tool, one work-around is to employ a two-stage approach:

Stage 1 – familiar single-asset class risk analyses to compare the current portfolio composition of each sub-portfolio to its benchmark.

Stage 2 – adapt mean-variance analysis to estimate the risk due to allocation between sub-portfolios. The covariance matrix can be computed from either actual returns to sub-portfolios or, if these are not available or thought to be unrepresentative, some proxy, such as a share-price index, a bond index or a hedge fund index. Note that exposures to asset classes should be expressed as economic exposures, taking into account the sensitivity of the sub-portfolio to its asset class as given by portfolio beta or duration.

A possible alternative for funds-of-hedge funds is available from a number of risk providers, who engage with hedge fund managers and absolute return fund managers to provide standardized risk profiles to prospective investors of their funds without divulging the actual fund composition.

A valid risk decomposition for a range of funds, all based on the same risk-modelling methodology, can give the fund-of-hedge funds manager the information needed to generate a comprehensive risk profile at both the asset allocation and fund selection levels, taking into account all interaction effects. This can be an ideal solution only if the following conditions apply:

- Enough potential sub-portfolios are covered by the service.
- The risk methodology is suitable to all the sub-portfolios.

If either condition is absent then the two-stage work-around is probably the best solution.

Summary

Accurate and credible investment risk measurement is necessary to manage and report risk. While a range of risk measures has come to be thought of as 'standard', not all risk measures are suitable for all types of portfolios, so applying them does not necessarily give the best information for either measuring or reporting investment risk. Because all risk measures have limitations, most risk analyses in practice comprise a battery of measures, often using more than one risk model to give more insight. At least as important as headline, or summary, portfolio risk measures is decomposition of the sources of portfolio risk to show which exposures are contributing to overall risk so as to help align sources of risk with sources of expected return, eliminate unwanted risk and thereby improve portfolio performance.

Case Study 1

This is a convertible bond arbitrage fund. Readers who are not yet familiar with convertible bonds are invited to read Appendix 6 that explains what they are and how they work.

The objective of the convertible arbitrage fund in this case study is to earn returns that are independent of conventional asset classes such as equities, fixed income and credit markets. It does this by buying convertible bonds and selling listed equities in each of the firms issuing the bonds. Equities are sold not on a one-for-one basis, but in a proportion derived from the delta of the option intrinsic to each convertible bond that equates small price movements in the bonds and the shares. In practice the value of the bought bonds is about twice that of the sold shares. This ratio is managed as a 'dynamic hedge', based on the formula for option pricing. This application of dynamic hedging tells the investment manager to sell shares as the share price rises and buy shares as it falls. As this means that the portfolio takes profits with each adjustment of the hedge, it benefits from more volatility and suffers if the share price is unexpectedly stable.

This portfolio strategy gives two possible sources of return:

- Any mis-pricing of the bond relative to the underlying share.
- Any unexpected volatility in the price of the shares.

Estimating the fair price and therefore the mispricing of the bond entails applying the theory of convertible bond pricing (see Appendix 6) with the bond price predicted by EMH and Black-Scholes option price theory. The result is a return forecast that, in principle, does not affect the risk of the portfolio because it carries no risk – it is the alpha in Equation 3.1 (Chapter 3). From the risk measurement perspective, the interest in this portfolio lies in attributing risk to different factors and capturing the contribution to expected return of the volatility of the underlying equity. This is a function of the optionality in the convertible bond and the implied optionality in the dynamic equity hedge.

A defining feature of convertible bonds is that, as the price of the underlying share rises, the bond correlates more closely with it as eventual conversion of the bond to the underlying equity becomes more likely. As the share price falls, the option to convert the bond to equity is less valuable (because the investor could buy the equity more cheaply in the open market than by forfeiting the convertible bond), so the convertible bond behaves more like a regular corporate bond issued by the same company. This means that the bond does not have a symmetrical return distribution: it participates in theoretically unlimited share price appreciation but is protected against price falls. It is exposed to credit risk too, which has limited upside, but can behave somewhat like a share in the extreme event of a default. It also has interest rate risk, which usually has more downside risk than upside, and possibly currency risk.

The task of the risk manager therefore is to represent this asymmetry in exposure. CAPM clearly won't work, but as there are lots of interacting asymmetrical effects – for example, credit risk with interest rate and currency risk, equity risk with credit risk and currency risk – only an advanced simulation methodology can capture the risk exposures adequately while showing the exposure to volatility. Because the fund was in the process of actively marketing itself, the risk profile had to be intuitive enough for investors to see how it would deliver positive returns and where the risks lay.

The system selected applied simulation with copula analysis to estimate the essential interactions. This allowed the risk profile to be displayed visually as shown in Example 6.5.

Example 6.5 Convertible bond portfolio risk profile

	99%	95%	84%	50%	16%	5%	1%
Portfolio	–6.74%	–5.32%	–2.29%	0.29%	3.37%	5.45%	8.26%
Interest rate	–6.33%	–5.25%	–3.42%	–0.47%	2.20%	2.92%	3.58%
Credit	–5.20%	–3.80%	0.22%	0.28%	0.35%	0.38%	0.45%
Equity market	–2.80%	–2.50%	–1.80%	–1.50%	3.20%	5.25%	7.46%
Currency	–1.79%	–1.37%	–0.97%	–0.37%	0.24%	0.64%	1.02%

The table in Example 6.5 shows the asymmetry in the portfolio outcome and how exposures to interest rates, credit, equity and currencies contribute. Note the asymmetry in each, reflecting the excess of downside over upside, especially at the extremes, of interest rate, credit and currency risk exposures. The positive skew of equity exposure dominates, however: despite also being correlated with the other exposures, the optionality in the convertible bond holding is sufficient to skew the overall portfolio result.

Case Study 2

This is a successful long-short fixed income hedge fund. Its return target is 12 per cent per annum, 70 per cent of which it aims to deliver from pure relative value strategies, with discretion to deliver up to 30 per cent of its return from directional positions in interest rate securities.

Typical relative value trades consisted of two to five legs, with off-setting bought and sold positions. The simplest entailed the sale of a government bond off-set by its forward repurchase three to four months in the future. This reflected the manager's view that the prevailing bond price was high relative to its fair value. The net position being risk neutral, profit was derived from the bond's re-sale at fair price or above and the close of the forward repurchase leg. This type of trade typically endured one to three months. Duration, currency of denomination and investment grade and credit spread for each leg are perfectly matched, so bought and sold legs cancel each other out perfectly, leaving the position risk neutral – apart from liquidity and counterparty risk, both of which were for small or off-setting for many holdings.

Another typical trade consisted of bought five-year bond futures in one currency off-set by the equivalent exposure in five-year bond futures in another currency, the intention being to capture perceived misalignment of five-year interest rate differentials, taking into account the currency differential, which was hedged or not according to the investment manager's views.

Similarly, a bought position in two-year bond future is off-set with a sold position in five-year bond future in the same currency, exploiting perceived mispricing between the two- and five-year bond prices. Importantly, the bought and sold positions were equated, not in terms of face-value, but in terms of duration equivalent, thus neutralizing exposure to general interest rate fluctuations and focussing on the differential between two- and five-year rates.

The manager also exploited opportunities for the 'carry trade'. This entails borrowing, by selling bonds for forward-purchase, in a low interest rate currency regime such as JPY, USD or GBP and investing an equivalent amount in a high interest rate regime, usually AUD. The net risk to the position is that the AUD will fall relative to the currency in which funds were borrowed. When this happened, which it did on a number of occasions, the manager's skill was in closing the position promptly, before losses were incurred, which in practice meant doing so before other carry-trade investors. As this was a popular strategy among relative value hedge fund managers, and because the choice of high interest rate currencies was limited, a slight fall in the value of the AUD relative to other currencies soon became a rout as hedge fund managers tried to close their positions simultaneously.

Another favourite was to combine bought and sold options on foreign currencies, such as EUR versus CHF. Short-term currency fluctuations are notoriously difficult to predict, so the key to controlling the risk of these positions is to ensure that any unexpected volatility works in the favour of the fund. This is relatively easy to do with options, by ensuring that the net option exposure is always positive, in other words, that, correcting for the option deltas, bought positions always dominated sold positions. The maximum loss was therefore capped at the net option premium paid, while gains could be several times as much.

The portfolio typically engaged in about 15 different strategies at any given time, necessitating between 50 and 60 individual holdings.

A number of common themes ran through all of the fund's strategies, which go a long way to explaining its success.

The most important was that the manager constructed all strategies from a risk management perspective. This meant neutralizing the risk of each strategy wherever possible. Any remaining risk, including liquidity and counterparty risk, was taken into account in order to ensure that it did not compound risk from the other strategies in the portfolio.

The manager saw to it that the expected payoff to a strategy should always exceed the maximum tolerable loss in a pre-defined ratio of approximately two to one.

Consistent with the risk-based selection process, each strategy was defined by a target payoff and a maximum tolerated loss, both estimated using conservative assumptions. Strategies were closed as soon as either condition was met, unless market conditions had changed to the point that they merited re-assessment. In these cases, the strategy was evaluated according to the same criteria that were applied to new strategies, in other words a new expected payoff and maximum tolerable loss were defined, which were then implemented rigorously.

The amount of risk assigned to any strategy was determined by the investment manager's confidence that the desired payoff would materialize. Even perfectly-matched positions implied some risk, in the form of liquidity or counterparty risk, and these were taken into account when allocating risk.

The investment manager confined his exposures to markets with which he was very familiar and confident that he commanded a competitive advantage. This limited opportunities on occasion, but ensured that all risk in the portfolio was well managed. Consistent with this discipline, exposures to currencies, where the investment manager considered his advantage to be not as strong, tended to be modest and where practicable, protected by options positions.

This portfolio posed an unusual challenge for the risk manager. Any application of mean-variance as a means of measuring risk was ruled out because it could not accommodate the instruments in the portfolio. Yet most off-the-shelf simulation systems, while capable of generating portfolio-level VaR and stress tests, were unlikely to show how individual holdings grouped to off-set the risk of each. Simulation was also unlikely to give a realistic profile of the risk attributable to each strategy.

Yet because the portfolio made extensive use of derivatives in combinations that to most people looked potentially very risky, successful seeding and marketing of the fund demanded a thorough and credible risk monitoring methodology and process, especially as it was clear that an unconventional risk-modelling and measurement methodology was required.

Because of the deliberate combination of positions in bonds of differing durations within each strategy, conventional leverage measures based on nominal monetary allocation would give a misleading picture of the risk of the portfolio. The only accurate representation was by economic exposure, in this case a measure of duration.

The risk manager assigned to this portfolio was chosen on the basis of her direct experience with many of the fund's strategies, especially those entailing options. She implemented a risk monitoring process that was sensitive to how the manager selected his portfolio, complementing conventional risk monitoring, which applied simulation, with a less conventional but more thorough process. This entailed direct access to the fund accounting system to inspect each of the 40 to 50 individual positions and then 'reconstructing' a sensible suite of strategies from them. Any positions or exposures that appeared unexplained by identifiable strategies were then discussed with the investment manager so that their intended contribution to the portfolio outcome was consistent with the other holdings. This procedure was carried out at the end of each reporting period, which was the end of the month, and at least once during the month at a time that was unknown to the investment manager. The risk manager was usually able to 'explain' about 90 per cent of the strategies, leaving one or two per analysis to be discussed.

As some positions in the portfolio had very short horizons, its composition was prone to change substantially within each monthly reporting period. Investors understandably sought to ensure that the risk snapshots that were reported were indeed representative of the portfolio at other times. This was given by a third component to the risk monitoring of the fund, which was a suite of simple summary risk measures (95 per cent and 99 per cent VaR and average duration) collected at the end of each trading day and presented in a line graph to show how stable or otherwise it was.

The thoroughness of this approach was sufficient for the risk manager to argue successfully that imposing an arbitrary and potentially counter-productive limit on the portfolio's leverage was both unnecessary and potentially damaging to the fund.

Another significant benefit was in marketing the fund. When interviewed by prospective investors as part of their due-diligence studies, the risk manager was able to explain the reasoning behind individual holdings as well as any intra-month fluctuations in summary VaR levels. This further added to the credibility of the investment management and risk management processes.

The fund was very successful, being continually voted a winner in its category. Nevertheless it was not without problems, arguably resulting from its success:

- Many people did not believe that the sheer consistency of its returns could be possible. In the wake of the Madoff revelations, the investment manager found himself devoting considerable time to working through the investment process with sceptical regulators.
- The real risk of the fund derived from investors finding it hard to accept low – but positive – returns in periods when the markets produced insufficient opportunities for very low-risk payoffs and demanding that the investment manager take on more risk in order to boost returns. With direct experience in the fund's preferred strategies, the risk manager agreed with the investment manager the need to resist pressure to assume risks with which the investment manager was uncomfortable, and this pressure at times was considerable: the fund saw significant redemptions in its first period of market doldrums.[1] The two together were able to argue that expanding into unfamiliar territory was not in the best interests of the fund and this pressure was largely resisted, ensuring the long-term success of the fund.

Endnote

1. The fund soon regained investors as this period saw it deliver modest, but positive, returns while its competitors delivered median returns of –8.0 per cent. The fund reached capacity and closed soon after.

7
Derivatives Risk Management

Imagine an investment product designed for individual, middle-class and working-class investors, whereby the investor acquires a risky asset worth more than twice the investor's annual revenues for a small initial outlay. The investor then undertakes to make regular payments of up to a third of his or her annual income over a defined, albeit extended, period. The only collateral demanded is the value of the risky asset itself. If the investor sells the asset before the end of the contract term he or she receives or pays the difference between the initial bought price and the initial sale price of the risky asset, which can be many times greater than the amount of the initial outlay.

A financial regulator might be forgiven for hesitating to approve an investment product that is both potentially volatile and geared for sale to relatively unsophisticated investors, yet home loans are considered one of the soundest of retail financial products.

In comparison, most derivatives transactions are tame. The risk of investing in derivatives is more to do with how they are used than with the instruments themselves. Derivatives are often defined as instruments that 'derive' their value from some physical asset or basket of assets. In this sense they are no different from a listed trust or a mutual fund. What is special about derivatives is that they delay settlement, so that the investor pays only a relatively small proportion of the face value when opening the position, settling the difference between opening and closing values at some later date. The delayed settlement feature means that derivatives can be used to gear exposure to the asset class. Because it is not necessary to buy the instrument before selling it, it is easy to take naked short positions using derivatives.

This chapter describes:

- How derivatives contribute to portfolio design, construction and on-going management.

- How to measure derivatives exposure.
- The different types of risk associated with derivatives.

Derivatives are sometimes thought to be more risky than their underlying physical assets because they facilitate gearing, or leveraging, and short selling. A sharp adverse market move can result in losses far exceeding the initial 'investment'. Short selling allows the investor to sell things he or she doesn't own, again with only a small initial payment, which can be dwarfed by the losses resulting from a sharp price appreciation. While these characteristics certainly can lead to extreme outcomes, investment portfolios (hedge funds are the notable exception) limit – indeed many are obliged to limit – their derivatives use in a way that avoids the risks of gearing and short selling. In practice most uses of derivatives significantly reduce the risk of the overall portfolio compared to conventional investment instruments.

How derivatives contribute to portfolio management

Nearly all investment portfolios can benefit from using derivatives, either as a complement to conventional assets or as the basis for a separate investment product, such as a hedge fund or guaranteed return fund, which can in turn complement investments in conventional funds.

Within conventional portfolios, derivatives are most commonly used for liquidity management, tactical shifts, return enhancement and to control risk.

Liquidity Management – liquid assets (cash) accumulated as a result of dividend and other income flows, and new investment that arrives in small amounts can be invested efficiently by buying appropriate futures as temporary exposure rather than leaving them un-invested. This protects the portfolio against market appreciation in the interim, with the accumulated cash making up the collateral. When market conditions are favourable, or an economic volume of cash is accumulated, the futures can be sold and physical instruments bought in an exchange-for-physical (EFP) transaction. Having negligible transactions costs, futures avoid the high costs of frequent trading of small volumes of physical instruments. They can even enhance return if they are bought and sold below and above their fair value relative to the underlying physical asset. The net effect is reduced risk and lower transactions costs.

Tactical shifts – as with liquidity management, simple futures contracts can effect short-term asset allocation shifts with negligible transactions costs. Thus a temporary shift from, say, equities to bonds can be achieved by selling share price index futures and buying bond futures. In this way futures contracts do not alter the risk of the portfolio, but can enhance return if bought below and sold above fair price; and by lowering transactions costs. For longer-term asset allocation shifts, asset swaps can be used in the same way as futures.

Return enhancement – futures and options can be used to enhance returns to conventional portfolios, both in combination with liquidity management and as return enhancements in their own right.

Futures in lieu of physical – these add risk-free return if they are bought at less than fair price, or are sold at greater than fair price. Fair price is easily calculated as a function of the price of the underlying asset, the interest rate, any income due to the physical,[1] such as coupons or dividends, and the time to expiry of the futures contract (see Appendices). This return enhancement can easily be achieved as part of liquidity management or tactical shifts.

Futures or swap – these can be used to 'transfer' alpha; for example, if the investor has some advantage in a particular asset class, such as a favourable tax position or better than average investment skill, then this can be 'transferred' to other asset classes. Physical securities are held in the favoured asset class, while futures are sold in that asset class and bought in another. For example, an investor may have particular skill in selecting European equities, but require some exposure to US stocks where his or her skill is only average. By combining bought physical European equities, selling futures on European equities and buying futures on US stocks, that investor can capture his or her European stock-picking skill while at the same time gaining a broad exposure to US stocks. This type of transaction is sometimes called a synthetic swap.

Bought call options – these can enhance return in two ways:

- By providing a cost-efficient substitute for the underlying physical instrument.
- By avoiding losses due to rises in the price of the underlying physical instrument.

Bought put options – these can also enhance return in two ways:

- By benefiting from a fall in the price of the underlying asset.
- By avoiding losses due to falls in the price of the underlying physical instrument. Bought out-of-the-money put options can be an effective hedge against extreme losses.

Sold options – these enhance return by attracting option premium, which the option seller retains if the options expire unexercised.

Simultaneous bought and sold options – these can provide a cost-efficient substitute for the underlying physical instrument while protecting against unfavourable movements in its price. For example, a bought call with an exercise price of \$5 combined with a sold call with an exercise price of \$10 gives exposure to share price movements in between. If the price of the underlying stock is \$5 or less at the time the options expire, then the investor loses only the net premium paid for the options. If, on the other hand, the share price is \$10 or more when the options expire, the investor gains \$500 (\$10 × \$5) less the net premium paid and foregoes further price appreciation.

Buying and selling options – according to their relative value (implied volatility), while ensuring that the overall position is market-neutral through delta-hedging, buying and selling options can be an important source of return enhancement that is independent of the return to the underlying physical investment. Being independent, this source of potential return enhancement does not necessarily affect the risk profile of the underlying portfolio.

Investment products based on derivatives strategies

Futures, swaps and options can help construct innovative investment products that meet specific risk-return objectives.

Smoothed return funds – options, with predefined decision rules, can help avoid the worst effects of sharp movements in physical asset prices and deliver portfolios with much reduced return volatility, for example, by participating in market appreciation while avoiding the worst deterioration. Investors can choose the balance that suits them best between greater protection against losses and lower participation in market growth, and vice versa.

Guaranteed minimum return funds – the demand for even more risk-averse investments can be achieved using options to deliver investments that will never fall below a specified value within a given timeframe. Using options to hedge these portfolios avoids the need for expensive reserve funds. It is also more efficient as the option can be tailored in a way that provides perfect protection, whereas reserves may turn out to be inadequate or a drag on overall returns. The downside is the cost of the option, which is established at the start of the protection period.

Tactical overlay – specialist mandates designed to effect short-term modifications to an existing balanced portfolio, possibly managed by a different investment management company, typically use futures and forwards but also swaps and options to effect asset allocation shifts without transacting physical instruments, thus saving on transactions costs.

Currency overlay – foreign exchange forwards and options are used to neutralize exposures to foreign currencies inherent in investment in physical assets in foreign markets. The currency hedge can be complete or partial and may or may not include some element of tactical protection.

Protection overlay – similar to tactical overlays, protection overlays substitute options for futures and forwards. The benefit is a cost-efficient hedge against unwanted volatility or unfavourable market movements without the cost of transacting physical instruments.

Hedge funds futures, swaps and options – these are ideal for use in hedge funds because they facilitate both gearing and short selling, are cheap to trade and therefore suit high turnover portfolios. Many hedge funds use futures, swaps and options to create off-setting long and short positions, giving a market-neutral portfolio that derives its return relative to the mispricing of similar assets rather than the direction of the market itself.[2] Derivatives facilitate short exposures without the need to borrow physical securities for delivery.

Risk control

Controlling risk usually means reducing it or capping it, in contrast with managing risk, which means using risk to best advantage. There are three ways to control investment risk:

- Cap it by means of risk limits, without derivatives.
- Hedge with forwards, futures or swaps.
- Insure against it using options.

Hedging with forwards, futures or swaps entails relatively simple purchase and sale of derivatives, for example sale of foreign exchange forwards to hedge unwanted currency exposure or the purchase of share price index or bond futures to gain temporary exposure to a rising market. The key to successful hedging is accurate estimation of the risk that needs to be hedged, which is discussed in detail in Chapters 5 and 6 on risk modelling and risk measurement. Hedging using forwards and futures of course eliminates not just the downside risk of the exposure, but any possibility of gain from the position.

Insuring risk using options allows the manager to hedge against downside risk only, leaving the possibility of a gain should the exposure prove to be favourable. The gain, of course, is reduced by the cost of the option. The manager can also choose the amount of loss to be hedged. The greater the loss that can be tolerated the cheaper the option. As with forwards, futures and swaps, hedging effectiveness depends on accurate quantification of the exposure to be insured.

Measuring derivatives exposure

There are two ways to measure derivatives exposure: economic exposure and capital employed. Economic exposure expresses it as a 'physical equivalent'; in other words its exposure to markets. Capital employed measures how much collateral is held against it.

Calculation of economic exposure

For forwards, futures and swaps, economic exposure is calculated as the number of contracts held, times the price of the contract, times the point value of the contract. For example, the S&P500 futures contract has a point value of $500. An investor who has bought five contracts has an exposure to US equities of $2500 times the level of the index. So if the S&P500 index is at 1010, the exposure is $2525 000. If it rises to 1017, it goes to $2542 500 (5 × $500 × 1017). It is the 'physical equivalent' because it is economically identical to $2525 000 invested in S&P500 physical shares.

For options, economic exposure is the same calculation with adjustment for the sensitivity of the option to a change in the underlying security. This sensitivity is given by the option delta (see Appendix 5). The initial position in the example given here, if effected using five at-the-money options – with a delta of 0.50 – in lieu of five futures, would be $1262 500 ($2525 000 × 0.5).

Capital employed

The accounting treatment of futures is based on the amount of capital actually posted in support of the derivatives position, as initial and any variation margins, (the latter are unrealized losses). This measure is intended to track cash flows, but gives no representation of economic exposure. Example 7.1 illustrates the differences.

Example 7.1 Economic exposure versus accounting treatment for forwards, futures and swaps

Point value of contract	$100
Initial margin per contract	$3000
Number of contracts bought	200
Number of contracts sold	0
Price at which futures traded	2743.4
Current futures price	2750.0
Available cash	$100 000 000

(Continued)

The valuation statement	Economic exposure	Capital employed
Initial margin	$600 000	$600 000
Unrealized profit and loss	$132 000	$132 000
Cash collateral	$54 268 000	$0
Futures exposure	$55 000 000	$732 000
Un-invested cash	$45 000 000	$99 268 000
Total	$100 000 000	$100 000 000

Example 7.1 shows a portfolio with a total value of $100 000 000, which is invested in share price index futures and cash. A total of 200 futures contracts were bought at $2743.4 and the current price is $2750.0. The point value of the contract is $100 and the initial margin per contract is $3000. The capital employed is equal to the initial margin paid plus any unrealized profit and loss, in this case 200 × $3000 + $132 000 (200 × $100 × (2750.0 – 2743.4)), or $732 000. The economic exposure on the other hand is 200 × $100 × 2750.0, or $55 000 000. A 1 per cent increase in equity prices will result in a further profit of $550 000 (200 × $100 × 27.50), or 1 per cent of the economic exposure. Note that the same price increase would represent a 75 per cent increase on the capital employed!

Example 7.2 Economic exposure versus accounting treatment for options

Point value of contract	$100	
Number of contracts bought	200	
Number of contracts sold	0	
Premium at which option was bought	500.0	
Current option premium	580.0	
Current futures price	2750.0	
Current option delta	0.55	
Available cash	$100 000 000	
The valuation statement	**Economic exposure**	**Capital employed**
Option purchase premium	$10 000 000	$10 000 000
Unrealized profit and loss	$1 600 000	$1 600 000
Cash collateral	$18 650 000	$0
Option exposure	$30 250 000	$11 600 000
Un-invested cash	$69 750 000	$88 400 000
Total	$100 000 000	$100 000 000

Example 7.2 shows a portfolio with a total value of $100 000 000, which is invested in options on share price index options and cash. A total of 200 option contracts were bought for $550 and their current price is $580. The point value of the contract is $100 and the option delta is 0.55. The capital employed is equal to the option premium paid, $100 000 000 ($100 × 200 × 500) plus any unrealized profit and loss, in this case $100 × 200 × (580 – 500)), or $1 600 000. The economic exposure on the other hand is the point value, times the number of options, times the current underlying futures price, times the option delta $100 × 200 × 2750.0 × 0.55, or $30 250 000. A 1 per cent increase in the underlying equity futures price will result in a further profit of $302 500 ($100 × 200 × 2750.0 × 1% × 0.55), or 0.55 times the economic exposure.

The delta-weighting method holds only for very small changes in the price of the underlying securities, and then only for a short period of time, because the option delta changes with both underlying price and the passage of time. The mis-estimation introduced by larger price movements can sometimes be tolerated for short periods and where the option exposure is a very small proportion (less than 5 per cent is a rule-of-thumb) of the portfolio's risk. Beyond that, more specialized methodology is needed, which is described in Chapters 5 and 6 on risk modelling and risk measurement.

Gross versus net

Portfolios often combine bought and sold positions in the same, or very similar, derivatives contracts. Investment managers often find this expedient for positions in over-the-counter derivatives such as swaps. Because it is sometimes difficult or costly to terminate the agreement early, it can make sense to transact a new agreement that exactly off-sets the first one. The result is two open positions that effectively cancel each other out giving a net position, in both economic and counterparty terms, of zero.

Even if the positions are not exactly off-setting, for example, a bought future in one delivery month that is off-set by an equivalent sold future in another delivery month is less risky than either the bought or sold positions by themselves. For this reason collateral is normally calculated against net rather than gross exposure so that enough is allocated to ensure against gearing, but not too much that the portfolio is in effect under-invested. For example, if an investor buys five S&P500 futures contracts and the price stands at 1020.0, the exposure is equivalent to $2 550 000 worth of US equities. If this position is augmented with three sold contracts, perhaps for a later settlement date, (equivalent to $1 530 000 in US equities), then the exposure of the position is reduced to $1 020 000.

When reporting aggregate derivatives exposures – for example, to provide exposure information to governance bodies – it is important that net exposures are given, since for off-setting positions, reporting only gross exposures is a misleading measure of exposure.

Derivatives risk

Derivatives are used to gain economic exposure to a risky asset class without the cost and other frictions associated with transacting physical assets. They therefore expose the portfolio to the same sources of investment risk as an equivalent exposure as the underlying physical securities would. The risks that are particular to derivative instruments and do not always apply to physical instruments include basis risk, counterparty risk and operational risks.

Investment risk

Investment risk for forwards, futures and swaps is estimated in the same way as for the underlying securities against which the derivatives are settled. This section therefore focuses on estimating risk exposures associated with options positions that, although settled against physical securities, embed the right of the holder to cap losses, which changes the risk profile of the option position relative to the underlying securities.

The asymmetrical outcome given by options, capped losses or limited gains demands specialist risk measures. The potential solutions fall into two main categories:

- Maintain the mean-variance risk factor approach used for conventional portfolios with delta-weighting modifications to accommodate options.
- Apply risk measures that do not rely on symmetrical return distributions.

Conventional mean-variance risk factor analysis with modifications for options – the delta-weighting method preserves the power of mean-variance analysis: that it facilitates risk decomposition by factors and holdings, and so allows risk to be targeted where it contributes most to expected return. The big limitation of delta-weighting is that it is suitable only for portfolios with very small options exposures.

Knowing that option deltas are not stable, it makes sense to measure the stability of the delta. This is given by the option's gamma, which is the change in delta for a small change in the price of the underlying asset. A positive gamma indicates that the portfolio stands to benefit from volatility in the underlying market, a negative gamma indicates that, other things being equal, the portfolio is likely to suffer (compared to the equivalent physical position) in volatile times. A low absolute gamma says that the delta, and the delta-weighted physical equivalent, will change only slightly with a change in the price of the underlying security. High absolute gamma values indicate the delta could change significantly with market prices and the delta adjusted risk measure should be complemented by other risk measures.

Risk measures that do not rely on symmetrical returns – for portfolios, such as smoothed-return portfolios, guaranteed return portfolios and hedge funds that comprise significantly or uniquely of options, a simple delta-modified risk factor approach is unsatisfactory because it does not accommodate asymmetric return distributions.

The other main methodology is simulation. Simulation has the big advantage that it can accommodate most investment instruments and is not confined to symmetric distributions. Its big disadvantage is that it can be poor at attributing risk to its sources, such as risk factors, countries, industries and sectors or individual holdings.

More detail about the relative merits of mean-variance and simulation methodologies is given in Chapters 5 and 6 on risk modelling and risk measurement.

Basis risk

Basis risk is the risk that the future or option contract is not a perfect hedge for the underlying assets. For example, the S&P500 futures contract is usually only an approximation for a typical portfolio of US equities. Basis risk is more common for exchange-traded contracts, as over-the-counter contracts can generally be tailored to the underlying portfolio of physical assets.

Counterparty risk

Over-the-counter derivatives, such as forwards, swaps and bought options are exposed to the risk that the investor or intermediary to the transaction is unable to honour the contract. This risk is managed in the same way as counterparty or credit risk for fixed interest securities in conventional portfolios and treasury operations: usually both by setting and enforcing limits on the exposure to any nominated counterparty or intermediary and ensuring periodic settlement of outstanding unrealized profit and loss that would render the portfolio vulnerable.

Operational risk

Apart from the risk of systems failures and disruptions, which impact all investment instruments, operations risk for derivatives comprises mainly:

- Instrument risk. This is the risk that derivatives will be used inappropriately, errors in valuation and the danger of selling call options for which insufficient underlying securities are held to ensure delivery. These risks are easily eliminated with appropriate management systems and procedures.
- Collateral management. Ensuring correct management of liquid collateral is the most common and basic risk-control measure. For example, sensible netting of positions can avoid posting too much collateral, which can earn less than market interest rates and therefore be a drag on return.

Evaluating the effectiveness of derivatives

This is about asking if derivatives are doing the job they were intended to do. There are two ways to do this:

- Performance analysis.
- Risk analysis.

Performance analysis – quantifies how much derivatives positions contributed to portfolio return.

This is necessarily a retrospective analysis, and while quantifying contribution to return is relatively straight-forward, it says nothing about the derivatives' effects on risk. One way to use performance analysis to evaluate the contribution of options is to see what the risk-adjusted result would have been with an alternative portfolio construction that did not use derivatives, but this is often not practicable. For example, the cost of options hedges appears only as a drag on performance if market conditions were favourable to the underlying exposure, thus rendering the option unnecessary in hindsight. The real value of the option hedge is of course its contribution to reducing the risk of loss, which is not captured by simple performance analysis.

Risk analysis – because it is a forward-looking exercise, risk analysis facilitates comparison of two alternative risk profiles: one with the intended derivatives positions and the other without.

By comparing headline portfolio risk with and without derivatives, the manager can see if any risk reduction is working – or if it is working too well. If the risk tool allows it, he or she can also see clearly whether or not the desired risk reduction is coming from the right sources, in other words whether it is modifying the intended exposures, and whether there are any unintended consequences of the derivatives holdings that demand action.

Summary

Derivatives are used increasingly in investment management because of their liquidity, cost effectiveness and flexibility. They are used both in conjunction with conventional, physical assets and as the basis for structured investment products. Common uses of derivatives include:

- Efficient portfolio management, or liquidity management.
- Tactical shifts between asset classes or individual securities.
- Return enhancement.
- Risk management and control.

Structured investment products usually fall into one of the following categories:

- Hedge funds.
- Smoothed return funds.
- Guaranteed minimum return funds.
- Tactical overlay funds.

Whether derivatives are used for efficient portfolio management, return enhancement or risk control, it is important to quantify accurately the economic exposure they achieve, and to distinguish between net and gross exposure.

The approach to risk measurement and management should reflect the objectives of using derivatives in the first place: for efficient portfolio management and tactical shifts, derivatives positions should not alter the risk of the portfolio. For return enhancement, naturally one would expect to see some increase in risk; while the effect of risk management should be clearly visible in the form of targeted risk and the elimination of unwanted risk.

Endnotes

1. More detail about forwards, futures, swaps and options is given in the Appendices.
2. When successful, this results in a true hedge fund, which, because it is fully hedged, is less risky than most conventional portfolios.

Part III

Risk-Based Portfolio Selection

8
Asset Allocation

During World War II, the Royal Air Force patrolled the Bay of Biscay in Sunderland aircraft. These giant aeroplanes were notable for having decks made of wood. This of course meant that airmen passed idle time polishing them.

Managing active asset allocation has been likened to patrolling the Bay of Biscay in a Sunderland: long periods of calm punctuated by furious bursts of action that ceased as abruptly as they began.

Asset allocation is deciding how much exposure a portfolio should have to each asset class, either:

- relative to a long-term multi-asset class benchmark or comparator portfolio; or
- absolute, typically compared to a benchmark interest rate such as LIBOR (London interbank offered rate) or some measure of inflation.

Risk-based investment management is about aligning risk with sources of expected return. The amount of investment risk that a portfolio aims for is of course determined by how much return it seeks to deliver. Risk-based asset allocation is about allocating this risk where it is most likely to contribute to the return objective of the portfolio. This in turn means allocating risk where the investment manager believes there is enough investment selection skill to warrant the extra cost and risk of active management. Where insufficient skill is available, then passive management is usually the most practical alternative. The active-passive decision is as relevant to asset allocation as it is to any asset class.

Passive allocation for a multi-asset class benchmark is where the portfolio asset class mix mirrors as closely as possible the benchmark asset allocation. Otherwise, asset allocation is managed actively, meaning that it seeks to add return to the long-term asset allocation by exploiting perceived transient under- and over-valuation of individual asset classes.

This chapter will address:

- Scope for adding value.
- Sources of risk and return.
- Modelling risk.
- Aligning risk and return.
- Passive asset allocation.
- Risk-parity portfolios.
- On-going management.

Scope for adding value

There are two ways of investing in a risky asset:

- Lend money by buying a bond (debt).
- Buy a share in its future profits (equity).

Debt is an investment that pays a predetermined income in the form of interest, with the principal repaid at the maturity of the loan or amortized over the life of the loan.

Equity is a fixed share in the growth in value of an enterprise in perpetuity or until the share is re-sold.

Both debt and equity come in many forms, such as domestic government bonds, listed equities and direct property. For the purposes of asset allocation, they are usually thought of as separate asset classes altogether. For example, property is usually thought of as a separate asset class from equities, although really it is another form of equity investment. The economic exposure of private equity, for example, is no different from listed equity; but it is usually more practicable to think of the two as distinct.

Investors benefit from including as many asset classes as possible in their investment universes. This allows the maximum chance of participating in asset classes that grow, and managing risk through effective diversification. According to the Fundamental Law of Grinold and Kahn,[1] the risk-adjusted return to a portfolio is a function of:

- The skill of the investment manager.
- The number of independent investment opportunities available to him or her.
- Time.
- Frictions, including transaction costs.

Note that Grinold and Kahn specify independent investment opportunities. Highly correlated investments may simply be different aspects of the same opportunity so do not add materially to the scope for adding value.

For most investors, asset classes include things like:

- Domestic equities.
- International equities:
  - developed markets;
  - emerging markets;
  - regional portfolios.
- Domestic fixed interest.
- Credit, including securitized debt.
- Sovereign bonds:
  - developed market;
  - emerging market.
- Private equity.
- Private debt.
- Real property.
- Hybrid asset classes such as convertible bonds.
- Infrastructure debt.
- Infrastructure equity.
- Pure alpha, including hedge funds.
- Cash.

The list does not include derivatives because derivatives are not an asset class, but vehicles for investing in physical asset classes. It also excludes structured investments, partly for the same reason; but also because some structured investments are designed to provide protection against falling asset prices, which can apply to any of the asset classes in the list.

How many asset classes, and which ones to include depend on:

- The size of the fund.
- Transactions costs in each asset class.
- The investor's tax regime.
- Any regulatory or legal limitations.

If they are obliged by their mandate to hold their investments in physical assets, large funds stand to benefit from a wider range of asset classes than do smaller funds. This is simple arithmetic: the absolute size of the smallest allocation needs to justify the costs of buying into that asset class. For example, a fund may allocate to 25 asset classes, with the smallest allocation set at 1 per cent. For a $1 000 000 000 fund, this implies an investment of $100 000 000, enough to achieve a well-constructed portfolio in most asset classes, but for a $50 000 000 fund, it is $500 000, which is often not practical.

This need not be a limitation for most funds, as exchange traded funds (ETFs) and derivatives can facilitate exposure to a wide range of asset classes with relatively low transactions costs.

Asset classes with high transactions costs, such as real property, can necessitate longer holding periods. For example, an investment needs to be held for a much longer period to justify a 3 per cent entry cost than one that costs less than 1 per cent to buy into. Transactions costs for some asset classes can vary according to the type of investor; for example, some public pension plans are exempt from government duties on domestic asset purchases and sales. Some stock exchanges impose differential charges and even trading rules on investors from different domiciles. Again, this need not be a limitation, as the availability of ETFs and derivatives can provide a practical, low-cost alternative to restricted or high-cost asset classes and for smaller funds.

The investor's tax regime can affect the choice of asset class, for example through his or her entitlement to dividend tax credits, which favour investment in domestic assets. This effect is usually captured in the asset class return forecast.

A fund may be subject to regulatory limits on its allocation and legal limitations can apply from time to time. For example, regulations governing the fund may dictate maximum holdings in some asset classes or in any single issuer of securities. Foreign exchange controls and mandatory allocation to particular asset classes such as government-issued securities may also apply. Legal and regulatory limits are usually incorporated in the fund constraints.

Sources of risk and return

This section describes some practical considerations entailed in aligning sources of risk and expected return by formulating portfolio asset allocation strategy, including:

- Some methods of forecasting returns.
- The role of the equity risk premium.
- Some theories about how extreme events occur.
- Currency effects and how they can be managed.
- The universal currency hedging ratio.
- The purposes and implications of frictional liquidity.

Forecasting returns

Investment managers differentiate themselves from their competitors by their skill in forecasting returns and identifying the best performing assets, but there are too many different techniques to attempt to describe them all here. Nevertheless, some generalization is possible.

For cash and bonds, the simplest forecast is to suppose that today's yield is the best predictor of future yields and that they are about as likely to rise as to fall. This has some obvious limitations; for example, yields cannot go below zero so, if they are already low, they are probably more likely to stay the same or rise than to fall. More sophisticated interest rate forecasting entails projections of macro-economic variables such as inflation, economic growth and currency projections.

For equities, returns are the sum of income paid out and growth in the value of the asset. The current price already discounts the consensus view of income and growth prospects, so the investment manager seeks assets whose true future value is either over-estimated or under-estimated by the market. To forecast future growth, he or she can:

- Extrapolate from historical returns.
- Calculate the aggregate value of future income from the asset class.
- Analyse macro-economic or fundamental trends.

Extrapolating from historical data can be as simple as saying that US equities returned 5 per cent in the past, and so will probably return 5 per cent in the future. A more thorough approach might be to separate real returns from inflation. For example, if inflation had been 2 per cent, then the real return to equities was 3 per cent. If inflation is expected to be 1.5 per cent this year, then extrapolating the real return will give an expected return of 4.5 per cent.

Using this method in isolation to forecast returns has some fairly obvious limitations. For one thing, the answer you get depends on what period of history you extrapolate from. Also it violates even the weak version of the EMH (which says that there can be no gains from analysing the price histories of securities). One needs only to inspect a chart of the history of equity market prices to see that projecting from the past can be hazardous, as shown in Example 8.1.

Example 8.1 shows how the results from simple extrapolation are affected by the period that is used for extrapolation.

- From January 2004 to September 2007 gives an annualized return of 8.6 per cent.
- From January 2009 to December 2012 gives an annualized return of 18.5 per cent.
- From January 2004 to December 2012 gives an annualized return of 2.5 per cent.

Of course there are much more robust ways of projecting from past returns to the future. One approach is to quantify durable relationships between

Example 8.1 Extrapolating from past returns

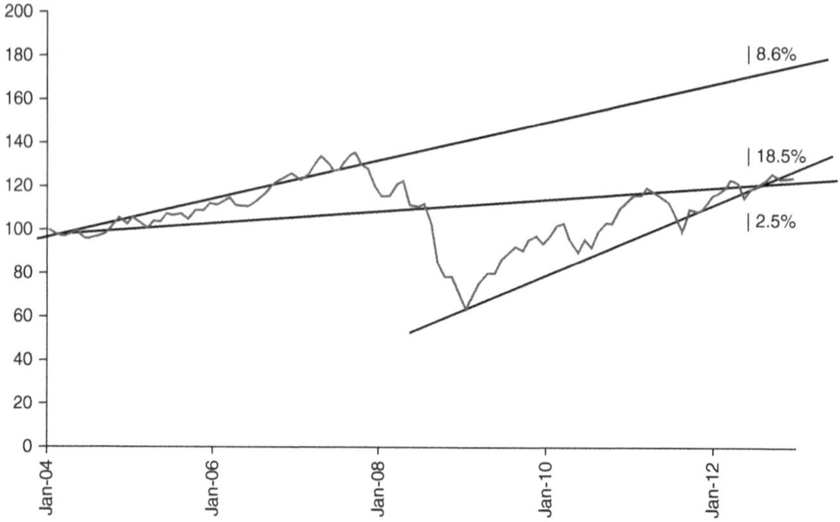

Source: FactSet

asset prices and the things that drive them, such as macro-economic variables, and combine them with forecasts of the macro-economic variables themselves to identify which asset class will benefit most from predicted macro-economic trends and orient the portfolio accordingly.

Or you can suppose that valuations to each asset class, as measured by things like earnings yield, dividend yield or rental yield, fluctuate around some long-term average, either in nominal terms or relative to inflation or some interest rate. The trick is to determine what the long-term average is; which means measuring past yields, ideally both forecast and observed. But the answer you get still depends on what period in history you choose to estimate the average from.

The equity risk premium

This is the return to equities that compensates investors for the risk of investing in equities rather than in low-risk bonds. Most methods of valuing equity assets imply some assumption about the equity risk premium. It can be thought of as a measure of aggregate investor risk-aversion.

The equity premium can be estimated:

- Ex-ante, it is the future difference between equity returns and bond returns that is implied by current equity valuations and bond yields.
- Ex-post, it is the equity risk premium implied by the observed market return differentials, the volatility of the differentials and aggregate investment in equities and bonds.

If you believe that aggregate risk aversion is relatively stable over time, a good estimate of the past equity risk premium should indicate the future long-term return differential between equities and bonds and therefore whether today's valuations are high or low in comparison.[2]

Professional investors find the equity premium a puzzle because there is surprisingly little consensus about what it should be, or even what it has been in the past. Evidence suggests that actual equity price levels (and therefore implied future returns) relative to bonds imply unrealistic risk aversion, in other words that equity returns have been higher than most models of risk aversion would imply. At least two reasons are proposed to explain the apparent anomaly:

- The observed outperformance of equities was substantially in excess of market expectations at the beginning of the relevant periods.
- More is invested in fixed interest bonds than would be predicted by the equity premium because of the requirement that many insurance companies and pension funds match their assets and liabilities.

The forward-looking equity risk premium relative to bonds through history is a function of:[3]

- Forecast real stock return given by stock dividend yields and an estimate of expected real dividend growth.
- Forecast real bond return given by bond yields and an estimate of expected inflation through history.

Extreme events

Extreme events seem to occur with increasing frequency, so are given plenty of attention. Forecasting crashes and crises is often thought of as a risk management task. But extreme events are in essence asset returns (large and negative, but returns after all). As it is the job of the portfolio strategist and the economist to forecast asset class returns, so the job of predicting crashes logically belongs with them too.[4] The risk manager's job is to estimate how the portfolio will fare if and when they happen.

There are four main theories of how extreme market events occur.

Chaos theory – studies how minor events can have much bigger consequences than intuition would predict, a phenomenon sometimes referred to as the 'butterfly effect'. This says that a butterfly flutters, which is a random event, starting a chain of tiny air vibrations that compound to develop into a hurricane. In the same way, small differences in values, such as those due to rounding errors, can yield widely diverging outcomes, rendering long-term modelling and prediction of extreme outcomes practically impossible. Chaos theory was first applied to financial markets by Benoît Mandelbrot, who discovered recurring patterns in cotton prices and found that the principle could be applied to other asset prices as well.

Financial instability hypothesis – borrows from J.M. Keynes, among others, although is usually attributed to Hyman Minsky, who took the view that financial markets in normal, stable, conditions contain the seeds of bubbles and therefore busts. This happens because, in prosperous times, when corporate cash flow rises beyond what is needed to pay off debt, a speculative euphoria develops and more is borrowed to invest in ever-more marginal projects. In time debts exceed what borrowers can pay off from their incoming revenues, which in turn produces a financial crisis. As a result of such speculative borrowing bubbles, banks and lenders tighten credit availability, even to companies that can afford loans, and the economy consequently contracts.

The same effect can be seen in the prices of assets such as shares and houses. As prices rise, lenders are willing to lend more to investors, pushing prices up further and increasing the appetite to lend, until the burden of debt becomes unsustainable and marginal buyers are forced to sell, triggering a downward spiral. While prices are rising, investors are happy to pay up, either because they believe the trend will continue or because they think other investors believe it will, and so will be happy to buy the asset from them at an even more inflated price: the 'greater fool' principle.

In 1974 Minsky wrote that:

> A fundamental characteristic of our economy is that the financial system swings between robustness and fragility and these swings are an integral part of the process that generates business cycles.[5]

Black Swans – Nassim Taleb's view is that extreme events are:

- Unpredictable.
- Not attributable to any identifiable process.

He concludes that investors can therefore never predict extreme events and should always avoid any exposure to them.[6]

Financial rogue waves – Steve Ohana draws parallels with rogue waves that cause maritime tragedy from time to time and observes that satellite technology has provided some insight into when and how they occur. They are not entirely random.

Like Minsky, Ohana draws on systems theory, which says that, in nature there are naturally-occurring processes, which are either self-correcting or self-perpetuating. For example, spontaneous bush-fires, which clear away old growth, make way for new plants to flourish and reduce the likelihood of a very big fire. Similarly, excess profit in a market segment attracts competitors whose effect is to push prices down until the sector's profit approximately compensates its financing costs. These are known as negative feedback systems: the occurrence of a fire makes another less likely and prices for goods and services self-stabilize, in normal market conditions, when supply and demand are in approximate equilibrium. Some feedback systems are positive, however, including rogue waves, where a small imbalance causes a wave to grow bigger than those about it. As it does so, it attracts water from the surrounding waves, becoming bigger still, until the wave collapses under its own weight. A similar system drives hurricanes and cyclones.

The implication is that, while not necessarily preventable, they can be observed and possibly even modelled from the early and intermediate stages of their development, allowing specific evasive or protective action to be planned.

Positive feedback systems can be observed in portfolios, when a small number of common risk factors explains progressively more and more of the portfolio's risk at the expense of other risk factors, giving an early signal to neutralize the exposure and avoid the direct effects of the subsequent extreme event.

One difficulty of course is in acting on the information before everybody else. Many investment managers have reduced their exposures to excessively bubbly market segments only to find themselves punished by investors who are disappointed in missing out on the gains from fast-rising asset prices. Only very brave (and sometimes soon-to-be-unemployed) investment managers cut their exposure to equities in early 2007, despite visible warning signals of a well-developed bubble.

Currency effects

Foreign exchange is not an asset class. To buy one currency you must sell another. But managed effectively currency exposures can be a source of active return. Unmanaged, they are a source of unnecessary risk. There are three broad strategies for dealing with currency:

- Neutral or passive.
- Hedged.
- Actively managed.

A neutral currency position is where the portfolio holds just enough foreign currency to buy the assets that are denominated in that currency. For example, if the portfolio has $100 million in Swiss equities and another $50 million in Swiss bonds, the fund should have $150 million worth of Swiss Francs.

The currency allocation of the portfolio is the sum of the currencies of the assets in it. This implicitly accepts that exposure to currency fluctuations is integral to the return to an asset and is not necessarily equal to currency allocation. Exposure to foreign currencies can therefore derive from holding assets denominated in the portfolio's base currency, as well as overseas holdings. If this seems counter-intuitive, consider a GB Pounds investor holding shares in BP. The investor accepts that the return to BP is due in part to its exposure to foreign currencies as well as it exposure to the oil price, which is in US Dollars.

Hedging to base currency aims to eliminate exposure to foreign currency fluctuations, leaving exposure to the returns to foreign assets only. Of course it is necessary to buy, say, Swiss Francs in order to buy physical Swiss equities and bonds, but the exposure to the Swiss Franc is neutralized by selling Swiss Francs.

Effective currency hedging depends on knowing what the portfolio's exposure to a currency is; which is usually not the same as the weight of assets denominated in that currency.

For example, a portfolio with allocation to the Swiss market will almost certainly have Nestlé in it. It is unrealistic to suppose that Nestlé is 100 per cent exposed to the Swiss Franc and has no exposure at all to any other currencies. Selling Swiss Francs according to the weight held in Nestlé would expose the portfolio to unmanaged risk and therefore unnecessary volatility. The strategy aimed at controlling risk would actually increase it.

In fact Nestlé's beta to the Swiss Franc is about 0.50,[7] so hedging its exposure according to its weight in the portfolio would result in selling twice as many Swiss Francs as necessary, with the excess in sold Swiss Francs representing a source of unmanaged risk to the portfolio. Meanwhile, Nestlé's – and the portfolio's – exposure to other currencies would also remain unmanaged.

Actively managed currency effectively treats currencies as a separate source of potential return. This approach of course demands skill in forecasting currency fluctuations and realistic modelling of currency exposures. Consistent with Grinold and Kahn, it can add significantly to the risk-adjusted return to the portfolio.

The two main theories of exchange rates are:

- Interest rate parity says that the difference between two currencies is a function of the difference between the interest rates in those currencies.
- Purchasing power parity says that the exchange rate should equate the price of identical goods in different currencies, after adjusting for transport costs and taxes.

Interest rate parity is used to estimate fair prices for forward exchange rates, but can also be useful in forecasting very short-term currency movements.

Example 8.2 Interest rate parity calculating the forward price

Spot exchange rate	
USD/GBP	£0.6500
GBP 90 day interest	2.00%
USD 90 day interest	2.50%
Time to expiry in days	90
90 day forward rate GBP/USD	£0.6492

In Example 8.2 the exchange rate in three months' time for GB Pounds to US Dollars is calculated using three-month interest rates for the two countries, using the following formula:

$$FX = SX \times (1 + r_{UK} \times d/365)/(1 + r_{US} \times d/365) \quad (8.1)$$

Where:

FX = forward exchange rate
SX = current or spot exchange rate
r_{UK} = UK interest rate
r_{US} = US interest rate
d = number of days between now and forward settlement

$= £0.6500 \times (1 + 0.02 \times 90/365)/(1 + 0.25 \times 90/365)$
$= £0.6492$

Being a very simple formula, the only assumption that may not always hold exactly in practice is that the interest rate differential remains constant during the forecast period.

Purchasing power parity says that tradable goods ought to cost the same everywhere, after taking account of differences in taxes between countries and transport costs. Probably the best-known illustration of purchasing power parity is the Big Mac Index, cited regularly in *The Economist* since 1986 as a mildly tongue-in-cheek estimate of the currencies' theoretical 'fair values'. It compares the cost in different countries of a Big Mac hamburger, the premise being that there is almost no difference in the quality of a Big Mac from Moscow to Melbourne to Manhattan, so any price differences, after adjusting for taxes and transport costs, reflect under- or overpriced currencies.

Example 8.3 shows the theoretical price of a hypothetical widget as a function of its cost in its place of manufacture (in this case the USA), transport costs, tax and the exchange rate. If the actual price of the widget is higher than the theoretical price then, other things being equal, the currency of that country is over-valued.

Example 8.3 Purchasing power parity

Currency	Exchange rate	Transport costs	Tax differential	Theoretical value of widget in local currency
US Dollars	1.0000	0.00%	0.00%	$1.00
Australian Dollar	0.9593	15.00%	0.00%	1.10
Canadian Dollar	1.0057	0.00%	0.00%	1.01
Danish Krone	5.5423	5.00%	2.50%	5.96
Euro	0.7427	5.00%	2.50%	0.80
Hong Kong Dollar	7.7541	7.50%	2.50%	8.53
Japanese Yen	90.9093	7.50%	2.50%	100.00
New Zealand Dollar	1.1943	15.00%	0.00%	1.37
Norwegian Krone	5.5222	5.00%	2.50%	5.94
Singaporean Dollar	1.2346	7.50%	2.50%	1.36
Swedish Krona	6.4583	5.00%	2.50%	6.94
Swiss Franc	0.9265	5.00%	2.50%	1.00
GB Pound	0.8715	5.00%	2.50%	0.94

In practice, neither interest rate parity nor purchasing power parity is a good predictor of currency rates. Funds flows and other transient effects cause them to diverge from both. They do however give a framework by which short- and long-term equilibrium rates can be estimated.

The universal currency hedging ratio

The universal currency hedging ratio was developed by Fischer Black in the late 1980s. It demonstrates that, somewhat contrary to intuition, the optimal proportion of currency hedging is a constant ratio defined by:

- The average across countries of the expected returns on the world market portfolio.
- The average across countries of the volatility of the world market portfolio.
- The average across all pairs of countries of exchange rate volatility.

It gives three possible solutions:

- Hedge foreign equity.
- Hedge less than 100 per cent of foreign equity.
- Hedge equities equally for all countries.

Assuming that:

- Investors see the world in light of their own consumption goods.
- Investors count both risk and expected return when figuring their optimum hedges.
- Investors share common views on stocks and currencies.
- Markets are liquid and there are no barriers to international investing.

Frictional liquidity

All portfolios must hold some liquid assets, usually very short term (less than three months) and low risk, typically issued by a government or a bank. The purpose is to:

- Meet short-term redemptions, management fees and costs.
- Meet margin calls for derivatives positions.

They accumulate from:

- Small amounts of new investment into the fund.
- Income from investments such as dividends and coupons.

The amount held in liquid assets is typically 5 to 10 per cent of the value of the portfolio, although it can be more if the portfolio maintains a large proportion of its exposure to risky assets through derivatives positions. From the investor's point of view, holdings in liquid assets are a dead-weight, as they cannot earn active investment returns. Relative to benchmark, they therefore represent a source of risk relative to the benchmark. Also, as management fees are levied on the whole of the fund, including un-invested cash, the investor can be paying active management fees on funds that are not actually invested and, strictly, should attract management fees at a much lower rate.

Modelling risk

While the expected return to the portfolio is simply the weighted sum of the returns to the assets classes in it, the portfolio's risk takes into account the volatility of asset class returns and the relationship between them, expressed as correlations or covariances.[8] This section discusses some of the issues that arise in modelling risk at the level of asset classes, and some approaches frequently used to manage them, including:

- Forecasting and formulating correlation matrices.
- What scenario analysis can add.

Correlation matrices

Forecasting correlation matrices is surprisingly difficult to do in practice, so investment managers tend to use some sample of historical returns as a guide. This of course supposes that the past is a good representation of what will happen in the future. The assumption is not entirely unreasonable, as correlations are more stable over time than asset returns, but they do vary, so the correlations you get depend in part on what historical data you sample from.

Too short a period risks excluding correlations that are relevant to the investment horizon, while choosing too much history risks including those that were important, but are now obsolete.

Example 8.4 shows that, while most asset classes exhibit stable relationships with each other, occasionally large changes occur. In this example the relationships between domestic government bonds and sovereign bonds has changed significantly, as has the correlation of developed market equities with domestic bonds, and developed market equities with emerging market equities.

A recurring issue in deciding what history to sample from is that atypical events can confound results. As the data sample rolls forward to each period, individual observations move further into the past until they 'drop out' of the sample. When an extreme event drops out, the risk of the portfolio can appear to fall abruptly. While their inclusion in the data sample causes obvious bias, leaving them out altogether can cause less obvious but no less important, biases. One way to deal with this is to place more importance on recent observations, and less on older data. There are a number of ways of applying differential weights to return, the simplest being to increase by an equal amount the importance of each consecutive observation, known as 'linear weighting'. Alternatively a more aggressive 'exponential' decay function can be applied. Thus recent data are much more heavily weighted than early observations, giving a more progressive evolution of correlations, and therefore of risk forecasts, that still conserves persistent asset class correlations.

For some asset classes, such as bonds, computation of asset class correlations can be done only on sector proxies. Calculation of correlations between pairs of assets demands that the returns to each are approximately symmetrical, which is not the case for individual bonds, but is a reasonable approximation for bond indices. This is because, unlike a physical bond, a bond index doesn't mature. Instead it tracks the price of a hypothetical bond with a constant maturity of, say ten years. The returns are not exactly symmetrical, but are usually close enough to allow estimation of correlations and volatilities.

Example 8.4 Comparing correlation matrices

	5 year correlation matrix	Risk %	1	2	3	4	5	6	7	8	9
1	Domestic fixed interest	4.06	1.00								
2	International sovereign debt	20.31	0.01	1.00							
3	Domestic corporate debt	4.59	0.93	0.27	1.00						
4	Domestic equities	14.43	0.15	0.68	0.38	1.00					
5	Developed markets equities	13.34	-0.01	0.67	0.21	0.92	1.00				
6	Emerging markets equities	26.49	-0.23	0.79	0.01	0.70	0.75	1.00			
7	Real property	16.53	0.05	0.47	0.22	0.56	0.48	0.48	1.00		
8	GB Pound	6.92	0.11	-0.27	0.03	-0.15	-0.08	-0.25	-0.01	1.00	
9	Euro	8.36	0.06	-0.24	-0.03	-0.21	-0.11	-0.26	-0.17	0.57	1.00
10	Japanese Yen	14.58	-0.02	-0.08	-0.10	0.10	0.26	0.05	-0.14	0.25	0.47

	10 year correlation matrix	Risk %	1	2	3	4	5	6	7	8	9
1	Domestic fixed interest	4.16	1.00								
2	International sovereign debt	17.67	0.14	1.00							
3	Domestic corporate debt	4.54	0.95	0.32	1.00						
4	Domestic equities	12.87	0.27	0.60	0.41	1.00					
5	Developed markets equities	12.75	0.17	0.56	0.30	0.84	1.00				
6	Emerging markets equities	23.94	-0.12	0.72	0.06	0.62	0.62	1.00			
7	Real property	17.13	0.17	0.43	0.28	0.59	0.52	0.50	1.00		
8	GB Pound	10.11	0.18	-0.11	0.10	0.00	0.19	-0.18	-0.06	1.00	
9	Euro	10.16	0.17	-0.20	0.08	-0.08	0.11	-0.23	-0.12	0.77	1.00
10	Japanese Yen	12.25	0.04	-0.13	-0.03	0.04	0.25	-0.02	-0.11	0.27	0.44

Scenario analyses

A full discussion of scenario analysis is given in Chapter 6 on risk measurement. Scenario analysis is widely used in asset allocation because it accommodates all instruments and strategies, both symmetrical and asymmetrical, and shows how much each asset class contributes to return in each scenario, making it appear intuitive.

The main limitation is that defining realistic scenarios is surprisingly tricky to do, while poorly defined scenarios give misleading results.

It is also impossible to ensure that all possible scenarios are included, so it can contribute to a false sense of security.

Aligning risk and return

Aligning sources of risk with sources of return so that incidental risk can be eliminated and returns enhanced entails:

- Distinguishing between exposure and weighting and accurate estimation of economic exposures.
- Realistically modelling interactions between asset allocation and asset class portfolio selection.
- Arguments for and against optimization and reverse optimization.
- What risk budgeting can add.
- Some observations on limits and constraints.

Exposure versus weighting

One of the most persistent misunderstandings in investment management is equating portfolio weights with economic exposure. Having 60 per cent of the portfolio invested in equities does not mean that the portfolio has an exposure of 60 per cent to equity market growth.

If an equity asset class sub-portfolio has a beta to the equity market of 1.05, then the portfolio's economic exposure to equities is 63 per cent (60 per cent x 1.05). Similarly if the bond holding of 30 per cent has a relative duration of 1.02, then the exposure to relative interest rate fluctuations is 30.6 per cent.

The exposure of one asset class portfolio to its asset class benchmark cannot compare with the exposures of other asset class sub-portfolios: the equity market beta says nothing about the sensitivity of that part of the portfolio to interest rates and bond duration has little to do with equities. Consequently, these do not add up to anything sensible at the level of the multi-asset class portfolio.

Example 8.5 compares portfolio weight and economic exposure for each asset class to its sector, calculated as the portfolio weight times the sector beta, less the benchmark weight. Note that the asset class benchmark in each case by definition has an exposure of exactly 1.0. The asset class portfolio exposure reflects the fact that the composition of each asset class sub-portfolio is different from the composition of its asset class benchmark. For example, the beta of the UK equities sub-portfolio to the UK equity benchmark is 1.22, suggesting a very actively-managed sub-portfolio that will overshoot returns to the UK equity asset class by 22 per cent in each direction. This is more than off-setting the 1 per cent underweight in that asset class, so the relative exposure of that part of the portfolio to UK equities is 0.20 per cent. The portfolio is slightly over-exposed to UK equities relative to the benchmark exposure of 25 per cent. The over-weight of 0.5 per cent in Developed Asia equities is compounded by the asset class beta of 1.12, giving an economic exposure to the sector of 0.92 per cent relative to the benchmark.

In practice asset allocation is usually subject to holding limits for each asset class, restricting the amount of over- and under-weight that is allowed.

The interaction between asset allocation and asset class selection

Asset allocation and stock selection are usually kept separate by the two-stage portfolio construction process, the end result can be off-setting and compounding decisions and risks within the overall portfolio, as is shown in Example 8.5. For another example, suppose that the asset allocations manager under-weights domestic equities and over-weights domestic bonds. If the domestic equity manager selects a portfolio with a beta to the local market or 1.04, then the effective exposure to domestic equities is 4 per cent greater than intended by the asset allocation manager, partially or completely negating the intentions of the asset allocation manager and reducing the chances of the portfolio meeting its return target. Meanwhile, if the domestic bond manager selects a portfolio with a relative duration of 1.02, then the bond portfolio effectively compounds the asset allocation decision. The additional exposure represents extra risk that is unmanaged at the level of the overall portfolio, so will cause unnecessary volatility in its returns.

The easiest and least ambiguous way to coordinate asset allocation of asset class portfolios is to specify that sub-portfolio exposures to their asset class benchmarks should always be neutral; for example, betas to equity markets equal to one and bond relative duration equal to one. In practice this specification is often not included in asset class investment mandates. Where asset class portfolios are invested via pooled vehicles, it may not be practicable to impose this condition on the physical portfolio. The other solution is to use derivatives to hedge away the unwanted exposure and so keep asset class exposures close to 1.0.

A valid measure of asset class beta is essential to a credible outcome. As we know, the beta measure is sensitive to which data sample it is measured from and how that data sample is treated. There is no 'right' answer

Example 8.5 Exposure versus weighting

Asset class	Portfolio weight	Benchmark weight	Asset class portfolio exposure to its sector	Relative exposure to sector	Relative weight
UK equities	24.0%	25.0%	1.22	0.20%	-1.00%
Developed European equities	4.0%	5.0%	1.08	−0.88%	-1.00%
US equities	10.5%	15.0%	1.24	−3.66%	-4.50%
Japanese equities	2.0%	3.0%	0.95	−0.96%	-1.00%
Developed Asian equities	3.5%	3.0%	1.27	0.92%	0.50%
Emerging European equities	1.4%	2.0%	1.08	−0.56%	-0.60%
Latin American equities	2.8%	2.0%	1.25	1.08%	0.80%
Emerging Asian equities	3.8%	2.0%	1.28	2.22%	1.80%
Domestic fixed income	28.5%	30.0%	0.68	−1.50%	-1.50%
Developed international fixed income	6.5%	5.0%	0.62	1.23%	1.50%
Emerging fixed income	5.0%	3.0%	0.88	1.60%	2.00%
Cash	8.0%	5.0%			3.00%
Equities	49.5%	57.0%			-7.5%
Fixed income	42.0%	38.0%			4.0%
Cash	8.0%	5.0%			3.0%
Total	100%	100%			-3.5%

to this. Taking more than one sounding of beta can help by indicating how stable or otherwise the asset class beta is, and therefore what margin of error should be factored into the exposure estimation.

The aim of all active management is to earn active returns by taking on active risk and aligning sources of risk with sources of expected return. Active return is earned by buying assets that are perceived to be below their fair price and selling assets that are above their fair price. When actual prices converge to their long-term fair price, the original allocation is restored and the active return realized.

Articulating, preferably in advance, the likely benefit to the portfolio of mispricing of assets, helps align return with risk. The next sections discuss how this can be done.

Optimization

One of the more powerful implications of CAPM is that it enables an efficient portfolio to be derived that has the best possible trade-off of return to risk. In practice investment managers have found that optimizers are far from ideal. Some things that limit their practical application are:

- Optimization assumes that efficient portfolios exist, when in fact they don't. Suppose you create an efficient portfolio as the market opens, using all the information you have at the time. The portfolio becomes inefficient as soon as prices move (and the portfolio weights change), or new information comes in (and the expected returns or risks change).
- Optimization assumes that all risk is equal, when in practice it isn't. Investment managers are paid to take risk, so their task is to distinguish intended from unintended risk. Unintentional risk should be eliminated as far as possible and intentional risk targeted and even increased. The optimizer assumes that all risk is equally bad and tries to eliminate even the intentional risk that is there in order to earn active returns.
- Optimization assumes that portfolio managers know exactly what their forecast returns are. In practice they rarely do. Rather than forecasting a single return, investment managers more often think in terms of ranges or rankings of returns, which do not fit neatly into an optimizer.
- Optimizers maximize errors. Errors can occur in either the return forecasts or the risk forecasts. Optimizers can't spot them, so will consistently select assets with over-optimistic return forecasts over more conservative estimates with the same risk. Similarly, they will favour low-risk stocks over high-risk stocks, other things being equal. This results in consistent selection of assets with over-estimated returns and under-estimated risk. The result is a portfolio with more risk and less return than the optimization results would imply – so can hardly be efficient.

Reverse optimization

A more robust and intuitive way to apply the power of CAPM is to reverse the optimization process. Starting with the investment manager's preferred asset allocation or exposure and assuming the same risk and correlations as for optimization, reverse optimization generates the return for each asset that is required for the portfolio composition to be efficient, either in absolute terms or relative to the benchmark.

The investment manager can then judge if the implied asset returns look reasonable. If they are too high, then the allocation or exposure to that asset can be reduced, and vice-versa. The advantages are:

- The investment manager starts with a realistic portfolio allocation or exposure.
- No explicit return forecasts are needed, ranges or even rankings can work just as well.
- Allocation can be expressed as exposure or holdings. Using exposure, as described in Example 8.5 is more powerful because it allows the interaction between the asset allocation decision and the asset class sub-portfolio composition to be taken into account.

The big benefit is that it gives an inherently risk-based portfolio selection process, ensuring that risk is allocated where the manager believes it will best contribute to return. Because it takes account of the asset class correlation matrix and asset class volatilities, its validity depends on realistic estimation of those parameters.

Risk budgeting

Another way to allocate risk without altering portfolio weights is by risk budgeting. Instead of adjusting the level of portfolio risk by changing the weight held in each asset class, the investment manager adjusts the riskiness, usually given by the tracking error or volatility of the asset class portfolio.

Example 8.6 illustrates with a simple two asset portfolio consisting of active and passive sub-portfolios invested in the same asset class. This combination of passive and active in the same asset class is known as core-satellite. The investment objective in the example is a portfolio wide active return of 1.5 per cent.

At a 50/50 weighting between the passive and active components of the portfolio, the expected return is 1 per cent and the expected tracking error is 2.83 per cent. The passive part has a tracking error of zero and zero expected active return, while the active component has an expected return of 2 per cent and tracking error of 4 per cent.

To increase the expected return of the combined portfolio, the investment manager can simply allocate more to the active part of the portfolio. If the allocation is increased to 75 per cent active and 25 per cent passive, the expected return goes up to 1.50 per cent. But many investors would be unhappy with a satellite that is bigger than the core, and might insist the core have at least 50 per cent in it.

The other way to increase the overall return is to keep the fund allocation at 50/50, and increase the tracking error of the active component to 6 per cent. As Example 8.6 shows, the expected return goes up to 1.5 per cent and the tracking error goes up to 4.24 per cent.

Example 8.6 illustrates risk budgeting by active versus passive within a single asset class. Risk budgeting for multi-asset class portfolios comprises the following steps:

- Define the long-term asset allocation. Risk budgeting assumes that this is efficient in terms of expected return and risk.
- Estimate, for each asset class portfolio, the expected information ratio, usually from the asset class manager's past performance.
- Apply a risk model that accommodates all asset classes in the portfolio. The best results depend on the structure of the risk model reflecting the selection process of the portfolio. In practice this can be difficult and/ or expensive to do and may imply some unrealistic assumptions about the interactions between the components of different sub-portfolios, particularly those with asymmetric return distributions. This subject is discussed in more detail in Chapter 5 on risk modelling.
- Reverse optimize it to obtain implied asset-class returns and, by applying defined information ratios to each, the risk budget for each asset class sub-portfolio.
- On-going management entails comparing the existing portfolio risk proportions with the risk budget and repeating the steps as necessary.

This brings the following advantages:

- It can improve risk return efficiency, especially if the portfolio is subject to tight holding constraints.
- It can help fine-tune performance targets for asset class managers and take into account the different opportunity sets for each. This means that the investment manager can take on more risk where he or she thinks it will contribute to active returns, and hold back in areas where there is more uncertainty.

Potential limitations include:

- Information ratios are assumed to be constant, which is almost certainly not true, as investment managers tend not to perform equally well in all market conditions.
- Modelling correlations between asset classes may not be possible if one or more have very asymmetrical return distributions. As the correlations are the core of the risk model, and therefore the main determinants of the output, this can be a fatal flaw.

Example 8.6 Risk budgeting

Portfolio	Expected alpha	Expected tracking error	Expected information ratio	Fund allocation
Passive core	0.00%	0.00%	0.00	50%
Active satellite	2.00%	4.00%	0.50	50%
Total	1.00%	2.83%	0.35	100%
Change fund				
Allocation				
Passive core	0.00%	0.00%	0.00	25%
Active satellite	2.00%	4.00%	0.50	75%
Total	1.50%	3.46%	0.43	100%
Change expected tracking error				
Passive core	0.00%	0.00%	0.00	50%
Active satellite	3.00%	6.00%	0.50	50%
Total	1.50%	4.24%	0.35	100%

- It assumes that the asset class portfolio exposures to their asset classes are the same as the holding. This is true only if each of the equity portfolios has a beta to its local market of 1.0 and each bond portfolio has a relative duration of 1.0. It is important to ensure that changes in volatility or tracking error of asset class portfolios do not alter the beta and duration to each asset class and therefore the effective asset class exposures.

Limits and constraints

Most funds are subject to some constraints either on the weight held in the portfolio or the exposure of the portfolio to an asset or a common factor. The aims are usually:

- To control risk.
- To limit or avoid investing in particular investment instruments or asset classes; for example, to comply with ethical, environmentally sustainable or corporate governance guidelines.
- To comply with relevant regulations.

Containing a fund's exposures to risky assets, and groups of risky assets, such as countries, currencies, industries, counterparties and so on, is often assumed to be an effective way to limit the damage incurred when the prices of those risky assets fall. But they can have precisely the opposite effect.

This is partly due to confounding portfolio weighting and economic exposure. Limits on portfolio weights are easily circumvented by choosing assets with high (or low) inherent exposure to the factor in question (in effect market beta for equities and duration for bonds) while complying with the aggregate holding limit. Constraints that can be circumvented in this way are ineffective, and so do not contribute to the intended risk control.

Limits or targets expressed as economic exposure can avoid this inconsistency. Measuring exposure to risk factors, by taking account of the beta to market or duration as applicable, is much harder to circumvent, so is a more effective way to control risk. But this solution is not free of contradictions either.

Limiting risk or economic exposure can come at the cost of returns foregone; and limits that are imposed without reference to how the investment manager selects his portfolio can increase, rather than reduce, risk by forcing him or her to seek returns where he or she is less confident of achieving them.

Limiting risks that will drive positive returns, necessarily limits those returns. Unintended risk, on the other hand, should be eliminated rather than just limited. Exposure limits can have other problems too.

One is that hard limits introduce the boundary problem: a small change in exposure tips the portfolio from being within tolerance to being outside it. This problem is compounded by the fact that all limits are necessarily arbitrary, and so can oblige the investment manager to carry out trades that serve only to ensure compliance, do nothing to benefit the portfolio and may in fact impede performance by departing from the manager's preferred positioning and increasing transactions costs – without actually reducing risk.

Yet many investors are uncomfortable with an investment mandate that imposes no limits or controls at all.

So now the question is about how tightly limits should be set. Setting limits too narrowly means that they will bite too frequently and so give rise to return-destroying transactions; while setting them too widely renders them meaningless

Moreover markets evolve and conditions change, and limits set in one environment can soon begin to have perverse effects in another.

The challenge is to find a stable solution that neither impedes the manager's ability to efficiently allocate risk nor gives rise to transactions that add no value to the portfolio. One way is to target risk directly.

Because targets can be matched to return objectives and forecasts, they are both more powerful and more robust than limits. Unlike limits, targets are neither arbitrary nor do they suffer from boundary error.

But even with impeccable management of risk exposures and concentrations, mishaps can occur, so some safety mechanism is usually desirable to contain the consequences of human error. The investor understandably would prefer to protect the portfolio against the investment manager getting it horribly wrong.

A practical solution that mitigates both boundary error and arbitrariness is to complement risk targets with dual limits, in effect a combination of:

- Narrow, soft, internal limits that serve as a warning and oblige the investment manager to formally explain or, within a defined time interval, take action such as to re-evaluate the portfolio's positioning.
- Hard, wide, external limits that oblige him or her to modify the position.

These limits too are arbitrary and suffer from the boundary problem, but are less likely to lead to artificial transactions. Corrective action can then be coordinated with on-going management. The internal limits can, indeed should, be breached regularly without automatically leading to counter-productive transactions. This way the external limits are breached only in extreme circumstances. The result is more efficient risk management, less vulnerability to shocks, lower portfolio turnover and more robust performance.

Passive asset allocation

If the multi-asset class investor does not have access to skill in allocating between asset classes, passive asset allocation is a logical strategy. It matches asset class exposures to those of the long-term benchmark and rebalances periodically to maintain that asset class mix. In principle, passive asset allocation assumes:

- There is little overall value to be gained, after costs, from trying to outperform the fund's long-term asset allocation by forecasting short-term returns to asset classes.
- Even if it were feasible to regularly predict returns, the costs in terms of economic and sector research of deriving the forecasts coupled with the transactions costs of implementing short-term asset allocation, outweigh any possible economic benefits.
- The long-term benchmark asset allocation is the best possible mix, given the long-term objectives of the portfolio.

Passive asset allocation has a number of benefits:

- Even if the investor takes the view that value can be added from tactical asset allocation, the portfolio can be better off keeping its physical

assets in their long-term asset allocation proportions and effect tactical asset allocation by means of a derivatives overlay, which is both cheaper and nimbler than trading physical assets.
- If active short-term asset allocation is carried out using a derivatives overlay, indexed asset class portfolios remove one source of complication in that their composition closely or exactly replicates the index against which the futures contract is settled. By contrast, actively managed asset class portfolios, when off-set by futures contracts, always leave some residual risk, known as basis risk, in place due to the mismatch in the composition of the physical portfolio and the index.
- Small to medium pension funds often find that passive allocation can reduce manager risk too. Because small funds are more likely to hire a small number of managers with balanced mandates (rather than a larger number of specialist managers), they are more prone to manager risk. Passive asset allocation removes one of the main sources of manager risk: that of poor short-term asset allocation, or market timing.
- For these funds the strategy can be ideal, allowing them to maintain their own mandate, rather than buying units in a large pooled investment vehicle.

Passive asset allocation can be combined with active or passive management of individual asset class portfolios, or in combination with these:

- As part of a balanced mandate.
- As a specialist mandate, with individual asset classes managed separately by specialist sector managers.

Central to passive asset allocation are rebalancing rules, which can be driven by:

- The time intervals at which the asset allocation should be reset to benchmark.
- The maximum allowable deviation between actual and benchmark allocation.
- Some combination of the two.

The investment manager generally has some discretion to override rules if he or she believes more frequent trades are justified by greater than normal deviation from expected tracking error between scheduled re-balances or if regular re-balances are not justified by the expected improvement in tracking error.

Most passive asset allocation mandates specify a mixture of both, so that the portfolio is rebalanced say every six months, with more frequent rebalances if and when any asset class weighting differs from the benchmark by, say 5 per cent or more. The mandate can also specify that natural cash flows be used to effect on-going rebalances whenever possible.

The frequency of resets, and the size of the allowable mismatch should reflect the investor's tolerance of deviation from long-term asset allocation, and likely transactions costs, which are determined largely by the asset classes themselves. For example, a large allocation to domestic fixed interest and equities implies low average trading costs, while a significant investment in less liquid assets, such as small capitalization equities and direct equity implies higher transactions costs. The availability and use of futures contracts can further reduce transactions costs by smoothing resets and managing liquidity.

Risk-parity portfolios

An alternative to allocating to asset classes by capital, risk parity seeks a portfolio composition whereby each asset class contributes the same risk to the portfolio. This is a passive approach, as it demands no asset class return forecasts but relies instead on accurate estimation of asset class return volatility and the covariance matrix of asset class returns to avoid unmanaged risk in the portfolio.

On-going management

This section describes some of the methods for maintaining and revising asset allocation and evaluating its contribution to return and risk.

Rebalancing

While all short-term asset allocation seeks to add value by departing from the long-term asset allocation mix, there is more than one way to do this:

- Physical re-allocation whereby the investment manager transacts physical assets with each revision of the short-term asset allocation.
- Tactical asset allocation overlay, whereby physical assets are held according to the long-term asset allocation and asset class exposure is adjusted by buying and selling derivatives contracts.

Buying and selling physical assets has the obvious appeal that it is conceptually simple. It also allows the investor to draw full benefits of any tax advantages, such as dividend credits, that accrue to physical holdings but usually not to derivatives. The downside is the cost and the time it can take to buy and sell physical assets, especially if the nominal amounts to be bought and sold are large. If these costs are great enough, they can tempt the investment manager to retain a particular asset allocation longer than is good for the portfolio, which can bias performance.

Derivatives can facilitate nimbler and more cost-efficient short-term asset allocation – and potentially a better return to risk profile. But it is not without its short-comings.

One danger is basis risk. Basis risk is the risk that the derivative instrument used will not deliver the same return as the physical assets it is meant to replace or off-set. For example, most equity futures contracts are based on a recognized share price index that mimics a well-diversified portfolio of shares, such as the S&P500 or the FT Allshare. Bond futures are usually based on a reference bond such as a hypothetical government issue which has ten years to maturity. To the extent that the actual portfolio differs in composition from the asset class index or reference bond or portfolio, the derivatives position can be only an approximation to the physical portfolio. The risk 'left over' is the basis risk. This of course can be a good thing if the investment manager is confident that the portfolio's active risk will contribute to active portfolio return.

If the number of futures to be transacted is estimated using portfolio weightings to asset classes, there will remain unwanted exposures to asset classes – both bought and sold – that are unmanaged. These will add to portfolio level risk and result in unnecessary return volatility.

Portfolio rebalancing always incurs costs to the portfolio. In order to add value to the portfolio, the expected benefits to the portfolio, in terms of an improved expected return to risk ratio – taking into account all sources of risk - should demonstrably outweigh the estimated costs of the anticipated transactions.

Performance measurement and attribution

The objective is to compare the portfolio's performance with that of the long-term allocation or benchmark and to quantify the contribution from each portfolio selection decision.

This should show which decisions added to return and which subtracted from it. Comparing the outcome with the rationale for each decision can give an insight into how much of the result is due to skill and good management and how much is due to chance.

Example 8.7 shows return attribution by contribution due to the exposure of the asset class sub-portfolio to the asset class and to pure stock selection within each asset class sub-portfolio (columns 9 and 10 respectively). This is calculated as follows:

Column 7	Return to asset class sub-portfolio weighted by portfolio holding	C2 × C6
Column 8	Return to asset class sub-portfolio weighted by relative holding	(C2 – C3) × C6
Column 9	Return to asset class sub-portfolio due to exposure to its sector	((C2 × C4) – C3) × (C5 – C5 total)
Column 10	Return to asset class sub-portfolio due to stock-selection	C8 – C9

The totals row, in Example 8.7, says that, of the portfolio out-performance of 0.054 per cent, 0.123 per cent was due to asset class exposure, while pure stock-selection within asset class sub-portfolios actually subtracted value. The information in individual rows shows that stock selection within the equities portfolios was responsible for the negative result, while the fixed interest portfolios gave positive results for stock-selection, though its results were mixed with regard to systematic (asset class exposure) contributions.

For this period at least, the investor would have been 0.07 per cent better off investing the equities asset classes in index funds.

Summary

Active asset allocation seeks to add return to the portfolio by departing from the portfolio's long-term or strategic asset allocation. In doing so, it incurs risk, which derives not only from the mismatch between the portfolio's exposures to each asset class and those of the benchmark, but also the interactions between asset class exposure mismatches and the composition of the asset classes themselves. Risk-based portfolio selection ensures that the risks entailed are commensurate with the extra value to be added.

Formulating the asset allocation strategy infers an assumption about the equity risk premium, which, implicitly or explicitly, is at the heart of most equity valuation methodologies. It also embeds an assumption about the contribution of foreign currencies to asset returns and therefore demands a clear strategy for currency management.

A range of methodologies can contribute to aligning return and risk, including optimization and reverse optimization, risk budgeting and scenario analysis.

In practice most asset allocation strategies take into consideration the possibility of market shocks and crises, usually entailing a forecast based on one or more of several theories about how they occur. A common

Example 8.7 Return contribution of short-term asset allocation

Asset class	Portfolio holding	Benchmark holding	Asset class portfolio exposure to its sector start of period	Return to asset class	Return to asset class sub-portfolio	Return to asset class weighted by portfolio holding	Return to asset class weighted by relative holding	Due to asset class exposure to its sector	Due to stock-selection
1	2	3	4	5	6	7	8	9	10
UK equities	24.0%	25.0%	1.05	1.80%	1.90%	0.456%	–0.019%	0.004%	–0.023%
Developed European equities	4.0%	5.0%	1.03	2.20%	2.50%	0.100%	–0.025%	–0.019%	–0.006%
US equities	10.5%	15.0%	1.08	1.60%	1.90%	0.200%	–0.086%	–0.059%	–0.027%
Japanese equities	2.0%	3.0%	1.02	0.50%	0.60%	0.012%	–0.006%	–0.005%	–0.001%
Developed Asian equities	3.5%	3.0%	1.12	3.60%	3.40%	0.119%	0.017%	0.033%	–0.016%
Emerging European equities	1.4%	2.0%	1.03	1.20%	1.50%	0.021%	–0.009%	–0.007%	–0.002%
Latin American equities	2.8%	2.0%	1.1	4.30%	4.60%	0.129%	0.037%	0.046%	–0.010%
Emerging Asian equities	3.8%	2.0%	1.11	5.40%	5.20%	0.198%	0.094%	0.120%	–0.026%
Domestic fixed income	28.5%	30.0%	0.95	0.30%	0.40%	0.114%	–0.006%	–0.009%	0.003%
Developed international fixed income	6.5%	5.0%	0.89	0.80%	1.00%	0.065%	0.015%	0.006%	0.009%
Emerging fixed income	5.0%	3.0%	0.92	1.40%	1.80%	0.090%	0.036%	0.022%	0.014%
Cash	8.0%	5.0%		0.20%	0.20%	0.016%	0.006%	–0.010%	0.016%
Equities	52.0%	57.0%		1.23%	1.13%	1.234%	0.003%	0.114%	–0.111%
Fixed income	40.0%	38.0%		0.88%	0.79%	0.269%	0.045%	0.020%	0.025%
Cash	8.0%	5.0%		0.80%	0.74%	0.016%	0.006%	–0.010%	0.016%
Total	100%	100%				1.52%	0.054%	0.123%	–0.070%

approach to controlling the portfolio's vulnerability to extreme events is to impose limits and constraints on the portfolio. Well formulated and managed, constraints can indeed provide some protection; however if they are imposed without consideration of the strategy by which the portfolio is selected, they can be at best ineffective and at worst a source of risk to the portfolio by compromising the investment manager's preferred positioning in favour of risks that he or she is less comfortable with.

Case Study

A large, conventional pension fund managed by a single investment manager as a balanced portfolio with an investment mix typical of pension funds, including domestic and international equities and domestic and international bonds, with some property.

Some years ago a meeting took place with the client where the consensus was that equity market appreciation was very likely. The economist had forecast 8 per cent plus. But everybody also agreed the outcome was far from certain and that a sharp decline was also possible over the six to nine month forecast horizon.

The strategist suggested exploiting the possibility of equity market growth with a simple option strategy known as a call spread, which would capture limited market growth and at the same time cap potential losses.

With the market trading at 3287 in mid-March, the strategy comprised the following transactions:

Buy September 3444 call options at 114
Sell September 3961 call options at 20
Buy December 3444 call options at 150
Sell December 3961 call options at 39

In other words, the market was expected to grow by between 8 and 20 per cent.

Example 8.8 Asset allocation call option spread

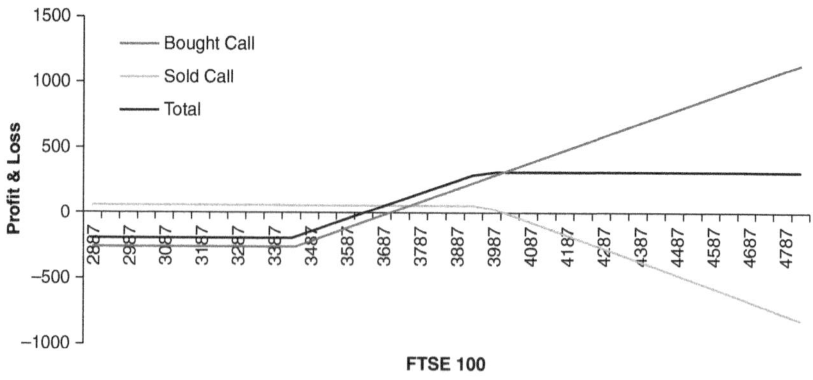

Payoff analysis	Index level	Change on initial level	Outcome	% of initial level
September				
Worst loss	3444	4.78%	94	2.86%
Break-even	3538	7.64%	0	0.00%
Maximum gain	3961	20.51%	423	12.87%
December				
Worst loss	3444	4.78%	111	3.38%
Break-even	3555	8.15%	0	0.00%
Maximum gain	3961	20.51%	406	12.35%

The bold line in the graph in Example 8.8 shows the aggregate payoff at option expiry to the strategy for each equity market index price. It is the sum of the two grey lines, representing the bought call and sold put option positions respectively. It shows that both maximum gain and worst outcome are capped. The positive slope of the bold line between 3444 and 3961 represents the net participation in equity market appreciation at the expiry of the options. This outcome is defined by the terms of the options, and the premiums paid and received for them. It is therefore known at the time the position is implemented.

The benefits of the strategy are:

- It exploits the forecast market rally: the portfolio benefits if the forecast is accurate, but the cost is minor if it is not. Even in the event of a sharp fall in equity prices, the maximum loss to this strategy is only the net premium paid.
- By selecting appropriate exercise dates and exercise prices, the strategist can target the forecast time period and return interval, but note that the further in the future the exercise date is, the less liquid the options tend to be.
- The same type of strategy can exploit forecast market falls too, by substituting put options for call options.
- Transactions costs are negligible for exchange-traded options, and market liquidity is generally enough for the strategy to be scalable, even for very large portfolios.
- This type of option trade performs best when the predicted market appreciation reaches or exceeds the exercise price of the sold call options at about the time of their expiry – in this case 3961 toward the end of September and or December.
- If the forecast growth takes place earlier than expected, the portfolio still benefits but by less.
- Split option settlement dates spreads risk of loss, so that if the forecast growth happens later than expected, the December positions still can capture it.

Endnotes

1. Grinold, R.G. and Kahn, R.N., *Active Portfolio Management: A Quantitative Approach for Producing Superior Returns and Selecting Superior Returns and Controlling Risk*. London: McGraw Hill Professional. 1999.
2. Again, it depends on what history is used as the starting point. See Elroy Dimson, Paul Marsh, and Mike Staunton, *Rethinking the Equity Risk Premium*. Research Foundations Publications. 2011: 32–52.
3. Arnott, Robert D. and Bernstein, Peter L., 'What risk premium is "normal"?'. *AIMR*. 2002.
4. Charging the risk manager with the task of predicting crashes is the same as saying that it is the risk manager's job to forecast negative returns and the strategist's job to forecast positive returns; which is inconsistent, if not just plain silly.
5. Minsky, Hyman P. 'The modeling of financial instability: An introduction'. *Modeling and Simulation*. Proceedings of the Fifth Annual Pittsburgh Conference. 1974.
6. Nassim, Taleb, *The Black Swan: The Impact of the Highly Improbable*. New York: Random House and Penguin. 2007.
7. R-Squared Global Equity Model.
8. Covariance is a function of correlations and volatilities.

9 Indexed Equities Portfolios

A finance professor started the semester with a challenge for his first-year MBA students. The 40 students were split into ten groups and each group told to compile a portfolio of investments from any sector of the economy, including things like lottery tickets and horse-racing bets. Over the length of the semester they could trade their portfolio as often as they liked, but all trade details were to be communicated to the professor as they occurred. The team with the best-performing portfolio at the end of the semester would be awarded an un-specified prize. In the meantime, the professor would compile his own portfolio, which would also compete for the prize.

At the end of the semester, the professor demonstrated that his portfolio had delivered the winning performance by passively investing, pro-rata, in each asset in each of the ten portfolios submitted, and held in the starting composition for the duration of the semester: in effect 'buy and hold'.

The second best performing portfolio was the only 'buy and hold' among the ten student portfolios. The team responsible for it claimed no particular skill or knowledge of the stock-market when they selected their portfolio.

If you find that, for some asset classes, you cannot identify a manager with enough skill to warrant risking part of your fund's return, you have two choices:

- Avoid the sector altogether. This is obviously not ideal, as the sector itself may be an important source of diversification for the fund, or it might be an important potential contributor to overall return.
- Invest in the sector passively, which means gaining exposure to the sector without paying a manager to add value to it by selecting the most promising assets within it.

Although conceptually simple, passive management and indexation are actually very easy to get wrong if not enough attention is given to detail. This chapter looks at:

- What is meant by passive management.
- The main reasons to invest in passive portfolios.
- The advantages of passively managed portfolios.
- What passive portfolios are used for.
- Some observations about passive portfolios.
- Methodology.
- On-going management.
- Enhanced indexation.
- Fundamental equity indices.
- Customized indices.
- Equally-weighted portfolios.
- Risk-parity portfolios.

What is passive management?

Passive investment management is any portfolio selection process that is primarily rules-driven and therefore not dependent on judgement on the part of the investment manager.[1] It includes:

- Indexed portfolios.
- Passive asset allocation.
- Dynamic hedging.
- Some stock-selection processes that depend principally on screening candidate universes according to fixed criteria.
- Automated trading strategies.

This chapter focuses on indexed equities portfolios. Passive asset allocation can be thought of as a special case of asset allocation, dynamic hedging is discussed in Chapter 15 on structured products, asset screening is discussed in the equity and bond portfolio selection and automated trading strategies in Chapter 17 on implementation.

Rationale

Indexed portfolios were originally developed in response to observations that:

- It is difficult to beat the market.
- It is even harder to beat the market after costs.
- Trading assets does not always add value.

Academic research into the relative performance of equity managers has indicated that few, if any, active managers consistently did better, after fees had been deducted, than the S&P500 – the market in which they invested. This seemed to suggest that active equity management represented poor value for money, and that simply replicating the market with modest but reliable performance was a better alternative.

This of course assumes that markets are broadly efficient in the sense that there are no opportunities to make excess returns from buying under-priced and selling overpriced assets. Returns can be improved only by assuming more market risk. Put another way, the alpha in the CAPM algorithm can only be equal to zero.

Advantages

It is not necessary to believe that markets are efficient in order to find advantages in indexation.

Because indexation creates a low maintenance buy and hold portfolio, it incurs minimal transactions costs. For example a portfolio of domestic equities with a turnover of 100 per cent can cost from 100 to over 250 basis points (hundredths of 1 per cent) each year in transactions costs. By contrast, indexed equities portfolios can turn over less than 30 per cent per year. How important this advantage is of course depends on the costs of trading the component securities. For an international portfolio the cost advantage is greater than for domestic equities, because both trading and custodian costs are significantly higher than for domestic portfolios. Some bonds have much lower transactions costs, so the cost advantage of indexation is less important.

Management fees for passive management tend to be much lower than for actively managed portfolios because the manager passes on to the investor the saving from not having to conduct expensive research and analysis of individual securities and forecasting asset class returns, economic analysis and so on. Management fees vary widely between markets and between managers. Lower management fees are of particular interest to small portfolios because, for actively managed portfolios, fees are usually higher for small portfolios as a percentage of funds under management.

As well as costing less, indexed portfolios are, *a priori*, less risky. While all long-only portfolios win and lose with the market in which they are invested, the active portfolio runs the additional risk that the securities it has bought will do better or worse than the market. By contrast, indexed portfolios and passive asset allocation deliver only the benchmark performance without the extra risk from security selection and asset class mismatches.

Applications

Some reasons for investing in indexed equities portfolios are:

- As part of a core-satellite investment strategy.
- To reduce costs and increase the efficiency of a global portfolio.
- As part of an asset swap transaction.
- As an exchange traded fund (ETF).
- As part of a short-term arbitrage transaction.

Large funds farm out management of their portfolios between several, sometimes dozens, of asset managers all operating in the same asset class or market. This leads to the problem that the portfolio selected by one manager can offset some of the risks in the portfolios selected by the others, with the result that the sum of active managers' investment decisions amounts to a very large indexed portfolio for which the fund pays active fees. This is known as a 'closet index' and is clearly not in the investor's best interests. The converse can also be true: managers' active risks can compound each other, resulting in unmanaged risk in the overall portfolio.

The investor can overcome this problem by adopting what is known as the 'core and satellite' approach. Within any given market, the fund invests a core of 50 or 60 per cent of its assets in a single indexed portfolio, with the rest allocated to a small number of satellite portfolios consisting of mandates to manage aggressively their portfolios with targeted sources of active return and therefore risk. Satellite portfolios can include hedge funds, long-short portfolios and other alternative investments, as well as specialist conventional portfolios such as small capitalization or emerging technologies. This approach, if effected properly, has a number of advantages:

- Better than market returns can be much easier to achieve with small to medium portfolios than for large ones, so the active portfolios are more likely to meet their given objectives.
- It reduces the likelihood of running a closet index because each satellite portfolio can be assigned a distinctive mandate.
- It facilitates the inclusion of hedge funds and other alternative investments in the overall portfolio structure.
- It recognizes the reality that all conventional portfolios consist of the benchmark plus a long-short portfolio representing the allocation differences between the portfolio and the benchmark.
- It minimizes the problem of market impact which otherwise could limit the investment manager's ability to assume the risks necessary to achieve acceptable returns.

- It facilitates the identification and reward of better than market performance by active managers.
- Overall management fees are reduced because the bulk of the portfolio attracts very low fees.

Global asset managers find indexation an attractive means of gaining cost effective exposure to international markets by indexing the securities within each target market. This way, management resources can be focussed on choosing which countries to invest in.

Most international portfolios are selected by some top-down process, where the primary allocation is by country or region because the managers believe they are skilled in picking countries or regions that will outperform the others. Unless they believe they have skills in choosing winning stocks within foreign markets, it makes sense to manage portfolios passively within countries and regions. The investment manager can eliminate the complexities of trying to manage portfolio specific risk in individual markets – often in an awkwardly different time zone. This leaves time to focus on optimizing and managing the risks attributable to the markets themselves and allocating between them.

Indexation offers the additional benefits of minimizing management, transactions and administration costs, which can be higher for international portfolios than for domestic ones.

Even if the country and region portfolios are managed by third party local investment managers (where skilled stock pickers may be available for hire), indexing can reduce manager risk.

Another way to invest in overseas markets is with asset swaps, which can be interesting for global portfolios that are subject to domestic tax. Asset swaps work as follows:

- Physical assets are held in a domestic indexed portfolio.
- With the help of a financial intermediary, the returns to the physical, domestic indexed portfolio are swapped for the returns to a portfolio of overseas assets.
- The global portfolio receives, over a fixed period of usually one, two or three years, the return to the agreed international asset or basket of assets and pays the return to domestic assets plus a margin.

The benefit to the portfolio is that, although it has the required international exposure, physical assets can be held domestically and so earn tax credits on dividends and where transactions costs and management fees are lower. Part of this benefit is given up in the form of the margin paid to the intermediary, but part is retained by the fund.

Indexed portfolios are often the underlying portfolios for ETFs. Indexed ETFs are funds holding physical assets indexed to replicate a market or a market segment. The investor in an indexed ETF effectively buys a share of the underlying physical portfolio.

These listed funds provide very low cost access to diversified asset class portfolios, making them particularly suitable for small investors. Because they can be sold short, they can be an excellent means of hedging asset class exposure and for effecting short-term asset allocation shifts. Indexed ETFs are not to be confused with exchange-traded notes (ETNs), which are discussed in Chapter 15 on structured products.

Observations

Indexed portfolios depend on active management. Security analysts constantly seek over- and under-priced assets, which active investors then sell and buy until the assets converge to their fair price. Collectively, this ensures that securities are approximately efficiently priced, at least most of the time. If all assets within a market were indexed then this information would not be used; it would be wasted, with the result that assets would soon diverge from their fair price. In such a world the indexed portfolio manager would have no business because rational investors would shun indexation and seek to profit by buying and selling mispriced assets.

The indexed asset class portfolio therefore can succeed only within a market that is kept efficient by the efforts of active portfolio managers, enjoying something of a free ride, benefiting from the efforts of active managers, while incurring only a fraction of the costs and risks in doing so.

Defining the benchmark is arguably more important for an indexed portfolio than for an actively managed one because the benchmark provides the only source of return to the portfolio. Desirable features for the benchmark are:

- It must meet the investment objectives of the investor. Usually this means that it must give a broad coverage of the market in which it invests. For some purposes this may necessitate a customized benchmark either within a recognized asset class or as a composition of different asset classes or parts of asset classes.
- It should be investable. In other words the securities that make up the benchmark should be freely traded on a recognized exchange.
- Availability of derivatives linked to it is a big help for liquidity management.

- Public quotation reduces ambiguity. While it is preferable to identify a benchmark that is quoted publicly, customized or less widely recognized benchmarks can work well provided the components are publicly quoted. This allows independent computation of benchmark performance by investor, investment manager and custodian; so avoiding confusion about the relative performance of the portfolio.

A benchmark that is hard to track will give an indexed portfolio a higher tracking error than it otherwise would have with a more investable benchmark. For the investor this introduces a source of potentially unmanaged risk.

Liquidity management is also more important for an indexed portfolio than for an actively managed portfolio. Any un-invested cash is a source of tracking error against a fully invested benchmark.

Methodology

The two main approaches to selecting an indexed portfolio are:

- Full replication, where the portfolio buys every security in precise index proportions.
- Sampling, whereby a subset of securities are selected to match as closely as possible the return of the benchmark index.

There are in turn a number of ways of selecting a sampled indexed portfolio, including:

- Optimization.
- Stratified sampling.
- Stratified sampling with optimization.

Sampling uses the following inputs:

- The composition of the benchmark.
- The tolerance for tracking error.
- The purpose and expected life of the index portfolio – long term or short term.
- The form of the existing portfolio – cash, shares and so on.
- Estimates of transactions costs for each security.
- A risk model.

The choice of methodology is usually determined by the composition of the benchmark and the nominal value of the portfolio to be indexed. For example, if the benchmark has a large number of securities in it, sampling can work best, particularly for small portfolios. If there are only a few dozen securities in it then full replication could be the answer, provided each component is sufficiently liquid and trading costs are not too high.

Full replication gives portfolio performance that is very close to but not identical to the benchmark. It is not identical because the composition of all benchmarks change from time to time and the replicating indexer must follow suit. Unlike the benchmark, the portfolio is subject to trading costs, which, together with administrative costs, ensure that the fully replicated portfolio always returns less than the benchmark it replicates. On the other hand, the portfolio may benefit from dividend tax credits that the benchmark doesn't.

Transactions costs for full-replication portfolios can be exacerbated if there are a large number of portfolios indexed to the same benchmark. Full replication demands that they undertake identical or near identical trades simultaneously, temporarily pushing up the prices of stocks to be bought and depressing the price of stocks to be sold.

Sampling can reduce the transactions costs of an indexed portfolio, particularly if there are a large number of assets in the benchmark. Because the composition of the portfolio is not the same as that of the benchmark, tracking error is usually higher for sampling portfolios than for full replication. Optimization, stratified sampling and a combination of the two seek to minimize this tracking error while preserving the benefits of lower transactions costs.

Optimization entails starting with the benchmark portfolio and applying a maximum number-of-stocks constraint to the optimization. The optimizer generates the most diversified portfolio possible within this constraint. Practical problems with optimization are discussed in more detail in Chapter 5 on risk modelling and Chapter 11 on optimization. For indexed portfolios, the main pitfall tends to be from illiquid stocks.

One issue is that optimizers have a knack for zooming in on the least tradable assets in a universe. This could be just chance, but is more likely to be due to the 'error maximizer' inherent in optimization. Because illiquid stocks trade infrequently, they appear to the optimizer to be less volatile. The optimizer will therefore favour them, along with other assets with under-estimated volatility. The result can be a portfolio that is impractical to implement and, even if it could be implemented, would be riskier, or more volatile, than the optimizer had indicated.

Screening by size seeks to overcome the problem of illiquid stocks by screening them out at the start of the process. Usually, stock size by market capitalization is a reasonable proxy for liquidity, although this is not fool-proof. Some large stocks trade relatively infrequently because they are majority owned by a parent company or dominated by very long-term investors, as in the case of some family companies. Some indexers prefer to adjust market capitalization by 'free float': the proportion of the company that trades regularly.

Of course screening out smaller stocks introduces size bias to the resulting portfolio, which is a potential source of tracking error. This bias must be off-set against the benefit of reduced transactions costs.

Simple screening by size can also introduce sector bias. This happens because some markets are dominated by a handful of very large stocks within a few sectors; leaving a long tail of unrepresented sectors that comprise medium-sized stocks that together make up a significant share of the benchmark by market capitalization.

Stratified sampling seeks to eliminate or at least reduce these sources of bias by selecting the largest stocks from each sector and scaling up their weight in the portfolio so that the allocation to each sector is similar to that of the benchmark while still excluding the most illiquid stocks. Some size bias will remain, but less than for the simple size screening method.

Example 9.1 compares size-only sampling (TOP100) and stratified sampling (SAMP100) for a 100 stock portfolio benchmarked to a 500 stock index.

Example 9.1 Stratified samples

	Benchmark		TOP100		SAMP100	
Industry Group	**Weight**	**Number of stocks**	**Weight**	**Number of stocks**	**Weight**	**Number of stocks**
Aerospace and defence	1.26%	7	1.12%	2	1.27%	2
Airlines	0.25%	4	0.00%		0.25%	1
Auto components	0.94%	13	0.69%	1	0.28%	1
Automobiles	0.27%	1	0.38%	1	0.28%	1
Banks	7.17%	28	7.33%	11	7.20%	5
Breweries and distillers	0.44%	3	0.56%	1	0.45%	1
Brokerage	0.25%	2	0.00%		0.25%	1
Business services and DP	7.00%	26	8.20%	5	7.04%	3
Chemicals	1.84%	15	1.84%	3	1.85%	2
Computers	5.21%	20	5.99%	6	5.24%	6

(continued)

Example 9.1 (Continued)

	Benchmark		TOP100		SAMP100	
Industry Group	**Weight**	**Number of stocks**	**Weight**	**Number of stocks**	**Weight**	**Number of stocks**
Conglomerate	1.39%	12	1.00%	2	1.40%	2
Construction materials	0.05%	1	0.00%		0.05%	1
Contracting and construction	0.09%	4	0.00%		0.09%	2
Electrical and electronic	8.48%	27	10.42%	7	8.52%	2
Electrical instruments	1.42%	14	0.60%	1	1.43%	3
Energy equipment and services	0.82%	6	0.45%	1	0.82%	2
Food manufacturing	2.97%	14	2.38%	2	2.98%	2
Food retailing	0.91%	5	0.76%	2	0.92%	2
Gold	0.13%	4	0.00%		0.13%	1
Health and personal care	7.34%	33	7.78%	9	7.37%	4
Household appliances	0.11%	4	0.00%		0.11%	2
Household products	0.34%	2	0.41%	1	0.34%	1
Industrial components	0.63%	5	0.48%	1	0.64%	1
Insurance	4.13%	23	3.28%	3	4.15%	2
Investment services	1.32%	5	1.43%	2	1.33%	2
Investment trusts	0.44%	1	0.61%	1	0.44%	1
Iron and steel	0.08%	5	0.00%		0.08%	2
Leasing and consumer credit	4.10%	8	5.31%	4	4.12%	2
Leisure and tourism	1.43%	11	1.27%	2	1.44%	2
Machinery and engineering	0.39%	7	0.00%		0.39%	2
Media and communications	2.29%	14	1.92%	3	2.30%	2
Metal fabricators	0.11%	1	0.00%		0.11%	1
Miscellaneous	0.46%	5	0.00%		0.46%	2
Miscellaneous basic industries	0.06%	3	0.00%		0.06%	2

(continued)

Example 9.1 (Continued)

	Benchmark		TOP100		SAMP100	
Industry Group	**Weight**	**Number of stocks**	**Weight**	**Number of stocks**	**Weight**	**Number of stocks**
Miscellaneous consumer goods	0.93%	4	1.02%	1	0.93%	1
Miscellaneous financials	0.30%	3	0.00%		0.30%	2
Miscellaneous transport	0.37%	4	0.00%		0.37%	2
Non-ferrous metals	0.48%	5	0.42%	1	0.48%	1
Office equipment and copiers	0.18%	3	0.00%		0.18%	2
Oil and gas	6.61%	24	7.09%	5	6.64%	4
Paper and forest products	0.49%	10	0.00%		0.49%	2
Pharmaceuticals	7.27%	11	9.63%	6	7.31%	3
Property	0.06%	1	0.00%		0.06%	1
Railways	0.13%	1	0.00%		0.13%	1
Recreation and other consumer services	0.45%	8	0.00%		0.61%	3
Stores and retail	5.93%	32	5.39%	4	5.96%	2
Telecommunications	7.96%	22	9.47%	8	8.00%	4
Textiles and clothing	0.13%	3	0.00%		0.13%	1
Tobacco	1.11%	3	1.41%	1	1.11%	1
Utilities	3.50%	32	1.36%	3	3.52%	2
Total	100%	499	100%	100	100%	100

In Example 9.1 the TOP100 portfolio does not hold stocks in all industry groups and is overweight in others relative to the benchmark. This is because some industry groups, such as banks and retail, are dominated by larger companies than others, such as recreation and textiles. By contrast SAMP100 has industry allocations very similar to the benchmark.

Example 9.2 compares the betas and tracking errors for TOP100 and SAMP100. SAMP100 is slightly better, with a tracking error of 1.87 per cent rather than 1.91 per cent. But both can be improved by optimization. Note that the process of sampling has by now eliminated the most

Example 9.2 Expected beta and tracking error – stratified sample and optimized

	TOP100	SAMP100	TOP100	SAMP100	SAMP120
		Stratified	**Optimized**	**Optimized**	**Optimized**
Expected beta	1.0300	1.0000	1.0000	1.0000	1.0000
Expected tracking error	1.95%	1.87%	0.91%	0.85%	0.74%

illiquid stocks – and therefore those most likely to have under-estimated volatility, so the error-maximizing tendency of the optimizer has been tamed.

Example 9.2 also shows how much improvement in expected tracking error can be achieved with optimization. It reduces TOP100 from 1.91 per cent to 0.91 per cent and SAMP100 from 1.87 per cent to 0.85 per cent. To see how this result can be further improved, the optimizer was allowed to select 120 stocks instead of just 100. SAMP120 has an even lower tracking error, of 0.74 per cent.

Optimization adds value by taking into account the return volatilities of individual stocks and risk factors as well as the correlations between them and stock betas to risk factors. How well it can reduce tracking error depends on the risk model it uses, especially how it defines and estimates common risk factors, factor returns and the correlations between factor returns. For the purpose of optimizing an indexed portfolio, the two main choices are:

- PCA factors versus pre-specified factors and the choice of factors.
- Periodicity of data sample used: daily, weekly or monthly.

The choice of risk model should reflect the use to which it is to be put. For example, PCA factors and very short data intervals can be ideal for defining a short-term tracking portfolio for the purpose of stock-index arbitrage or otherwise for implementing a very short-term portfolio to track closely a given share price index.

For most investment portfolios, which are designed to be held for more than a few hours or days, data intervals of at least a week in conjunction with a pre-specified factor model with intuitive factor definition usually give the most stable results.

The optimizing indexer must therefore judge if the portfolio defined by the optimizer looks sensible and is tradable. So even this most passive of investment techniques entails some judgement.

On-going management

Indexed portfolios are managed typically according to decision rules that govern rebalancing, response to corporate actions and any return enhancements to the portfolio. This section provides some detail of the practical considerations.

Rebalancing

If the portfolio is to be held long enough to need rebalancing, then some policy about when and how to do this needs to be determined. For a full-replication portfolio, this is determined by when the composition of the benchmark portfolio is updated. Sampling allows more lee-way.

Rebalancing frequency depends on transactions costs and the amount of specific risk that can be tolerated: high-risk tolerance allows less frequent rebalancing because the cost of a rebalance will be justified less often by the expected reduction in tracking error, while low-risk tolerance requires more frequent rebalances. Rebalancing will also be a function of the frequency and timing of cash flows to the portfolio. Co-ordinating rebalancing with cash flows can sharply reduce the costs of doing so.

Rebalancing rules can stipulate:

- Fixed time intervals.
- When portfolio composition diverges from benchmark by a fixed amount.
- When forecast tracking error breaches a defined limit.
- When sufficient cash flows have accumulated to warrant purchase of a basket of physical stocks.
- Whenever the benefit of rebalancing, in terms of reduced tracking error, outweighs the costs of rebalancing.

Implementation of indexed portfolios can entail a large number of small transactions. These can be effected in the following ways:

- One-by-one as for many active equity portfolios.
- Simultaneously by means of a basket or block trade, whereby an aggregate trade 'price' is indicated by the broker, who then executes the trades. Basket trades can ensure much smoother execution from the perspective of the portfolio, partly because they effectively transfer the risk of implementation to the broker.
- Futures can be used to smooth the implementation process by providing short-term exposure to the required asset class pending full

implementation of the physical portfolio. The physical portfolio can subsequently be bought or sold in an exchange-for-physical (EFP) transaction.

The investment manager generally has some discretion to override rules if he or she believes it is justified by greater than normal deviation from the expected tracking error between scheduled re-balances, or if regular re-balances are not justified by the expected improvement in tracking error.

The aim of rebalancing a portfolio is to improve ongoing performance net of costs, so any trading activity should demonstrate expected benefits that outweigh the costs.

Corporate actions

Response to corporate actions is in principle passive; the theory being that what affects the portfolio also affects the benchmark in exactly the same way. This is not always strictly true in practice, especially for sampled portfolios.

- Takeovers require no action so long as the portfolio holds both the offeror and the offeree companies. The indexer will usually wait until the takeover proceeds to compulsory acquisition or the bid fails.
- In principle stock splits require no action because there is no change to the value of the company or the benchmark. The exception is if, as a consequence of sampling, the portfolio holds significantly more or less in the stock than the benchmark, in which case rebalancing may be justified.
- Cash dividends accumulate liquid assets, which must be invested across the portfolio as soon as practicable, either by buying physical assets or an equivalent position in share price index futures.
- Stock dividends are accepted in the form of physical shares, as the dividend represents an increase in the issued capital of the company.
- Share buy-backs are accepted because the value of the firm remains unchanged by the action.
- Rights issues can present an opportunity for risk-free or low-risk return enhancement. If the investment manager estimates that the rights are under-priced relative to the physical shares he or she can sell shares, buy rights and then exercise the rights to restore the correct weight in the physical shares. If the rights are over-priced, then the investment manager can sell them and buy the shares – or not – on the rights exercise date.

Enhancements

Opportunities for enhancements include:

- Mispriced derivatives – such as share price index futures and options and listed stock options.
- Rights issues.
- Dividend re-investment plans.
- Tax anomalies.

Mispriced derivatives are rare in mature markets, and when they occur the mispricing is usually so small as to be mostly un-exploitable. However they can still be spotted in immature markets, and markets with particularly high transactions costs. The classic example is known as stock index arbitrage. This takes advantage of stock index futures, trading either above or below fair price.

For example, an investment manager seeking exposure to the stock-market has two ways of doing so: buy shares or buy futures and place the cash on deposit, as shown in Example 9.3.

In Example 9.3, the level at which the stock-market closes on 29 December is irrelevant because the futures contract is settled at the level at which the

Example 9.3 Stock index arbitrage

Date now	7 July
Physical share price index	2202
SPI futures	2215
Expiry date of futures	29 December
Futures settle at	2210
Dividend yield	3.2% p.a.
Interest rate	6.8% p.a.

Strategy	**Buy shares**	**Buy futures**
Profit (loss) on shares	8	0
Profit (loss) on futures	0	(5)
Dividend income	33.8	0
Interest income	0	71.8
Profit (loss)	**41.8**	**66.8**
Percentage of initial investment	1.90%	3.03%

physical index closes that day; however for the sake of illustration we will say that the market closes at 2210.

The investment manager is clearly better off buying futures and investing, in short-term interest-bearing securities, the cash that would have been used for buying physical shares. Even if the portfolio was already fully invested in physical shares on 7 July, it could benefit by selling shares, buying futures and investing the cash received from the share sale in interest-bearing securities so long as the transactions costs thus incurred are less than 1.1 per cent (3.0 – 1.9) on the round trip.

Opportunities to exploit share-price-index arbitrage in mature markets are in practice available only if the transaction coincides with natural cash flows, where transactions costs can be disregarded because they would be incurred anyway. The collective activity of arbitrageurs ensures that share price index futures contracts tend to trade in a range – determined by transactions costs – about their fair price. And although less mature markets can show apparent opportunities for share price index arbitrage, the 'risk-free' returns to be earned are often offset by high trading costs and risks associated with poor regulation and lack of market transparency.

Dividend re-investment plans (DRPs) – shares which probably would have to be purchased anyway, are effectively bought with dividends foregone, saving transactions costs and adding to return if the DRP shares are issued at a discount to the price of existing shares, which they often are.

Tax anomalies – the foreign investor sells stock to a local tax payer immediately before the ex-dividend date and repurchases the stock immediately after, usually hedged in the meantime with some kind of repurchase agreement to protect both parties from unwanted fluctuations in the share price. Usually there is some sharing of the imputation benefit to give the non-local taxpayer incentive to undertake the transaction. Alternatively the stock may be transferred as part of an asset swap or a stock lending agreement. The advantage to the portfolio is similar.

Fundamental indices

So far this chapter has been all about portfolios designed to track publicly quoted market indices. Most market indices are designed to give a broad representation of a market in order to capture as many of the price movements as possible in the wider market. Usually the components of share price indices are weighted according to their market capitalization.

Critics of this methodology point to the inherent inefficiency in capitalization weighted indices due to the fact that securities that are over-priced relative to their intrinsic value are given an 'unfairly' large representation in the index and under-priced stocks are unfairly under-represented. These misrepresentations are self-perpetuating, as indexers – and many active managers – are obliged to buy more of the over-priced stocks and less of the under-priced stocks than they would have if the stocks were correctly priced.

In consequence, standard capitalization-weighted market indices, such as the S&P500, are inherently inefficient most of the time, so they can give returns that are too low for the index's risk and risk that is too high for the index's return. If this is the case, it follows that any portfolio that is benchmarked to the indices must also be inefficient. The problem is logically more acute for indexed portfolios because, unlike actively-managed portfolios, they have no scope to compensate for the inefficiency through active stock selection.

Fundamental indices attempt to correct this bias by applying weights to stocks that reflect the 'fair' value of each stock relative to its peers. The trick is how to define a measure of 'fair' value that can be applied frequently to virtually every stock in the market. Fundamental indexers favour measures such as:

- Dividends.
- Earnings.
- Sales.
- Book value.

Unsurprisingly, fundamental indices tend to have a bias toward smaller stocks – or at least away from very large stocks – relative to the comparable market capitalization index. This is not much more than simple arithmetic, and is not, by itself, a short-coming of fundamental indices.

A more substantial limitation is that fundamental indices can be difficult to compose accurately if reliable accounting data are not available for all listed stocks in the market. So far, fundamental indices have been applied mostly in the USA, where accounting data are reported relatively frequently and with relatively small time lags. Even in many European markets, company reporting can be less frequent and often less timely, so the index weight risks being obsolete soon after it is reweighted.

Another issue concerns turnover. One of the main reasons for investing in indexed portfolios is that they usually have low turnover relative to actively-managed portfolios. However if the weight of a stock changes with reported earnings, for example, the weight of individual stocks can fluctuate significantly from one reporting period to the next, giving rise to unacceptably high turnover. If a large change in weighting is combined with a significant lag between the end of a reporting period and the publication of the accounting information, the portfolio will have been effectively out of balance for some time, which defeats much of the purpose of the fundamental index.

Customized indexed portfolios

Indexed portfolios are easily customized to accommodate restrictions on investments – for example, in order to comply with ethical, environmental or corporate governance constraints; or if a company pension fund is not allowed to invest in the shares of the company itself.

Investment embargoes are usually applied at the stock level, but can also be applied to common factors if suitable factors can be identified.

Stock-level embargoes typically work by eliminating offending stocks from the investment universe from which the portfolio is selected. The screening process typically eliminates stocks that derive a significant part of their revenue from embargoed activities, or that fail to meet defined ethical or governance criteria. The risk is that the process of elimination causes the universe to shrink by so much that it becomes difficult to select a suitably diversified portfolio.

Restricting exposure to common factors can work if a suitable common factor can be identified. Industry groups allow the investment manager to control things like tobacco production and sales. Restricting by common factors applies to economic exposure rather than to stock classification or according to detailed analysis of its sources of revenues and costs. The benefit of screening by economic exposure to factors is that it captures stocks with significant but indirect exposure to the embargoed activity. In practice some embargoed activities can be surprisingly difficult to screen out, either by common factor or at the stock level, without seriously limiting the investment opportunity set. For example, alcohol distribution is often embedded in the travel and leisure sectors, while pornography is hard to split out from telecommunications. Quality of corporate governance can be hard to capture by means of common risk factors.

Equally-weighted portfolios

One way around the problem of bias in capitalization-weighted indices is to give every stock in the portfolio the same weight. The investment manager then has to choose how many stocks to hold. If he or she chooses every stock in some broad market proxy, then the portfolio risks the problem of holding the smallest stocks in the market in unrealistically large proportions, which can introduce issues of liquidity and tradability as well as – if the portfolio itself is big – being a large shareholder in the firm. The portfolio will also have significant sector bias, overweighting sectors that are made up of a large number of small stocks and underweighting sectors where a few large firms dominate.

If the smaller number of shares is held in equal proportions, the large shareholder problem disappears and the question then focuses on the inherent sector and market capitalization size biases, and the potential performance of the portfolio compared to alternative portfolio structures.

The advantages of equally-weighted portfolios are that the portfolio methodology is simple, has no apparent estimation error and accords with many investors' preferences for equal weighting. Because it entails no skill at all on the part of the investment manager, it attracts very low management fees.

On the other hand, it ignores any forecasting skill that is available and takes no account of volatilities and covariances between assets and common factors, liquidity and so on.

Overall, the evidence on the practical merit of equally-weighted portfolios is mixed.

Risk-parity portfolios

A conceptually similar way to select a passive portfolio, while avoiding the inefficiency of market capitalization weighting, is to assign portfolio risk equally by risk factor rather than to assign weightings equally.

Again, this is in principle very simple and demands no forecasting skill. The investment manager is in effect saying that he or she cannot foresee which risk factors will outperform and which will underperform.

The portfolio is thus defined by:

- The number of assets it holds.
- The amount of portfolio-level risk it can have.
- The risk model used.

As no factor forecasts are needed, this type of portfolio can in principle be derived using PCA factors, which in theory will allocate risk with maximum efficiency.

Because it demands no skill, it attracts passive-level management fees.

Pitfalls

Constructing and managing indexed portfolios can look deceptively simple, and some index portfolios are indeed very easy to look after. This perception is associated with the continuing downward pressure on management fees. Some pitfalls include:

- One approach does not fit all. Often this means that the indexer goes for full replication without considering the implications for the costs of running the portfolio in question.
- Using the optimizer or other stock selection software as a 'black box' is usually a bad idea. Experienced indexers choose their optimizer according to the market to be indexed and also exercise some care about how data are sourced and results interpreted.
- It is important first to screen the universe of securities for investability, in order to ensure that the optimal portfolios obtained are practical and cost efficient to implement.

Once the portfolio is up and running the indexer needs to take care to:

- Manage liquidity.
- Avoid unwanted portfolio turnover.

And beware that:

- Corporate actions can occasionally cause problems by landing the portfolio with securities that are not required for diversification and merely add to transactions and administration costs.
- Large changes to the benchmark holdings, often resulting from privatized utilities or other publicly owned entities, can oblige the indexer to buy large parcels of stock at inflated prices.

Summary

The original rationale for investing in indexed portfolios is that in practice investment managers usually do not deliver consistently positive active returns after costs. However there can be other advantages and applications of indexed portfolios that do not demand that markets be inefficient. Strategies that use indexation include core satellite portfolios, complex global portfolios, swap transactions and ETFs.

Although conceptually very simple, implementing them entails consideration of a number of potential complexities. There is also considerable scope for departing from standard market capitalization weighted indices by indexing to alternative market proxies through customization and fundamental indices. Other variants of passively managed portfolios include equally-weighted portfolios and risk-parity portfolios.

Epilogue

The epilogue to the MBA professor's challenge to his class is that, at the start of the following year, one of the students gave the secret to winning the 'prize' to the incoming MBA class. Nobody believed her, so they all delivered sub-optimal performance too.

Case Study

This is a small corporate pension fund that is a subsidiary of a major multinational corporation in the food manufacturing sector. Company policy and local regulation demand that it maintain an employee pension scheme. There are 800 employees, many of whom are nearing retirement. It is anticipated that the fund will decline from its current value as members retire and pensions pay-outs exceed new contributions.

The scheme is obliged to appoint a board of trustees to oversee the fund. The board of eight trustees is made up of at least 50 per cent member representatives, including production-line workers, food technicians, truck-drivers and so on. Because of the time commitment required of trustees, the company observes a policy of 'revolving' trusteeships, whereby each member trustee is elected by the fund membership to serve on the board for two years. Thus two new members are elected to the board every year.

The full-time secretary of the board is therefore always concerned with educating member trustees. This he finds to be a double-edged sword. While new member trustees tend to be naturally suspicious of many investment practices, notably those involving derivatives, the constantly changing board composition means that the fund's investment structure is always being scrutinized from a new and different point of view, encouraging transparency and discouraging complacency.

To achieve the best investment results, given its size and the necessity of containing costs, the fund needs to be as flexible as possible regarding investment alternatives. The secretary recognizes the contribution of derivative-based strategies to cost control for such a fund. Bearing in mind the suspicion of derivatives harboured by many members, he is keen to ensure that a high level of discipline is applied, and is seen to be applied, to management of the fund in general, and especially to its use of derivatives.

What concerns the secretary, even if it is less on the mind of the other trustees, is the risk of poor manager selection, cognizant that poor investment performance is perfectly achievable without the help of derivatives. The best way to reduce manager risk is of course to hire multiple managers, but the scope for this is limited in a fund that is small and shrinking.

The fund is invested in six asset classes, as shown in Example 9.4.

Example 9.4 Long-term strategic asset allocation

Asset class	Long-term asset allocation
Domestic equities	25%
International equities	20%
Domestic fixed interest	20%
Listed domestic property	15%
Inflation-linked bonds	10%
Small stocks	10%
Total	100%

Given the small size of the fund, specialist mandates are out of the question, except by buying units in pooled investment vehicles. Even this would turn out to be expensive, because it would necessitate a specialist asset allocation mandate to coordinate asset allocation, which might cost at least 0.5 per cent of the fund's value each year, which would be unacceptable to the fund's members.

The only workable solution is to split the fund into a number of balanced mandates. The consultant believes that three would provide enough manager diversification. To try to minimize the likelihood of active asset allocation strategies cancelling each other out, and thus delivering effectively an indexed fund with active fees, the consultant suggests that one mandate be managed using passive asset allocation and passive asset class management. The other two mandates are to be defined respectively as conservative and aggressive active: a version of core-satellite. This mix of mandates is prescient as it prepares the fund for the introduction of 'member choice', whereby members can switch, at minimum cost, their pension from aggressive to conservative and then to passive as they near retirement and their natural risk tolerances fall.

Managers are selected primarily according to past performance and demonstrated competence in each investment style. They are also required to manage as much as possible of the portfolio in individual accounts rather than via units in pooled vehicles. This is to satisfy the fund's requirement that the fund's assets should be held, wherever possible, directly in the name of the fund. This turns out to be feasible for most asset classes. The exceptions are international equities, inflation-linked bonds and small stocks, which together comprise 40 per cent of the long-term allocation. The portfolio is simply too small to

Example 9.5 Portfolio structure

Asset class	Passive		Conservative active		Aggressive active	
Percentage of Fund	40%		30%		30%	
Domestic equities	Passive	Individual	Active	Individual	Active	Individual
International equities	Passive	Pooled	Active	Pooled	Active	Pooled
Domestic fixed interest	Passive	Individual	Active	Individual	Active	Individual
Listed domestic property	Passive	Individual	Active	Individual	Active	Individual
Inflation-linked bonds	Active	Pooled	Active	Pooled	Active	Pooled
Small stocks	Active	Pooled	Active	Pooled	Active	Pooled

enable these asset classes to be managed economically as individual accounts by each manager.

The passive manager is able to offer three of the six asset classes as passively managed individual portfolios, but the portfolio is too small to manage international equities, inflation-linked bonds and small stocks in this way. International equities are invested by buying units in the investment manager's pooled fund, which was passively managed; but only actively–managed pooled vehicles for inflation-linked bonds and small stocks are available. Example 9.5 summarizes how each asset class was managed within each mandate.

All three mandates specify the same benchmark allocation, to which active managers are to add active return. The conservative active portfolio is given a target return of 3 per cent per annum above the benchmark. The aggressive mandate seeks 5 per cent.

After-costs performance of the fund over four years is set out in Example 9.6 which shows that with a return of 9.63 per cent per annum, the passive part of the fund comfortably outperforms both active parts over a four-year period. In fact, only over a one-year period did the conservative active part of the fund do better than the passive strategy. While tracking error for a passive portfolio is in theory zero, the fact that it isn't in this case is due to the portfolio having some active components, and the fact that even pure passive management shows some tracking error because of transactions costs.

Normally you would expect to see much higher tracking errors for the active portfolios. For this type of active portfolio, information ratios of 0.5 are the normal expectation, implying tracking errors of 6 per cent for the conservative portfolio and 10 per cent for the aggressive portfolio. The conservative portfolio's tracking error of 1.43 per cent, for example, implies that the fund would deliver the target 3 per cent above benchmark only about once every 40 years. Two thirds of the time it will be within the range of the return to the long-term allocation plus or minus 1.43 per cent. Similarly, the aggressive portfolio, while slightly more aggressive, is quite unlikely ever to deliver 5 per cent annual out-performance. Its tracking error indicates that it will outperform the return to the long-term benchmark by 1.88 per cent one year in six, or 16 per cent of the time, and will outperform by 3.76 per cent one year in 40, or 2.5 per cent of the time.

It is worthwhile noting, too, that the tracking error of the overall fund is measured at 0.81 per cent, considerably less than the weighted average of the tracking errors of the component portfolios, which is 1.06 per cent. This highlights the off-setting effects of the variance of the component funds, resulting in overall portfolio risk that is reduced by engaging three managers with different investment mandates. But since aggregates and averages can conceal as much as they reveal, closer inspection of the results is warranted. A rudimentary four-year attribution analysis, in Example 9.7, tells an interesting story.

Example 9.6 Portfolio performance

Performance summary	Benchmark	Passive asset allocation		Conservative active		Aggressive active		Total portfolio	
Percentage of Total Fund		40%		30%		30%		100%	
	Return	Return	Variation	Return	Variation	Return	Variation	Return	Variation
4 Years	9.69%	9.63%	–0.06%	9.50%	–0.20%	5.35%	–4.35%	8.21%	–1.48%
3 Years	15.51%	15.45%	–0.07%	14.63%	–0.89%	10.73%	–4.79%	13.67%	–1.84%
2 Years	14.37%	14.33%	–0.04%	13.51%	–0.86%	11.62%	–2.75%	13.21%	–1.16%
1 Year	16.35%	16.33%	–0.02%	17.00%	0.65%	13.37%	–2.99%	15.66%	–0.70%
Tracking error		0.16%		1.43%		1.88%		0.81%	

Example 9.7 Attribution analysis

Return contribution by manager	Passive	Conservative	Aggressive	Total
Asset allocation	0.04%	0.70%	−0.28%	0.16%
Stock selection	0.00%	0.23%	−0.23%	0.02%
Transactions costs*	−0.10%	−0.81%	−2.18%	−1.00%
Residual	0.00%	−0.32%	−1.65%	−0.67%
Total	−0.06%	−0.20%	−4.35%	−1.48%

**Asset Allocation only. Transactions costs associated with stock selection are included in sector performance.*

Example 9.7 shows that the conservative manager indeed adds value from asset allocation, but not enough to cover the transactions costs of implementing asset allocation changes. The aggressive manager fails to add value from either asset allocation or stock selection over the four-year period, although there are periods of outperformance within the four years. The problem was again transactions costs. The aggressive shifts in asset allocation turned out to be very costly to implement.

Both active portfolios suffered at some point from poor stock selection, and closer inspection shows that this was nearly always in international equities. Both managers had a policy of actively managing currency risk. In practice this often consisted of hedging foreign currency exposures to base currency. This could well have been due to the common mistake of confounding currency exposure with aggregate weight by domicile, discussed in Chapter 8 on asset allocation, which results in significant unmanaged risk.

Endnote

1. Except insofar as the investment manager decides the decision rules in the first place.

10
Equities Portfolios

The conversation between colleagues during after work drinks at a local pub turned to what drives markets. The local market at the time was in a particularly optimistic phase and the stockbroker asserted that sentiment was far more important to stock prices than fundamental analysis of likely future company profitability. The investment manager disagreed and, in keeping with the *zeitgeist*, a bet was made that the stockbroker could cause the price of any randomly-selected stock to at least double in price in the space of a few weeks on the strength of rumour alone.

The following day the broker scoured stock listings and found a suitable candidate (rarely) trading on a minor regional exchange that engaged in gold exploration in an unlikely prospect area. He began a rumour that the firm had decided to abandon its quest for gold in favour of the patent it had acquired for a process that transformed used automobile tyres into a substitute for rare earths used in the manufacture of electronic devices.

Within a few days the stock price had risen by more than 50 per cent on spectacularly increased trading volume. The stock-market overseers contacted the directors of the company for an explanation for the sudden activity and price volatility. The directors, genuinely ignorant of, but hardly unhappy about, the source of the new interest, said they had no comment to offer. This sent trading into a frenzy, causing the price to double once more before abruptly crashing to below its starting level.

The broker won his bet, although it could be said that in the end both he and the investment manager were right: rumour can indeed drive market prices, but only so far, and only for so long. In the end fundamental profitability must determine investment returns.

This chapter looks at what goes into the selection of an active equity portfolio before describing some popular types of equity portfolios, covering:

- Why invest in equities?
- Types of equities portfolios.
- Return forecasting.
- Aligning risk with return.
- On-going management.

Rationale

For many investors, listed equities are the most important assets in their portfolio. Partly this is because they are familiar, being reported daily in the media. Partly it is because of the received wisdom that equities represent the main source of long-term returns.

Listed equities offer investors:

- Participation in the future growth of the economy. Being real assets, equities share in the growth of listed firms and thereby in that part of the economy represented by listed equities.
- Some protection against long-term inflation[1] because the value of real assets grows in nominal terms.
- A means of meeting the liabilities of a defined benefit pension fund, which are often linked, explicitly or implicitly, to inflation and wages.[2]

Types of equities portfolios

For the purposes of this chapter, portfolios are distinguished according to the issues relevant to them, although there are various other criteria by which equity portfolios can be distinguished.

- Long only portfolios include:
  - conventional portfolios,
  - low volatility portfolios, high yield portfolios.
- Long-short portfolios include:
  - market neutral portfolios,
  - sector neutral portfolios,
- 130–30 portfolios.
- International equities portfolios, which can be long or long-short.

Conventional portfolios

Conventional equities portfolios are usually primary components of pension funds, multi-asset class mutual and trust funds as well as single asset class trusts and funds. Typically they hold only long, or bought, positions and do not sell stocks they don't already own. In fact many equity investment mandates forbid short selling, except of derivatives for hedging purposes.

The aim is usually a diversified mix of stocks that will deliver the return to the equity market as a whole plus some active return. Active returns are earned by positioning the portfolio toward selected stocks or common factors, usually relative to some benchmark or comparator portfolio. The benchmark therefore can serve:

- As a point of comparison by which investment managers' performance can be evaluated.
- As an objective proxy for the asset class in the context of the overall portfolio.
- As an unbiased representation of the equity opportunity set.

Active returns can be added to the market return by over- and underweighting the portfolio holdings according to:

- Industry group.
- Style (value versus growth).
- Size bias.
- Countries or regions.
- Global themes.

Portfolios can also be tailored to meet investor demand for investments that conform to ethical guidelines, environmental sustainability and corporate governance that aim to avoid investing in firms engaging in unethical or environmentally unsustainable businesses or whose corporate governance falls below a defined standard.

As well as avoiding naked short-selling, conventional, long-only portfolios usually:

- Are fully invested, retaining enough liquid assets only for frictional purposes.
- Do not allow borrowing or any other kind of leverage.
- Have a beta to their market or benchmark of about one.

Low-volatility portfolios

Some conventional equities portfolios are structured deliberately to be less sensitive to market fluctuation than conventional portfolios: that is, they have a beta to their market significantly below 1.0, while still delivering positive active returns. They seek to exploit the 'low volatility anomaly'.

The low volatility anomaly was identified by academics, investors and investment managers who observed that, over several decades, low-beta stocks have given better performance than would be predicted by CAPM. A number of possible explanations have been proposed, such as leverage constraints, agency effects and the widespread use of benchmarks, so far with no conclusions about why it persists.

The portfolio is selected usually by first screening the candidate universe of stocks for stocks with low betas to their market. Combined with some forecast stock or factor returns, the screened universe is then optimized or otherwise configured to give a low volatility portfolio.

Low volatility portfolios can be expected to have significant sector bias relative to the market in which they are invested, because some industry groups, such as utilities and health care, are by their nature inherently less sensitive than others, such as banks, to overall market fluctuations.

The investor benefits from a portfolio that participates in equity market growth with less risk than for a conventional equity portfolio and relatively low transactions costs. If the anomaly holds, the Sharpe ratio – the ratio of return to risk – will be greater than for a conventionally-managed equities portfolio investing in the same market and similar expected active return.

High yield portfolios

High yield equities portfolios are conventional portfolios that are managed in a way that gives better than market income. They can be attractive to pension funds that must pay income to their members and to foundations whose members demand income-paying investments.

The portfolio is selected usually by first screening the candidate list of stocks for stocks that usually pay higher than average dividends and optimizing or otherwise configuring the portfolio to give the best balance of income to risk. Some investment managers find that better results can be achieved by including some low-dividend stocks in the portfolio. While not contributing to the portfolio's dividend yield, these stocks can have a diversifying effect that reduces the portfolio's volatility, enough to give a better overall outcome.

High yield portfolios nearly always have significant sector bias relative to the market because some sectors, such as utilities and banks, tend to pay more of their earnings in dividends than others, such as technology stocks.

Share prices anticipate dividend payments by gradually increasing up to the ex-dividend date (the day when investors are eligible to receive the dividend), after which they 'correct' by, on average, the amount of the dividend. This allows the investment manager to artificially enhance the portfolio's yield through a process known as 'dividend stripping'. Dividend stripping is where the investor buys a share immediately before the ex-dividend date, in other words cum-dividend, and sells it immediately after, or ex-dividend. This crystalizes a capital loss of about the same amount of the dividend gained, plus transactions costs, effectively converting the portfolio's capital to income and incurring transactions costs in doing so. If the investment objective of the portfolio is expressed solely in terms of a yield that is greater than that achievable in the overall market, then the investment manager may be tempted to engage in some dividend stripping to help achieve it. The portfolio suffers through reduced capital returns and hence reduced nominal income in subsequent periods.

A well managed high-yield equities portfolio gives the investor:

- The potential to benefit from equity market appreciation.
- The steady income with the liquidity of equities but without the vulnerability to upward pressure on interest rates, exposure to credit or sovereign risk that would be associated with high yield bonds.
- Relatively low transactions costs.

Dead weight

Any portfolio that is compared to a benchmark index or comparator portfolio can be thought of as comprising the benchmark plus an active, long-short portfolio. The weights for each stock in the original portfolio are the sum of the benchmark weight and the active weight. The active position is bought for overweight stocks and sold for underweight stocks. Put another way, the weighting of each stock in the active long-short portfolio is its original portfolio weight less its weight in the benchmark. The sum of stock weights in the benchmark is 100 per cent and the sum of the stock weights in the long-short active part of the portfolio is zero.

Only the active component of the portfolio benefits from the skill of the investment manager. The part represented by the benchmark is in effect 'dead weight' because it does not benefit from portfolio selection skill. The investor can easily and cheaply achieve the return to the benchmark component by buying an ETF or futures, or investing in the combination of a futures portfolio and a market neutral portfolio, any of which would reduce the management fees paid for the same outcome.

Short selling

In pure economic terms there is no difference between a bought position in a stock and a sold position: they are precise mirror images of each other. However, there are material practical differences between underweight (but still bought) stock positions and short selling.

Firstly, short selling incurs a cost. In order to sell a stock short, you first need to borrow the stock from another investor in order to deliver it and receive settlement. This incurs borrowing costs, which are determined by prevailing short-term interest rates and the availability of the stock for loan. The lender of the stock bears the risk that the borrower will be unable to return the stock at the end of the loan, so he or she has counterparty risk against the borrower or the intermediary if one is used to arrange the loan. To off-set this counterparty risk, the lender or intermediary usually demands margin payments or collateral to guarantee the stock's return or compensate for its non-return.

Secondly, it entails extra risk. If the price of the stock rises sharply, the investor who is sold short may have difficulty in repurchasing the stock in order to contain losses. The price of a stock cannot fall below zero, but it can in theory rise indefinitely, so potential losses to a short position are unlimited. Short-sellers, being required to post increased margins and collateral may, in a tight market, be unable to raise funds to do so and be forced to liquidate other positions, including those that they otherwise would have retained. The collective actions of short-sellers trying to cover their positions can lead to severe shortages of the stock in the market place, which can be exploited by other investors who are not so constrained. The result is known as a 'short squeeze'.

Because of the costs and risk associated with naked short sales, short positions can usually be held only for limited periods, within which the anticipated underperformance or price falls must occur in order for the position to pay off.

By contrast, for the investor who is merely underweight a sharply rising stock can simply wait until the stock price 'corrects', presenting an opportunity to buy more of the stock. He or she is not obliged to meet margin calls or to effect transactions that otherwise might compromise the performance of the portfolio.

Portfolios that allow short-selling include:

Market neutral portfolios – sometimes known as 'pure alpha' portfolios, the aim is to deliver active return with no exposure to the market at large. In theory, market-neutral, with a beta of approximately zero, corresponds to the active component of a conventional portfolio – although in practice many 'market neutral' portfolios retain some market exposure measured as the portfolio's beta to its market. Ideally the investor pays only for the investment manager's selection skill and not for market exposure that he or she can achieve easily and cheaply elsewhere. Market neutral portfolios do not embed the 'incidental' short positions that can compromise the performance of conventional portfolios selected from stock-level research. Because of the explicit costs of short-selling, short positions in long-short portfolios are deliberate (in contrast to many conventional portfolios, where the underweight positions are often incidental), usually with a specific target outcome and time-frame. On the other hand, they are subject to the additional costs and risks inherent in short-selling and the necessity to borrow stock for delivery. Many equity market neutral portfolios are structured as hedge funds in order to allow borrowing to lever the skill of the investment manager.

Sector neutral portfolios – conceptually similar to market neutral portfolios, they aim for zero net exposure to sectors or industry groups within the market as well as market neutrality. In practice sector neutral investment managers often select their portfolios by pairing stocks within a sector; for example, by matching a bought position in one retailer with an off-setting sold position in another retailer.

130–30 portfolios – a sort of hybrid conventional and long-short portfolio, where bought positions represent 130 per cent of the portfolio's investment and the extra 30 per cent is 'funded' by selling short stocks worth 30 per cent, giving a net exposure of 100 per cent. By buying an extra 30 per cent and selling an extra 30 per cent of invested funds, the portfolio effectively levers the skill of the investment manager to deliver enhanced return with the same level of market risk as a conventional long only portfolio.

International equities – many investors retain a distinction between developed and emerging international equities portfolios, but as the demarcation of developed and emerging markets continues to blur, this section makes no distinction between them, since broadly similar issues affect both, especially from the perspective of investment risk.

The main reason to invest outside the portfolio's home market is to expand the scope for active returns: a broader universe of assets offers more opportunities. This argument is stronger if:

- The home market is small.
- The home market is concentrated in or dominated by a few sectors.
- Some sectors aren't represented at all in the home market, for example if they are state-owned or otherwise not listed.

Considerations specific to international equities portfolios include:

- Explicit exposure to currency risk.
- Home bias.
- International equities benchmark composition.
- Foreign ownership restrictions.

Assets outside the home market are likely to expose the portfolio to foreign currency risk, which can be:

- Managed passively, by accepting currency risk as inherent to the returns to foreign assets.
- Hedged to the portfolio's base currency.
- Actively managed.

Effective management and hedging of currency risk depends on accurate estimation of the portfolio's exposure to each currency. In practice this means distinguishing between the portfolio's currency of exposure and its currency of denomination.

The universal currency hedging ratio was developed by Fischer Black in the late 1980s. It demonstrates that, somewhat contrary to intuition, the optimal proportion of currency hedging is a constant ratio defined by:

- The average across countries of the expected returns on the world market portfolio.
- The average across countries of the volatility of the world market portfolio.
- The average across all pairs of countries of exchange rate volatility.

It gives three possible solutions:

- Hedge foreign equity.
- Hedge less than 100 per cent of foreign equity.
- Hedge equities equally for all countries.

Assuming that:

- Investors see the world in light of their own consumption goods.
- Investors count both risk and expected return when figuring their optimum hedges.
- Investors share common views on stocks and currencies.
- Markets are liquid and there are no barriers to international investing.

For most investors, the investable universe outside their home borders is many times the size of the home market and can multiply several times, the effective scope for earning active returns. Yet many if not most multi-asset class portfolios hold more of their assets in the home country than can be justified on the basis of economic efficiency. This home bias persists even in the face of evidence showing that it costs the portfolio in terms of risk and return. The persistence of the home bias can be due to a number of reasons:

- The home market is more familiar than overseas markets.
- Investors feel more confident about identifying and monitoring skilled investment managers close to home than overseas.
- Domestically-listed firms may have extensive overseas investments and therefore provide significant effective international diversification.
- Transactions and custodian costs are higher for overseas investments.
- There may be tax incentives to invest at home.
- There may be capital controls and regulatory restrictions that mandate domestic investment.

More subtly perhaps, investors tend to judge investment managers on their performance against the local stock-market, which is one of the most visible investments for many people. Being more visible, it may be considered more important and therefore worthy of more allocation.

While the home bias is observable in most equity markets, it is more evident in some home markets than in others. For example, Britons have traditionally been happier than, say, Americans to invest outside their home country. This could be due to history: Britain's relationship with its erstwhile colonies was defined largely by trade and investment, and many of the relationships have survived. Another explanation is that the USA, being a much larger and more diverse economy than Britain, offers more investment scope within its borders than does Britain, so there is less incentive to invest abroad.

An effective benchmark reflects the investor's investment universe and is investable, meaning that it is practicable for the investor actually to invest cost effectively in all its component securities in their benchmark allocations. An important distinction between international equity indices is how they allocate to countries, which can be by:

- Gross domestic product (GDP) allocation, which has the advantage that it is not affected by stock-market valuations and can be said to represent the contribution of each economy to world output. On the other hand it can result in large allocations to countries with relatively small stock-markets, with the consequence that the benchmark is less investable.
- Market capitalization, which inherently embeds any pricing inefficiencies of markets relative to each other. Because this gives greater allocations to markets that are over-priced, it builds in inferior returns.

In practice investability trumps efficiency: the most popular international equities benchmarks apply market capitalization.

Many authorities limit the types of shares that can be held by foreigners. For example by:

- Limiting the size of the investment by foreigners in some industries that may be deemed strategic or otherwise politically sensitive, such as banking, media, energy and defence.
- Limiting the voting rights exercised by offshore investors, obliging companies wishing to attract foreign investment to issue non-voting or limited-voting shares in parallel with normal shares for domestic investors.

To circumvent these limitations, some large firms seek multiple listings; for example, in London, Hong Kong and New York, where trading is less costly and relatively unrestricted. One way to do this is to set up a trust in a developed market, the sole assets of which are shares in the target company. The trust holds the shares indefinitely, and units in the trust are traded on the market where it is listed, so the rules and settlement procedures of that market apply. American depository receipts (ADR), traded in New York, are examples of this.

Another way to manage limitations caused by foreign ownership restrictions is through ETFs, which are in effect funds that invest in a diversified portfolio designed to give the return to a sector of country. As with ADRs, the fund is listed on an exchange and holds indefinitely the portfolio of shares. Investors gain exposure to the diversified portfolio by buying units in the trust. Some ETFs are actively managed so the investor gains not just the return to the market in question, but also some active return resulting from security selection within the market. Other ETFs guarantee index fund-like performance, so the returns to the investor reflect the market return only.

ADRs and ETFs are particularly useful to some regulated funds, which may be prohibited from trading in less regulated markets, which otherwise would impair their scope to invest in some emerging markets.

Return forecasting

All active investment managers have their own approach to selecting assets to give above-market returns. Despite their diversity, most return forecasting models can be thought of as a variation on one of the following:

- Trend analysis:
    - technical analysis,
    - momentum models.

- Fundamental analysis:
  - dividend discount models,
  - single stock models,
  - arbitrage pricing theory.
- Stock screening:
  - ratio models,
  - mean-variance screening.
- Risk based:
  - factor models.

Technical analysis

Also known as charting, technical analysis assumes that future share prices can be predicted by studying patterns of earlier share price movements. According to technical analysts, stock prices tend to form repeating and recognizable patterns from which future price fluctuations can be predicted.

Efficient market adherents point out that if it were that easy, the share price would very quickly adjust to the predicted price, so the pattern would soon disappear. The case in favour of using charts of historical price movements is described in an article by Andrew Lo et al. (2000) in the *Journal of Finance*.[3]

Practitioners of technical analysis concede that the economic rationale for persistent trends in stock prices may be weak, but that the method works despite this because other investors believe it does. From this, it follows that while studying past share prices gives no clue about the prospects for future company growth it can predict buying and selling behaviour by other investors, and therefore short-term share price performance.

Momentum or moving average models

In their simplest form, moving average models are not unlike technical analysis in that they also use historical price data. To this they add a line describing a moving average, which is the average price over some recent period, such as rolling one month or three months. When the price line and the moving average line intersect, a change of trend is indicated, which is interpreted as a signal to buy or to sell the stock, as shown in Example 10.1.

Momentum models take this one step further by applying the slope of the line in Example 10.1 describing price movements over some rolling period, such as three, six or twelve months.

Momentum is a puzzle because it seems to contradict the EMH. Widely-available information, such as past performance, should be quickly arbitraged away. Its persistence has been explained by the observation that

Example 10.1 Analysis of moving average

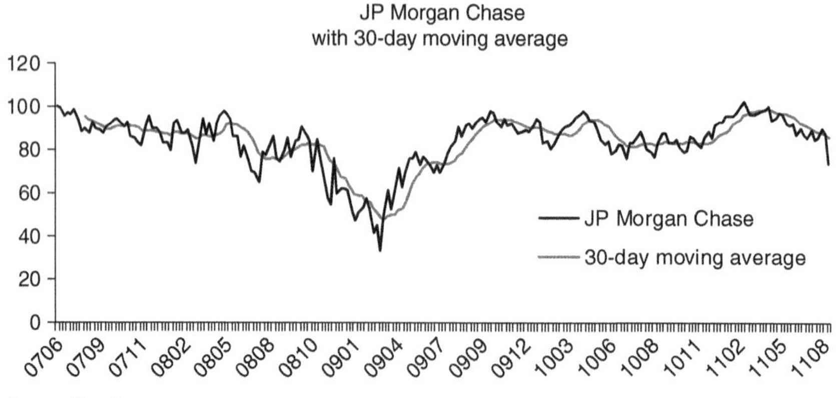

Source: FactSet

investors choose managers who have performed well in the recent past. Those managers invest the new funds in stocks they like. Because those managers have performed well, their favourite stocks are likely to be those that have done well, causing momentum to persist longer than investment theory would predict.

In practice momentum is used more often in stock screening and as a factor in factor return models than as the sole criteria for security selection. In the lead-up to the global financial crisis of 2007–08, momentum was one of the most prominent factors in many risk models, explaining a surprising amount of portfolio risk. So while momentum seemed to defy the most basic economic theory, investment managers ignored it at their peril, which of course further helped it to become, in a sense, self-perpetuating.

Dividend discount models

Dividend discounting says that the current value of the firm is by definition the value in current money of what investors will ultimately receive from it. Bonds are priced in exactly the same way. Unlike bonds, whose coupons are known in advance, equity dividends vary according to the profitability of the firm. Not only that, but, in common with bonds, the discount factor, which reflects, among other things, the market's estimation of the riskiness of the dividend stream, fluctuates too. The skill in applying dividend discounting is in forecasting growth in dividends as well as the likely discount rate.

Example 10.2 shows the effect of simple discounting over 100 years. The present value of the last dividend in the analysis is \$0.01 ($2.00 \times ((1 + 2\%)^{100})/((1 + 7.5\%)^{100})$, as opposed to the current dividend payment

Example 10.2 Dividend discounting

Current dividend	$2.00
Annual dividend growth rate	2.00%
Discount rate p.a.	7.50%
Assumed time horizon in years	100
Present value of last dividend in horizon	$0.01
Present value of all future dividends	$38.90

of $2.00. The dividend is assumed to be growing at 2 per cent per year, and the assumed discount rate is 7.5 per cent, the sum of 100 years of discounted dividends gives a current value for the share of $38.90. Note that, in this example, the discount rate is constant for the 'life' of the firm. This implicitly assumes that the current discount rate is the best predictor of future discount rates. In practice, dividend discount models expand on this by using information contained in market yield curves and swap spreads to capture expectations of future interest rates and risk.

Single stock models

The future profitability of the firm is predicted from what is known about its current and prospective business mix, market share, cost structure and competitive and regulatory environment, as well as the strength of its balance sheet and borrowing costs. Example 10.3 gives a simplified example.

The model in Example 10.3 shows the relationships between the firm's revenues and costs, and its resulting profitability. It allows the analyst to test different assumptions about revenues and costs to see what effect they have on the firm's profitability. For example, if long-term interest rates rise by 0.5 per cent, earnings per share falls from $2.18 to $2.17, while if hourly labour costs rise to $9 per hour, earnings per share goes down to $0.61.

Stock modelling is often combined with dividend discount models, ratio analysis and macro-economic analysis. It can also help estimate the firm's exposure to common risk and return factors.

Arbitrage pricing theory (APT)

In theory the value of any asset is the sum of the value of its parts. This is helpful when a listed company owns parts of other listed companies: the value of the parent company should be the sum of the value of its holding in subsidiaries plus the value of any operations it carries on directly. If

Example 10.3 A simplified single stock model

Inputs to the Firm		Outputs	
Number of Shares on issue	15 000 000	Market price per unit	$15.75
Current share price	$50.00	Units sold	105 000 000
		Capacity utilization	87.50%
Short-term interest rate	4.50%	*Total revenue*	$1 653 750 000
Long-term interest rate	**6.50%**		
Flat rate of corporations tax	40.00%	Materials costs	$367 500 000
Fixed labour costs	$15 000 000	Labour costs	$684 375 000
Hourly labour costs	**$8.50**	Marketing costs	$535 000 000
Hours of labour per unit	0.75	Administration Costs	$8 500 000
Fixed marketing costs	$10 000 000	Operating costs	$1 595 375 000
Unit cost of marketing and sales	$5.00		
Administration costs	$8 500 000	Operating profits	$58 375 000
Actual capital investment	$55 000 000	Interest costs	$3 800 000
Actual working capital	$5 000 000	Tax	$21 830 000
Units production Capacity	120 000 000		
Raw materials costs per unit	$3.50	*Net profit*	$32 745 000
		Earnings per share	**$2.18**
Market price per unit	$15.75		
Units sold	105 000 000		

there is a discrepancy between the fair price thus estimated and the price at which the company's shares are traded, there exists an opportunity for arbitrage, or risk-free profits, by buying the under-priced assets and selling the overpriced assets in off-setting quantities. When market prices converge to their fair relationship, the investor reverses or unwinds the position and realizes the same amount of profit regardless of any market fluctuations in the meantime.

In Example 10.4, the market value of the company is $171 250 000 000, or $68.50 per share. It has direct operations with an estimated value of

Example 10.4 Arbitrage pricing theory

	Shares on issue	Market price of shares	Market valuation	Valuation estimate	Percent owned by parent	Value of parent holding	% of theoretical value of parent
Parent company:	2 500 000 000	**$68.50**	$171 250 000 000		100%	$147 716 250 000	100.00%
Direct operations #1				$58 000 000	100%	$58 000 000	0.04%
Direct operations #2				$36 000 000	100%	$36 000 000	0.02%
Subsidiary #1	2 150 000 000	$45.50	$97 825 000,000		52%	$50 869 000 000	34.44%
Subsidiary #2	980 000 000	$75.00	$73 500 000 000		58%	$42 630 000 000	28.86%
Subsidiary #3	850 000 000	$62.25	$52 912 500 000		32%	$16 932 000 000	11.46%
Subsidiary #4	730 000 000	$98.50	$71 905 000 000		25%	$17 976 250 000	12.17%
Subsidiary #5	1 050 000 000	$91.50	$96 075 000 000		20%	$19 215 000 000	13.01%
Theoretical share price of parent company		**$59.09**					

$94 000 000, a very small percentage of the company's overall worth. Most of its value is in its holdings of other listed companies, here known as subsidiaries #1 to #5. The sum of the market value of these holdings and the direct operations come to only $147 716 250 000, or $59.09 per share. This would imply that the parent company is over-priced relative to its subsidiaries.

The investor can make a risk-free profit by buying the subsidiaries, in proportion to their 'weighting' in the parent, and selling shares in the parent company; and reversing the transaction when the market price and the theoretical price of the parent company are the same or similar. In theory profits are the same regardless of the direction of the overall market. The risk is that the value of the direct operations is underestimated, increasing the theoretical value of the parent, and reducing commensurately the potential gains to the strategy.

The appeal of APT is that it is independent of any other market conditions and relies on conceptually fairly simple analysis. Because it is so simple, and relatively unambiguous, opportunities for true arbitrage are rare.

Like fundamental stock analysis, it can be labour intensive and therefore difficult to extend to a large number of stocks.

Ratio models

Ratio models rely on balance sheets to provide information about the current state of the firm. The advantage of this type of analysis is that it allows large numbers of securities to be analysed simultaneously. Unlike single stock models, which involve painstaking analysis of individual securities, the analyst can simply purchase balance sheet information from a data supplier, such as a stock exchange, load it into a model or even a spread-sheet and, by a simple screening process, derive a list of promising assets that can then be researched in more detail.

The following are examples of ratios used for forecasting:

- Price to book is the ratio of the current market price of the share to its book value (usually the price at which it was issued, adjusted for stock splits and other relevant corporate actions).
- Payout ratio is the ratio of the dividend paid per share and the earnings per share for the same period.
- Gearing ratio is the ratio of total debt to the current market value of the company (measured as total debt plus market value of total equity).
- Debt to equity is the ratio of total debt to the current market value of total equity.

- Dividend yield is the ratio of dividends paid annually to the current market price of the share.
- Earnings yield is the ratio of annual earnings per share to the current market price of the share.
- Interest cover is the ratio of total earnings (usually EBIT) to interest payable over the same period.
- EBIT is earnings before interest and taxes.

The skill of the investment manager is in determining which ratios, or combinations of ratios, to screen and what to look for.

Screening stocks according to their reported ratios is subject to issues of data reliability and timeliness, and standardization of company reporting between jurisdictions. To say that the portfolio is investing heavily in high price to book stocks may not be helpful if the book value is calculated only once a year, reported with a significant delay and in any case can mean different things in different markets.

In practice, most security screening processes distinguish between ex-post versus ex-ante. For example, dividend yield, earnings yield and EBIT can change significantly from one period to the next. The investment manager is more interested in what they will be in the future, so using past information is of limited appeal – unless you believe that past performance is a good guide to future performance.

Mean-variance screening

Another screening technique that seeks stocks with unusual ratios of expected return to risk is mean-variance screening. If all stocks in the market are efficiently priced, then they should all have a more or less predictable ratio of risk, expressed as return volatility, and the return that most investors expect of them. This relationship can be seen by plotting them on a graph, with risk along the x axis and expected return on the y axis, as shown in Example 10.5, which does so for US equities. Expected returns are represented by consensus return forecasts, which can be purchased from a data vendor, while risk is given by the past volatility of the stock.

The diagram in Example 10.5 shows typical clustering of returns between 0 per cent and 5 per cent (the mean consensus expected return relative to the benchmark is 0 per cent and the standard deviation is 0.7 per cent), with risk between 20 per cent and 80 per cent (the mean observed volatility is 37 per cent and the standard deviation is 11 per cent). Most of the stocks lying within this cluster area can be considered to be close to their fair price, given their risk; but stocks outside the cluster could be either too dear or too cheap.

Example 10.5 Risk and return

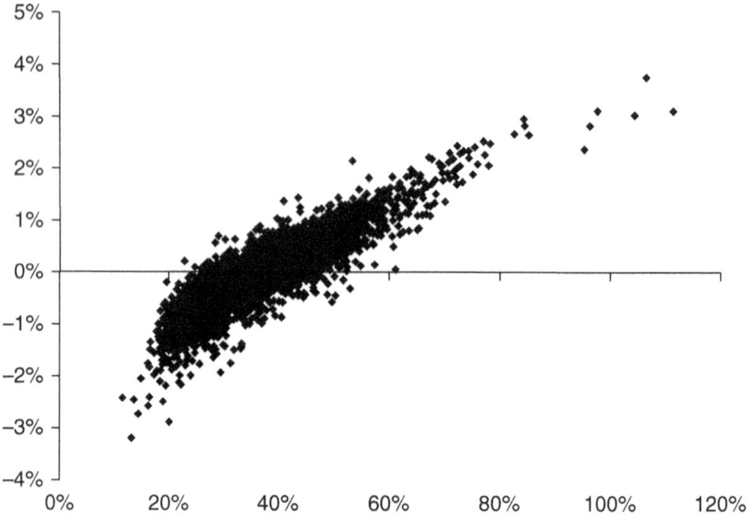

Source: R-Squared Risk Management

In Example 10.5 the outliers appear to have an unusual balance of risk and return, which can be due to:

- Stock idiosyncrasies, such as being a possible takeover target, that justify the existing expected return to volatility ratio.
- There is a liquidity premium because the stock trades rarely so is more costly to buy and to sell than other stocks.
- The stock is genuinely mispriced. This can be due to lack of attention to the stock from stock analysts.
- Data error.

Only liquidity premium and genuine mispricing can usually justify an active position in the stock.

Because it has 'screened out' most efficiently priced stocks, this method can cover a wide range of stocks, freeing the investment manager to focus on stocks that may be promising sources of expected return. Skill in fundamental analysis can in theory then be harnessed very effectively, although in practice most investment manager stock analysis resources are specialized in a particular sector or stock type, such as value-growth or size; therefore they are not always versatile enough to fully exploit the range of potential opportunities thrown up by mean-variance screening.

Another limitation is that the outliers that suffer relative inattention from most stock analysts are in effect so illiquid as not to be tradable in practice. So, while they are genuinely mispriced, this cannot be translated into a practical investment opportunity.

Factor models

Conceptually similar to, and ideally – for the purpose of risk-based portfolios selection – closely aligned with factor-based risk models, the investment manager identifies a set of factors that he or she believes are important drivers of stock returns and for which he or she has skill in forecasting.

Sensitivities, usually expressed as betas, are estimated for each stock to each factor and, together with the investment manager's return forecast for each factor, an expected return is calculated for each stock.

In addition to its systematic or factor related return, individual stock returns are affected by characteristics that are specific to the stock, such as an impending change in chief executive or its potential as a takeover target.

The beta to each stock can be estimated either from what is known about the current business mix and financial position of the firm or from past returns in the same way that time-series factor betas are estimated for risk modelling.

Return factors are things like:

- Style (for example, Fama–French) factors.
- Market (country) factors.
- Currency factors.
- Industry factors.
- Commodity factors
- Macro-economic factors.

Style factors generally originated with the observation by Eugene Fama and Kenneth French that value factors tended to outperform growth stocks over time. While Fama and French identified two style factors, book-to-price ratios and market capitalization, the number of style factors has grown. Examples of other style factors include:

- Value factors:
  - dividend yield,
  - book-to-price ratio,
  - cash-flow-to-price ratio,
  - earnings-to-price ratio.
- Growth factors:
  - earnings growth,
  - revenue growth,
  - book value growth.
- Size.

- Leverage.
- Momentum.
- Liquidity.
- Quality:
  - return on equity,
  - cash flow to sales ratio,
  - sustainable growth.

The distinction between ex-post versus ex-ante is important to style factor definitions. Dividend yield, cash-flow-to-price and earnings-to-price are useful for forecasting only if they are themselves forecast. Even so, many models substitute ratios from the past as an approximation of the immediate future.

Stock betas to style factors are usually derived from what is known about the firm at the time of the analysis. There are two ways of doing so. The first is to carry out detailed fundamental analysis of each stock. The obvious limitation is that most investment managers have the resources to do this for only a small section of the possible investment universe, which can effectively eliminate many stocks from the opportunity set, reducing the scope to earn active returns.

The second is to read them from a database of published company information. This allows all or nearly all stocks in a market to be covered.

Market, or country, factor betas can be estimated in one of two ways. The first is to assign a binary one or zero, according to whether or not the stock belongs to the market. This is deceptively simple because it doesn't allow for stocks that are sensitive to more than one market. This happens if the stock has multiple listings or because its revenues and costs derive from different parts of the world. Think of Unilever, which is listed in both London and Amsterdam but has operations around the world. The second way to estimate stock betas to countries or markets is to use time-series regression to see how sensitive the stock price is over time to each market. Neither method is fool-proof, but the time-series method is less prone to anachronistic results as it recognizes the multiple market exposures of many stocks as well as differences in their leverage.

Currency betas can also be defined as binary or derived from past stock return history. As with stock betas to countries, assigning a beta of one or zero according to a stock's currency of denomination is often unrealistic. Shell, for example, is traded in both GB Pounds and Euros, but its profits are derived mostly from production of oil, which is priced in US Dollars. It is therefore sensitive to all three currencies.

Industry factors can be estimated in the same ways, with the same issue regarding binary betas. Stocks tend to be assigned one industry classification. This is mainly to facilitate data sorting and doesn't always describe all the stock's sources of profitability; for example, some large automobile manufacturers have significant finance subsidiaries in order to help customers buy their cars. General Electric, too, has a large finance subsidiary, so using the time-series method it has betas to more than one industry group, which better reflects reality.

Commodity factors similarly can be estimated either from binary scoring or by time-series regression. Clearly, giving a simple one or zero score to any single commodity factor for BHP or Rio Tinto would be unrealistic, so time-series is probably likely to give more robust results.

The inherent contradiction of binary scoring for market, currency, industry and commodity factors can be mitigated by assigning stocks multiple betas; for example, giving Shell a beta of 0.5 to GB Pounds and 0.5 to Euros. This method has two limitations. First, it depends on some amount of research into the operations of the firm, so is not really scalable. Second, there is no reason the betas of a stock to currencies, say, should sum to one. In this sense it remains arbitrary and is probably not a valid estimation of the sensitivity of the stock's return to the factor.

Time-series regression to derive stock betas to country, industry, currency and commodity factors is made easier by the fact that these factors tend to have ready-made return series in the form of published market and industry indices, and past currency and commodity returns are readily available. This adds transparency to the beta estimation process, which can help to spot and avoid errors.

Macro-economic factors can, in theory, be estimated from published data using time-series regression. This however is complicated by the fact that macro-economic data tend to be released some time after the period to which they apply, so direct relationships between stocks and things like inflation and employment statistics can be tricky to quantify with any accuracy. The other method, which is to estimate stock sensitivities to macro-economic factors by fundamental analysis, suffers the limitation that it is labour intensive and likely to cover only a small proportion of the universe of investable stocks, thus reducing potential scope to add active returns.

Clearly, the success of any factor model for forecasting stock returns hinges on the choice of factors and of course the returns forecast for them. Desirable characteristics of return factors are:

- The more of the security's or the portfolio's return they can account for collectively the better.
- They should accord with factors that the manager has skill in forecasting.
- They should be uncorrelated. Return factors that are correlated with each other do not represent different sources of potential return, but different aspects of a single opportunity. For example, having exposure to both Taiwan and semiconductors is not two but one single source of return because Taiwan and the semiconductor industry are highly correlated with each other.

The advantages of factor models include:

- They can cover a wide universe of candidate stocks and therefore the scope to earn active return.
- They concentrate portfolio selection in a relatively small number of decisions, those of selecting return factors and forecasting returns to them. This focuses investment management resources, so can improve the quality of each forecast and lessen the chance of damaging errors.
- Estimation of factor betas for individual stocks can be carried out using databases of stock returns and stock balance sheet information, so can be scalable. Errors in beta estimation for individual stocks, while relatively likely, need not be damaging to the overall forecast, since most errors will cancel out at the portfolio level – provided the errors in beta estimates are not all or mostly in the same direction.
- Risk-based factor models integrate easily with risk models to facilitate true risk-based portfolio selection. The investment manager is therefore in a strong position to align sources of return with sources of risk and eliminate unwanted sources of risk.
- Risk-based performance attribution follows naturally. This can show clearly how much performance is due to skill and how much to chance.

The disadvantages of risk-based models are:

- They are very dependent on the choice of return factors.
- Errors in factor return forecasts flow straight through to the portfolio outcome.

Aligning sources of risk with sources of return

No return forecast is infallible and, even with the most prescient return forecasts, the portfolio can fail to achieve its return targets if risk is not accurately aligned with sources of return. Many talented investment managers underperform, despite good asset selection skill, because unintended, and therefore unmanaged, risk dominates the active returns they achieve from intended exposures.

It is therefore important to measure accurately the sources of risk in the portfolio in order to eliminate unwanted risks that compromise the manager's information ratio and expose the portfolio to extreme risk.

The ideal way to align risk and return is to match the factors in the factor return model with those in the risk factor model that measures and analyses risk. The risk model will show what sources of risk remain in the portfolio that are not associated with deliberate exposures. It will also show how much they contribute to risk. The investment manager can decide whether to remove them either by diversification or by hedging. This can leave the investment manager in the happy position of being able to allocate more risk to deliberate exposures, so making more effective use of his or her skill without increasing the risk to the portfolio itself.

If a factor model is not used to forecast stock returns – for example, if the investment manager selects stocks by fundamental stock analysis – a risk model with well constructed factors can still highlight sources of unwanted risk provided the risk factors themselves are intuitive and the model transparent. This usually is doable because investment managers tend to favour stocks with particular characteristics, which often correspond to factors such as value and growth, industry clusters and so on.

Whichever method is used to forecast returns, a good way to build in risk control to the portfolio construction process is to articulate target outcomes for key positions. For example, an overweight to one retailer paired with an underweight to another retailer should have a stated net outcome, either in terms of price differential or target return; together with a maximum tolerable loss from the mismatch. More risk can be allocated to positions that promise the best outcomes and of which the investment manager is most confident.

On-going management

Corporate actions

Corporate actions are changes to firms' capital bases, such as declaring and paying a dividend, issuing rights and merging with or taking over another firm. The investment manager is interested in how a corporate action can change the value of the firm, how it affects different classes of shareholder and therefore the portfolio's holding in the stock.

Dividends reduce the size of a firm but by themselves do not directly impact the value of the investment. Other things being equal, the price of a \$50 share after a \$0.20 dividend has been paid will be \$49.80. The investor still has an investment worth \$50.00, but now 20 cents of it is held in cash. It has however reduced the size of the firm by 0.40 per cent (\$0.20 / \$50.00).

Stock splits and bonus issues are simply an increase in the number of shares on issue, causing the price of the shares to adjust so that the value of the firm remains unchanged. If a firm with shares trading at \$50 announces a 1 for 20 bonus issue its shares will fall to \$47.62, so that an investor who held 20 shares at \$50, worth \$1000, now holds 21 shares at \$47.62, worth \$1000.

Rights issues are in effect call options on the firm's stock. The value of the firm will increase when and if investors take up their rights by buying newly-issued shares at the rights exercise or take-up price. The amount by

Table 10.1 A typical rights issue

Announcement date	1 April
Share price at announcement date	\$56.50
Number issued	one for four
Ex-rights date	16 May
Rights start trading	1 June
Rights exercise Date	30 December
Rights exercise price	\$55.00

which the firm's value increases is the number of rights taken up multiplied by the take-up price of each right, plus (or minus) what investors think the company plans to do with the extra cash. A typical rights issue looks something like Table 10.1.

In Table 10.1 shareholders are typically allocated rights in proportion to their holdings of common stock as at the close of trading on 16 May (the ex-rights date). 'One-for-four' means that for every four shares held, the holder is allocated one right. Between 1 June, when the rights begin trading, and 30 December, when the rights expire, rights holders are entitled either to sell their rights or to hold them as a continuing investment in the company. When the rights expire, rights holders choose either to exercise or abandon their rights. In this case, rights holders will exercise if the share price is trading above \$55.00 on 30 December, paying \$55.00 to convert each right held into one common share.

If the share price has by then fallen below \$55.00 the investor is better to abandon the rights and buy the shares more cheaply in the open market. The capital base of the firm increases if rights are exercised, by the number of rights taken up times their exercise price. If no rights are taken up, then the capital value of the firm is not affected by the rights issue.

In principle, a firm with a sizeable cash balance will want to buy back its shares if it estimates that they are trading below what it thinks is their fair price. If the shares really are under-priced, then the firm makes a profit on the shares it has bought back – as do investors who didn't sell their stock. Share buy-backs can in theory send a positive signal to the market: that the firm, which presumably has superior information about its own prospects, believes it to be worth more than the current share price would imply.

Re-balancing

In principle, equities portfolios are reviewed and re-positioned in response to new information about the prognosis for stocks or common factors, or whenever the investment manager estimates that re-balancing its holdings will result in better returns.

Re-balancing of course incurs costs in terms of transactions fees, taxes, bid-ask spreads (the difference between the purchase and sale price) and custodian fees. Investment managers can usually estimate the costs to the portfolio of trading each asset in it. They are also able to estimate the benefit, in terms of improved forecast return and/or reduced risk that will result from the re-balance. It therefore makes sense to ensure that the benefits of any prospective re-balancing clearly outweigh the estimated costs.

Further discipline can be introduced to the re-balancing process by calculating the actual cost of transactions after they have been completed.

Performance measurement and attribution

Investors, prospective investors and investment managers are interested to know how a portfolio has performed:

- To see if it is on track to achieve its investment objectives.
- To see how it compared with other, similar, portfolios.
- To see if the risks it is taking are actually contributing to returns.
- To see how much of the results it achieved were due to skill and how much to chance.

Conventional performance measurement for equity portfolios usually compares the value of the portfolio at the end of the investment period with its value at the beginning, with time-weighted adjustments for cash flows that occurred during the period. But return in fact tells you very little about the portfolio's performance, as shown in Example 10.6.

Example 10.6 Return measurement

Period	Portfolio	Benchmark	Difference
3 Months	1.92%	1.82%	0.10%
6 Months	3.93%	3.82%	0.12%
12 Months	15.53%	15.81%	-0.28%
2 Years	22.74%	22.42%	0.32%
to 31 May			
3 Months	0.00%	0.09%	-0.09%
6 Months	6.68%	7.07%	-0.40%
12 Months	16.63%	17.05%	-0.42%
2 Years	18.25%	18.18%	0.07%

Each period in Example 10.6 appears to tell a different story, so in practice, portfolio returns are usually accompanied by risk measures, usually observed tracking error and some return to risk ratio.

The most frequently used measures of return to risk ratio are:

- The Sharpe ratio, which is the absolute return to the portfolio divided by its observed volatility.
- The information ratio, which is the return differential of the portfolio and benchmark divided by the tracking error.

These two measures are often used as an indication of the skill of the investment manager and to compare portfolios. Of course they embed some important assumptions about the portfolios being compared, such as that the investment mandates and scope are comparable, which may not be true in practice.

Performance is measured and analysed not only to see what the returns to it were, but also which parts of the portfolio contributed to the returns and by how much.

One way to do this for a single period is to multiply the weighting in each asset in the portfolio by the return to that asset over the period. These will sum to the return to the portfolio. The product of the asset weighting and its return is a measure of that asset's contribution to portfolio return.

For a portfolio with relatively few holdings this is a simple and intuitive method of return analysis. However many equities portfolios have dozens or even hundreds of holdings. If they are compared to a benchmark, then the assets in the benchmark, which may number in the thousands, represent active positions in the portfolio, and therefore affect how the portfolio performed against the benchmark, even if the portfolio doesn't actually hold them.

To better understand which portfolio elements are contributing to return, assets can be grouped by some common characteristic, such as industry classification. According to this method, the contribution to return of the industry is the weighted sum of the contributions to return of the assets in that industry group.

This introduces an extra level of analysis because the industry weighting in the portfolio will be more or less than that of the benchmark; and the composition of the industry group will be different for portfolio and benchmark. This gives you:

- The return contribution from allocation to industry.
- The return contribution from stock selection within the industry group.

For a single period return analysis, returns from subgroups will sum to the portfolio and benchmark returns respectively, and give a clear picture of which groups contributed and detracted from portfolio return.

This clarity is deceptive however, because what the analysis cannot tell you is how much risk was assumed within each group in order to achieve the results. It also falls into the trap of confounding weight with exposure and arbitrarily assigning stocks to a single industry classification when in fact their sources of return may be attributable to multiple industries.

Holdings-based return attribution cannot say by how much the sources of risk in the portfolio at the start of the period actually contributed to the result, which was one of the main reasons to analyse return in the first place. It therefore cannot help the investor distinguish between the contributions to the result of skill and chance.

Risk-based performance attribution overcomes these shortcomings by computing how portfolio exposure to risk factors contributed to return over the period. For a single period the contribution to the portfolio's return from each risk factor is its beta to that factor at the start of the period times the return to the factor over the period.

To see how much each source of risk contributed to return, you simply compare the percentage contribution to portfolio risk from each risk factor at the start of the period with the percentage contribution to return from that factor over the period.

If the portfolio has been constructed using, for example, a factor based stock selection model, then there is a compelling argument to apply the same set of factors to performance attribution. This allows the investor and the investment manager to evaluate the success or otherwise of the manager's factor-based strategy.

Another interesting question to ask is whether intra-period trading added value or not. This is done by comparing the actual return with the outcome that would have been achieved had the portfolio been held constant over the period in its start-of-period composition.

Unsurprisingly, this analysis sometimes appears to show that the portfolio would have been better off if the investment manager had done nothing. This is not necessarily a valid conclusion however, as the transactions may have been carried out with a longer horizon in mind.

Summary

For many investors, equities are the most familiar asset class. They are important to pension funds because they are often perceived to be the main source of return necessary to achieve the investment objectives. Being real assets, they arguably also give some protection against inflation.

Investment managers use a range of methodologies for forecasting asset returns. Whichever methodology is used, the result is stocks favoured by the investment manager usually on the basis of common characteristics, which frequently can be identified as common factors. Risk-based portfolio selection seeks to align these stock selection factors with risk factors so that risk is concentrated where the investment manager is confident of delivering positive returns. Unwanted risk can then be eliminated in order to reduce portfolio return volatility and improve performance.

Case Study 1

This is an example of simple but very effective application of pragmatic, risk-based performance selection.

International investors in the Australian market aim to gain exposure in commodities markets, either because it taps into growth in China and India, or for general exposure to growth in commodities.

As a result of home bias, Australia-based investors have a disproportionate exposure to commodities, which can make their portfolios more volatile and less efficient than they would otherwise be.

The local stock-market index, widely used by local investors as the benchmark for domestic equities, is the All Ordinaries Index (AOI). The AOI classifies stocks as either industrials or resources, representing roughly 70 per cent and 30 per cent respectively of the All Ordinaries itself. Unsurprisingly the two sectors behave very differently. For example, the resource sector tends to be very volatile and is dominated by a small number of jumbo stocks favoured by offshore investors; while a long tail of very small stocks in the sector are plagued by chronic illiquidity. The industrial sector is dominated by banks, which also attract much attention from international investors, but otherwise is more diversified, with a high representation of local investors, such as local pension and trust funds.

By contrast, the global stock-market comprises only about 10 per cent in resource stocks.

Example 10.7 Comparison of return and volatility for Australian All Ordinaries, All Industrials and All Resources Indices

	All Ordinaries total return		All Industrials total return		All Resources total return	
	Return	Volatility	Return	Volatility	Return	Volatility
1 Year	20.19%	11.51%	24.94%	9.21%	11.69%	18.48%
2 Years	4.77%	13.59%	4.49%	12.49%	5.49%	18.97%
3 Years	16.85%	14.28%	15.34%	13.22%	20.33%	19.43%
5 Years	15.91%	13.79%	16.03%	13.41%	15.96%	17.78%

	All Ordinaries total return		All Industrials total return		All Resources total return	
	Return	Volatility	Return	Volatility	Return	Volatility
10 Years	12.85%	20.82%	13.53%	20.13%	11.76%	25.87%
15 Years	12.56%	20.52%	17.18%	18.86%	7.31%	26.41%

From Example 10.7 it would appear that the best solution would be simply to exclude resource stocks altogether, but a closer look at the data suggests that this would be unacceptable to investors. The returns to year 14 and year 15, set out in Example 10.8, show that in some market conditions, resource stocks can greatly outperform industrials, so an industrials-only strategy would occasionally disappoint.

Example 10.8 Comparison of return and volatility for Australian All Ordinaries, All Industrials and All Resources Indices: years 14 and 15

	All Ordinaries total return		All Industrials total return		All Resources total return	
	Return	Volatility	Return	Volatility	Return	Volatility
Year 14	45.36%	13.47%	40.53%	12.71%	56.55%	18.00%
Year 15	–8.67%	14.35%	–12.61%	13.23%	–0.37%	19.31%

So what proportion of industrials to resources gives the best risk-return balance across all test periods? The conclusion drawn was that the global proportion would probably be a good place to start. So the same calculations were carried out using a portfolio comprising 90 per cent resources and 10 per cent industrials, with the results shown in Example 10.9.

Example 10.9 Results for Australian All Ordinaries, All Industrials and All Resources Indices and 90/10 portfolio: years 14 to 17

	All Ordinaries total return		All Industrials total return		All Resources total return		90/10 Portfolio return	
	Return	Volatility	Return	Volatility	Return	Volatility	Return	Volatility
Year 14	14.60%	8.60%	19.82%	9.27%	4.11%	11.31%	18.22%	8.91%
Year 15	12.23%	16.72%	24.57%	16.77%	–17.23%	20.99%	19.76%	16.69%
Year 16	11.63%	11.46%	17.47%	11.16%	–11.22%	21.78%	14.45%	11.17%
Year 17	16.10%	11.42%	10.77%	10.54%	49.80%	27.53%	14.50%	11.01%
Years 14–17	13.63%	12.41%	18.05%	12.35%	3.47%	22.29%	16.71%	12.30%

The risk-return trade-off for the four hypothetical portfolios is illustrated graphically in Example 10.10

Example 10.10 Risk-return trade-off for Australian All Ordinaries, All Industrials and All Resources Indices and 90/10 portfolio from 1980 to 1999

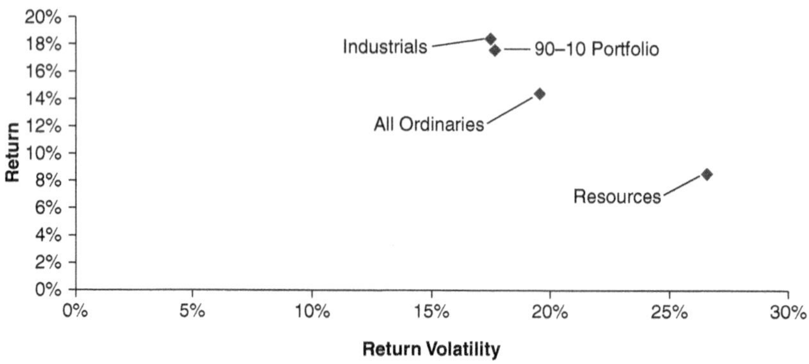

Example 10.10 shows that the 90/10 portfolio and the All Industrials index are quite close together, demonstrating a very high return to risk ratio. The All Ordinaries shows a slightly lower return with higher risk, while the position of the All Resources index suggests that the long-term rewards to this portfolio by itself cannot justify the return volatility.

The simplicity and transparency of the strategy put an unsurprising downward pressure on management fees, since physical assets were held in indexed sub-portfolios. To reflect the value-added by the investment manager's insights and research, it was agreed to augment passive fees with performance-based fees, with performance measured against the AOI. The fee structure included a 'catch-up' clause, whereby any underperformance would have to be matched by subsequent, equal outperformance before the performance-based fee could be re-activated.

To demonstrate on-going value-added, the investment manager sought to develop a 'switching mechanism' to forecast periods when resources were indeed likely to do better than industrials. The portfolio would then 'switch' to the benchmark 70/30 allocation.

Development of the switching mechanism turned out to be much more difficult to do. After considerable research using historical data, a factor-based model emerged based on a number of macro-economic indicators and resource price indices. The model was shown to have some predictive value on past data, but was not subject to sufficient live testing ('out-of-sample') – using current prices – to be proved of unequivocal value. In fact, the switch signal was never activated, and the portfolio remained at its initial 90/10 allocation. The good news was that portfolio returns delighted the members and the trustees of the fund, not to mention the investment manager. It soon had a number of imitators.

Case Study 2

This is a pooled trust designed to give indexed exposure to developed markets with minimal non-market risk. The bid-ask spread of units was set at 0.5 per cent, compared to 1.5 per cent to 2.0 per cent for other indexed international equities trusts.

The fund sought to enhance returns in three ways:

- To keep transactions costs low, the manager held share price index futures instead of physical shares.
- Because most of the physical assets of the fund would be held in short-term interest bearing instruments, the fund could earn additional returns by investing in short-term investment grade bonds and bills rather than simply holding cash deposits in order to enhance return by earning interest.
- Monitoring futures prices enabled the investment manager to add value when rolling futures contracts from one settlement month to the next. The portfolio manager, being able to calculate the 'fair' value of the difference in price from one settlement month to the next, executed the required trade when the tradable spread was advantageous. Spread trading could earn between 0.20 per cent and 0.50 per cent per annum.

Investing in futures rather than physical shares limits the countries in which the portfolio could invest to those with suitable futures markets. Most major markets were included, as shown in Example 10.11. Country allocations, in terms of weighting, were maintained as closely as possible to benchmark, with consideration for regional allocations. For example, the shortfall in Singapore was compensated by overweighting Japan, and the lack of futures contracts in smaller European countries was compensated by increased allocations in UK, Germany, France, the Netherlands and Switzerland.

Example 10.11 Composition of the international index fund and benchmark

	Portfolio	Benchmark
Australia	1.56%	1.48%
Austria		0.30%
Belgium	0.76%	0.72%
Canada	2.50%	2.38%
Denmark		0.43%
Finland		0.12%
France	4.14%	3.93%
Germany	4.17%	3.96%
Hong Kong	1.76%	1.67%
Ireland		0.00%

(continued)

	Portfolio	Benchmark
Italy		0.96%
Japan	25.78%	24.50%
Netherlands	2.12%	2.01%
New Zealand		0.18%
Norway		0.19%
Portugal		0.00%
Singapore		0.78%
South Africa		0.09%
Spain		1.17%
Sweden		0.76%
Switzerland		2.78%
UK	2.93%	11.29%
USA	11.88%	40.31%
World	42.42%	100.01%

For the first few years of its life the fund worked splendidly. Not only were transactions costs low, but custodian fees were kept to a minimum because the number of transactions was much reduced. Each re-balance entailed 11 transactions, compared to an average of about 1,000 for a portfolio of physical shares. After about five years however the fund began to under-perform the benchmark and investors began to demand explanations.

Example 10.12 Performance of the international index fund and benchmark: years 1 to 8

Twelve months to:	Portfolio	Benchmark	Difference
Year 1	−4.95%	−5.15%	0.21%
Year 2	19.00%	21.38%	−2.38%
Year 3	10.00%	6.57%	3.42%
Year 4	23.72%	21.81%	1.91%
Year 5	16.97%	14.34%	2.62%
Year 6	13.75%	16.72%	−2.97%
Year 7	22.15%	25.97%	−3.81%
Year 8	21.53%	26.18%	−4.65%
Inception to, annualized:			
Year 1	−4.95%	−5.15%	0.21%
Year 2	6.35%	7.30%	−0.94%
Year 3	7.55%	7.05%	0.50%

(continued)

Twelve months to:	Portfolio	Benchmark	Difference
Year 4	11.39%	10.57%	0.82%
Year 5	12.48%	11.31%	1.17%
Year 6	12.69%	12.20%	0.49%
Year 7	14.00%	14.07%	-0.07%
Year 8	14.91%	15.52%	-0.60%

A detailed performance attribution (Example 10.12) was carried out, which showed that the performance problem had a number of sources, including a mismatch in its allocation to individual markets, and the fact that within markets the portfolio did not match the benchmark return. It was also significant that the benchmark assumed the full benefit of dividend tax credits even though the fund, as a foreign investor, was not able to earn those credits.

Example 10.13 Summary attribution analysis of the international index fund

	Country allocation effect	Security selection within country	Residual
Year 1	0.48%	1.55%	-1.83%
Year 2	-0.98%	1.31%	-2.71%
Year 3	-0.32%	2.49%	1.25%
Year 4	0.34%	2.53%	-0.97%
Year 5	-0.60%	3.21%	0.01%
Year 6	0.68%	-1.15%	-2.50%
Year 7	-0.80%	-0.77%	-2.24%
Year 8	-0.79%	-2.03%	-1.83%

Sources of variation

Country allocation		Contribution to return variance
Year 2	Spain	-0.26%
	USA	-0.22%
	Singapore	-0.17%
	Italy	-0.14%
	Others	-0.23%
Year 7	Italy	-0.56%
	Spain	-0.36%
	Others	0.13%
Year 8	Finland	-1.05%
	Sweden	-0.53%
	Others	0.78%

(continued)

Security selection

Year 6	USA	−0.91%
	UK	−0.09%
	Japan	−0.05%
	Germany	−0.16%
	Australia	−0.03%
	Others	0.09%
Year 7	USA	−1.20%
	UK	−0.10%
	Japan	0.28%
	Germany	−0.18%
	Australia	−0.02%
	Others	0.44%
Year 8	USA	−0.99%
	UK	0.15%
	Japan	−0.86%
	Germany	−0.17%
	Australia	−0.01%
	Others	−0.15%

Example 10.13 shows that country allocations effects contributed to underperformance in years 2, 3, 5, 7 and 8, mainly due to the lack of liquid futures contracts in countries such as Spain, Italy, Finland, Sweden and Singapore. Security selection within countries contributed to underperformance in the USA, UK, Germany, Japan and Australia where the share price index contract on which futures contracts are based under-performed the benchmark index in those countries.

The mismatch within countries is of course due to differences in the composition of the country portfolio with the benchmark index and the notional portfolio against which the local futures contracts are settled. For example, the Topix index in Japan is an equally-weighted index, so has significant differences from the capitalization-weighted share price index of the benchmark.

The manager was able to show that, by applying a global risk model to the portfolio with its country weights constrained to the benchmark weights, the portfolio could not hope to achieve a tracking error below 2.6 per cent. She was also able to show that this could be reduced to about 0.7 per cent by allowing country weights to vary from those of the benchmark, and that this reduction in tracking error would resolve much of the portfolio's underperformance.

Endnotes

1. They offer only limited protection however, because beyond a certain, ill-defined point, inflation – or rather inflation volatility – becomes a source of uncertainty. Economic uncertainty makes it hard for companies to invest and grow, so while a stable level of inflation is considered healthy, galloping inflation works as a brake on economic growth.
2. Financial assets, such as bonds, can hedge annuity-like liabilities where periodical payments are fixed in nominal terms.
3. Andrew Lo, Harry Mamaysky and Jiang Wang, *Journal of Finance*. August 2000, cited in *The Economist*. 19 August, 2000, p. 76.

11
Optimization for Equity Stock Selection

Say you have $1,000 to invest in the equities market. Your favourite stock is Blue Sky Ventures (BSV), which you believe will return about 18 per cent next year. In the past it has been quite volatile, at about 30 per cent. You buy $1000 of BSV and you expect to earn 18 per cent plus or minus around 30 per cent.

Now you have another $1000 from an unexpected source. You still like BSV but think it prudent to spread your bets. Another stock, Purple Profound Productions (PPP), has been recommended to you. It is expected to earn about 15 per cent with about 25 per cent volatility. The two businesses are quite different, so you estimate that the correlation between the two stocks is about 0.25. Will the 50/50 mix give the best overall outcome?

The graph in Example 11.1 shows risk on the x axis and return on the y axis for a range allocations to BSV and PPP summing to 100 per cent. The highlighted points represent 100 per cent in BSV, 100 per cent in PPP

Example 11.1 Risk and return

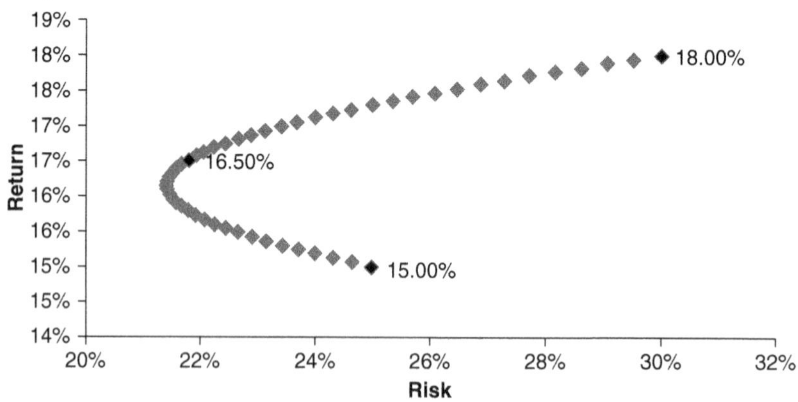

and 50 per cent in each stock. Note that the return to the 50/50 combination is 16.5 per cent, which is less than the risk of the less risky of the two stocks. Put another way, if you had started with 100 per cent allocation to PPP you could have both increased your return and reduced your risk by investing some of your money in BSV, a more risky stock. This result is possible because of the relatively low correlation between BSV and PPP. The graph shows that risk can be reduced even further by investing 38 per cent in BSV and 62 per cent in PPP, giving expected risk of 16.14 per cent and expected return of 21.4 per cent.

Add a third asset and the task of allocating between stocks to achieve the best ratio of expected return to expected risk becomes much more complicated.

By the time you have a dozen or so assets in your portfolio, it is no longer feasible to calculate manually the expected risk of each possible combination of assets in order to decide which gives the right balance of return to risk for your preferences, even if you have a reliable estimate of the risk of each asset and the correlations between them. An easier way to do it is to get an optimizer to do it for you.

This chapter sets out to show:

- How optimization works.
- What can go wrong with optimization.
- What optimization is used for in practice.
- How it helps select portfolios.
- Re-sampling.
- Reverse optimization.
- The Black-Litterman model.

How optimization works

Mean-variance optimization is in fact a special case of linear optimization, which is used widely in engineering and production management. It finds the portfolio with the highest expected return for a given level of risk – or the lowest risk portfolio for a given level of return – using what it knows about the universe of assets from which it can select. Like all linear optimizers, it does this by making small, incremental changes to some given starting position, such as the existing portfolio, calculating the return and risk for each new configuration, then trying another combination until it has found a range of portfolios with the best expected return for each risk level. This set of portfolios is said to be mean-variance efficient and lies on the efficient frontier. They are efficient in the sense that no other portfolio can give more return for each level of risk or less risk for each level of return.

To calculate the expected risk of each portfolio a basic mean-variance optimizer takes into account:

- The weight in the portfolio of each asset.
- The estimated volatility, or risk, of each asset.
- The correlation, usually expressed as the covariance (which takes account of volatilities as well as correlations) between each pair of assets.

For portfolios with relatively small numbers – up to a few dozen – of assets in them, the basic optimizer works well, since covariance matrices of up to a few dozen square are reasonably tractable. In practice however most equities portfolios hold dozens and even hundreds of stocks. Benchmark indices can hold thousands, so even a relatively small portfolio can have thousands of implied active positions when compared with a benchmark. When the number of assets extends to the hundreds or thousands, computing the covariance matrix is no longer feasible. One reason for this is that the number of observations in the data sample must exceed the number of rows and columns in the covariance matrix, so for example, a portfolio with 100 assets needs at least 101 return observations to compute a viable covariance matrix. As the covariance matrix is central to risk estimation for each portfolio, any errors in it will compromise the optimization results. To optimize a portfolio with more than a few dozen stocks it is necessary to reduce the covariance matrix to a more workable size.

William Sharpe in 1963 developed the single index risk model, which exploits the fact that, for most portfolios invested in a single market, the stocks in the investment universe all co-vary to some extent with the market in which they trade. To estimate the risk of a portfolio, you therefore need only to estimate the risk of the market and the beta (the covariance of the stock with the market divided by the variance of the market) of each stock to the market.

This innovation allowed portfolios of large numbers of stocks to be modelled relatively easily. But academics and practitioners noticed that stocks co-vary with things other than the market. It followed that including their effects in the risk estimation algorithm would improve the results. Multi-factor risk models both gave more valid estimates of portfolio risk and better optimizations.

Multi-factor mean-variance risk models used for most investment portfolios include factors like:

- Style (Fama–French) factors.
- Market (country) factors.
- Currency factors.
- Industry factors.

- Commodity factors.
- Macro-economic factors.
- Statistical factors.

For some applications, such as short-term indexed portfolios, PCA factor risk models can give the best results.

With the addition of multiple factors, the risk computation was expanded to include:

- The weight of the stock in the portfolio and the benchmark.
- The beta of each stock to each risk factor.
- The risk or expected volatility of each risk factor.
- The risk factor covariance matrix.

In other words, the same things that go into any multi-factor mean-variance portfolio risk model.

Limitations of optimization

When optimization was used to select actual portfolios, it became clear that it had some problems. Investment managers found that:

- It could be very sensitive to quite small changes in inputs, especially expected returns.
- It almost always delivered counter-intuitive results and too often depended on constraints to produce an acceptable solution.
- It tended to select impractical portfolios that had unrealistic holdings in small, illiquid and often very risky stocks, giving portfolios that no investor would be happy to hold even if they could be implemented, which often they couldn't.
- It was often unstable from one model update to the next, resulting in unacceptably high portfolio turnover.

On-going research suggested a number of possible causes for the apparently counter-intuitive results:

- Errors in return estimates.
- Errors in risk estimates.
- Data issues.
- Unintended consequences of constraints.
- Error maximization inherent in optimization.
- The efficient portfolio fallacy.

Errors in return estimates

For each portfolio generated by the optimizer, the expected return is the sum of the expected return to each stock weighted by its percentage holding. An error in this simple calculation is of course easily spotted and corrected.

Expected returns for individual stocks inevitably have errors in them, but they don't necessarily bias portfolio results if they cancel out at the portfolio level. Errors in stock return forecasts can happen in at least two ways.

The first is that in practice most investment managers do not forecast stock returns as point estimates. Rather, they tend to think of ranges of expected returns. Optimizers cannot work with ranges, so most investment managers tend to choose the mid-point of their range for the purpose of the optimization. If the range for a stock is wide, then the error built into the return estimate is wide too, and is not necessarily averaged out by the optimizer because of the tendency of the optimizer to favour high return stocks.

Another source of errors in stock forecasts, from the point of view of the optimizer, is to do with the information used by investment managers to forecast returns.[1]

Stock returns can be thought of as comprising a number of factor-related components plus a stock alpha. Even if the investment manager is not consciously selecting according to factor-related returns, the stocks he or she favours nearly always have a number of characteristics in common, which usually correspond to common factors. Typically he or she uses both the factor exposures, implied or otherwise, and the expected alpha to select stocks.

The number of criteria investment managers use to select stocks tends to be small and might include value, growth, liquidity, size or momentum characteristics, as well as country or industry membership. In other words, things you often see in multi-factor risk models. As well as these, he or she might choose stocks for stock specific reasons.

In practice stock selection models can be useful even if they forecast only a relatively small proportion of the total return to a stock. Risk models, on the other hand, need to capture all the common factor and stock specific risks in the portfolio to be useful, so they typically have many more factors in them. This means that the resulting portfolio is exposed to many other factors apart from those used to select the stocks in it.

Unsurprisingly it is hard for a portfolio optimizer to distinguish between the factor exposures that a manager wants to make, and those that are incidental, which poses a problem for the optimization results.

The optimizer assumes that all risk is bad and therefore should be minimized – including the risks that the investment manager includes on purpose in order to earn active return.

Errors in risk estimates

The chapter on risk modelling describes the possible sources of risk estimation error as:

- Estimates of stock betas to risk factors.
- The estimated risk factor covariance matrix.

Estimates of stock betas to factors – being numerous, these are rarely if ever perfect. They need not be, so long as any errors are not systematic and cancel out at the portfolio level. In practice this is often the case, but not always.

Style factor betas, which are derived from the most recent company financial reports, can be unstable; for example, earnings surprises can cause discrete jumps that translate to sharp changes in the stock beta estimates from one model update to the next. This usually has little effect on the portfolio if the surprises are in different directions for different stocks because they will cancel out at the portfolio level. But often things like earnings revisions and surprises work in the same direction across stocks at the same time, causing instability in the factor betas at the portfolio level. Most investment managers would not be too worried to see instability from this source: in fact, they would expect it if market conditions were causing large changes in estimates of future stock earnings.

Industry, country and currency beta estimates for individual stocks can be estimated either from time-series regression against a published return series for the factor or from what is known about the current sources of earnings for each stock. In practice, many risk and optimization model providers apply a short-cut of assigning stock betas according to industry classification, country of domicile or currency of quotation rather than the very labour-intensive process of analysing income sources. This gives a binary score of one or zero for each stock to each factor, so that each stock is sensitive to only one country, one currency, one industry and so on.

When an optimizer encounters two UK retailers, one with an expected return of 8 per cent and the other with 5 per cent, it assumes that both retailers have exactly the same risk and will therefore allocate more to the retailer with 8 per cent expected return. If, as is likely, this is the more risky of the two retailers, then the allocation between the two stocks is necessarily inefficient. This source of error does not cancel out at the portfolio level, so will bias optimization results.

The time-series method of estimating stock betas, described in Chapter 5 on risk modelling, to factors is obviously also subject to estimation error, for example, due to data sources. But its ability to capture the differences in factor sensitivities that would mark the 8 per cent retailer as the more risky stock arguably outweighs the effect of this source of error, particularly at the portfolio level. In addition, the results it gives are not affected by changes in industry classification that occasionally affect large stocks, for example Nokia's metamorphosis from a forestry stock to a telecoms stock.

Errors in the covariance matrix – these can be due to two things.

The first is poor choice of factors. Factors are most useful when they are relevant to the universe from which portfolios are selected. Factors that are irrelevant to the portfolio or its market are unlikely to explain most of the risk in the portfolios generated by the optimizer. A risk model that explains only part of the risk of the portfolio is likely to underestimate it. Think of how relevant a dividend yield factor is to the Japanese market.

Yet even the most apposite set of risk factors is bound to underestimate some portfolio risk. The shortfall can be remedied by including statistical factors to ensure that all factor-related risk in the portfolio is accounted for, and risk under-estimation is therefore less likely.

Factors that are correlated with each other can cause instability too because the optimizer perceives them as, in a sense, substitutes for each other. This means that even relatively small changes in return forecasts can cause risk to 'flip' between correlated factors from one model update to the next.

The other main source of error in the covariance matrix is poor estimation of factor returns. Two reasons for this are data issues and factor construction.

Factors are constructed according to the binary beta estimation method build in the distortions of the beta estimation itself, so they will cause systematic biases in the factor covariance matrix. For example, currency factor returns derived only from the returns to the stocks in the investment universe that have a beta of one to the currency won't correspond to any published returns to that currency. The covariance of that currency factor with the other risk factors will therefore not be realistic.

Data issues

Estimating risk from samples of historical data assumes that that data set is a valid indicator of what the forecast horizon will be like. So what history you use is important.

If the data are sampled from too short a history, then important investment cycles may be omitted that can prejudice the result – as happened in the lead-up to the 2007–08 crisis, when markets were atypically calm and risk widely underestimated.

On the other hand, data samples that go too far back can build in structural changes in markets and so confound the sample with irrelevant events. They also embed stock survivorship bias.

There is no unambiguously right answer. However the problem can be mitigated by weighting recent observations more heavily than earlier ones. This also helps resolve the problem caused when extreme events 'drop out' of the rolling data sample with each model update, when they do, they can cause arbitrary 'jumps' in the results that can add to the sense of instability.

How long or short the time is between sample observations dictates how far into the future you can project. Most mean-variance risk models estimate risk using monthly or weekly return observations from which they extrapolate to give annualized risk forecasts. Some models however extrapolate from daily observations to give annualized estimates. While some extrapolation is unavoidable, too much can give invalid results because of the propensity of asset prices to overshoot and over-correct in the very short term. This results in 'white noise' that is not relevant to investment horizons calibrated in months or years. On the other hand, frequent observations and short forecast horizons are the most appropriate way to support construction of portfolios with very short horizons.

Constraints

Investment managers usually constrain optimizations in order to avoid allocation to illiquid stocks, to limit concentrations in individual stocks or groups of stocks, to limit the number of stocks in the portfolio and so on. Inevitably constraints reduce the efficiency of the resulting portfolios, as shown in Example 11.2.

In Example 11.2, the constraints keep the portfolio allocations close to benchmark, but in doing so have limited the portfolio's range of risk and return outcomes and therefore the choices available to the investor. By doing this they can also compromise the investment manager's ability to add active return. Not only are high-risk, high-return outcomes excluded but also low-risk, low-return outcomes, as a result of the constraints. Constraints can have unintended consequences, such as:

- By disallowing or limiting allocation to some assets, the investment manager may in effect force the optimizer to allocate or over-allocate

Example 11.2 Constrained and unconstrained optimization

	Original portfolio	Benchmark portfolio	Expected return	Minimum constraint	Maximum constraint
American International	7.00%	10%	–0.05%	7.50%	12.50%
AOL Time Warner	8.16%	10%	–11.58%	7.50%	12.50%
Citigroup	9.16%	10%	1.50%	7.50%	12.50%
Exxon Mobil	11.21%	10%	–2.50%	7.50%	12.50%
General Electric	17.65%	10%	18.00%	7.50%	12.50%
Intel	7.61%	10%	5.00%	7.50%	12.50%
IBM	7.43%	10%	–5.64%	7.50%	12.50%
Microsoft	13.30%	10%	5.00%	7.50%	12.50%
Pfizer	10.01%	10%	12.00%	7.50%	12.50%
Walmart	8.47%	10%	15.00%	7.50%	12.50%
Portfolio	100%	100%	3.673%		

Optimization summary	Efficient portfolios				
	1	2	3	4	5
Unconstrained optimization					
Relative return	0.000	3.582	7.164	10.745	14.327
Tracking error	0.000	2.828	5.863	9.962	17.490
Information ratio	0.320	1.267	1.222	1.079	0.819
Constrained optimization					
Relative return	0.000	0.458	0.916	1.374	1.832
Tracking error	0.000	0.362	0.732	1.200	2.259
Information ratio	0.000	1.267	1.251	1.145	0.811

Source: R-Squared Risk Management

to other assets that are less attractive in terms of their return and risk characteristics.

- Constraints that are too restrictive can in effect determine the shape of the portfolios generated by the optimizer, so defeating the purpose of finding portfolios that have superior return to risk properties.
- Over-restrictive constraints can be impossible to satisfy, causing the optimization to fail because it cannot identify any portfolios that satisfy all the constraints imposed on it.

Example 11.2 illustrates a fairly typical set of holding constraints. The objective is to keep the portfolio allocations reasonably close to the benchmark weights.

Some optimization systems allow the investment manager to superimpose his or her own risk factor covariance matrix. This has the obvious advantage of harnessing the insights of the investment manager. However it does not guarantee that the covariance matrix is viable or consistent. If the covariance matrix is unrealistic or inconsistent it can cause the optimization to fail.

Error maximization tendency of optimizers

Optimizers tend systematically to maximize errors. Presented with two assets with the same risk and different returns, the optimizer chooses the one with the higher return. If this return is an over-estimate and the other one is not, then the over-estimation is incorporated in the optimization results. In the same way, an optimizer given the choice of two assets with the same expected return but different risks will choose the one with the lower risk. If the risk is an under-estimate, then the risk under-estimation will find its way into the optimization result. There is no scope to off-set errors of this kind, which there are bound to be in practice. They therefore result in 'optimal' portfolios that are inefficient in a risk-return sense.

The efficient portfolio fallacy

Efficient portfolios exist in theory but not in practice. Even if you create an efficient portfolio as the market opens, using all the information you have at that moment, it becomes inefficient as soon as prices move (and the portfolio weights change), or new information comes in (and the expected returns or risks change).

Optimizers regard all return as equally attractive, and all risk as equally bad. This contradicts the purpose of active portfolio management, which is to earn active return by assuming calculated risks, or, put another way, distinguishing between good (intentional) risk and bad (incidental) risk.

Uses of optimization

Indexed funds – short term and long term

For indexed portfolios that do not aim to fully replicate the index they are designed to match, optimization can add value by reducing the tracking error of a tracking portfolio that has been compiled using some sampling process.

Long-term tracking portfolios, for example, as part of a core-satellite structure, are usually selected using a combination of optimization and sampling, usually to ensure that industry and/or factor exposures are not too different from those of the benchmark index. Optimizers based on multi-factor risk models, using monthly, weighted return observations, tend to do this best, as they allow the investment manager to inspect factor exposures and concentrations of risk in order to contain the error-maximizing tendency of the optimizer and achieve an intuitively practical portfolio.

Short-term tracking portfolios – for example, those used by investment bankers to effect very short-term hedges – can achieve good results using PCA-based optimizers and daily return observations because they can forecast risk accurately and tend to give the lowest possible short-term tracking error for a portfolio of a given number of stocks. Counter intuitive factor concentrations, in this context, usually have little impact on very short-term portfolios.

Low volatility portfolios

The ability of optimizers to identify portfolios with the best return to risk profile can be very helpful in selecting low volatility portfolios. These portfolios are intended to give low sensitivity to fluctuations in equities markets, offering investors a 'low risk' exposure to the market.

Low volatility portfolios are selected from a list of candidate stocks that typically have been screened for lower than average betas to their market and acceptable liquidity. The investment manager specifies a target number of stocks and the optimizer selects fully-invested portfolios with low forecast beta. It usually does this with a multi-factor risk model and almost always some intervention on the part of the investment manager.

Quantify cost of constraints

Optimization can help define the terms of investment management mandates. By generating sets of 'efficient' unconstrained portfolios and comparing their return and risk profiles with those of sets of portfolios generated by optimization with various different sets of constraints, the investment manager can demonstrate the likely 'cost' of different sets of constraints in terms of portfolio expected return and risk. This can help design more stable constraints that satisfy investment guidelines and restrictions without unduly compromising the ability of the portfolio to meet its investment objectives.

Portfolio construction

To use an optimizer to construct a portfolio, the investment manager provides the following information:

- Some starting portfolio, such as the existing portfolio, benchmark allocations or cash. Portfolio allocations can be represented as the number of shares held, holding value or percentage of total portfolio value. Benchmark holdings are represented as percentage holdings.
- The universe of permitted investments.
- Forecast returns for each asset in the portfolio and benchmark.
- Any constraints to which the portfolio is subject, such as total number of assets or maximum exposure to industry groups.

Most commercially-available optimizer systems compute stock betas to risk factors and the factor covariance matrix using the risk model embedded in them, although some systems allow the investment manager to super-impose his or her own.

Because the optimizer works by making small changes to the existing portfolio, the composition of the starting portfolio is important. An investment manager seeking to adjust an existing portfolio would prefer to start with that portfolio and look for the smallest required changes to reach optimality in order to minimize turnover. Initial index tracking portfolios usually start the optimization process with the benchmark composition. Initial low volatility portfolios are more likely to start from a position of 100 per cent holding in cash.

The universe of permitted investments tells the optimizer which securities can be held and which are to be excluded, for example because they are embargoed or because they are difficult to buy or incur very high transactions costs.

If asset return forecasts are omitted, the optimizer assumes that all securities have equal returns and so will seek the minimum risk portfolio, which is suitable for an indexed or low volatility portfolio. Alternatively, if forecast returns are not available, as is often the case in practice, stock rankings can work well in their place.

Re-sampling

Re-sampling aims to reduce the problems of instability in optimizers through a process combining statistical re-sampling, simulation and averaging to derive more information from the data sample used in the original optimization. By effectively extracting more information from the same data sample, the investment manager can reduce the effects of overestimation of return and underestimation of risk due to quirks in the original data sample. Re-sampling does not directly address the optimizer's tendency to maximize errors.

Reverse optimization

The other way to derive the benefits of optimization while avoiding some of its limitations is by reverse optimization.[2] Reverse optimization was first built into portfolio risk tools in the early 1980s.

Whereas optimization asks the question: what holdings make the portfolio efficient? Reverse optimization asks the question: what returns make the portfolio efficient?

Reverse optimization starts by analysing the risk structure of the portfolio, which shows whether the manager:

- Has the right amount of risk overall (for the mandate).
- Has the right kinds of risk (the deliberate bets).
- Has the right proportions of risk (for efficiency).

The analysis then gives the implied returns required for efficiency, which can be compared with the manager's expected returns to determine which holdings do not efficiently reflect his or her views, given his or her forecasting ability. This avoids one of the main problems with optimizers.

This is that they demand point-value estimates of expected returns for each stock. These are then treated as if they are known for certain. The optimizer then generates a set of precise portfolio holdings.

In practice, investment managers usually forecast returns as 'fuzzy' ranges that embed more information than is possible with a single number. Investment managers also tend to think of stocks as ranked from favourite to least favourite. For those managers, portfolio inefficiency consists of not having their favourite stocks too far down the list, and their less favourite stocks being near the top

Alternatively, if the investment manager forecasts stock returns by explicitly using factors or common stock characteristics, then he or she usually has an idea of how important each of these is relative to the other.

A very practical solution is to run the optimization backwards. The process begins with the portfolio manager's preferred portfolio composition, which is assumed to be mean-variance efficient. To this is added stock betas to factors and the factor covariance matrix to give the expected return for each asset in the portfolio and benchmark that is implied by the given preferred portfolio composition.

The investment manager can then judge if the implied returns are within the range that he or she believes is reasonable for the investment horizon, given what he or she knows about the stocks and whether they contribute their 'fair share' of risk.

The benefits of reverse optimization include:

- It allows fine tuning of portfolio holdings (or factor exposures) without doing a full optimization.
- In the limit, managers don't even need to quantify their return forecasts, as the analysis generates an implied ranking of assets (or factors).
- Ranking the assets in a portfolio from high to low by their contribution to return gives us the implied ranking of assets by their relative attractiveness.

Portfolios are often selected and managed with constraints. Reverse optimization is still useful:

- If holding sizes have been constrained to a minimum or maximum, then a stock's implied return becomes an upper or lower limit on its expected return.
- The same will apply to groups of holdings, such as those in a particular country, industry or sector.
- It also applies to the implied risk premium for a constrained factor, where the constraint is applied to the portfolio beta to that factor.

Portfolio managers often find the output of portfolio optimization counter-intuitive or puzzling. Often this intuition is correct and the puzzling result is because the optimizer is unable to use all of the manager's intuition. Reverse optimization effectively allows as much insight as possible to be used in the portfolio construction process.

Reverse optimization can be applied to the portfolio, the benchmark or the portfolio relative to the benchmark.

- Applied to the portfolio, the assumption is that that portfolio is efficient.
- Applied to the portfolio relative to the benchmark, the assumption is that the differences in holdings comprise an efficient long-short portfolio.

By applying reverse optimization to the benchmark, the investment manager can see, from what he or she knows about the stocks in it, whether the weights in the benchmark are reasonable – in effect how different his or her views of stocks are from those of the market.

If the return to a stock that is implied by the reverse optimization seems too high to the investment manager, then the holding in that stocks should be reduced to better reflect his or her view. If the implied return looks too low, then an increase in the portfolio's holding is indicated.

In Example 11.3, the implied return is the return you would expect from the stock, given the target portfolio relative return, (which in this example is 2 per cent) if the portfolio was efficient relative to the benchmark.

The implied alpha can be considered 'true alpha' in that it is independent of factor effects, so is the return that is expected due to pure stock-selection.

The magnitude of the contribution to relative implied return should correspond directly to the investment manager's views on the specific value of the stock. If it is larger than can be justified by his or her confidence in his or her views on that stock, then reducing exposure might be considered. Conversely, if it is less than he or she thinks warranted by his or her views, an increase in the portfolio's exposure to it may be called for.

The same process can be applied at the level of factor exposures to help align sources of factor risk with sources of return and eliminate unwanted risks.

The implied risk premium is the return, relative to the portfolio expected return, the investment manager would expect from that factor, given the target portfolio relative return (in Example 11.4, 2 per cent), if the portfolio was efficient relative to the benchmark. For example, the relative exposure of the Swiss Franc of 0.11 implies that the manager expects the Swiss Franc to appreciate by 5.17 per cent (2.00 + 3.17) relative to the Euro. If the manager thinks this 5.17 per cent is too optimistic, he or she can reduce the allocation to Swiss Francs, which will also reduce the exposure.

The magnitude of the implied risk premium should correspond directly to the investment manager's views on the factor. If it is larger than can be justified by his or her views on that factor, then reducing the portfolio's exposure should be considered. Conversely, if the implied risk premium is less than he or she thinks warranted by his or her views, an increase in the portfolio's exposure may be called for.

Reverse optimization adds value to stock-by-stock portfolio selection, for example, for portfolios selected using return forecasts derived from fundamental stock analysis. By highlighting apparent inconsistencies between the implied stock and factor returns and the views of the

Example 11.3 Reverse optimization by stock

	Percentage holding	Relative holding	Relative risk	% risk and return	Implied return	Implied alpha	Contribution to relative return
Stock 1	0.01%	0.00%	0.00%	0.00%	0.00%	0.00%	0.00%
Stock 2	0.75%	0.75%	37.71%	0.76%	0.00%	0.00%	0.00%
Stock 3	0.43%	0.43%	36.69%	0.48%	2.04%	0.02%	0.02%
Stock 4	0.69%	0.69%	33.26%	0.83%	2.21%	0.02%	0.01%
Stock 5	0.02%	0.02%	39.92%	0.01%	2.40%	0.02%	0.02%
Stock 6	1.16%	1.16%	32.37%	1.02%	1.48%	0.00%	0.00%
Stock 7	1.53%	1.53%	38.99%	2.00%	1.76%	0.04%	0.02%
Stock 8	1.53%	1.53%	35.35%	2.13%	2.61%	0.03%	0.04%
Portfolio	100%	0%	18%	100%	2.00%	0.03%	2.00%

Source: R-Squared Risk Management

Example 11.4 Reverse optimization by factor

Factor	Relative beta to factor	Factor risk	% risk and return	Implied risk premium	Contribution to return
Swiss Franc	0.11	8.51%	17.10%	3.17%	0.34%
Sweden large	–0.04	15.63%	6.69%	–3.69%	0.13%
Japanese Yen	–0.03	15.69%	3.98%	–2.31%	0.08%
France small	–0.02	16.20%	3.40%	–3.88%	0.070%
Building and construction	–0.02	17.11%	3.06%	–4.32%	0.061%
Finland	–0.02	18.67%	2.98%	–4.60%	0.064%
Biotechnology and pharmaceuticals	–0.02	12.09%	2.43%	1.22%	0.05%
Statistical factor 1	0.00	26.72%	2.12%	4.09%	0.04%
Switzerland small	–0.04	15.12%	1.83%	–5.02%	0.041%
Italy large	0.03	20.41%	1.73%	–1.63%	0.03%
Long-term price momentum	–0.01	3.31%	1.69%	1.09%	0.03%
Sweden small	–0.05	17.13%	1.63%	–6.29%	0.03%
Health care	–0.01	12.36%	1.52%	–2.06%	0.03%

Source: R-Squared Risk Management

investment manager, the manager can achieve a portfolio that reflects his or her selection skills and avoids the dampening effect on portfolio active return from inadvertent and unmanaged risks.

For portfolios selected stock-by-stock, the process can add material value in terms of reduced risk and improved information ratios by quantifying unwanted risks that arise from underweights and under-exposure to risk factors that are due to stocks that are in the benchmark but not held in the portfolio.

It is important to note that the effectiveness of reverse optimization depends on the validity and reliability of the risk model embedded in the reverse optimizer. Errors in estimation of the covariance matrix will be reflected in unreliable estimates of implied stock and factor returns.

Black–Litterman

The Black–Litterman model was developed in 1990 at Goldman Sachs by Fischer Black and Robert Litterman to help overcome some of the limitations of optimization, as applied to asset allocation. It starts with the assumption that the portfolio allocation should be proportional to the market values of the available assets, and then modifies that to take into account the investment manager's 'views' to improve on that position.

Like reverse optimization, it seeks to address some of the issues of fitting investment managers' expected returns to optimizers. Instead of expected returns, the Black–Litterman model assumes that the initial set of expected returns corresponds to existing market efficiency. The investment manager then says how his or her assumptions about expected returns differ from the market's, together with his or her degree of confidence in the alternative assumptions. From this, the Black–Litterman method computes the desired (mean-variance efficient) portfolio allocation.

In fact the Black–Litterman model can be thought of as a special case of reverse optimization, with the added assumptions that:

- The World Markets portfolio is efficient as defined by the international CAPM.
- Currency influences aren't a problem, in other words, the universal currency hedging constant is valid and can be determined accurately enough.
- Given any known return such as US T-bills, the investment manager can derive the implied equilibrium returns for all other markets.

With the Black–Litterman model:

- Implied returns allow managers to use information about their expected ranges of returns rather than having point forecasts misrepresent their real views.
- Equilibrium returns give the manager additional information about the extent to which his or her views differ from those implied from market information.
- Both the implied and equilibrium returns effectively provide a reality-check on the consistency of the original forecasts.

Summary

The ability to derive portfolios, using a relatively simple algorithm, with the best possible return to risk profiles is unambiguously compelling.

However in practice the methodology encountered limitations, such as its tendency to maximize errors implicit in many of its inputs, causing it to deliver counter-intuitive results and 'optimal' portfolios that could not be implemented in practice. These practical problems affect some portfolio selection tasks more than others, so optimization still finds a number of practical uses.

A number of approaches have been proposed and are used in practice to overcome the practical limitations for most actively-managed equities portfolios, including re-sampling and reverse optimization.

Endnotes

1. The insights in this passage draw heavily on a talk by Jason MacQueen of R-Squared Risk Management, titled 'To optimize or not to optimize? The case against optimization', given at a meeting of the London Quant Group in May 2010.
2. This section is also informed by the insights of Jason MacQueen.

12
Fixed Interest Portfolios

> But now I would like to come back as the bond market. You can intimidate everybody.
>
> James Carville, political advisor to President Clinton

All interest rate instruments are loans. For a standard interest rate transaction the borrower, provided he or she meets all repayment obligations, retains the right to the assets he or she owns. The lender has no call on the assets of the borrower, except for the amount of the loan and interest earned. This chapter is about portfolios comprising fixed interest instruments, including bonds, bills and notes, issued in the currency of the investor by government, semi-government organizations and banks, which are usually assumed to have negligible or very low risk of default by the issuer. It discusses:

- The rationale for issuing and investing in bonds.
- Some observations about the interest rate.
- Why the yield curve is important.
- How yield curves are modelled.
- How bonds are priced.
- Measuring the risk of bonds.
- Construction of bond portfolios.
- Some notes on inflation-linked bonds.
- Some notes on asset-liability management.
- Implementing bond portfolios.

Rationale

Issuers of bonds are borrowers such as governments, semi-government organizations, banks and companies that are large enough to raise capital from bond markets directly rather than indirectly, via a bank loan. The difference between a private loan and a bond, bill or note is that the latter three are traded on the secondary market.

Many fixed interest instruments that are traded on the secondary market are loans initially by a bank to a company. The bank records the loan as an asset, which can then be resold in the secondary market. The bank can resell it in its raw form, in which case it will describe it as company ABC, maturity x, coupon y and so on. The investor knows that if company ABC is unable to honour the loan, he or she could lose all or part of his or her investment. Alternatively, the bank can sell it at a higher price by first endorsing it. In endorsing the loan, the bank is effectively saying that, 'if company ABC cannot pay up, we'll guarantee performance of the loan'. The investor's risk is then against the bank rather than against company ABC.

Investors are lenders such as pension funds, hedge funds, mutual and trust funds and insurance companies who seek an income-bearing, low volatility and often low risk investment, either to help diversify a multi-asset portfolio, to offset pension or annuity liabilities, as part of relative value or arbitrage strategy or as collateral to support derivatives positions.

Investment and pension funds hold portfolios of interest rate instruments:

- To meet regulatory requirement to hold a given quota of government bonds.
- To modify the risk of or diversify their overall portfolio: fixed interest is usually thought of as being less risky than, and relatively uncorrelated with, equities.
- As collateral for positions in futures, options and other derivative instruments.
- In anticipation of high returns to bonds relative to other assets.

The interest rate

Central to active management of fixed interest portfolios are assumptions and forecasts about the behaviour of interest rates.

An interest rate for a borrower is the value of present versus deferred consumption. For the lender it is the reward for delayed consumption. The interest rate for a bond of a given term is a function of:

- Inflation.
- Expected future inflation.
- Time value of money.
- Opportunity cost.
- Uncertainty.

- Default likelihood.
- Supply and demand.
- Expected future supply and demand.
- Government policy.

Nominal interest rates are the sum of the real interest rate and inflation. As interest rates are nearly always quoted as nominal, whereas for many investment and econometric purposes the real yields is more relevant, it is necessary to derive the real yield by subtracting the inflation rate from the nominal yield. For example, a nominal interest rate of 4.5 per cent coupled with an inflation rate of 2 per cent gives a real yield of 2.5 per cent.

The yield of a bond is the rate of return to the investor, taking into account its coupon, maturity and the price paid for the bond, which if purchased on the secondary market can be either more or less than the face value of the bond.

An investor who is prepared to tie up his or her money for a long period of time can usually demand a higher effective rate of interest. The relationship between the time to the maturity of bonds and their yields is described by the yield curve.

The yield curve

The yield curve shows several yields or interest rates across different contract lengths for a given class of borrower, such as a government, semi-government, bank or company.

Fixed income analysts, who analyse bonds and related securities, use yield curves to understand conditions in financial markets and to seek trading opportunities. Economists use the curves to understand economic conditions.

An important function of the yield curve is to price other investment instruments. The government or LIBOR yield curves are often used as the approximation for the risk-free rate of interest used by most asset pricing models, including CAPM and the Black-Scholes option pricing formula. Given their central role in investment theory and practice, it is perhaps surprising that yield curves are not directly observable, but must be estimated, as discussed further in this chapter.

No single yield curve describes the cost of money for everybody. Each yield curve is defined by its:

- Currency of issue.
- Credit quality, usually given by the bonds' credit rating.

Example 12.1 A yield curve

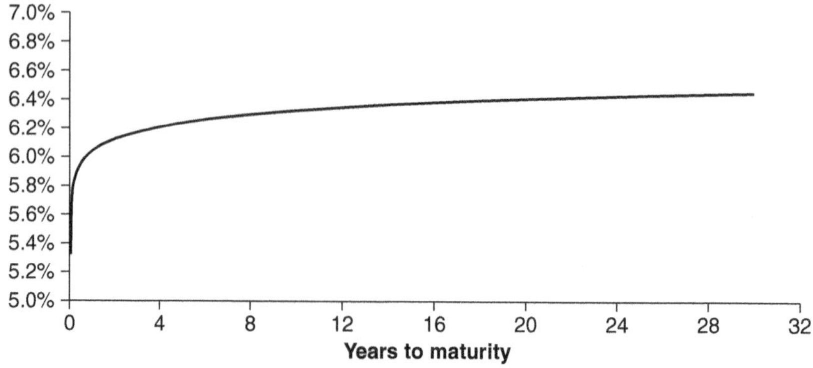

For a given currency of issue, the credit quality of a yield curve is usually described by one of the following:

- Bonds issued by governments, which are called the government bond yield curve, or the government curve.
- Banks with high credit ratings (Aa/AA or above), which borrow money from each other at the LIBOR rates. These yield curves are typically a little higher than government curves. They are the most important and widely used in the financial markets, and are known variously as the LIBOR curve or the swap curve.
- Corporate, or company, curves, constructed from the yields of bonds issued by corporations. Since corporations usually have less creditworthiness than most governments and most large banks, these yields are typically higher. Corporate yield curves are often quoted in terms of a 'credit spread' over the relevant swap curve.

Yield curves are usually upward sloping so that longer maturities attract higher yields, with diminishing marginal increases. As Example 12.1 shows, the curve flattens out toward the right. There are two common explanations for upward sloping yield curves:

- The market is anticipating a rise in interest rates. If investors hold off investing now, they may receive a better rate in the future, so investors who are willing to lock their money in now need to be compensated for the opportunity cost of the anticipated rise in rates, resulting in the higher interest rate on long-term investments.
- Longer maturities entail greater risks for investors who demand a risk premium to compensate for the fact that at longer durations there is more uncertainty and a greater chance of a rise in inflation or an

extreme event that causes the value of the bond to fall. This effect is referred to as the liquidity spread. If the market expects more volatility in the future, the increase in the risk premium can cause an increasing yield, even if interest rates are expected to fall.

The actual shape of the yield curve is determined by:

- The liquidity premium.
- Expected inflation.
- Expected economic growth.
- Expected demand for bonds for each maturity – for example, if there is a large demand for long bonds, such as from pension funds to match their fixed liabilities to pensioners.
- Expected supply of bonds for each maturity. Shortages of supply can happen in times of economic stress, as firms shelve investment plans and so have less need to borrow, or when governments have balanced budgets and so do not need to borrow money to finance deficits.

Frequently seen yield curve shapes include:

- Normal.
- Steep.
- Flat.
- Humped.
- Inverted.

The normal yield curve

In normal economic conditions the yield curve slopes positively from left to right, reflecting investor expectations that the economy will grow in the future and, importantly, that inflation will rise rather than fall, and consequently that:

- Higher inflation will cause the central bank to tighten monetary policy by raising short-term interest rates to slow economic growth and dampen inflationary pressure.
- Higher inflation creates a need for a risk premium associated with the uncertainty about the future rate of inflation and the risk this poses to the future value of cash flows.

Investors price these risks into the yield curve by demanding higher yields for maturities further into the future. In a positively sloped yield curve, lenders profit from the passage of time since yields decrease as bonds get closer to maturity (as yield decreases, price increases); this is known as 'roll-down' and is a significant component of profit in fixed-income investing.

Steep yield curve

Steep yield curves are where the difference between long-maturity bonds and short-maturity bonds is unusually large.

Steep yield curves can herald an economic expansion, often following a recession. In this scenario the period of economic stagnation will have depressed short-term interest rates while growing economic activity stimulates latent demand for long-term capital to finance new investment.

Flat or humped yield curve

The yield curve may also be flat or hump-shaped, due to anticipated interest rates being steady, or short-term volatility outweighing long-term volatility.

A flat yield curve is when all maturities have similar yields, whereas a humped curve results when short-term and long-term yields are equal and medium-term yields are higher than those of the short-term and long-term. A flat curve sends signals of uncertainty in the economy.

Inverted yield curve

An inverted yield curve occurs when long-term yields fall below short-term yields. Under unusual circumstances, long-term investors will settle for lower yields now if:

- They think the economy will slow or even decline in the future, causing future interest rates to be lower than they are now. Inverted yield curves are widely thought to be good predictors of recessions.
- They believe inflation will remain low.
- They believe that deflation is possible, which would make current cash flows less valuable than future cash flows.
- They anticipate a flight to quality or a global economic or currency situation that leads to an increase in demand for bonds on the long end of the yield curve, causing long-term rates to fall. This effect can be strong enough to offset a positive risk premium.

Despite its record in presaging recessions, an inverted yield curve is not necessarily a precursor to an impending economic slowdown. For example, if short-term interest rates are already close to zero, then long-term rates cannot fall lower because nominal interest rates cannot be negative.

Explanations of yield curve shapes include the following:

Expectations hypothesis – this says that long-term interest rates reflect what short rates are expected to be at that time in the future, allowing for the provision that they normally should be a bit higher to compensate for the other uncertainties that increase over time, such as expected inflation. This hypothesis is sometimes helpful when long-term rates are lower than short rates: it says that short rates are expected to fall. For example, if investors have an expectation of what one-year interest rates will be in a year's time, the two-year interest rate can be calculated as the compounding of this year's interest rate by next year's interest rate.

Liquidity preference hypothesis – investors prefer to get their money back sooner, and so demand higher compensation for tying it up for long periods.

Preferred habitat hypothesis – in addition to interest rate expectations, investors have distinct investment horizons and require a meaningful premium to buy bonds with maturities outside their 'preferred' maturity, or habitat. Short-term investors dominate over short-term borrowers most of the time, so supply and demand causes longer-term rates to be higher than short-term rates, for the most part, but short-term rates can sometimes be higher than long-term rates.

Market segmentation hypothesis – this is similar to the preferred habitat hypothesis. It says that financial instruments of different terms are not substitutable. As a result, the supply and demand in the markets for short-term and long-term instruments are determined largely independently. Prospective investors decide in advance whether they need short-term or long-term instruments. If investors prefer their portfolio to be liquid, they will prefer short-term instruments to long-term instruments and higher prices and lower yields for longer-term instruments will result. Because the market segmentation theory says that the supply and demand of the two markets are independent, it fails to explain fully the observed fact that yields tend to move up and down together.

Yield curve modelling

The yield curve is actually only known with certainty for a few specific maturity dates, while the other maturities are calculated by interpolation. The curves must therefore be modelled either from prices available in the bond market or the money market.

- Yield curves built from the bond market use prices only from a specific class of bonds such as bonds issued by the government.
- Yield curves built from the money market use:
  - prices of 'cash' from today's LIBOR rates, which determine the 'short end' of the curve, that is for maturities of less than three months,
  - futures which determine the middle of the curve for maturities of longer than three months and less than 15 months,
  - interest rate swaps which determine the 'long end' comprising maturities of greater than one year.

A LIBOR curve is constructed using either LIBOR rates or swap rates and is the most widely used interest rate curve because it represents the credit worth of private entities at about A+ rating, roughly the equivalent of commercial banks. Substituting the LIBOR and swap rates with government bond yields gives the government curve, which is typically used in practice to approximate risk-free interest rates for a given currency for the purpose of pricing other investment instruments such as equities (think CAPM) and derivatives. The spread between the LIBOR or swap rate and the government bond yield, usually positive, means that private borrowers must pay a higher rate of interest than the government to borrow money for a similar term. It is therefore a measure of risk tolerance of the lenders or, put another way, it is the price of risk paid by the non-government borrower.

Practitioners use different techniques to solve different areas of the curve, for example:

- Some kind of sampling at the short end of the curve, where there are few cash flows from coupons.
- Regression can be used to find the curved line that minimizes the aggregate distance between it and observed bond yields at the long end of the curve.
- Cubic spline is a method that decomposes the observed yield curve to segments and then fits curves to each segment that vary only slightly from their neighbours to give a smooth overall curve.

Example 12.2 illustrates the relationship between a modelled yield curve and the individual bonds from which it is estimated. It shows how some bonds fit better than others.

Yield curve modelling is an inexact science, with the perfect solution often unobtainable in practice, necessitating a trade-off between:

- Market structure.
- Data integrity.

- Estimation accuracy.
- Computational efficiency.
- Cost effectiveness.

Example 12.2 A simple fitted yield curve

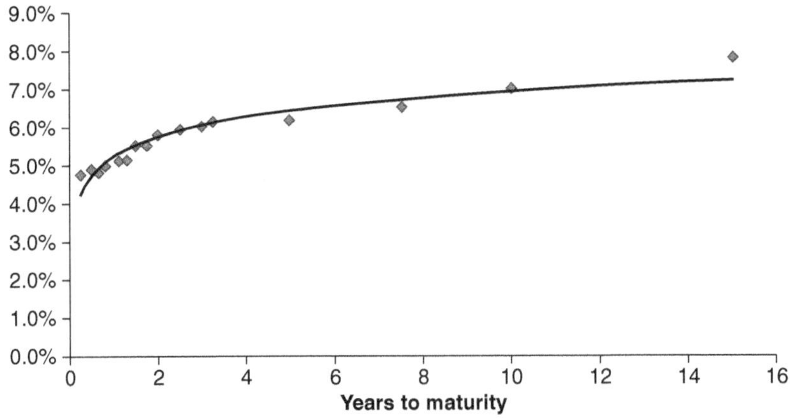

As illustrated in Example 12.2, the process of modelling a curve is an attempt to fill the gaps in the observed yield curve, and to sift through the 'noisy' data in maturities where market prices fluctuate around the 'fair price' according to short-term pressures of supply and demand. Yield curve modelling also tries to eliminate the reinvestment risk inherent in observed bond prices, by deriving what is known as the 'zero coupon curve'. A successful yield modelling exercise will have the following characteristics:

- It will fit the available data.
- It will not be too 'noisy'. That is, it will not have too many small bumps in it. These bumps are usually a symptom of 'over-fitting', and indicate that more smoothing is necessary.
- There should be consistency between the normal yield curve and the zero coupon curve. In other words, the prices of the two should not allow any arbitrage opportunities.

Panels

Panels are often used to estimate yields where information from actual transactions is not available. This entails asking a number of banks and brokers to quote prices for a range of bonds. The prices quoted are then averaged to derive a consensus price. This is better than nothing, but is prone to bias because the panel members usually know that they are not quoting for a real transaction, and so the price they give may not be one they would be prepared to deal at in any significant volume.

Reinvestment risk

Yields at which bonds are traded incorporate reinvestment risk because the bond settlement price assumes that all coupons will be reinvested at the bond's current yield to maturity. This of course is often not realistic because by the time coupons are paid or the bond matures interest rates are likely to have risen or fallen.

Pricing

The prices of all fixed interest instruments are calculated using some derivation of discounted cash flows. The differences in methodology are in compounding to reflect the timing of interest accruals and the timing of any cash flows from coupons.

Discount securities

The simplest interest rate instruments are discount securities, usually with maturity of less than a year, no coupon payments and interest therefore effectively paid at the end of the loan. Typically the investor pays and the borrower receives, at the start of the loan, the face value of the loan 'discounted' by the interest rate adjusted for the term of the loan. At the end of the loan, the borrower pays, and the investor receives, the face value.

Example 12.3 Discounting

The price of a simple one-year discount instrument is:

$$P = FV / (1 + i) \tag{12.1}$$

Where:

P = the price of the bond
FV = the face value of the bond
i = the interest rate on the bond

For a \$100 bond at 8 per cent interest, this is:

= \$100 / 1.08
= \$92.59 now.

In other words, \$92.59 invested for one year at 8 per cent will result in an investment worth \$100.00. Working backwards,

$$\begin{aligned} \$92.59 \text{ now} &= \$92.59 \times 1.08 \\ &= \$100 \text{ in a year's time} \end{aligned}$$

In practice, most interest payments are compounded at some specified interval such as daily. For example, 8 per cent is 0.0219 per cent (8 / 365). Compounded daily, the loan described in Example 12.3 would be as shown in Example 12.4.

Example 12.4 Compounding monthly over one year

$$P = FV / (1 + i / p)^{p} \qquad (12.2)$$

Where:

P = the number of interest payments per year

For a \$100 bond at 8 per cent interest, this is:

$$\begin{aligned} &= \$100 / (1 + 0.08/12)^{12} \\ &= \$92.34 \end{aligned}$$

The effective interest rate is 8.30 per cent, or $(1 + 0.08/12)^{12} - 1$.

Example 12.5 Compounding daily over more than one year

$$P = FV / (1 + i / p)^{p \times y} \qquad (12.3)$$

Where:

y = number of years

For a \$100 bond at 8 per cent interest over three years, this is:

$$\begin{aligned} &= \$100 / (1 + 0.08/365)^{365 \times 3} \\ &= \$78.73 \end{aligned}$$

When interest rates are used to help price other investment instruments, such as equities and derivatives, normal practice is to compound continuously.

Example 12.6 Continuous compounding

$$P = FV / (1 + e^{iy}) \qquad (12.4)$$

For a \$100 bond at 8 per cent interest over three years, this is:

$$= \$100 / (1 + e^{0.08 \times 1})$$
$$= \$78.66$$

Bonds with coupons

Most bonds issued for more than about one year have fixed nominal coupons paid at regular intervals, such as quarterly, semi-annually or annually. The formula for pricing a bond with fixed coupons is a special case of the familiar discounted cash flow (DCF) formula.

Example 12.7 Calculating the bond price

$$P = v^{(f/d)} (c(x + a_n) + 100v^n) \qquad (12.5)$$

Where:

P = the price per \$100 of the bond's face value
v = $1 / (1+ i)$
c = the periodic coupon payment per \$100 of the bond's face value
x = 0 if the bond is ex-interest, 1 if it is cum-interest
a_n = $(1 + v^n) / i$

For example, a bond with the following characteristics:

Settlement date	20 January 2021
Maturity date	30 September 2040
Next coupon	30 March 2021
Last coupon	30 September 2020
Coupon rate %pa	8.00%
Coupons per year:	2
Cum-interest	0
Yield to maturity %pa	8.35%

has a settlement price of \$99.10 per \$100 face value.

The settlement date is rarely the day on which the bond is transacted. By convention, settlement for bonds is 't + 2', in other words, two days after the deal is struck; and bonds are typically priced on this understanding. Should the buyer or the seller request later settlement, the settlement price of the bonds is adjusted using discounting to reflect the delayed settlement.

Ex-interest means that the next interest payment is not included in the price of the bond. By convention, there is an ex-interest period before any coupon payment. If the bond trades during this period, the original holder, not the purchaser receives the coupon.

Risk measurement

There are various measures of pure interest rate risk.

Portfolio value per basis point (PVBP) – also known as the Dollar value of 0.01 per cent (DV01), is the simplest measure of interest rate risk. As the name suggests, it measures the change in the portfolio's value if the interest rate changes by one basis point (0.01 per cent).

It is the difference between the settlement price of the bond at the current interest rate and the settlement price of the current rate plus 0.01 per cent.

Although this measure is useful for very small segments of the yield curve and for very small changes in the interest rate, it cannot be used for larger changes in interest rates because the PVBP alters according to the interest rate, as described in Example 12.8.

Example 12.8 Portfolio value per basis point for three bonds

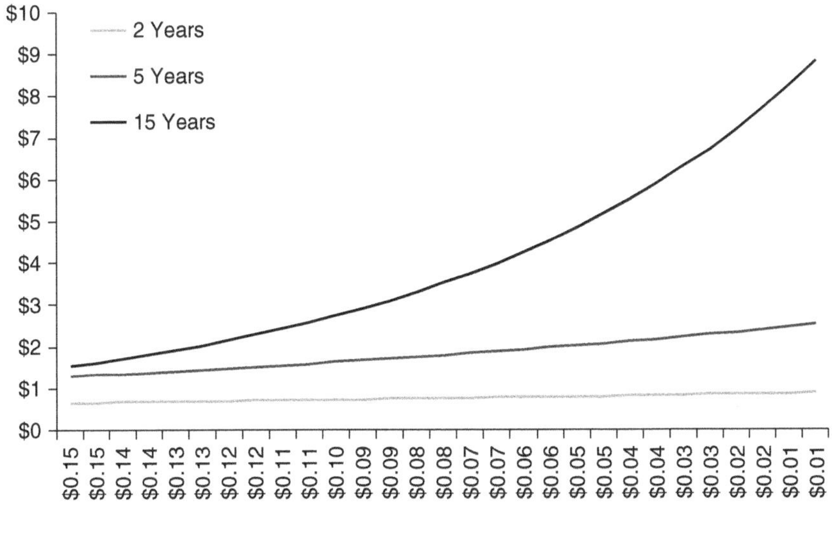

Maturity – the maturity of a bond is simply the time until it matures and the principal and any outstanding interest become due. The maturity of a portfolio is the weighted average of the maturity of the bonds in it. This of course tells you something about the portfolio because, other things being equal, long-maturity bonds are more sensitive to interest rate fluctuations than short bonds. But other things are usually not equal. Bond sensitivity to interest rate fluctuations is also affected by how much interest is outstanding and maturity says nothing about that: a five-year bond paying an annual coupon of 6 per cent is less sensitive to interest rate fluctuations than a five-year zero-coupon bond (which pays all interest at the end of its life), yet both have the same maturity.

Duration – this measures the weighted-average time until bond cash flows are paid. Because it gives information about both the maturity and the cash flow of a bond, it is the most commonly used bond descriptor. The duration of the portfolio is the weighted average of the duration of the bonds in it. Example 12.9 illustrates the price, PVBP and duration of different coupon rates for two otherwise identical bonds.

By providing useful comparisons between bonds and portfolios, duration can indicate which are more or less risky. A portfolio with a higher duration is more sensitive to an interest rate rise than a low or short duration portfolio.

Example 12.9 Duration for two bonds

	Bond 1	Bond 2
Face value	$100	$100
Settlement	20 January 2021	20 January 2021
Maturity	30 September 2040	18 June 2032
Coupon per annum	8.00%	5.75%
Coupons per year	2	2
Next coupon	30 March 2021	18 June 2021
Last coupon	30 September 2020	18 December 2020
Cum interest? (1=yes, 0=no)	1	1
Yield to maturity	8.50%	6.00%
Interest rate change	0.01%	0.01%
Bond price	$97.72	$98.47
Portfolio value per basis point per $million	$457.04	$403.59
Duration	4.6773	4.0986

Example 12.10 Convexity of two bonds

	Bond 1	Bond 2
Face value	$100	$100
Settlement	20 January 2021	20 January 2021
Maturity	30 September 2040	18 June 2032
Coupon per annum	8.00%	5.75%
Coupons per year	2	2
Next coupon	30 March 2021	18 June 2021
Last coupon	30 September 2020	18 December 2020
Cum interest? (1=yes, 0=no)	1	1
Yield to maturity	8.50%	6.00%
Interest rate change	0.01%	0.01%
Bond price	$97.72	$98.47
Portfolio value per basis point per $million	$457.04	$403.59
Modified duration	4.6773	4.0986
Convexity	0.3323	0.2091

Slope – this measures the sensitivity of the bond or portfolio to a change in the slope of the yield curve. The slope describes the difference in yields between bonds of increasing maturity.

Convexity – this measures the sensitivity of duration to fluctuations in the interest rate. The more convex the bond or portfolio, the more its value changes with bigger yield fluctuations (Example 12.10).

As the bond reaches maturity its value converges to its par, or face value. This effect is called the 'pull to par'.

Pull to par – there is a time dimension to the analysis of bond values. A ten-year bond at purchase becomes a nine-year bond a year later, the following year becomes an eight-year bond, and so on. Each year the bond moves incrementally closer to maturity, resulting in lower volatility and shorter duration and demanding a lower interest rate when the yield curve is positively sloped. Since falling rates create increasing prices, the value of a bond initially will rise as the lower rates of the shorter maturity become its new market rate. Because a bond is always anchored by its final maturity, the price at some point must change direction and fall to par value at redemption. Example 12.11 illustrates the pull to par effect for 8 per cent yield to maturity.

Example 12.11 Pull to par

	Annual coupon paid semi-annually		
Maturity in years	**6.00%**	**8.00%**	**10.00%**
20	80.21	100.00	119.79
15	82.71	100.00	117.29
10	86.41	100.00	113.59
8	88.35	100.00	111.65
5	91.89	100.00	108.11
3	94.76	100.00	105.24
2	96.37	100.00	103.63
1	98.11	100.00	101.89
0	100.00	100.00	100.00

Portfolio construction

Selection of fixed interest portfolios tends to be inherently top-down, in that the investment manager first decides the portfolio level profile with respect to its exposure to:

- A rise or fall in the general level of interest rates affecting all markets and levels of credit quality equally, also known as a 'parallel shift'.
- A change in the shape or slope of the yield curve.
- Changes in yield curve spreads.
- Changes in inflation.

This provides the starting position from which instruments can be selected to reflect the investment manager's views; for example, by over-weighting long maturity bonds to benefit from anticipated flattening in the yield curve.

The yearly 'total return' from the bond is the sum of:

- The bond's coupon.
- The capital gain from the changing valuation as it slides down the yield curve.
- Any capital gain or loss from changing interest rates at that point in the yield curve.

This implicitly assumes that inflation remains unchanged. An increase in inflation has the effect of reducing the real value of the bond's principle as well as of future coupon payments.

Aligning sources of risk and return is therefore a matter of ensuring that larger exposures, in terms of likely active return and risk, reflect the investment manager's confidence in each view – and that the views are as independent of each other as possible.

The difference between a portfolio's weighting and its exposure to any strategy is determined primarily by the duration. The duration of the portfolio or any group of assets within the portfolio is the weighted sum of the duration of the bonds that comprise it.

Investors such as pension funds and annuity funds often have liabilities linked to inflation, which they seek to hedge with inflation-linked bonds.

Inflation linked bonds

Inflation linked bonds, also known as inflation-indexed bonds, are bonds where the principal is linked to a defined index of inflation. They are thus designed to cut out the inflation risk of an investment.

The bonds pay a periodic coupon that is equal to the product of the inflation index and the nominal coupon rate. For some bonds the coupon is also adjusted for inflation. A rise in coupon payments is a result of an increase in the inflation index.

For example, if the annual coupon of the bond is 5 per cent and the underlying principal of the bond is $100, the annual coupon payment is $5. If the inflation increases by 10 per cent, the principal of the bond increases to $110. The coupon rate remains at 5 per cent, resulting in an interest payment of $110 times 5 per cent, which is $5.50.

The real yield of any bond is its annualized growth rate, less the rate of inflation over the same period. This calculation is often difficult in the case of a nominal bond, because the yields of such a bond are specified for future periods in nominal terms, while the inflation over the period is an unknown rate at the time of the calculation. However when index linked bond yields are specified as a margin over inflation, the real yield can be easily calculated using a standard bond calculation formula.

Asset-liability management

Managers of defined benefit pension funds usually set their investment objectives to meet the known and expected liabilities of their fund. A starting point for this process is to define the fund's liabilities in terms of bonds, in other words, a stream of future cash flows, possibly including lump-sum payments.

The fixed interest portfolio can then be constructed so that its profile matches the aggregate projected 'bond' given by the liability profile.

Any surplus can then be invested relatively aggressively to maximize the potential for active returns.

If the liability horizon is relatively distant, there can be a case for exposing a higher proportion of the fund to higher-growth assets in order to further improve returns.

Implementation

Unlike most equities, physical bonds usually are not traded on a central exchange, but on a bi-lateral basis between investors and brokers. Traditionally this has been done over the telephone, although screen based services are also available in some markets.

Important features of bond markets are:

- There is no exchange standing between buyer and seller, which means that markets often lack transparency. Most big bond investors and intermediaries publish some traded prices, but these are generally indicative only and so are not necessarily a representation of prices at which deals are or could have been struck.
- Commissions are not levied directly, but are implicit in the bid ask spread of the bond.
- The lack of an exchange means that investors need not transact through an intermediary. In fact in many markets, the bulk of wholesale fixed interest is transacted directly between investors.
- When transacting directly with the other party, the investor is taking it on faith that that party is able to honour the purchase or sale of the bond. Normally this is not a problem. If bank XYZ has just confirmed the sale of $10 million of US Treasuries, the investor assumes that they actually have these securities on hand to deliver. But since settlement is usually one or two days after the transaction is confirmed, there is ample time for XYZ bank to discover a rogue trader in its ranks and go bust. The investor won't have paid for the bonds yet, so the implications may not be dire. But another source of US Treasuries would be required, which might be tricky to find in a market where a major bank has just defaulted. Similarly, XYZ bank has taken it on trust that you have the means to pay for the bonds. The risk that settlement obligations will not be honoured is the counter-party risk, which is discussed in Chapter 13 on credit portfolios.
- Most fixed interest traders and investors try to control their counterparty risk by placing absolute, Dollar value limits on open exposures to each issuer, investor and intermediary with whom they deal regularly.

Markets for domestic government bonds are typically deep in developed countries, so shortages of supply are rare. They can happen; for example, if the government budget is in balance, the government may have no need to issue new bonds and may even repurchase bonds it has already issued. From a pure macro-economic and political point of view, this is usually considered a good thing because it drives down borrowing costs for private investors, potentially stimulating new investment and therefore employment.

It is not necessarily a good thing from the perspective of investment markets for two reasons. The first is because investment returns are driven down, making it harder for pension funds and savers to achieve their investment objectives. The second is that it can pose problems for asset pricing because the 'risk-free' asset used ubiquitously in asset pricing, effectively becomes unobservable.

Conversely, shortages of investors in government securities can occur for a number of reasons. Governments often try to ensure demand for their bonds by obliging certain categories of regulated investors such as banks and insurance companies to hold defined quotas of government securities.

Use of derivatives

The global market for interest rate derivatives is by some measures of staggering dimensions. Often the numbers quoted overstate the real position because they confound gross and net exposures.

Effective exposure

From the perspective of risk calculations, exposure achieved through derivatives should, as a rule, be calculated in the same way as the underlying physical instrument, which means applying the appropriate pricing formula to the terms of the notional bond or combination of bonds, described by the futures or swap contract, and adjusting for the delta if options are included. This allows the derivative exposure to be counted in the same portfolio-level calculation of durations, convexity and so on.

A common practice for swaps is instead to use the outstanding margin value of the position. This in effect is a measure of the unrealized profit or loss on the position. It is of course important to the portfolio's estimation of counterparty risk; but counterparty risk does not contribute to the portfolio's active return. Portfolio active return is achieved through exposure to interest rate fluctuations. This measure of swap exposure, gives no information about the contribution to the portfolio return of interest rate exposures, which is the main objective of a fixed interest portfolio. It can also give misleading information when used to report derivatives exposure for the purpose of risk governance.

Even correcting for the confusion about how to measure and report an open position in an interest rate derivative, the size of the global market is remarkable. The main reason for the growth of interest rate derivatives usage (which started in the early 1980s) is their practical usefulness.

The main uses of derivatives in fixed interest portfolios are for:

- Liquidity management.
- Hedging.
- Arbitrage.

Liquidity management – this is the simplest use of derivatives. As coupon income accumulates, for example, and other cash flows in and out of the portfolio, futures contracts can be used to ensure that the portfolio is fully invested but is not geared.

Hedging – this can reduce exposure to particular segments of the yield curve without trading physical instruments. This could be to compensate for a temporary drying up of the supply of physical bonds in a particular segment of the yield curve or because the investment manager anticipates that conditions will change soon and therefore seeks only a temporary change in the portfolio's positioning.

Arbitrage – in equilibrium, the yield on a five-year bond should be equal to the yield on a four-year bond compounded by the yield on a one-year bond in four years' time. If it is not, then an arbitrage opportunity exists, at least in theory. This can be exploited with a combination of bought and sold positions in the relevant physical futures (if available) and swaps.

Summary

Investors hold bonds mainly to provide a low volatility 'cushion' to complement exposure to riskier equity asset classes, but also as a source of active return, to satisfy regulatory requirements and as collateral for derivatives positions.

Central to positioning a fixed interest portfolio is to understand the current state of the relevant yield curves, which give information about expectations regarding future economic conditions. All active positions in fixed interest embed a view about future interest rates or interest rate differentials, or spreads.

For any given interest rate, instrument and portfolio sensitivities can be calculated using the appropriate variant of discounted cash flows. From these, risk exposures are easily derived arithmetically.

Portfolio construction for fixed interest portfolios, being essentially top-down, lends itself naturally to aligning sources of risk with sources of return, so is almost by definition a risk-based process.

Case Study

An expensive lesson was learned by a bond trader who thought he had spotted an arbitrage opportunity.

Example 12.12 Put-call parity in terms of yield

Face value of contract	$100 000	
Maturity in years	10	
Coupon per annum	10%	
Coupons per year	2	
Interest rate change	0.01%	
	Yield	Futures price
Current futures price	11.00%	89.00
Exercise price of call option	6.00%	94.00
Call option premium	1.50%	1.50
Exercise price of put option	6.00%	94.00
Put option premium	5.80%	5.80
Strategy		
Buy futures		0
Sell call		1.50
Buy put		-5.80
Exercise call		0
Exercise put		5.00
Outcome		0.70

Put-call parity theory tells us that the net premium for a bought call and a sold put option on the same underlying instrument for the same settlement date and exercise price is equal to the difference between the current asset price and the exercise price of the option. In this case, –4.30 per cent (–5.80 + 1.50) and 5.00 (11.00 – 6.00), giving a 'risk free' outcome of 0.7 per cent, as shown in Example 12.12.

This appears to be a no-risk transaction. The settlement price for an option premium however is calculated by multiplying the Dollar value for one basis point (DV01) by the quoted value of the option. Applying the settlement price can change the attractiveness of the transaction.

Example 12.13 Put-call parity in terms of settlement value

	Yield	Futures price	DV01	Settlement value
Current futures price	11.00%	89.00	$24.82	$59 786.19
Exercise price of call option	6.00%	94.00	$34.44	$74 442.74
Call option premium	1.50%	1.50	$34.44	$5 166.18
Exercise price of put option	6.00%	94.00	$34.44	$74 442.74
Put option premium	5.80%	5.80	$34.44	$19 975.88
Strategy				
Sell call		1.50		$5 166.18
Buy put		–5.80		–$19 975.88
Exercise call				$0.00
Exercise put		5.00		$14 656.56
Outcome		0.70		–$153.15

What appeared to be a riskless profit of 0.70 per cent per contract, turns out to lose $153.15 per $100,000 of bond face value instead, as Example 12.13 shows.

13
Credit Portfolios

Credit portfolios invest in corporate and sovereign bonds, which are bonds issued by corporations, usually for a term of more than a year.

The issuer of a corporate bond retains full title to its assets and their future growth in value so long as the terms of the bond, including timely payment of interest and capital, are honoured. The investor in a corporate bond earns no more than the interest on the bond, so shares none of the growth prospects of the issuer. By contrast, if the issuer is unable to honour the terms of the bond, the investor risks losing all or part of the investment.

This chapter discusses the characteristics of credit portfolios that distinguish them from portfolios of bonds issued by governments and banks, including:

- The rationale for issuing and investing in credit instruments.
- Who issues credit instruments?
- Terms and conditions that often apply to credit instruments.
- A description of structured debt instruments.
- A note on credit quality.
- What usually happens when an issuer defaults?
- Pricing individual securities.
- Risk measurement and construction of credit portfolios.
- A note on model complexity.
- Some hedging strategies for credit portfolios.
- Some observations on counterparty risk.

Rationale

There are two main ways for a company to raise debt capital to finance its operations:

- Borrow from a bank.
- Issue bonds directly on the market.

Large corporations seeking to raise a significant amount of capital usually choose the latter because it allows them to tap a larger pool of investment funds, which is more likely to meet their requirements.

Corporate bonds can be listed on major exchanges but most trading in developed markets takes place in decentralized, dealer-based, over-the-counter markets.

Pension and trust funds invest in corporate and sovereign bonds mainly to benefit from the higher income they offer over government bonds and bank debt. Hedge funds invest in the bonds of distressed companies to benefit from capital growth that the bonds deliver if the company issuing the bonds recovers and the price of the bonds increases.

Issuers

In addition to corporate bonds, credit portfolios include bonds issued by:

- Special purpose entities.
- Governments.
- Non-profit organizations.

Terms and conditions

A corporate bond is defined principally by its:

- Issuer.
- Time to maturity.
- Coupon rate.
- Currency of issue.

Other parameters that distinguish a bond include:

- Seniority.
- Call provisions.
- Covenants.
- Credit rating.

Seniority

The bond's seniority defines its position within the issuer's capital structure and therefore the order in which investors in the bond are paid or compensated in the event of a default or partial default by the issuer. Senior debt holders recover their money before other bond-holders and equity holders, but usually after any tax or other liabilities due to the government and usually after wage and salary-earning employees of the company have been paid.

Junior, or subordinate, debts holders recover after senior debt holders, government and employees but before trade creditors and equity holders.

Call provisions

Some corporate bonds have an embedded call option that allows the issuer to redeem the bond on specific dates or according to specified conditions before its maturity date.

Other provisions can include the right of the investor to demand full repayment of the bond in the event that the issuer's financial position changes materially, as defined by say its debt-to-equity ratio, its interest coverage ratio or its credit rating.

Covenants

Issuers sometimes seek to enhance the marketability of their bonds by including other conditions or restrictions; or are obliged to provide the lender with reassurance that the debt will be honoured by adhering to covenants, such as:

- That the company periodically reports its financial condition.
- That it refrains from paying dividends, repurchasing shares, borrowing further or other voluntary actions that alter the company's capital structure or might have an adverse effect on its financial position.

Credit rating

Issuers often seek to support the attractiveness of their bonds by obtaining a credit rating from a credit rating agency. The credit rating ideally is an independent assessment, resulting from detailed fundamental analysis, of the issuer and or the bonds, of the likelihood that the bond will be honoured.

The credit rating takes the form of a discrete 'score' reflecting the assessed quality of a security, or the issuer of a debt security, ranging from high quality and therefore low risk, indicated by a rating of AAA or Aaa, through to very risky or vulnerable to default, corresponding to a rating of C.

Investors use credit ratings to help decide how volatile the bond price is likely to be and to estimate a fair value of the interest rate spread and therefore which yield curve, relative to the government or LIBOR curve, is most relevant for the purpose of deriving a fair price for the bond.

Structured debt instruments

Structured debt can be:

- A collection of bonds of different credit quality issued by a single entity.
- A collection of obligations of similar credit quality issued by different entities.

Single issuer structured debt instruments

Structured debt can be attractive to firms wishing to raise large amounts of capital in the debt markets. Unlike a normal bond, where the borrower pays a single interest rate on the entire principal of the bond, structured financial transactions are in effect either a series of bonds with different conditions, or a suite of small loans with similar conditions packaged into a series of 'tranches'. Each tranche is ascribed its own credit rating on the strength of its constituent bonds.

By dividing the total debt into tranches with different levels of credit quality, the issuer can achieve a lower overall cost of borrowing even if the lowest of the tranches pay higher interest rates than the firm's average cost of borrowing. Ratings agencies are often consulted on what composition of each tranche would result in a desired rating, and therefore interest rate.

Multiple issuer structured debt instruments

Another type of structured transaction entails bundling many small loans into securitized instruments for re-sale on the secondary market as a collateralized debt obligation (CDO). Rating agencies are often consulted on the composition of these assets in order to achieve the most favourable rating and therefore the highest price in the market.

CDOs can entail the bundling of hundreds or thousands of similar, and similarly rated, securities – for example, credit card receivables or student loans – into a single investment instrument. While the probability of technical default can indeed be low, the concentration of similar risks can be such that even a slight change in the probability of default can cause significant volatility in the price of the bundled security. This means that, even though the original opinion is accurate that the chance of default of the structured product is very low, a slight change in the market's perception of the risk of that product can cause the price of a highly rated security to collapse without there being any default or significant chance of default. This undermines the assumption that high ratings correspond to low volatility and high liquidity.

CDOs that are assigned an AAA rating can in fact comprise bonds of much lower quality. Indeed the appeal of the CDO is that its rating is not wholly dependent on the quality of the underlying bonds, but of the CDO itself. CDOs are usually paid out in a 'waterfall' style fashion, where income received gets paid out first to the most senior tranches, with the remaining income flowing down to the lower quality tranches.

Credit quality

Credit quality is defined either by the credit rating of the bond, provided by a credit rating agency or given by its credit spread. Credit spreads are determined by the market's assessment of the risk of the bond, taking into account:

- The riskiness of the company's business.
- Its financial position, as indicated by its debt to equity, interest coverage and so on.
- The seniority of the bond.
- Call provisions of the bond.
- The bond's covenants.
- Supply and demand.

Credit ratings agencies

A credit rating agency is a company that assigns credit ratings for:

- Bonds.
- Other debt instruments, including structured investments, which can comprise multiple tranches by a single issuer or a basket of broadly similar debt obligations from many different issuers.
- Issuers of debt instruments.

Credit ratings are used by:

- Investors.
- Issuers.
- Investment banks.
- Broker-dealers.
- Governments.

Ratings use by bond issuers

Issuers rely on credit ratings as a theoretically independent verification of their own credit-worthiness and the value of the instruments they issue. Bond issues that are not rated by a recognized agency risk being undersubscribed or attracting a lower price, and consequently higher effective borrowing costs, to the issuer or of raising less capital than was sought.

Issuers also use credit ratings in structured finance transactions. For example, a company with a very high credit rating wishing to undertake a particularly risky research project can create a legally separate entity with its own assets, known as a special purpose entity (SPE), which issues bonds in its own name. Being separate from the parent company, the SPE attracts its own credit rating, which, because the particular project is riskier than the parent's other operations, is lower than that of the parent, effectively quarantining the risky project from the parent, and so preserving its higher rating.

Conversely, a company with a low credit rating can borrow on better terms by forming an SPE, transferring significant assets to that subsidiary and issuing secured debt securities. Investors have recourse to the assets owned by the SPE in the event of default, so its cost of borrowing is lower than that of the parent company.

The same issuer can have different credit ratings for different bonds according to:

- The structure, terms and conditions and any covenants of each bond.
- Whether and how each bond is secured.
- How senior or subordinate each bond is to other debt issued by the same issuer.

Credit ratings agencies can usually advise an issuer on how to structure its bond offerings and SPEs so as to achieve the desired credit rating and therefore cost of borrowing. This can create a conflict of interest if it implies any obligation, direct or indirect, on the part of either the agency or the issuer. For this reason some agencies maintain a policy of not rating issues on which they have previously advised.

Under both Basel II and Securities and Exchange Commission (SEC) regulations, issuers of bonds must choose a rating agency that is:

- Objective.
- Independent.
- Transparent.

The purpose of this is to avoid moral hazard that might result from bond issuers choosing agencies that are likely to give them the most favourable ratings for their debt.

In the USA bond issuers can choose their own rating agency, which is then scrutinized by the SEC, which determines whether ratings from that particular ratings agency are widely used and considered 'reliable and credible'.

Ratings use by government regulators

Government regulators often demand that bonds be rated for the purposes of estimating the capital adequacy of a bank or other regulated financial institution that invests in them. The reasoning is that, the riskier the bond, the more capital should be set aside to guard against the possibility that its price will collapse. Rather than accept the bond holders' own estimations of the riskiness of their bond portfolios, regulators seek an 'independent' estimation of the risk. For example, under Basel II, an AAA rated securitized asset requires capital allocation of 0.6 per cent, a BBB requires 4.8 per cent, a BB requires 34 per cent, whilst a BB(-) securitized asset requires a 52 per cent allocation.

This assumes that the risk of portfolios of risky bonds is equal to the sum of the risks of the bonds in them. It therefore ignores diversification effects and concentrations of risk in different types of bond issuer, currency and other common factors, at the portfolio level.

Credit rating agency business models

Most credit rating agencies follow one of two business models.

The first is described as '**subscriber-based**', where the agency provides the ratings to subscribers to its publications, and subscription fees represent the main source of revenue for the agency. Smaller agencies tend to use this business model. It has the advantage that it is not subject to potential conflicts of interest. Its disadvantage is that few investors may be willing to pay for ratings on any but the very largest bond issues and issuers, so the universe of assets covered can be limited and the ratings that are provided are not widely available to investors.

The second is the '**issuer-pays**' business model, in which most of the agency's revenue is from fees paid by the issuers themselves and most ratings are provided to the public free of charge. The advantage is that it encourages most issuers to seek ratings, making more information available to prospective investors. The disadvantage is that it embeds a clear conflict of interest.

Wikirating is a third model based on collaboration between investors. The online community credit rating platform aims to provide a transparent, freely available source of credit rating information for a broad range of bonds, reviewed by a worldwide community and free of conflicts of interest.

Benefits of credit ratings

The benefit to investors of independent and well-researched bond credit ratings is that they gain cost effective access to a wide pool of investment instruments. Even the largest institutional investors have finite research resources and so are unlikely to be in a position to evaluate as large a universe of bonds as can be covered collectively by commercial ratings agencies.

This in turn increases the total effective supply of risk capital in the economy, leading to greater liquidity, higher capital formation and stronger economic growth. It also opens the capital markets to categories of borrower who otherwise would not have access to the research, allowing them to invest efficiently in corporate bonds.

The collective efforts of ratings agencies thus provide some of the services that the investment research departments of large stock-brokers and investment banks provide to investors in the equities markets.

Observations on credit ratings

Because they are discrete scores, credit ratings can be subject to a time lag between the market's assessment of a change in the riskiness of a bond and the adjustment of its rating.

The lowering of a credit score by a rating agency can create a vicious cycle and be a self-fulfilling prophecy. Not only can interest rates for that company increase, but other contracts with financial institutions may be affected adversely, causing an increase in the issuer's cost of borrowing and consequent deterioration in its credit worthiness.

In some cases, a large loan to a company contains a clause that makes the loan due in full if the company's credit rating is lowered beyond a certain point, usually to a 'speculative' or 'junk bond' rating. The purpose of these 'ratings triggers' is to ensure that the lender is able to lay claim to a weak company's assets before the company declares bankruptcy and a receiver is appointed to divide up the claims against the company. The effect of such ratings triggers can however be disproportionate because, once the company's debt is downgraded by a ratings agency and the company's loans become due in full, a 'death spiral' can result, whereby a company that is experiencing temporary liquidity problems can be forced into bankruptcy despite being otherwise solvent.

Investment mandates often specify limits on portfolio exposure or allocation to non-investment grade bonds, and sometimes embargo them altogether. This means that a small change in the profile of a bond can trigger a sell-off as investment managers, all subject to similar mandate restrictions, are forced to shed the assets, exaggerating the bond's volatility and adversely affecting portfolio performance.

Because the rating agency business is reputation-based, and the finance industry pays little attention to a rating that is not widely recognized, the business is subject to high barriers to entry and therefore limited competition and diminished incentives to innovate.

Most rating agencies do not draw a distinction between a rating of AAA on structured finance and AAA on corporate or government bonds, although they do typically specify the type of instrument. For example, a CDO with an AAA rating is generally understood to be in the same class as US government bonds. Because the structure of the Basel II agreements causes CDO capital requirements to increase 'exponentially' with ratings downgrades, CDO portfolios can be particularly vulnerable to multiple downgrades, essentially precipitating large margin calls. For a number of reasons, often having to do with inadequate resources and the complexity of CDO structures, many institutional investors rely solely on the ratings agencies rather than conducting their own analysis of the risks these instruments pose, so magnifying the effects of a change in rating.

Credit ratings issued by the main three credit rating agencies are strictly snapshots or 'point in time' opinions of the quality of any debt instrument. This means that no guarantee is attached to the likely volatility of the bond, and its effective quality can change with any alteration in the financial position of the issuer or of the constituent bonds of the security in the case of a structured transaction.

Ratings arbitrage

Structured transactions that entail rating agencies being consulted on the composition that would result in the most favourable rating, and therefore the highest price in the market, can provoke issuers to 'shop around' for the best ratings for their CDOs or to add and remove loans of various quality until they meet the minimum standards for a desired rating.

Because regulatory capital requirements are often linked to assets' credit ratings, regulated financial institutions have an incentive to hold the riskiest assets within a ratings band in order to achieve the highest return for a given capital allocation. Because the structure of the Basel II agreements causes CDO capital requirements to increase 'exponentially' with ratings downgrades, CDO portfolios can be particularly vulnerable to multiple downgrades.

Market-sourced alternatives to credit ratings

Market-sourced alternatives include:

- Average credit yield spread over a comparable credit-risk-free bond, such as a domestic government bond or LBOR curve.
- Option-adjusted spread, which uses option modelling to estimate the yield spread that explains the difference in price between a corporate bond and a comparable credit-risk-free bond.

One limitation of market-sourced measures of credit risk is that they depend on a transparent and liquid market in securities linked to the bond in question, so cannot always be easily applied to all bonds.

Default

Default occurs when the issuer of a bond cannot or will not honour the terms of the bond. This happens when a corporate issuer is illiquid or insolvent, or when a sovereign issuer has insufficient foreign currency reserves to meet interest payments or is unable to raise new debt in the capital markets in order to retire maturing debt.

Default by a corporate issuer

Corporate default can result in one of the following:

- The bankruptcy of the organization.
- Sale of the firm to another entity, often a competitor, who assumes responsibility for the outstanding debt.

In the event of bankruptcy, the assets of the company are liquidated, usually by a court appointed receiver or administrator, who then distributes the proceeds to the firm's creditors according to the seniority of their claims, which is usually in order of: government, employees, senior debt holders, subordinate debt holders and trade creditors. Equity holders, who are at the end of the queue, typically receive nothing after a bankruptcy.

It is unusual for a company to have no saleable assets at the time of bankruptcy, so bond holders usually recover some of their investments.

The percentage they receive of the value of the outstanding bond is called the recovery rate. If they believe that the firm has a future as a going concern – for example, if the bankruptcy is the result of illiquidity rather than insolvency – they may accept equity in lieu of a low percentage recovery of their investments.

The terms of some bonds stipulate that all holders of each level of debt seniority should be treated equally, which means that, if one bond holder declines early offers of partial settlement or of equity and subsequently is paid a higher proportion of his outstanding investment, then other investors in the same level of debt seniority are entitled to reimbursement at the same rate, even if they had already accepted a lower settlement.

Default by a sovereign issuer

Sovereign debt can be issued either in the currency of the issuer or in another currency, such as a reserve currency.

Sovereign bonds issued in the currency of the issuer are much less likely to default because the government can simply print more of its own money, keep paying interest and avoid a technical default. This is not without costs however:

- The value of the bonds fall in terms of investors' currencies, imposing losses on the investors.
- The sovereign's credibility in international capital markets can suffer, making it more expensive to borrow in the future.
- Currency devaluation causes higher inflation and therefore potential damage to the sovereign's home economy.

Default on sovereign bonds issued in a currency other than that of the sovereign, or where, for some reason the government is unable to devalue, usually results from a shortage of foreign currency reserves, in turn often the result of imbalances or distress in the local economy.

Unlike companies, countries cannot be wound up: so a way must be found to keep them going. The response of creditors is usually one of the following:

- Seek a consortium of lenders, possibly led by the International Monetary Fund (IMF) to restructure the debt, usually meaning to repay it from the proceeds of newly issued bonds.
- Accept partial settlement from available reserves.
- Seek a higher level of recovery through asset sales.
- Forgive the debt.

Debt restructure usually is tied to conditions by which the government agrees to some package of economic reforms. These can in turn harm the political standing of the government at home, possibly to the extent of causing political unrest, with attendant costs and risks to any economic recovery.

Credit default swaps

Credit default swaps (CDS) are over-the-counter derivatives instruments linked to the default on a debt instrument. They are used by holders of credit instruments who seek to protect against the effects of a default on the debt. For this protection they pay a premium, akin to the premium paid on an option.

Sellers of protection receive the premium in the same way that the seller of an option does. CDS are characterized by the definition of what comprises a default on the debt, and therefore under what circumstances it pays out.

The importance of CDS in financial markets is that they provide a mechanism for discovering the price of default risk that is determined dynamically through forces of supply and demand.

A crucial consideration when structuring any over-the-counter derivative transaction, such as a CDS, is that both parties agree to settle the derivative against valuations that are derived independently by a third party. For most over-the-counter derivatives, valuations for settlement purposes are computed using a defined formula and parameters derived from observable market prices, such as LIBOR or an equity index price. This is not always the case for CDS because they are settled against a corporate or sovereign bond or a basket of corporate and/or sovereign bonds. The absence of an observable price can make independent valuation tricky and some investment managers settle for the short cut of accepting the intermediary's valuation. This can introduce a serious conflict of interest, especially if the intermediary is also the counterparty to the transaction, and therefore has an interest in biasing the valuation. A number of commercial providers of independent prices for this kind of over-the-counter transaction can obviate the problem.

Most CDS agreements are International Swaps and Derivatives Association (ISDA), and therefore over-the-counter, agreements that link bonds to a specified yield curve, but otherwise the agreements tend to be tailored to the demands of the two parties to the agreement. This means that they are not standardized with respect to the face value of the swap, the term, coupon or a common definition of an event that would be recognized as a default and therefore trigger a payout – although in practice many CDS share similar definitions. Tailoring of swap agreements is one of the advantages over futures agreements, which are standardized.

The natural consequence of bespoke, over-the-counter transactions is that they are opaque to the outside world and there is no central counterparty, so it is hard for supervisors to keep track of outstanding exposures as they can with the conventional banking system. This can become a problem when outstanding exposures become very large, with the consequent possibility of systemic risk.

Pricing individual securities

Most corporate bonds are priced using an application of the model proposed by Robert Merton, which says that a corporate bond consists of a normal bond, plus a put option on the equity of the issuing company. This reflects the fact that, in the event of default on the bond, the investor can find him- or herself holding the firm's equity.

This framework allows the value of the bond to be thought of as comprising:

- The current market yield or spread of the bond.
- A forecast of the future spread.
- An estimate of the likelihood of the bond being re-rated up or down.
- An estimate of the likelihood of default.
- An estimate of the recovery rate in the event of a default.
- The effects of any other call provisions or covenants of the bond.
- The volatility of the underlying equity.

The Merton model assumes that there exists a listed equity instrument for the bond's issuer. For most large bond issuers this is the case. For bonds without an associated equity instrument, investment managers choose as a proxy a listed company or the average of a basket of listed equities with a similar business mix and profile to the issuer of the bond.

Other considerations when pricing a bond include:

- Expected changes in the general level of interest rates, or parallel shift.
- Inflation, which reduces the real value of future fixed cash flows. An anticipation of inflation, or higher inflation, may depress prices immediately.
- The bond's liquidity and the risk that there may not be a continuous secondary market for the bond, whereby the investor could have difficulty selling it at, or even near to, a fair price.

- Supply of the bond, whereby heavy issuance of new, similar bonds may depress their prices.
- Expected changes in the tax code that can affect the value of the bond to investors and consequently its market value.

Taking account of all determinants of the price of a credit instrument can necessitate building a detailed model of the issuer and, from that, estimating the instrument's fair price. Simulation is frequently used to derive a range of fair prices under different assumptions and market conditions.

Modelling default risk for companies

There is no generally accepted standard for measuring the likelihood of default and the likely recovery rate. One widely used method is the Z Score method, developed by Ed Altman of New York University in the 1970s, who identified cross-sectional statistical relationships between balance sheet information and imminent failure of companies. From this work he quantified the predictive value of various financial ratios of bond defaults.

The limitation is its dependence on reliable and timely balance sheet information. Altman worked with US bonds, where the necessary information tends to be easily available, timely and of good quality. The USA also happens to be the biggest market for corporate debt. The Z Score is harder to apply in many other markets, where data are often less granular and less timely.

Modelling default risk for sovereign issuers

From the purely economic point of view, some macro-economic variables that affect the probability of sovereign debt rescheduling are:

- Debt service ratio.
- Import ratio.
- Investment ratio.
- Variance of export revenue.
- Domestic money supply growth.
- Currency of issue.
- Currency management policy; for example, floating or pegged.

Estimating the probability of default by a sovereign issuer is complicated by the effects of political risk, which is hard to model and therefore quantify.

Political risk is both internal to the country and external to it.

- Political risk from inside the country includes the policy orientation of the government, for example whether it is populist or technical, how its central bank is managed – for example, how independent it is and what targets it aims for – and the stage the country is at with respect to its electoral cycle, if there is one.
- For example, a populist government in conditions of economic stress may see default on foreign-owned bonds as a practical and popular expedient to easing internal imbalances.
- Political risk from outside the country is to do with who owns how much of the bonds on issue and who holds exposure through derivatives linked to the bonds. This can determine whether there would be flow-on effects to other economies, for example, through the international banking system.
- If the consequences of default by a sovereign issuer are considered a systemic danger to the international economy, then the likelihood of a bail-out by an international consortium is greatly increased with the result that default will be avoided. Building this into a default prediction model is not straight-forward.

Distressed debt

Distressed debt is seen by some investors as an opportunity. By buying the bonds of companies in or near default at a fraction of their face value, profits can be earned if the issuer's health recovers and the prices of the bonds increase significantly.

Distressed debt in this way behaves somewhat like an equity investment because the distribution of potential returns is nearly symmetrical. Portfolio-level risk for portfolios consisting only of distressed bonds can be reduced using the same diversification methods used for portfolios of equities.

Risk measurement and portfolio construction

Estimating the risk of a portfolio of corporate and sovereign bonds necessitates first modelling the return distribution of each bond, then aggregating them and modelling interaction effects.

Portfolio-level risk can be thought of as deriving from portfolio-wide effects, bond-specific effects and interactions effects. Portfolio-wide risks include:

- A rise in the general level of interest rates, known as a 'parallel shift' of interest rates.

- Inflation, which reduces the real value of future fixed cash flows and can depress prices immediately.
- Currency devaluations, which depress the price of bonds denominated in the relevant currency.
- Widening of the interest rate spread between government and corporate bonds.

Portfolio-level risk that derives from individual bonds includes:

- Widening of the interest rate spread of the credit yield curve to which the bond is aligned.
- Re-rating of the bond to a lower yield curve caused by increased market estimates of its riskiness.
- Liquidity risk that can cause the bond to be difficult to sell at its fair price.
- Default on the bond.
- Changes in taxation that can adversely impact the value to investors and consequently its market value.

Interaction effects can be between:

- Individual bonds and portfolio-wide effects; for example, the likelihood of any issuer defaulting on a bond is heightened if the bond's interest rate rises. This can happen because of an increase in the general level of interest rates, an increase in inflation or an increase in the credit spread.
- Two or more individual bonds, which is usually driven by exposures of individual bonds to common factors. For example, an increase in the oil price adversely affects the profitability and risk of all transport companies and airlines together, as well as most oil-importing countries.

Investment managers select the bonds they think will deliver the best returns. These bonds typically share common characteristics that the investment manager will recognize at the portfolio level as well as at the level of individual assets.

Concentrations of risk from interaction effects can accumulate quickly because credit portfolios are usually selected one bond at a time, rather than top-down, which would entail specifying desirable risk exposures early in the portfolio selection process. Unintended and therefore unmanaged sources of risk that can result from stock-by-stock selection are a drag on portfolio performance because they introduce more volatility than is necessary to achieve the portfolio's investment objectives. Sources of risk at the portfolio level that do not accord with the investment manager's favoured characteristics can be hedged.

Because of the asymmetry of returns inherent in corporate bonds, it is not possible to use mean-variance techniques to estimate interaction effects. Instead, some kind of simulation is normally adapted, whereby the returns to individual bonds are simulated to give return distributions and the portfolio effect is taken as the sum of these. Advanced simulation systems use copula analysis to capture interaction effects and thereby quantify concentrations of common factor risk.

Model complexity

A further source of risk comes from the sheer complexity of the modelling techniques needed to capture the provisions of very different instruments and exposures and the interactions between them, which may not be well understood by the analysts and managers who base investment decisions on their output. They are vulnerable to:

- The quality of the data from which statistical estimates are derived.
- The assumptions underlying the model, which may become unrealistic or obsolete as market conditions change.
- Routines to simplify the more complex computations, intended to reduce computing time may corrupt the model to the point that the results it gives are invalidated.

These risks are compounded by the lack of transparency of very complex models, so are hard to monitor and manage.

Hedging strategies

The main hedgeable sources of risk in a credit portfolio boil down to:

- Interest rate risk.
- Currency risk.
- Credit risk.

Once quantified, each can be hedged in part or in full:

- Interest rate risk can be hedged using bond index futures contracts or interest rate swap positions.
- Currency risk is easily hedged using foreign exchange forward contracts.

- Credit risk can be hedged in two ways:
  - The credit risk of individual bonds can be hedged using (CDS) contracts on individual bonds.
  - Risk associated with the credit spread can be hedged using index CDS contracts that protect against the volatility in a basket of corporate bonds.

Counterparty risk

Counterparty risk is the risk that a counterparty to a transaction will not meet its obligations on a bond, credit derivative, trade credit insurance or payment protection insurance contract. Counterparty risk can be thought of as a special case of credit risk, which concerns only the event of a default since it is unaffected by day-to-day volatility that characterizes stable markets. Investment managers tend to think of counterparty risk as being associated mostly with derivatives positions, especially over-the-counter derivatives positions.

Exposure to counterparty risk is typically measured as the net nominal exposure of open positions. Investment managers usually impose a nominal limit of exposure to each counterparty, which is monitored regularly as part of the risk governance process.

Most investment managers ensure that all significant exposures to counterparties are comprehensively documented, usually by means of an ISDA agreement. The ISDA agreement in principle sets out how settlement should be calculated and the recovery amounts to each party to an over-the-counter derivatives position.

But because counterparty risk is principally concerned with default, and because defaults are most likely to occur in stressed market conditions, ISDA agreements don't necessarily give water-tight protection if an extreme event should occur. Financial institutions don't usually default in isolation: because of the interconnectedness of global financial markets, other institutions and possibly whole banking systems can be affected, invoking the 'too big to fail' clause in the unwritten supervisory code, effectively insulating some parties to ISDAs.

This means that in practice, counterparty risk is likely to come from exposures that might not be covered by an ISDA agreement. It is also exacerbated by concentrations of exposure, also known as 'wrong way risk'.

Even if a portfolio is relatively free of concentrations of counterparty risk, counterparty risk can interact with the portfolio's exposure to corporate and sovereign bonds, and indeed with exposures in its equity portfolios. These concentrations can magnify the effects on the portfolio in an extreme event.

Summary

Credit instruments are issued by corporations, sovereign borrowers and financial institutions, usually to raise capital to finance investment, but also as part of securitization transactions. For investors, they can provide a stream of income that is higher than that achievable by investing in government bonds. Credit instruments are defined by their terms and conditions as well as their credit quality, as given by their credit rating or the interest rate spread at which they trade relative to the government or LIBOR rate of interest.

Credit ratings agencies are central to the market for credit instruments because of the broad coverage they can offer and because of their use by regulators and supervisors and in structured instruments, as well as in investment mandates, although market based alternatives to credit ratings are becoming more widely used.

Pricing of individual securities and portfolio selection usually employs simulation methodology to estimate their fair price under different assumptions and market conditions, to identify and quantify risk concentrations and to inform hedging strategies. Portfolio risk is estimated by aggregating simulations of individual securities.

14
Property Portfolios

A well-known practice in some parts of the world is for the aging owner of a house or apartment to enter into an agreement with a younger person, whereby the youngster pays an agreed sum each month to the older one for the rest of his or her life in return for the property when the older person dies. Of course it is by no means unheard of for the older person to outlive the youngster, which can of course be unfortunate for both.

The property owner gains income while he or she can use it and the youngster gains an entry to the property market with a relatively small outlay.

In this case the owner of the apartment was aged 70 and the buyer about 40 when the deal was struck. The owner lived to be 122, and for several years held the title for the oldest, living person in the world with proof of age and of course comfortably outlived the less comfortable buyer.

This is in fact an example of a property derivatives transaction, which are described later in this chapter. In the meantime, it discusses:

- Rationale.
- Types of exposure.
- Types of instrument.
- Characteristics.
- Pricing and valuation.
- Risk estimation and portfolio construction.
- Property derivatives.

Rationale

Investors hold property assets in their portfolio because:

- It is considered a 'safe' asset.
- It usually has relatively low volatility of returns.

- It can deliver a steady income most of the time.
- It combines some of the qualities of both equities and bonds.
- It can give exposure to economic growth in specific regions and localities and particular sectors within them.
- It can provide a hedge against inflation.
- It can diversify the risks of other assets.

Returns to property are generally thought to be less volatile than equities and other real assets. The value of physical property assets are composed mostly of tangible assets. By contrast a significant proportion of the value of an equity investment can comprise intangible assets such as goodwill or forecast future cash flows. The high percentage of tangible assets in real property provides an effective floor to the price by linking the asset to productive, revenue generating potential. This means that, notwithstanding short-term fluctuations in market sentiment and short-term volatility, the asset has an intrinsic economic value, which must ultimately be priced by the market.

Because of relatively low observed volatility and income generating capacity, property although a real asset, tends to behave somewhat like a bond, yet is often regarded by investors as a sort of hybrid that can help diversify exposures to both equities and bonds.

Because the value of real estate rises with economic growth, property investment is a way of participating in the growth of the economy. In addition, it can present a distinct set of growth opportunities whereby the investor can target specific regions and sectors within regions. This is harder to achieve with equity investments, because they tend to be linked to industries that operate on an economy-wide, regional or local scale. Within regions, property can give the opportunity to target local industries, which is also harder to do with equities.

Types of exposure

Property as an asset class is usually thought of as comprising a number of sectors, including:

- Residential.
- Retail.
- Commercial.
- Industrial.
- Tourism.
- Agricultural.

Residential

Portfolio investment in residential property usually entails the purchase of existing or the development of new housing estates or apartment blocks.

Purchases of existing residential properties can also include those that have been repossessed as a result of defaults on mortgage payments.

Retail

Investment in retail property usually entails the purchase, re-development or development of shopping malls, high street properties or urban properties either for re-sale or as a source of continuing income.

Commercial

Office space can be bought for leasing, re-development or re-sale. Pension funds often buy a whole building or a block of neighbouring buildings, which can generate multiple sources of income in addition to the income from rental leases; for example, from leasing the naming rights to buildings. Commercial developments often incorporate retail space, which can add extra revenue from this source.

Industrial

Investment in factories, warehouses and industrial parks can give the portfolio exposure to the growth of specialized local economic clusters such as industrial design and specialist manufacturing.

Tourism

Investment in hotels, restaurants, resorts and casinos gives targeted exposure to geographically promising areas and a specific region or locality, potentially benefiting from growth in a specific group of prospective tourists.

Agricultural

Farming properties give participation in the growth of food and other primary products and can target growth in demand from specific consumers or primary produce.

Types of instrument

Property investment is usually thought of as the direct purchase of a property such as a shopping mall, office block, factory or industrial park, hotel, resort or farm. Physical property assets need not be a simple passive investment – often it entails active on-going management of some kind as in the:

- Purchase of an existing property for lease.
- Purchase of an existing property for re-development and re-sale.
- Greenfield development for lease or re-sale.

Most developments are purchased in their entirety, but some larger developments issue part ownership rights, where the investor can buy a share of revenues and capital gains. In fact, exposure to property can take a number of forms, including:

- Direct property – whole ownership.
- Direct property – part ownership.
- Indirect property – listed property instruments.
- Indirect property – derivatives.

Purchasing a part interest in a development can be attractive from the point of view of diversification because it ties up a smaller nominal sum, thereby allowing smaller funds to spread their exposures across a greater number of assets. This advantage may be off-set by the increased difficulty of re-selling the interest.

The alternative to buying buildings or parts of buildings is to invest in a listed property vehicle, such as a Real Estate Investment Trust (REIT). For US investors, REITs can confer some tax advantages if most of the income they generate is distributed to investors as dividends. Offsetting this is that:

- Listed instruments typically comprise bundles of investments, giving the potential advantage of built-in diversification, but at the same time depriving the investor of the ability to target particular sectors within defined localities.
- Listed property securities trade in stock-markets in the same way that equities do. Often they are closed funds, which means that the price at which they trade can depart materially from the aggregate value of the underlying properties. This type of listed property vehicle is therefore not generally a good substitute for direct property investment.

Listed property vehicles are traded on a number of stock exchanges worldwide and, in some markets, instruments that target particular market segments are available.

Effective exposure to the property market can also be achieved using property swaps. Property swaps can be structured to deliver the return to a single property or development or, more frequently, linked to the return to a property index that is compiled by a commercial real estate index provider. Property indices are constructed to reflect the returns either to economy-wide property markets or to economic segments, defined by sector, such as residential, retail, commercial and so on; or by geographic regions or urban areas within an economy.

Characteristics

Most property investments held by institutional investors are in holdings of physical land and buildings, where the portfolio is the sole owner. This means that direct property investments have a number of characteristics that are not generally shared with other asset classes, for example:

- They are unique.
- They are illiquid.
- They are not listed on an exchange.
- They tend to be large in terms of nominal value invested.
- They are often subject to some kind of regulation.
- They must usually be managed while the investment is held.

They are unique. While other houses, apartments, hotels, shops, factories warehouses, office blocks and car-parks may be similar, no two are identical. As the investor is the sole owner, the price of the investment can be discovered only when it is sold. Intermediate valuation of the asset for the purpose of portfolio valuation is therefore only an estimation.

Turnover in physical property is very low. In most jurisdictions, the process of buying and selling physical property is labour intensive, slow and expensive, in terms of commissions, taxes and legal costs, but also in terms of management time. Because property is traded effectively over-the-counter, there is no exchange or screen market where traders can find each other and exchange information, compare prices and otherwise expedite the process of finding suitable properties for sale and willing buyers. Instead the process is conducted with the help of brokers and agents. It entails sometimes lengthy negotiations over price and the terms of contracts, settlement terms and so on, the complexity of which is magnified by the fact that each property – and sometimes the terms of its title deed – is unique.

As with all over-the-counter instruments, purchase and sale of physical property implies an element of counterparty risk, albeit mostly during the actual periods of purchase and sale. Counterparty risk in this context is the risk that the purchase fails because of some problem with the sale contract or property title, which can leave the buyer with un-invested funds; or the risk that the prospective buyer of the property is unable to complete the transaction, which can leave the investor with the opposite problem if the proceeds have already been committed to purchasing another asset.

The uniqueness of property investments can be magnified when large properties are leased to multiple lessees. For example, leases for office space are typically negotiated and re-negotiated one by one. The negotiation or re-negotiation determines the amount of rent to be paid (usually by the square metre or square foot), the term of the lease, early termination clauses, renewal options and even fit-out of the space. Because the terms are determined largely by the supply of similar properties for lease in the locality and the demand from other prospective lessees, the terms of consecutive leases can vary significantly. This means that leases held concurrently by different lessors in the same building can also have quite distinct terms and conditions.

Property investments can be subject to regulations in ways that generally don't apply to other asset classes. For example, zoning restrictions can limit the use to which land and buildings can be put; health regulations can affect tourism developments; while retail developments can be restricted to protect existing local commerce and subject to health regulations. Being specific to particular localities, property developments can be affected by the sensibilities of local residents' groups and environmental issues. The risk and cost profile of the investment can also be affected by a heritage listing, which can enhance its investment appeal but also impose additional maintenance costs. Even without a heritage listing, buildings can acquire iconic appeal, as happened with the Rockefeller Centre in New York City, which can affect their continuing value as well as the uses to which they can be put, what shape any re-development can take and even to whom the buildings can be sold.

Once acquired, buildings, factories, hotels and so on must be managed for the term of the investment. While some large investment management firms maintain a team of building managers in-house, the norm is to engage third party property managers. Property managers tend to concentrate on particular types of properties, such as shopping malls, office and retail complexes, hotels, resorts and casinos, often specializing within sectors according to a particular target market, such as budget hotels or five star resorts.

This means that the contracts for on-going management and the relationships with managers must be managed throughout the term of the investment, in the same way that office leases are. And unlike shares and bonds, buildings are subject to on-going physical maintenance, depreciation, improvements, re-development and insurance, all of which impose management and other holding costs that are not entirely predictable at the time the property is bought.

Pricing and valuation

In theory the price of a property and the rental income it can attract should be tightly linked. The rent commanded by a property should be about the same as the interest that would apply to finance the property plus other holding costs, such as maintenance and management. If this is not the case, economic theory says that owners of overpriced property will profit from the discrepancy by selling and, if necessary, renting accommodation at the relatively cheap rental rates available. If property is too cheap relative to market rents, renters will buy property rather than rent, thereby correcting the imbalance.

In practice, imbalances in property markets rarely correct quickly or smoothly, but can persist for extended periods because:

- The cost of buying and selling property impedes liquidity, which can result in 'sticky' prices.
- Controlled rents prevent rental income rates from adjusting.
- Subsidized mortgage interest rates artificially depress the cost of buying.
- The difficulty some would-be property buyers have in financing purchases of property impedes the upward adjustment of prices.

Because the price of most direct property investment can be discovered only when the property is sold, interim pricing for the purpose of portfolio valuation must be based on estimates. As with other equity investments, the fair price of a property is determined by:

- An estimate of the present value of future net income.
- The market's estimate of the risk of future net income.
- Estimated inflation.
- Supply and demand.

Future net income is a function of current net income and the expected future growth of net income. Income comprises rental income plus any other income, such as from renting building naming rights, advertising space, the space for mobile network masts and so on. Income is offset by holding costs, including maintenance, management, depreciation, improvements, property taxes and insurance to give net income.

Risks to future net income embedded in the discount factor used in the present value calculation are determined by:

- Anticipated volatility in interest rates, which affect confidence in economy-wide property income forecasts.
- Uncertainty regarding future micro-economic conditions specific to the property asset that could affect the stream of income and capital growth in the asset's value.
- Inflation which affects both the nominal value of future income and the discount factor, but not necessarily equally.

Supply and demand for property are driven by:

- Factors that affect property as an asset class.
- Sector related factors.
- Region and locality related factors.
- Effects that are specific to the individual property.

Economy-wide factors include the interest rate at which banks can borrow, expected inflation and anticipated economic growth. These factors in turn affect things like the overall profitability and growth of the corporate sector, employment and mortgage rates, which determine the ability of households to borrow and repay home mortgages and to pay rent. Other factors that affect residential property throughout the economy are:

- Whether mortgage rates tend to be fixed or floating.
- Tax incentives for owner occupation.
- Tax on capital gains of various classes of property.
- The percentage of owner-occupied compared to rental property.

At the regional and local levels, factors that determine property values include infrastructure and transport links, which affect the region's attractiveness to particular industries and residents and therefore the availability of local employment. These, along with the quality of local schools and other amenities and crime rates, in turn affect the attractiveness of the region to households.

Factors that affect the prices of individual properties, independently of economy, region and sector effects include:

- The design and state of the building.
- The purposes to which it can be put.
- The particular location with respect to local amenities or beauty spots.

- Suitability of the building to local economic activity.
- The terms of any existing leases and maintenance contracts.

Commercial and industrial rents are driven by the profitability, and therefore the ability to pay, of prospective tenants. Rents on retail properties are sometimes linked to revenues earned by the retailer, so are influenced by the purchasing power of the local population and demand for the specific range of merchandise carried by the retailer.

Observing economy-wide, regional and sector related factors is not usually doable. In practice, valuations for individual properties are usually estimated from regional or local averages for recent transactions involving similar properties, adjusted for the particular locality and features of the property that distinguish it from the average.

This process attempts to capture the effects of supply and demand specific to the property, but is subject to obvious limitations to do with the depth and quality of recent local data and is dependent on the judgement of the individual valuer.

Investors like property because, among other things, it is considered less volatile than equities but, like equities, gives participation in economic growth. Like bonds, it gives a steady stream of income but with more potential for capital gains and less potential for losses than bonds usually have.

In fact, some of property's reputation for volatility is due more to its low turnover and the fact that the actual values of individual properties are usually not visible in practice. Estimates of property price volatility are usually derived from the returns to published property indices, which capture economy-wide factors if they are national indices, and regional and sector-wide factors if they are regional or sector indices. They do not capture the extra price variations that are specific to the property, which tend to average out at sector, region and economy levels. The extra volatility is therefore not reflected in published property index returns. The same is true of equity and bond index returns, which capture volatility at the index level but cannot reflect the volatility of individual asset returns. The result is that the actual returns to individual properties are almost certainly more volatile than they are thought to be. Of course this matters only when the investor comes to buy or sell a property, but that is after all what matters to portfolio performance.

Income streams to property investments are generally steadier than to equities because leases for commercial and industrial properties and management contracts for hotels and resorts tend to run for terms of several years, with the effect that rents are held constant in nominal or real terms during that interval. Equities, by contrast, pay variable dividends quarterly or semi-annually. Income from property investments, although steadier than equities, does in fact fluctuate, but usually in discrete jumps rather than continuously – although the jumps are somewhat smoothed at the portfolio level.

Risk estimation and portfolio construction

As an asset class, the appeal of property is its combination of relatively low risk, steady income and participation in future economic growth. In fact it can also be an important source of active return by allowing the investment manager to target specific growth opportunities that may not be available through listed vehicles such as equities and listed property securities.

For example, the investment manager may have particular expertise in researching regional development within the economy, so investing in particular localities can give suitable, focussed exposure. The ability to determine lease terms can enhance the quality and timing of income and capital growth. These investment selection and management strengths can be further enhanced using property derivatives.

Property derivatives can also help manage liquidity risk, and reinvestment liquidity risk is the risk of underinvestment in a rising market. Underinvestment can result from accumulated liquid assets from rents or new investment into the portfolio. It can also come from the failure of a planned acquisition. Reinvestment risk is the risk that funds remain idle following the sale of a property. It is magnified by the lead times in effecting new property acquisitions.

Property derivatives

The market for property swaps has developed since the mid-2000s, particularly in the UK, where they are regularly used by institutional investment managers.

Property swaps tend to be settled against property indices that are published by third party index providers and describe returns to national property markets or to segments within them. Property swaps can be useful for:

- Managing liquidity and reinvestment risk.
- Targeting property exposures, and aligning sources of risk with sources of return.

An example of how property swaps can help invest accumulated liquid assets is given in Example 14.1. An investor with £5 000 000 to invest has yet to identify a suitable property for purchase. The funds are held on deposit where they earn interest until an appropriate property is found. But if property prices are rising, the portfolio will suffer from underinvestment relative to its peers.

A swap can be entered into whereby:

- The portfolio pays LIBOR plus 0.40 per cent per annum.
- The portfolio receives the return to a publicly quoted property total return index.

Suppose that, six months later, property prices have appreciated by 2 per cent and still no suitable property has been found. In the meantime the portfolio has accumulated a further £3 000 000, so the investment manager enters into another, similar swap transaction and places the £3 000 000 on short-term deposit to earn approximately the LIBOR rate of interest.

Another six months later the property market has risen a further 5 per cent and a suitable property for purchase has been found and negotiated. The investment manager can either close out the swap agreements early or, if the terms of the swaps don't permit this, enter into a swap for £8 000 000 that cancels out the two open swap agreements. The funds flows for the transactions are summarized in Example 14.1.

In Example 14.1 the net outcome of £455 059 off-sets the increase in property prices that occurred while the investment manager was

Example 14.1 A property swap

Day	Property index	Cash flow	LIBOR interest +	Interest earned
			0.40%	
0	100	5,000,000		
180	102	3,000,000	–135,000	125,000
360	107	350,000	–270,000	250,000
360	107	147,059	–162,000	150,000
Total		497,059	–567,000	525,000
Net Total		455,059		

searching for suitable properties. Note that the 0.40 per cent margin represents the fee to the intermediary who arranges the swap, and who may also be the counterparty.

Property swaps can also help target and align portfolio risk and return. Suppose that the investment manager expects property to underperform other asset classes in the medium term, and so prefers to hold less than the benchmark allocation in property. Within this lacklustre market, he or she has identified a very promising property niche, which is expected to do well despite the overall outlook for property. The investment manager would like to earn extra return from this insight and can indeed do so by buying the property in question through a conventional asset purchase and hedging the general property market exposure by entering into a swap whereby the portfolio pays the return to an agreed general property index and receives the interest rate less a margin. The transaction is almost the mirror image of the one given in Example 14.1, with the exception that instead of receiving LIBOR plus a margin, the portfolio receives LIBOR minus a margin.

The net effect of this transaction is that, while funds are tied up by the purchase of the physical asset, the portfolio as a whole is under-invested because most of the exposure to the property market has been hedged away by the swap. The investment manager can effectively 'invest' this amount by buying futures or swaps in a more promising asset class, such as equities or bonds.

An important consideration in structuring any over-the-counter derivative transaction is that the investor and counterparty agree to settle the derivative against a valuation that is derived independently of either party. In practice most property swaps are settled against a published property index.

The appeal of property derivatives to UK institutional investors is enhanced by the ruling that the transactions are admissible for the purpose of calculation of solvency ratios for insurance companies, provided that:

- The positions are covered.
- The counterparty to the transaction is approved.
- They are valued independently.

Summary

Property is an attractive asset class for investment portfolios because it is perceived to be relatively stable, giving relatively consistent streams of income while at the same time participating in economic growth.

In fact, individual property returns may be less stable than they appear, and income streams are not always consistent.

Another potential attraction of property investment is that it can allow effective harnessing of investment selection skills because individual properties can give exposure to specific economic and geographical growth niches where the investment manager may have particular expertise.

The use of derivatives in the form of property swaps can further enhance the manager's skill in targeting specific opportunities. They also can be an effective way of eliminating the perennial performance drag caused by liquidity risk and reinvestment risk.

Case Study

This is a large tourism related development carried out in an area of considerable natural beauty with, in principle, significant earnings and capital gains potential. The investor was a large and well-established corporate pension fund with investments spanning several domestic and international sectors, with both listed and unlisted assets, including property.

Planning permission was obtained to develop a casino as well as a hotel complex, with the aim of earning higher revenues than a simple resort, both for the investor and the government. Local regulations limited the granting of casino licences, further enhancing the project's earning potential.

Keen to exploit the casino licence as much as possible, the project was designed to be much bigger than other tourist resorts in the area. Local residents voiced concerns that such a large development would be incongruous with existing structures, and would potentially damage the environment, which was the source of many of their livelihoods. Moreover they were unsure about having a casino, especially such a big one, because they thought this might affect the friendly and relaxed atmosphere of the local village, which they felt added to its appeal for visitors.

Owners of existing tourist resorts were even less happy at the prospect of a huge new competitor that could potentially undercut them by subsidizing food and accommodation from gambling income.

The slightly scaled down project took a lot longer to complete, and cost a lot more to build than had been planned. Operating profits of the completed development turned out to be lower than expected, owing to various concessions to local concerns, lower than expected occupancy rates (due either to widespread public disapproval of the project or the very high accommodation rates being charged) and higher than expected operating costs.

The investor had planned to revalue the property annually, in keeping with its policy for its other direct property investments, but a year after the completion of the project, the independent valuation was less than the cost of the project. Then a slowdown in regional tourism resulted in negative returns to the project for the following year too. The trustees of the pension fund were becoming impatient.

The investor was under pressure to do something quickly. The most expedient thing to do was to carry out valuations less frequently, so a three-year valuation cycle was imposed – as luck would have it, just as regional tourism began to pick up. With the value of the project held at its last nominal valuation, it was now significantly under-performing similar projects elsewhere.

Now there was pressure to sell the property, if for no other reason than to free up funds for more promising investments elsewhere. The problem was that, for such a large investment, there were not a great number of potential buyers at short notice. The investor decided on a moderately innovative solution, which was to turn the property into a trust and list it on the stock-market. This process could be achieved in a matter of months, whereas an outright sale of the property might have taken a year or more. This solution had the additional benefit that the property could be partially sold with some interest retained by the investor in order to reap the rewards that would no doubt materialize in the longer term.

The trust was formed with the original investor owning all the units in it. These were then offered on the stock-market at a price that would imply a higher valuation than the overall cost of the project. In other words, the price at which the investor was prepared to sell the units would guarantee a nominal profit for the overall project. The problem was that hardly anybody was prepared to buy the units at that price, so most of the units stayed with the original investor. Things were becoming tense, but the investor was reluctant to sell the units at a loss because this would signal a big failure on its part to other investors, with consequent damage to its reputation.

The property was still classified in the investment portfolio as property, where it was acting as a noticeable drag on the overall returns to that sector. This could be fixed by reclassifying the investment as equity and putting it in the much larger equity component of the portfolio, where its impact would be less noticed. This did not please the equity manager, whose performance, and hence her reputation and remuneration, were to be affected by this drag on her investment returns.

Arguments ensued, with the property being moved to various different sectors, as units were gradually sold on market. Eventually it formed the kernel of a sector devoted to 'alternative investments', which were supposedly directed to long-term profitability, and which were not required to deliver competitive returns in the short term.

15
Structured Products

In a restaurant, a man asks for a glass of milk. The waitress brings the milk, but as the man brings the glass to his mouth, he sees that there is a mouse in it. He calls the waitress and draws attention to the mouse, upon which the waitress puts her hand in the milk, removes the mouse and hands the glass back to her customer. Astonished, the man refuses the milk:

– I can't drink that!
– Well I don't understand: you don't want the milk with the mouse, and you don't want it without the mouse!

Seemingly benign investment structures can have surprising things in them and still comply with the letter of their label. A glass of milk with a mouse in it is still, strictly speaking, a glass of milk.

Some investment products seem to promise positive outcomes without apparent downside. Risks that are not apparent or poorly understood can be more damaging than risks that are known and understood.

Structured products are sometimes not well understood. This chapter sets out to describe:

- What structured products are.
- Different types of structured products.
- What they are used for.
- Advantages and disadvantages.
- The risks that are often inherent.
- Some common hedging strategies.

What they are

Structured products are also known as market linked investments. The term covers a wide variety of investment products, which are typically linked to some physical asset or a portfolio of physical assets and often incorporating some capital protection or guaranteed minimum return. Although the returns they are designed to deliver may be linked to equities, commodities or other kinds of assets, the structured product itself is a bond.

The first structured products were issued as a means of raising debt capital cheaply. This had typically been achieved with the convertible bond, which gave the bond holder the right to convert the bond to equity. By adding features such as capital protection, the issuer's cost of borrowing could be reduced further. Packaged into a single, tradable security, it became a structured product.

While there is no single definition of a structured product,[1] common features include:

- They consist of a debt instrument with cash flows derived from the performance of an underlying asset or a portfolio of underlying assets.
- They combine derivatives such as options, forwards and swaps designed to provide investors with highly targeted investments tied to specific risk profiles that may not be otherwise achievable in the marketplace.
- They are usually insured by the issuer, and thus have the potential for loss of principal if the issuing company is unable to meet its obligations.

Different types of structured products

These include:

- Exchange traded notes (ETNs):
  - interest rate-linked notes and deposits,
  - credit-linked notes and deposits,
  - individual equity-linked notes and deposits,
  - equity market-linked notes and deposits,
  - FX and commodity-linked notes and deposits,
  - hybrid linked notes and deposits.
- Constant proportion debt obligations (CPDOs).
- Constant proportion portfolio insurance (CPPI).

Exchange traded notes (ETNs)

An ETN is a debt security with a maturity date, which is backed by the credit of the issuer. When held to maturity, the investor receives a cash payment that is linked to the return of a physical asset or index or a portfolio of physical assets, less management fees. As debt securities, ETNs don't actually own the assets they are linked to. Unlike other debt securities, interest is not paid during the term of most ETNs and unlike other structured products they typically do not offer principal protection. They are traded on an exchange and can be sold short.

The management fee for an ETN is based on the value of the physical asset or assets to which it is linked. This means that, if the value of the underlying asset decreases or does not increase significantly, the investor may receive less than the principal amount of investment at maturity or upon redemption.

Advantages of ETNs

- They are tax efficient. Because the note itself does not own the underlying assets it is not obliged to trade them or to distribute income. Capital gain or loss is realized when the investor sells the ETN or it matures.
- There is no tracking error. The investor receives, in theory, the return to the underlying assets less the management fee.
- They are traded on exchanges. ETNs can be bought and sold during normal trading hours on a securities exchange and many are liquid. For large redemptions, investors can generally offer their ETN for repurchase by the issuer. Being traded securities, market prices of ETNs are directly observable. In this sense, ETNs resemble ETFs.
- They can allow cost-efficient access to a wide range of markets and strategies. ETNs can provide access to hard-to-reach exposures such as commodities, exotic equities markets and packaged strategies such as 'momentum' portfolios (which invest only in assets that have done well in the recent past), and option trading strategies such as volatility trading.
- They can be geared. Some ETNs offer leverage instead of directly tracking a benchmark's performance, which can enhance returns, especially in a rising market.
- They can be sold short. ETNs are relatively easy to sell short in the market. In addition they can embed sold positions in the physical assets, so the buyer of the ETN benefits from falls in prices of the underlying assets.

Disadvantages of ETNs

- They can embed credit risk. ETNs, as debt instruments, are subject to risk of default by the issuing bank or counterparty.
- They can be illiquid. Not all ETNs enjoy high liquidity.
- They are dependent on credit ratings. Deterioration in the credit rating of the issuer can cause the performance of the ETN to vary materially from that of the underlying assets.

- They may be linked to unprofitable trading strategies. The performance of the fund is dependent on the success of the trading strategy underlying it.

Trading strategies and hedging mismatches

Although ETNs usually are linked to a basket of physical assets, they do not hold them. The provider of the ETN may or may not hedge the obligation inherent in the product by holding the portfolio of assets itself or entering into a swap with a third party who in turn hedges the underlying exposure. The structured product can be backed by any basket of physical assets or derivatives contracts – or none at all.

If the provider is an investment bank it may find it expedient not to hedge the ETN. This is because most investment banks maintain a 'facilitation portfolio' of physical assets and derivatives instruments in order to meet quickly big sell and buy orders from wholesale clients. The facilitation portfolio can be expensive to fund, and may include illiquid instruments. One way to off-set the holding cost is to use the securities in the facilitation portfolio as an (imperfect) hedge against an ETN – a sort of holding pen. This presents a potential conflict of interest. Being only imperfectly hedged exacerbates the risk that the ETN will deliver a significant net loss to the issuer, possibly even to the point where the note will not be honoured if the investment bank runs into trouble.

Constant proportion debt obligations (CPDO)

A CPDO is designed to deliver long-term exposure to corporate bond returns in a highly rated debt security.

Because physical corporate bonds and CDS linked to them have finite maturities, the investor seeking long-term exposure to this asset class is obliged to reinvest at the maturity of each bond. CPDOs give the investor continuous exposure.

CPDOs are formed by first creating a special purpose vehicle (SPV), which issues debt. The SPV holds an index of debt securities, such as credit default swap indices. The index of debt securities must be rolled periodically, obliging the SPV to buy protection on the maturing index, and sell protection on the new index in order to maintain the hedge. Because the composition of the new and maturing indices are not identical, the CPDO is exposed to rollover risk, since the maturing index may trade at a different credit margin to the new index. If the rollover incurs a loss, then the hedge adjustment entails an increase in leverage, thereby increasing its vulnerability to future losses.

Constant proportion portfolio insurance (CPPI)

CPPI is a trading strategy that allows the investor to maintain an exposure to the upside potential of a risky asset with limited downside risk. The outcome of the CPPI strategy is somewhat similar to that of buying a put option, but the strategy does not make use of option contracts. CPPI can be used to give protection on any liquid, risky asset, index or portfolio of risky assets, including multi-asset class portfolios. The way CPPI works is described in more detail later in this chapter in the section about hedging strategies.

What structured products are used for

A primary function of structured products is to transfer risk, for a fee, from those who do not want to bear it to those who are willing to bear it. They are used to:

- Achieve exposures to markets and strategies that are not easily achievable using standardized financial instruments available in the markets.
- Gain exposure to a direct investment, as part of the asset allocation process to reduce risk exposure of a portfolio.
- Exploit a view on the likely returns to an asset class or basket of assets.
- Implement arbitrage strategies.

Advantages of structured products

- They protect the principal investment.
- They give tax-efficient access to fully taxable investments.
- They can deliver enhanced returns within a single investment instrument.
- They can deliver an investment with reduced volatility, or risk.
- The can earn a positive return in low yield or flat market environments.

Disadvantages of structured products

- They are subject to credit risk. Structured products are unsecured debt usually issued by investment banks.
- They sometimes lack liquidity. Once issued, some structured products rarely trade so investors seeking to sell before maturity can be obliged to sell at a significant discount.
- They can be difficult to price. If prices cannot be discovered directly from on-market transactions they must be estimated by modelling the structured product using current prices for the underlying assets. Often the modelling process necessitates assumptions about future interest rates and asset price volatility, so can be subject to bias.

- They can be highly complex. The complexity of the modelling and return calculations can be such that they are not widely understood. Return forecasts relative to the underlying assets therefore can be subject to significant bias.

The risks often inherent in structured products

To the investor:

- Counterparty risk.
- Liquidity risk.

To the issuer:

- Counterparty risk if hedged with an over-the-counter derivative such as a swap.
- Hedging mismatch if hedged directly.

Counterparty risk

Because a structured product is essentially a debt instrument, it is vulnerable to the risk that the issuer will be unable to honour its obligations.

Hedging mismatches

Although structured products are usually linked to a basket of physical assets, they do not hold them. The provider may hedge the obligation of the product by holding the portfolio of assets itself or entering into a swap with a third party who in turn hedges the underlying exposure, but this is not necessarily the case. The issuer of the structured product can be applying any hedging strategy or none at all.

Hedging strategies for embedded protection guarantees

The simplest hedge works as follows: an investor can achieve a capital guaranteed investment that is linked to the returns to a risky asset class simply by buying a bond and a call option. For example, with $100 to invest, the investor buys a risk free bond with a sufficient coupon rate to grow to $100 at the end of a five-year period. This bond might cost $80 today. With the $20 leftover the investor buys call options in the target risky asset. If the options expire worthless, the investor has $100 as a result of the $80 bond plus the interest it has earned. If the risky asset grows, the investor has $100 plus the value of the call option on the risky asset.

All portfolio protection is in fact a type of insurance, or option, that transfers some of the risk of an asset, index or portfolio to the provider of the insurance or protection. As with any other type of insurance, reduced risk entails some cost, either in the form of an initial payment or premium, or foregone future returns. The cost of the insurance is not recouped if it turns out not to have been needed. (In the same way, your house insurance premium was 'wasted' if your house did not burn down.) As with any general insurance the price of protection depends on the value of the goods insured, how likely the event insured against is, the period covered and the excess or deductible. In portfolio protection terms, these correspond to the amount of the investment to be insured, the riskiness of the investment, the period of protection and the minimum return required.

This section describes how capital guarantees and guaranteed minimum returns are hedged in practice. Hedging strategies include:

- Hold physical risky asset and buy put options.
- Hold riskless asset and buy call options.
- Replicate a bought option using dynamic hedging.
- CPPI.

Hold physical risky asset and buy put options

The investment manager holds the physical portfolio and buys a put option or put options to protect it against falls in market prices. The exercise price of the option determines the worst outcome for the portfolio. Below that point the increase in the value of the option off-sets falls in the value of the physical portfolio. Above the option exercise price, the portfolio return is the same as for an unprotected portfolio less the option premium paid.

The portfolio-plus-put configuration in some ways resembles a tactical asset allocation overlay in that the physical portfolio remains invested as normal, with the put option effectively an overlay.

Hold riskless asset and buy call options

A similar outcome can be achieved by holding cash-like instruments and buying a call option or a portfolio of call options to protect against being uninvested in a rising market.

As with the simplest hedge described already, the call option replaces the physical portfolio. It is valueless below the exercise price of the option but above the option exercise price it appreciates at the same rate as a fully invested portfolio. Above the option exercise price, the portfolio return is the same as for a portfolio of the underlying physical risky assets less the option premium paid.

Economically there is no difference between the two configurations, except that they incur different transactions costs and, in most jurisdictions, taxes. The former is more suitable for a portfolio that is already invested in risky assets, the latter for a portfolio not yet invested, the assets of which are cash-like instruments.

Example 15.1 shows the outcome for both strategies under four different market scenarios.

- Scenario 1 is a strong market appreciation.
- Scenario 2 is a moderate market appreciation.
- Scenario 3 is a stable market.
- Scenario 4 shows what happens if the market drops sharply.

This example ignores transactions costs, so the hold-physical-and-buy-put strategy appears to cost slightly less than it would in practice because of the relatively high cost of transacting physical assets. Costs for options transactions are usually negligible.

Example 15.1 Hold shares and buy put options versus sell portfolio and buy call options

Market data				
length of period in days	153			
Initial value of equities held	$100 000 000			
At start				
Short-term interest rates	7.50%			
Dividend yield	1.50%			
Physical market	1 328.7			
Point value of futures	$500			
Option exercise price	1 375.0			
Estimated volatility	25%			
Call option price	79.55			
Put option price	92.41			
At end	**Scenario 1**	**Scenario 2**	**Scenario 3**	**Scenario 4**
Market move	25%	5%	0%	–25%
Physical market	1 660.9	1 395.2	1 328.7	996.5

Hold physical and buy put option				
Number of put options purchased	151			
Face value of options	$100 318 360			
Option premium paid	$21 631 427			
Value of equities held	$125 000 000	$105 000 000	$100 000 000	$75 000 000
Value of put option	$0	$0	$3 494 140	$28 573 730
Cost of option	$6 976 727	$6 976 727	$6 976 727	$6 976 727
Interest income	$0	$0	$0	$0
Dividend income	$628 767	$628 767	$628 767	$628 767
Value of portfolio	**$118 652 040**	**$98 652 040**	**$97 146 180**	**$97 225 770**
Sell physical and buy call option				
Number of call options purchased	151			
Face value of options	$100 318 360			
Option premium paid	$13 110 363			
Proceeds of sale of equities	$100 000 000	$100 000 000	$100 000 000	$100 000 000
Value of call option	$21 585 450	$1 521 778	$0	$0
Cost of option	$6 005 663	$6 005 663	$6 005 663	$6 005 663
Interest income	$3 143 836	$3 143 836	$3 143 836	$3 143 836
Dividends received	$0	$0	$0	$0
Value of portfolio	**$118 723 623**	**$98 659 951**	**$97 138 173**	**$97 138 173**

For each scenario in Example 15.1 the difference between the two strategies is minimal. Both benefit from market appreciation but are protected against falls. The apparent difference results from the fact that the number of options purchased does not give a face value exactly the same as the starting portfolio, with the result that interest income and dividends do not exactly off-set the price difference between call options and put options. In both cases, the portfolio is very slightly under-protected, so the precise difference in the two outcomes depends on whether the market goes up or down.

The level of protection depends on the choice of option exercise price. The more risk that the portfolio can bear (in effect a higher call option exercise price or a lower put option exercise price) the cheaper the protection.

Critical to the effectiveness of this hedging strategy is buying the right amount of protection. If, as is usually the case, options on market indices are used to effect protection, the hedge should be calculated against the portfolio exposure to the market, or markets, in question rather than against the nominal value invested in each. In other words, it should take into account the beta of the portfolio to equities markets and the relative duration of the portfolio in bond markets.

Option on a portfolio versus a portfolio of options

Protecting a portfolio using purchased options is conceptually a very simple strategy. There are however two ways to do it for a multi-asset class portfolio. One way is to buy options on each asset class individually. This has the advantage that counterparty risk is negligible because the counterparty to each option is an exchange on which the options are traded. Being exchange traded, the positions are subject to frequent margin calls, ensuring that all positions have collateral lodged against them, so counterparty risk is negligible. Also, prices are observable, making valuation of the position straightforward. Another advantage is that, being liquid, the positions can be closed easily and cheaply. The disadvantage is the cost: simple bought options can be expensive.

A more cost-efficient way to achieve the same protection is to configure an option on the portfolio of risky asset classes, instead of options on each asset class. This is cheaper because option prices increase with the volatility of the underlying asset. As the volatility of a portfolio is nearly always less than the average volatility of the assets in it, an option on the portfolio costs less than the sum of options on the component asset classes.

Example 15.2 An option on a portfolio of assets versus a portfolio of options

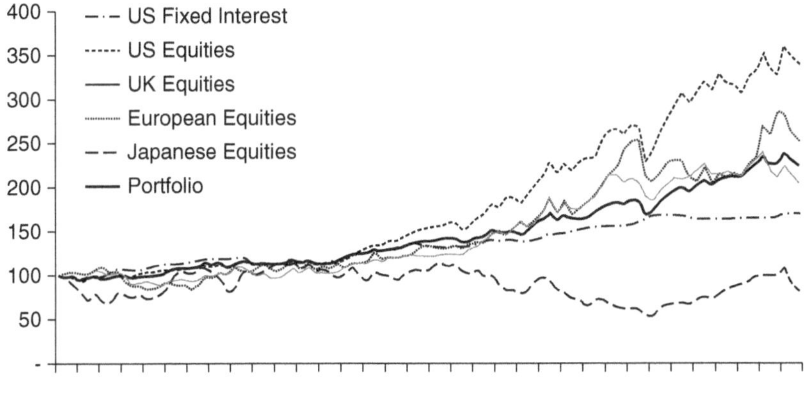

Portfolio value	\$100 000 000
Length of option in days	153
Exercise price of option	\$100 000 000

Asset class	Strategic benchmark weighting	Estimated asset volatility	Option price
US fixed interest	25%	4.16%	$260 589
US equities	35%	12.84%	$1 125 560
UK equities	10%	13.40%	$335 646
European equities	10%	14.86%	$372 175
Japanese equities	15%	23.30%	$874 966
Cash	5%	0.32%	
Total		11.85%	$2 968 936
Portfolio		8.60%	$2 155 357

Example 15.2 illustrates the effect: the weighted average of the volatilities of individual asset classes is 11.85 per cent, compared to the volatility of the multi-asset class portfolio, which is 8.6 per cent. Buying options on each asset class separately would cost 2.97 per cent of the portfolio's value, compared to 2.16 per cent for an option on the portfolio.

Replicate a bought option using dynamic hedging

Portfolio protection can take the form of an option purchased on market or over-the-counter, or an option can be replicated using a mix of the risky asset or portfolio of assets to be protected and cash-like instruments. The risky asset is usually approximated with futures contracts to resemble as closely as possible the protected portfolio. Using futures contracts in lieu of physical assets can introduce basis risk, the risk that the return to the portfolio of futures is different to that of the underlying portfolio, but this is usually preferable to the high costs of transacting physical assets.

The proportion of the portfolio invested in risky assets is determined by the option's delta. The option delta is a value between zero and one that represents the change in value of the option corresponding to a small change in the value of the underlying portfolio. A value of one represents lockstep and a value of zero represents no co-movement. In the case of a bought call option, the value of the delta increases as the price of the underlying asset appreciates until the amount invested by the replicating portfolio is close to 100 per cent of the portfolio's value. As the prices of the underlying physical assets fall, the option delta decreases, and the replicating portfolio sells risky assets, until it is invested only in cash. This means that the replicating portfolio is buying in a rising market and selling in a falling market.

Example 15.3 Replicating options and actual options

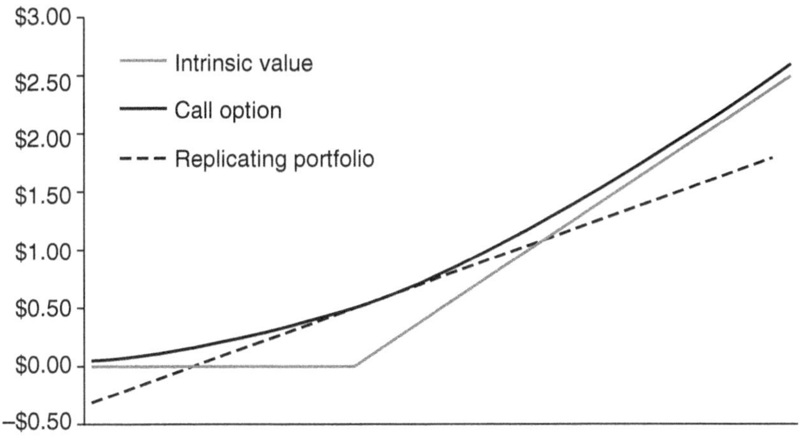

In Example 15.3 the curved line on the graph describes the value of the option as the price of the underlying risk asset moves about. The straight line tangential to the option describes the replicating portfolio at a given asset price and point in time. Whether the risky asset rises or falls, the replicating portfolio always does worse: rising by less or falling by more than the actual option it is replicating. As the investment manager adjusts the hedge to the new price and the new hedging ratio, the small losses of the replicating portfolio relative to the actual option are crystalized, adding to the cost of the hedge. This effect can be exaggerated if the prices of the underlying asset zig-zags, even if individual price changes are small. This gap risk is the main source of hedging costs for replicating portfolios. To minimize them, the investment manager must adjust the hedge frequently enough to minimize each loss, but not so frequently that excessive transactions costs are incurred.

Because of hedging risk, replicated options rarely deliver exactly the same payoff as the options they aim to replicate. Hedging risk is due to a number of assumptions built in to options pricing theory.

- Interest rates are assumed to be constant over the life of the option, whereas in practice they fluctuate.
- The volatility of the underlying asset is assumed to be known in advance and constant over the life of the option. In fact, asset price volatility fluctuates, sometimes significantly, with the result that the wrong percentage of the portfolio can be held in risky assets.
- Transactions costs are assumed to be zero. The fact that they are not can make a big difference to any dynamic hedging strategy, which entails frequent trading.

- Asset prices are assumed to move in infinitely small increments, whereas in practice they do so in discrete jumps.

Managers of dynamic hedging strategies try to mitigate the risk and cost of discrete price jumps by buying options in the market when prices are perceived to be relatively low. This effectively transfers the gap risk to the seller of the option.

The main difference between an option purchased on market or over-the-counter and a replicated one is that the cost of the purchased option is known at the outset, while the cost of the replicated option can be only estimated in advance. Most investment managers do not replicate options themselves but enter a swap whereby a third party promises the payoff to a defined option for an agreed option premium and assumes the risk of managing the dynamic hedge. The risk to the investment manager therefore is the counterparty risk against the third party that promises the payoff. This gives the investment manager the benefit of knowing the cost of the option at the outset of the transaction.

Partial protection

In practice, purchasing options can be expensive. There are a number of ways to reduce the cost. One way, already described, is to accept slightly more risk by adjusting the exercise price so that protection cuts in at a higher or a lower level. Another way is to protect only part of the portfolio.

Example 15.4 compares three portfolio protection structures under the same scenarios as in Example 15.1. The three protection structures are:

- Strategy 1 – a simple call option covering all the portfolio (the same as in Example 15.1).
- Strategy 2 – the same call option covering only half the portfolio.
- Strategy 3 – a call option with full participation that becomes effective only after a small rise in the market.

Example 15.4 Cost of option for partial protection

Market Data	
Length of period in days	153
Initial value of equities held	$100 000 000
At start	
Short-term interest rates	7.50%

Dividend yield		1.50%		
Physical market index		1 328.7		
Point value of futures		$500		
Estimated volatility		25%		
	Scenario 1	**Scenario 2**	**Scenario 3**	**Scenario 4**
Market move	25%	5%	0%	–25%
Physical market index	1 660.9	1 395.2	1 328.7	996.5
Structure 1				
Participation rate	100%			
After market	0%			
Appreciation of exercise price	1 350.0			
Number of call options Purchased	151			
Face value of options	$100 318 360			
Call option price	90.88			
Option premium paid	$6 861 077			
Cash collateral held	$100 000 000	$100 000 000	$100 000 000	$100 000 000
Value of call option	$23 472 950	$3 409 278	$0	$0
Cost of option	$6 861 077	$6 861 077	$6 861 077	$6 861 077
Interest income	$3 143 836	$3 143 836	$3 143 836	$3 143 836
Value of portfolio	$119,755,709	$99 692 037	$96 282 759	$96 282 759
Structure 2				
Participation rate	50%			
After market	0%			
Appreciation of exercise price	1 350.0			
Number of call options purchased	75			
Face value of options	$49 827 000			
Call option price	90.88			
Option premium paid	$3 407 820			
Cash collateral held	$100 000 000	$100 000 000	$100 000 000	$100 000 000
Value of call option	$11 658 750	$1 693 350	$0	$0
Cost of option	$3 407 820	$3 407 820	$3 407 820	$3 407 820
Interest income	$3 143 836	$3 143 836	$3 143 836	$3 143 836
Value of portfolio	$111 394 766	$101 429 366	$99 736 016	$99 736 016

Structure 3				
Participation rate	100%			
After market Appreciation of	5%			
exercise price	1 425.0			
Number of call options purchased	151			
Face value of options	$100 318 360			
Call option price	60.07			
Option premium paid	$4 535 267			
Cash collateral held	$100 000 000	$100 000 000	$100 000 000	$100 000 000
Value of call option	$17 810 450	$0	$0	$0
Cost of option	$4 535 267	$4 535 267	$4 535 267	$4 535 267
Interest income	$3 143 836	$3 143 836	$3 143 836	$3 143 836
Value of portfolio	$116 419 019	$98 608 569	$98 608 569	$98 608 569

Example 15.4 shows that less than full market participation can reduce the cost of protection significantly. The third structure is most effective if the market moves sharply up, as in scenario 1, which is almost the same as for full participation. The second structure can also save costs, and gives at least some participation for all positive market moves.

Constant proportions portfolio insurance (CPPI)

Constant proportions portfolio insurance (CPPI) works by ensuring that the portfolio always holds enough risk free assets to retain an agreed percentage of its value in the occurrence of a pre-defined event or crash. As with option replication, it relies on a dynamic hedging strategy. Unlike an option it is not dependent on forecasts of asset volatility but does demand that the investor specify the outcome he or she needs to protect against.

In order to guarantee the capital invested, the seller of portfolio insurance maintains a position in cash like instruments, together with a leveraged position in a 'risky asset', such as a market index. CPPI is defined by its:

- Cushion or floor.
- Maximum tolerable discrete loss, also known as a multiplier.
- Duration of protection.

The amount invested is calculated as:

$$\text{CPPI} = \text{M} \times (\text{CPPI} - \text{C}) \tag{15.1}$$

Where:

CPPI = the value of the portfolio
M = the multiplier
C = the cushion

For example, say an investor has a \$100 portfolio, a floor of \$90, which is the sum invested in bonds to guarantee \$100 at maturity, and a multiplier of 5, which ensures protection against a drop of at most 20 per cent. Then on day one, the writer will allocate (5 × (\$100 – \$90)) = \$50 to the risky asset and the remaining \$50 to the riskless asset. The exposure will be revised as the portfolio value changes, with fluctuations in the prices of the risky assets.

The bond floor is the value below which the value of risky assets in the CPPI portfolio should never fall in order to be able to ensure the payment of all future due cash flows, including the notional capital guarantee at maturity.

The multiplier is the factor by which the cash in the CPPI portfolio is geared. It is five in the example accompanying Equation 15.1.

The gap is a measure of the proportion of the equity part compared to the cushion. It is the proportion that the manager attempts to keep constant through dynamic hedging.

Dynamic hedging of CPPI portfolios

As with option replication, CPPI is subject to hedging risk in that the investment manager is always 'following' the market. The investment manager aims to trade as often as necessary to maintain the constant hedge proportion, but not so often that excessive transactions costs are incurred. CPPI managers usually define a band of tolerances to control the frequency of trading and allowable hedging mismatches, which works as follows.

If the gap remains between an upper and a lower trigger band, the strategy does not trade. Aiming to be within a band rather than at a single point within it reduces the frequency of trading and therefore transaction costs. However when trades do take place, they can incur greater losses because in the CPPI strategy is obliged to buy at a higher price and sell at a lower price. The leverage inherent in the strategy exaggerating the losses.

As dynamic trading strategies assume that capital markets trade in a continuous fashion, gap risk can be significant relative to the theoretical value of the strategy. A sudden drop in the value of the risky assets can

Table 15.1 Comparison of four protection methods

	Purchase option	Replicate option	CPPI	CPDO
Cost	High	High	Moderate	High
Cost known in advance	Yes	No	No	No
Vulnerable to price gapping	No	Yes	Yes	No
Fixed term	Yes	Yes	Yes	No
Forecast asset price volatility required	Yes	Yes	No	No
Predefined crash specified	No	No	Yes	No

reduce the overall CPPI net asset value below the value of the bond floor needed to guarantee the capital at maturity. Failure to deliver the principal at maturity can also be due to sudden price moves that make it impossible to adjust the hedge in time. Providers of CPPI protection generally charge a 'protection' or 'gap' fee to cover this risk, usually as a function of the notional leveraged exposure.

CPPI is 'path dependent', meaning that the future value of the portfolio at any time depends on what has happened so far. If markets exhibit a sharp fall early in the protection period, the portfolio divests a large proportion of its risky assets and holds mostly cash. If the risky assets subsequently recover abruptly, the portfolio doesn't participate fully because of the large cash holding. Conversely, if the price of the risky asset rises sharply early in the protection period, the investor has the choice of maintaining the existing level of protection or effectively 'locking in' the gains by setting a new, higher floor. Staying with the same level of protection affords the portfolio a higher level of participation of further appreciation in the risky asset, but this benefit is off-set by the possibility of losing all gains to date if the market subsequently falls. Resetting the floor means reducing the portfolio's exposure to further rises in the price of the risky asset, but ensuring a higher minimum return for the portfolio (Table 15.1).

Summary

Structured products are exchange-traded debt instruments, the returns to which are linked to some physical asset, index or portfolio of risky assets; often incorporating a guarantee of capital or a guaranteed minimum return. As a debt instrument, a structured product carries counterparty risk against the issuer, who may or may not hedge the obligations of the security.

Guarantees of capital and of minimum returns can be hedged using a number of methodologies including the purchase of actual options, portfolios that replicate option payoffs, constant proportion debt obligations and constant proportion portfolio insurance. None deliver a perfect hedge and all entail some cost to the investor.

Case Study

The market conditions favourable to offering capital guaranteed funds are often not the same as those giving rise to demand for such funds, and vice versa. Investors seek the reassurance of a capital guarantee in times of market volatility, which are the very conditions that make capital guarantees difficult to offer at attractive rates.

In an environment of general uncertainty, high interest rates, a negative yield curve and a lively local options market, some innovative investment managers launched funds with guaranteed minimum returns. Most of these funds were constructed conservatively in that they invested the portfolio in long-term, low-risk assets, and used part of the (relatively safe) interest income to buy options on equity instruments. They were therefore able to guarantee that the fund would always earn the long-term interest rate less the cost of the option. The minimum return they offered ranged from 4 to 5 per cent per annum (7 to 8 per cent annual interest income less 3 per cent per annum for the equity options).

The success of these funds sparked competition and, unsurprisingly, some of this came from the traditional investing institutions, which saw that they were in danger of losing some of their market share. They responded by offering capital guaranteed equity products of their own. To ensure that theirs would be more attractive to investors, they offered higher minimum returns.

Although aware that this strategy could prove very risky, the risk was considered worth taking because, following one of the longest periods of stock-market appreciation in living memory, they held excess reserves against their traditional investment products. These reserves were estimated to be sufficient to make up any shortfall in returns between what they had promised their investors by way of capital guarantees and what was actually achievable in the market. Relying on reserves, it was thought, avoided the cost of purchasing options. Part of the cost could be passed on to investors and part would represent profit to the institution. So no off-setting options or other risk control measures were thought necessary, and none were implemented. Because equity markets had given the best recent returns, equity linked funds were the most attractive to retail investors, so about 70 per cent of the fund was allocated to equities, with the rest invested mostly in short-term bonds.

It was estimated that a call on the institution's capital was unlikely, as this would happen only if both interest rates rose and the equity markets failed to deliver attractive returns.

The fund was, unsurprisingly, a hit. The combination of attractive, guaranteed minimum returns and the reassurance of a long-established and well-respected investment manager was irresistible to many investors.

Example 15.5 Capital guarantees

	Years 1–2	Years 3–4	Year 5
	Annual return	**Annual return**	**Annual return**
Return to equities	15.0%	12.0%	-8.0%
Return to fixed income	8.0%	8.0%	-4.0%
Option cost	3.0%	3.0%	3.0%
Return to investors	18.5%	15.5%	6.5%
Return to reserves	n.a.	10.8%	-6.8%
Shortfall	n.a.	4.7%	13.3%

As shown in Example 15.5, the returns delivered by the markets in the ensuing few years were not extraordinary. As often happens following extended periods of above-trend returns, local bond and equity markets delivered sharply negative returns at the same time.

The return guaranteed to investors of 6.5 per cent exceeded the return earned by the reserves of –6.8 per cent by 13.3 per cent in year five. The success of the fund of course exacerbated the liability and threatened the survival of a large and well-established institution.

Endnote

1. The US Securities and Exchange Commission defines structured securities as 'securities whose cash flow characteristics depend upon one or more indices or that have embedded forwards or options or securities where an investor's investment return and the issuer's payment obligations are contingent on, or highly sensitive to, changes in the value of underlying assets, indices, interest rates or cash flows', a definition that could include many other investment products apart from structured products.

16
Hedge Funds and Funds of Hedge Funds

A woman goes to her bank manager for a personal loan to buy a car. Seeking to make conversation while completing the documentation, the loan officer asked his client what kind of car she intended to buy. With little interest in, or knowledge of, car makes and models – a friend having identified a suitable used car for her – the client replied, 'Um ... well ... a green one.'

The colour of a car is by no means unimportant: navy blue needs washing more often than other colours; black can trap the heat in summer; grey can be hard for other motorists to see; and so on. But the colour of a car will not affect its performance and reliability.

How a fund is packaged or wrapped can make it more attractive to investors, but it does not determine its performance.

This chapter describes the distinctive characteristics of hedge funds, private equity funds and funds of hedge funds, including:

- What they are.
- What they are used for.
- Hedge fund strategies.
- Private equity fund strategies.
- Notes on funds of funds.
- Their correlation with conventional asset classes.
- The role of prime brokers.
- Some observations on risk management.
- Fees.

What they are: characteristics of hedge funds and private equity funds

Hedge funds and private equity funds are characterized more by their structure than any common element in their approach to investments.

Characteristics common to most hedge funds and private equity funds are:

- They seek absolute return, benchmarked to cash rather than an index or comparator portfolio of risky assets.
- Their returns are enhanced by leverage.
- They are usually managed by specialist, boutique investment managers.
- They often have a minimum investment period.
- They often have a high minimum investment.
- They usually specify a maximum fund size.
- They are unregulated in most jurisdictions.
- Their returns tend to be very volatile.
- Their investment strategies usually rely in part on short selling.
- They usually levy performance-based management fees.

While they tend not to be compared to market indices in the same way that conventional portfolios are, hedge funds typically specialize in a particular market or sector, they do not necessarily expose the portfolio to the sector. Most hedge fund investors seek returns that are derived from unusual investment selection skill that is independent of directional exposure to conventional markets.

Private equity funds also tend to specialize in market sectors, but as they can give geared exposure to returns to the sector, comparison to a conventional, risky asset class is usually valid.

Hedge funds and private equity funds are usually managed by firms that specialize in the genre, often focussing on a relatively narrow range of funds. However some large investment managers offer both hedge funds and conventional funds under the same roof.

Most funds set some minimum initial investment period, often one year, with fairly long notice periods for subsequent withdrawals. These limitations allow the investment manager to maintain minimal liquidity balances, so keeping the fund fully invested most of the time.

It is common for hedge funds and private equity funds to set a maximum size for the fund, beyond which no further investment is accepted. This is mainly because the most successful investment strategies accommodate only limited investment before the best investment opportunities disappear. It also signals success on the part of the investment manager, potentially attracting further interest in the fund as and when existing investors withdraw, and in subsequent funds launched by the same investment manager.

Hedge funds and private equity funds were initially developed to provide high return investments to wealthy investors with high tolerances for return volatility and relative illiquidity. Confined to this market, hedge funds traditionally were mostly unregulated. In recent decades their investor base has expanded to include conventional funds such as pension funds, trust and mutual funds, whose investors in turn tend to have lower risk tolerances. Expansion of the investor base has prompted some authorities to consider regulation of the sector. Meanwhile, many hedge funds, seeking further expansion and diversification of their investor base, voluntarily seek regulatory status; for example, under the European Undertakings for Collective Investment in Transferable Securities (UCITS) umbrella.

Expansion of the hedge fund and private equity fund investor universe to include conventional investors such as pension funds and mutual funds is the result of two factors:

- The perception that conventional asset classes, such as equities, bonds and property, will deliver only modest returns in the future, which are unlikely to meet the investment objectives and obligations of their investors.
- Increased awareness that high volatility in one investment does not necessarily translate to high risk at the portfolio level if the risky investment is uncorrelated with other investments in the portfolio. High risk, high return investments can add to return without necessarily adding to risk.

Hedge funds typically charge performance-based fees, whereby the investor pays a regular management fee that is augmented by a share of the performance of the fund above some agreed return such as LIBOR. Typically the flat fee is 1 to 2 per cent of funds invested per year, with a further 10 to 20 per cent of returns above some threshold. Funds of hedge and private equity funds usually attract an extra layer of fees, typically 1 per cent and 10 per cent flat fee and performance fees respectively.

What hedge funds and private equity funds are used for

- To give high return with concentrated risk sources.
- To give returns due to pure alpha, independent of market related returns.
- As a complement to conventional portfolios, including pension, trust and mutual funds.
- As part of a core satellite investment structure in a multi-asset class portfolio.
- In funds of hedge funds and funds of private equity funds.

Hedge fund strategies

Hedge fund strategies are known for their variety, yet most can be described by one of the following:

- Relative value.
- Market neutral.
- Sector neutral.
- 130–30.
- Event driven.
- Bear funds.
- Volatility trading.
- Convertible hedge.
- Commodities.
- Distressed debt.

Each type of hedge fund strategy is typically qualified by specializing in a country, region, sector or investment style corresponding to the portfolio selection strengths of the hedge fund manager.

Relative value

Relative value funds typically invest in fixed interest, although theoretically relative value can apply to any asset class where bought positions are matched against sold positions. The investment manager models the theoretical price differential between physical assets, between physical assets and derivatives and between different types of derivatives. When the theoretical price differential deviates from the market price differential, an arbitrage opportunity exists. If the securities are sufficiently liquid, then the opportunity can be traded. If the original analysis is accurate, the strategy will yield a profit regardless of the general direction in the underlying markets.

In practice many relative value hedge funds also include some directional exposure to the markets in which they invest.

Market neutral

Sometimes known as 'pure alpha' funds, market neutral funds aim to deliver active return with no exposure to the market at large. In theory, market-neutral equity funds should have a beta to the market in which they invest of close to zero. In practice however many 'market neutral' portfolios retain some market exposure as measured by the portfolio's beta to its market. As with all long-short equity portfolios, market neutral funds are subject to the additional costs and risks inherent in short selling and the necessity to borrow stock for delivery. The risk and costs specific to short selling are described in more detail later in this chapter in the section on risk management.

Sector neutral

Sector neutral portfolios are conceptually similar to market neutral portfolios, but aim for zero net exposure to sectors or industry groups within the market as well as market neutrality. In practice sector neutral investment managers often select their portfolios by pairing stocks within a sector, for example, by matching a bought position in one retailer with an offsetting sold position in another retailer when the investment manager estimates that their price differential will change materially. If he or she is right, the portfolio benefits whether the general direction of the market is up or down.

130–30

130–30 portfolios are a sort of hybrid conventional and long-short portfolio. Bought positions represent 130 per cent of the portfolio's investment. The extra 30 per cent is 'funded' by selling short stocks worth 30 per cent, giving a net exposure of 100 per cent and therefore a beta to its market of about 1.0. By buying an extra 30 per cent and selling an extra 30 per cent of invested funds, the portfolio effectively levers the skill of the investment manager to deliver enhanced return with the same level of market risk as a conventional long only portfolio.

Event driven

Event driven, also known as 'deal arbitrage', is effectively another type of long-short strategy, which aims to benefit from price discrepancies that occur in the lead up to mergers and takeovers, changes in regulations and other structural changes in the market.

It is commonly understood that, during the lead up to a takeover bid, the shares of the target company go up relative to those of the acquiring company. This can happen for two reasons. The first is because its shares were under priced to begin with, which may be the reason for it being bought. The second is that the acquiring company often needs to pay a premium over the market price to secure a controlling interest. There is evidence that the price of the resulting entity often then under-performs similar assets, as the costs of effecting the merger exceed expectations, and projected synergies prove less beneficial than had been anticipated.

Other event driven strategies derive from changes in regulations governing an industry, or some other major structural change in a market or industry.

Bear funds

Bear funds profit from falling markets. Most bear funds invest in equities markets, although theoretically they can operate in any liquid market that allows short selling or where liquid derivatives markets facilitate short exposures. Physical assets are invested in short-term, interest-bearing securities, which provide collateral for sold physical assets and/or short futures positions in one or more markets, profiting from a fall in the market and losing if the market appreciates. In addition to being exposed to market directional risk, bear funds are subject to the costs and risks that attend short selling of physical assets.

Volatility trading

The portfolio sells expensive options and buys cheap ones, benefiting from small inconsistencies in the market volatilities implied by different series of options within a market. In theory volatility trading does not expose the portfolio to the direction of prices of the underlying risky assets. The strategy can entail buying and selling actual options or a combination of actual options and dynamic hedging.

Convertible arbitrage

The portfolio buys the convertible instrument and sells short the underlying equities, usually in proportions given by the delta of the option embedded in the convertible bond. The resulting position is thus a bought corporate bond, a bought actual call option and a sold replicating call option. Many managers also hedge away the corporate bond risk using CDS contracts to isolate the potentially lucrative option effect.

The convertible arbitrage portfolio benefits from the hedging risk resulting from the dynamic option replicating strategy. The gap risk that works against the manager of option replicating portfolios, described in Chapter 15 on structured products, works in favour of the convertible arbitrage manager. This is because, rather than being sold the actual option and bought the replicating option, the convertible arbitrage manager is bought the actual option and replicates a sold option. Consequently instead of crystalizing a loss each time the hedge is adjusted, the convertible arbitrage manager crystalizes a profit.

Commodities

Commodities funds seek to exploit the returns to commodities themselves, commodities derivatives, the relationship between the two and the relationships between different commodities derivatives. Commodities fund managers can find opportunities through analysis of macro-economic trends, supply and demand and substitution effects.

Distressed debt

Distressed debt is common to both hedge funds and private equity funds. Investments in distressed securities include:

- Investments where debt securities are bought with the aim of gaining control of the target company in the event that it recovers. These are also called 'distressed-to-control' and 'loan-to-own' strategies.
- Purchase of debt and equity as a form of rescue financing to companies undergoing operational or financial challenges. These strategies are known as 'special situations' or 'turnaround' strategies.
- Active trading of bonds issued by distressed companies.

Distressed securities are securities of companies or government entities that are either already in default, under bankruptcy protection or in distress and heading toward such a condition. The most common distressed securities are bonds and bank debt. While there is no precise definition, fixed income instruments with a yield to maturity in excess of 10 per cent over the risk-free rate of return, or government borrowing rate, are commonly thought of as being distressed. A related category is stressed debt yielding between 6 per cent and 8 per cent over the government borrowing rate. Distressed securities often carry ratings of CCC or below from agencies such as Standard & Poor's, Moody's and Fitch.

Investors in distressed securities often try to influence the process by which the issuer restructures its debt, narrows its focus or implements a plan to turn around its operations. Investors may also invest new debt or equity capital in the company.

The success of a distressed debt investment depends on the target company's ability to improve its profitability, as well as whether the restructuring process, which frequently requires court supervision, benefits one class of securities more than another.

Private equity fund strategies

By definition, private equity funds invest in equity securities that are not publicly traded on a stock exchange; however some private equity companies do sometimes invest in publicly traded companies. They can also invest in debt securities.

Private equity funds include venture capital and angel investors as well as private equity itself. All provide working capital in order to facilitate expansion, new product development or restructuring of the company's operations, management or ownership.

Private equity strategies include:

- Leveraged buyouts.
- Growth capital.
- Mezzanine capital.
- Venture capital.
- Distressed and stressed investments.

Leveraged buyouts

A leveraged buyout is the purchase of majority control of an existing or mature firm.[1] In a leveraged buyout transaction, an investor agrees to acquire a firm without itself committing all the capital required for the acquisition, instead raising debt, the interest cost of which he or she anticipates will be off-set by cash flows from the target firm. The debt raised is often non-recourse to the investor and so has no claim on other investments he or she manages. The investor benefits in a number of ways:

- The investor gains the benefits of leverage while limiting the risks of borrowing.
- The investor needs to provide only a fraction of the capital for the acquisition.
- The investor earns positive returns so long as the return on the target's assets is greater than the cost of the debt.
- By retaining the debt that financed the acquisition, the investor can off-set interest costs against the profits of the company, thus reducing, or even eliminating, tax.

The amount of debt used to finance a transaction varies between transactions, but tends to be between 60 per cent and 90 per cent of the purchase price. Risk can be further reduced by hedging the debt with CDS contracts.

Growth capital

Growth capital entails the purchase of a, usually minority, equity investment in relatively mature companies aimed at expanding or restructuring operations, entering new markets or financing a major acquisition.

Being mature, the target company is usually able to generate revenue and operating profits but unable to generate sufficient cash to fund major investments. In this sense its risk profile is distinct from other direct equity investments.

Mezzanine capital

Mezzanine capital is subordinated debt or preferred equity securities that typically are junior to other debt obligations but senior to the company's equity. Mezzanine debt can reduce the amount of equity capital required to finance a leveraged buyout or major expansion. Mezzanine capital is also used by smaller companies as an alternative to the bond markets to which they may not have access. It can allow them to raise capital beyond the levels that banks are generally willing to lend.

Venture capital

Venture capital is an investment in equity that helps finance less mature companies, including:

- The launch of start-up companies.
- Early stage development.
- Expansion of a young business.

Unlike leveraged buyouts, venture capital investors tend not to seek control of the target company.

Distressed and stressed investments

Distressed debt is common to both hedge funds and private equity funds. Investments in distressed securities include:

- Investments where debt securities are bought with the aim of gaining control of the target company in the event that it recovers. These are also called 'distressed-to-control' and 'loan-to-own' strategies.
- Purchase of debt and equity as a form of rescue financing to companies undergoing operational or financial challenges. These strategies are known as 'special situations' or 'turnaround' strategies.
- Active trading of bonds issued by distressed companies.

Investors in distressed securities often try to influence the process by which the issuer restructures its debt, narrows its focus or implements a plan to turn around its operations, including, if necessary, investment in new debt or equity capital in the company.

The secondary market in private equity

Investments in existing private equity assets or portfolios of direct investments can be bought from existing investors. This can improve diversification in a number of ways:

- By broadening the range of available investments.
- By giving exposure to new and mature investments, with different revenue and cash flow patterns.
- By giving access to the best performing funds, which otherwise are inaccessible as a result of being oversubscribed.
- By allowing the investor to avoid being limited to investments with structural impediments such as long lock-up periods, lack of transparency, unlimited leverage, concentrated holdings of illiquid securities and high investment minimums.

By its nature, the private equity asset class is illiquid, intended as a long-term investment. Secondary market transactions in private equity interests are typically effected through third party fund vehicles, which are structured as a fund of funds, although private equity fund interests can also be transacted directly between buyer and seller. Most secondary market transfers of private equity interests entail the buyer assuming the funds' unfunded commitments as well as the investments in the fund.

There are two types of secondary private equity transactions:

Limited partnership interests – which include the sale of an investor's interest in a private equity fund or portfolio of interests in various funds by transferral of the investor's limited partnership interest in the fund or funds. Transfer of the limited partnership interest typically allows the investor to receive some consideration for the funded investments and can include a release from any remaining unfunded obligations to the fund.

Direct interests – also known as 'secondary directs' or 'synthetic secondaries', these are the sale of portfolios of direct investments in operating companies, rather than limited partnership interests in investment funds.

Sources of return to private equity investments

Returns on private equity investments are derived from:

- Debt repayment.
- Cash accumulation through cash flows from operations.
- Operational improvements that increase earnings over the life of the investment.

- Multiple expansion, which results from selling the company for a higher multiple of earnings than was paid at acquisition.
- An initial public offering (IPO), in which shares of the company are offered to the public, giving immediate crystallization of profits to the investor as well as a public market into which it can later sell additional shares.
- A merger or acquisition, where the company is sold either for cash or for shares in another company.
- A recapitalization, where cash is distributed to the shareholders, meaning the investor and its private equity funds, either from cash flow generated by the company or through raising debt or other securities.

Measuring exposure to private equity investments

The most common ways of measuring the size of a private equity fund are by:

- The amount of capital raised.
- The total value of companies purchased by the fund.
- Estimation of the size of the fund's active portfolio plus capital available for new investments.

As with any measure of nominal investment, these give no information about the contribution to return from each investment, nor do they give any insight into the concentrations in risk of the fund or sources of vulnerability.

Private equity versus hedge funds

Typically private equity investment groups are geared towards long-term investment strategies in illiquid assets, such as whole companies, large-scale real estate projects or other tangible assets not easily converted to cash, where they can exercise more control or influence over operations or asset management.

By contrast, hedge funds usually focus on short- or medium-term liquid securities, which are more quickly convertible to cash and are less likely to have direct control over the business or asset in which they are investing.

Both private equity firms and hedge funds often specialize in specific types of investments and transactions. Private equity is primarily concerned with managing assets while hedge funds are mainly concerned with managing capital.

Funds of funds

Individual investors can gain access to hedge funds and private equity funds via funds of funds. Funds of funds can provide better diversification across funds than is generally available to individuals. They can also give access to hedge funds and private equity funds that are otherwise closed, having reached their maximum capacity.

Most funds of hedge funds and funds of private equity funds select portfolios to give broad coverage and to diversify the risks associated with a single investment fund. However some funds of funds invest in a single fund in order to give ordinary investors access to an otherwise hard to invest in fund.

There are a number of benefits to the individual investor of using funds of funds instead of investing directly in one or more alternative investment funds, including:

- Researching and selecting managers to identify the funds that are most likely to deliver the best results.
- Conducting due diligence on the funds prior to investment and periodically while the investment is held.
- Allocating between funds to give the best mix of investments given the different strategies available.
- On-going scrutiny of individual funds' investments.
- Diversification across strategies.
- Diversification across several or many funds reduces manager risk, enabling the fund of funds to achieve its objectives, even if one or more individual investment managers fail to achieve theirs.
- The fund of funds manager can exploit its size to negotiate significant fee reductions.
- Access to successful, hard to invest in funds that may be closed to new investment or that impose long investor lock-in times.

Funds of funds levy fees for their services in addition to the hedge fund's management and performance fees. The fee to the fund of funds manager can be 1 per cent on the value of the fund with a performance fee of about 10 per cent.

Correlation with other asset classes

One of the main attractions of hedge funds and private equity funds is the low correlation of their returns with those of conventional asset classes. The effect of this is to add to the scope of the investment universe and thereby help enhance the returns to multi-asset class funds without materially adding to risk, instead often helping to diversify risk.

In theory, hedge funds investing in the following strategies should have little or no correlation with conventional equity and bond market returns because all have more or less off-setting bought and sold exposures, which largely neutralize exposure to the market in which they invest.

- Relative value.
- Long-short equity.
- Market neutral equity.
- Sector neutral equity.
- Event driven.
- Volatility trading.
- Convertible arbitrage.
- Commodities.

In practice however, they can exhibit surprisingly high correlations, not just with conventional asset class markets, but also with each other.

One reason is that in fact they tend to retain some directional exposure to the markets in which they invest; for example, relative value fixed interest funds often have directional exposure to interest rates and currencies; and equity long-short funds typically have a beta to the market in which they invest of about 0.40.

This can be disappointing for the investor for two reasons:

- The funds do not give the additional investment scope and diversification potential that is usually expected of them.
- The investor is paying very high fees for exposure that he or she could easily achieve simply by buying futures contracts or ETFs.

For private equity funds, low correlation with conventional asset classes can be due more to their low return volatility than any inherent diversification potential. They are, after all, still investing in equities or corporate bonds, generally with no off-setting sold exposures. The reported low volatility, in turn, may be due more to the fact that the assets are priced less frequently than those of similar companies with equity that is listed on an exchange. There is no reason to suppose that unlisted equity is less volatile than listed equity. The difference is more likely to do with the fact that the volatility in the value of unlisted assets is visible only when the asset is traded.

Private equity fund returns, and therefore the correlation of their return with other asset classes, are also affected by the fact that often they are not fully invested. Part of any private equity fund is likely to remain idle while new investment targets are sought. Idle cash is of course a drag on performance.

The role of the prime broker

Nearly all hedge funds engage one or more prime brokers to provide a range of services, including:

- Providing a centralized securities clearing facility to allow netting of collateral requirements across all open positions, which can reduce the fund's cost of funding its collateral.
- Maintaining a centralized, master account of the fund's investments that facilitates trading with multiple brokerage houses for IPO allocations, research, best execution, conference access and other products.
- Global custody, including clearing, custody and asset servicing.
- Securities lending.
- Financing to facilitate leverage.
- Risk management advisory services, including risk analytic technology, sometimes supplemented by risk consulting.
- Capital introduction to expand the fund's investor base.
- Consulting services, typically provided to 'start-up' hedge funds, to help with regulatory establishment requirements.
- Providing daily and real-time reporting of open positions.
- Operational support, including liaising with other broker dealers.
- Office space leasing and servicing.

Prime brokers typically do not charge a fee for the bundled package of services they provide to hedge funds. Rather, revenues are typically derived from:

- Spreads on financing, including of margins and security lending.
- Trading commissions.
- Fees for clearing transactions.
- Fees for the settlement of transactions.

Prime brokers represent a source of counterparty risk to hedge funds. For example, if the prime broker or its parent defaults, the hedge fund may be unable to reclaim collateral lodged with it. For this reason, most hedge funds maintain relationships with more than one prime broker. Using more than one prime broker is also not without its problems. From the operational perspective it adds complexity, obliging hedge funds to devote extra resources to managing multiple relationships. From the investors' perspective, having more than one prime broker complicates the due diligence process, necessitating reconciliation of open positions and trades between the fund's administrator and its counterparties.

Hedge funds are a source of counterparty risk to prime brokers too because prime brokers facilitate hedge fund leverage, primarily through loans secured by the long positions of their clients. This exposes the prime broker to the risk of loss in the event that the value of collateral held as security declines below the loan value, and the client is unable to repay the deficit. The prime broker is also exposed to operational risk and reputational risk.

Risk management

Hedge funds and private equity are generally perceived to be more risky than conventional investments, so it follows that risk management deserves particular attention. To be effective, risk management must be tailored to the investment strategy of each fund, so there is a limit to how much generalization is possible. Nevertheless, some observations about risk management for hedge funds and private equity investments are:

- Risk management is not the same as risk minimization. Risk that is expected to lead to extra return should be nurtured and managed.
- Otherwise it should be eliminated. Failure to understand risk management means some sources of risk remain unmanaged, leaving the fund vulnerable to unnecessary losses.
- Risk measurement should include the portfolio's gearing and counterparty risk as well as market and factor risk. In combination they all affect portfolio outcomes.
- VaR, CVaR, tracking error or volatility can be used to estimate:
  - everyday risk, which is effectively the likelihood of the investment target return being achieved,
  - extreme loss, which is the vulnerability of the portfolio to crashes.
- The time frame should be appropriate to the investment strategy and horizon. For example, a one-month VaR is unhelpful if the investment horizon is three years, and vice-versa.
- Risk measurement should quantify the main sources of expected return as well as potential points of weakness; for example, hedge fund managers typically have four to six themes in their portfolios. Too few themes and the fund may be too concentrated. Too many themes can be hard to manage, increasing volatility (if the risks compound each other) or dampening returns (if they are off-setting). Themes should be as independent as possible so as neither to off-set nor compound each other.
- Risk measurement should distinguish between the likelihood of both gain and loss, and the sources of any asymmetry.

- Risk controls should be integral to each theme or strategy. Explicit target returns and loss limits, as distinct from stop-losses, for individual themes signal that the portfolio manager actively links risk with return. A stated exit strategy for each theme, for both good and bad outcomes, reflects discipline.
- A robust risk management process can complement and enhance the portfolio manager's investment selection skills. By quantifying the compounding and offsetting relationships in the portfolio, a skilled risk manager can suggest ways to target risk to improve the overall outcome.

Short selling

In pure economic terms there is no difference between a bought position in a stock and a sold position: they are precise mirror images of each other. However there are material practical differences between underweight (but still bought) stock positions and short selling.

Firstly, short selling incurs a cost. In order to sell a stock short, the investment manager first needs to borrow the stock from another investor so as to deliver it and receive settlement. This incurs borrowing costs, which are determined by prevailing short-term interest rates and the availability of the stock for loan. The lender of the stock bears the risk that the borrower will be unable to return the stock at the end of the loan, so he or she has counterparty risk against the borrower or the intermediary if one is used to arrange the loan. To offset this counterparty risk, the lender or intermediary usually demands margin payments or collateral to guarantee that the stock will be returned or compensate for its non-return.

Secondly, it entails the risk of a short squeeze. If the price of the stock rises sharply, the investor who is sold short may have difficulty in repurchasing the stock at short notice in order to contain losses. The price of a stock cannot fall below zero, but it can in theory rise indefinitely, so potential losses to a short position are unlimited. Short-sellers, being required to post increased margins and collateral may, in a tight market, be unable to raise funds to do so and be forced to liquidate other positions, including those that they otherwise would have retained. The collective actions of short sellers trying to cover their positions can lead to severe shortages of the stock in the market place, which can be exploited by other investors who are not so constrained.

Because of the costs and risk associated with naked short sales, short positions can usually be held only for limited periods, within which the anticipated under-performance or price falls must occur in order for the position to pay off.

By contrast, for the investor who is merely underweight a sharply rising stock can simply wait until the stock price 'corrects', presenting an opportunity to buy more of the stock. He or she is therefore not obliged to meet margin calls or to effect transactions that otherwise might compromise the performance of the portfolio.

Fees

Hedge fund fees usually have two components:

- A fixed percentage, usually 1 to 2 per cent of the funds under management. This means that, as the fund grows, either with new investment in the fund or simply as a result of market appreciation, this portion of the fees earned by the hedge fund manager grows correspondingly.
- A performance linked fee, typically 10 to 20 per cent of the return earned by the fund over some agreed level, such as LIBOR. Usually performance fees are subject to some kind of 'claw back', whereby underperformance must be recouped before further performance fees can be accrued.

This dual fee structure can help explain why many relative value and long-short hedge funds retain directional exposure to the markets in which they invest. For a fund investing in a rising market, say equities, where the performance fee is calculated relative to LIBOR, the fund can earn fees of 10 to 20 per cent simply as a result of market appreciation, as well as the flat 1 to 2 per cent fee, even with mediocre performance. Add in the fact that most hedge funds are geared, and attractive fees to the hedge fund manager are all but guaranteed so long as the market continues to rise, irrespective of any portfolio selection skill.

Summary

Hedge funds and private equity funds were conceived first to give high returns to wealthy individuals and family offices with high tolerances for return volatility and relative illiquidity. Investors now include conventional multi-asset class portfolios owned by pension, trust and mutual funds and funds of funds. While the investors in those funds do not normally have the appetite for the risk inherent in most hedge funds and private equity funds, the funds can be an attractive source of return and diversification within a multi-asset class portfolio, so long as correlations with conventional asset classes remain low. Correlations between hedge funds and between hedge funds and conventional asset classes are not always as low as is generally supposed, which can compromise their suitability for inclusion in investment portfolios seeking diversification of market risks. Hedge funds and private equity funds with genuinely low correlations with conventional asset classes can however materially improve the risk–return profile of a multi-asset class portfolio.

Unlike most conventional portfolios, hedge fund managers are usually paid according to how big their fund is as well as how well they perform against an agreed comparison rate of return, such as LIBOR.

Case Study

Until the dot.com boom of the late 1990s, it was widely accepted that stock prices nearly always rose fairly slowly but fell quite sharply: 'up by the stairs and down by the elevator'. This pattern can sometimes be exploited using exchange-traded options on risky assets. A trader noticed that stock options on many stocks were trading at implied volatilities in the range of 40 to 80 per cent, compared to usual levels of 20 to 30 per cent.

His strategy was to sell at-the-money call and put options simultaneously on a number of individual stocks and to sell short the underlying shares. Selling at-the-money options yielded the maximum option premium. The risk was that the share price would move sharply up, in which case the calls would end up in-the-money and be exercised, forcing the trader to buy shares in the market and resell them at a loss. The loss, equal to the difference between the price at which the shares would be repurchased and the exercise price of the options, would be compounded by the loss on the sold physical shares, which would be repurchased at a higher price than that at which they were sold at the outset of the trade.

Example 16.1 Short call and put at the same exercise price with short stock position

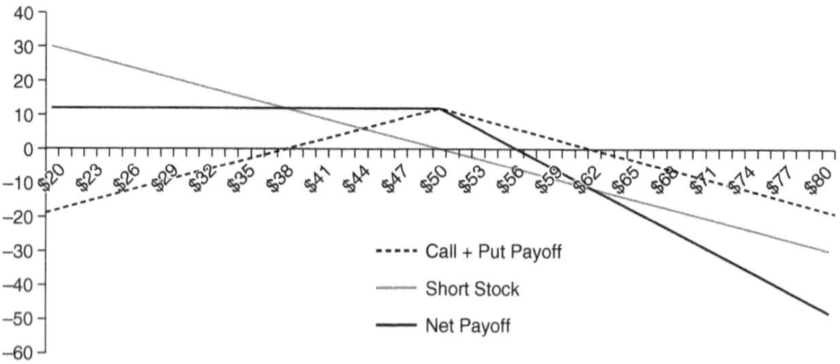

Example 16.1 shows that the position is immune to a fall in the share price, but that an increase above $56 would start to incur serious losses.

The transaction took place in an exchange operated by 'open outcry', meaning that bids and offers are communicated orally in the hall of the stock exchange.

Open outcry can be very labour intensive, as each transaction must be carried out individually. In this case, each transaction had three 'legs': the sold call, the sold put and the sold physical share. As with many exchanges, the options are traded in a separate part of the exchange to physical shares. As the options were usually less liquid and therefore more difficult to transact, these were put in place first, the idea being to sell the shares, which generally could be effected quickly, when the options transactions had been completed.

Selling the options took longer than expected however and the bell signalling the close of business sounded before the physical shares were sold. This was thought not to be a problem because, for one thing, the sold share positions were merely intended as a safety net, so not critical to the success of the strategy; and second, all the stocks in question were major companies, which could be traded in other time zones. The shares could thus be sold on another market within a few hours. The trader instructed his colleague to place orders to sell the shares on another market, and then left for the day.

The position of the fund at the close of the day therefore looked like that shown in Example 16.2.

Example 16.2 Short call and put at the same exercise price without short stock position

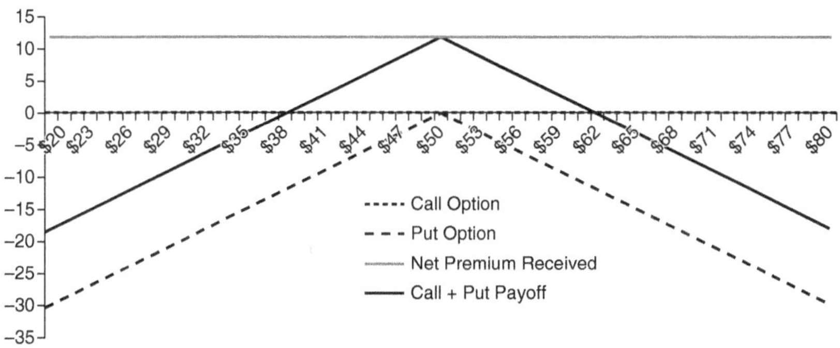

In other words, it was exposed to potentially unlimited losses in both market directions and would deliver a positive outcome only in a steady market.

More experienced traders had seen this strategy before, and had seen just how risky it could be in volatile markets. They also knew that unusually high implied volatilities in options markets usually signals impending unusually high volatility in the underlying securities. Some traders had even named this strategy an 'airport spread', observing that the best next move for the trader would be to head for the airport and leave the country.

By coincidence, this trader was obliged, for reasons unconnected with this transaction, to travel overseas for two weeks. He caught a flight out that evening.

Meanwhile the colleague, confident that selling parcels of leading shares would not pose a problem, decided to delay placing the sale order until the following day, when he would have more time to calculate and check the precise quantities required. The following day, the share index opened 40 per cent lower. The sold put options were very much in-the-money.

Example 16.3 Pay off to option strategy

Payoff with 40% drop in price	
New stock price	30.09
Value of call option	$0.24
Value of put option	$19.16
Profit/loss on calls	$6.22
Profit/loss on puts	($13.84)
Total theoretical Loss	($7.62)

Put options exercised	
Loss on sale of stock	($20.06)
Premium received	$11.78
Net loss	($8.28)

As Example 16.3 shows, the trader had sold put options at an exercise price of $50 when the current share price was $50.15, obliging him, upon exercise by the buyer of the options, to buy the shares at $50, regardless of their market value. Buying at $50 and selling the shares at $30.09 incurred a loss of $19.91 per share. This transaction was highly geared because the actual exposure of the position was many times the amount of the capital required to put it in place. The initial margin requirements for short option positions was about $1 per option, so for each share equivalent, the transaction was backed by capital of about $2, giving a return on investment of –406.5 per cent.

Endnote

1. This is distinct from a venture capital or growth capital investment, in which the investors, typically venture capital firms or angel investors, invest in young or emerging companies, and rarely obtain majority control.

Part IV

Peripherals

17
Implementation

Modern investment theory depends to a greater or lesser extent on the efficient functioning of markets. But in practice few markets are perfectly efficient. This chapter describes how the functioning of markets contributes to or compromises efficiency, covering:

- Centralized versus decentralized markets.
- Exchanges.
- Off-exchange: dark pools.
- Block trades.
- Algorithmic trading.
- Front running.
- Soft dollars and directed commissions.
- Portfolio transition.
- Stock lending.

Implementation of portfolios can be effected:

- Via a centralized exchange, such as a stock exchange or a futures exchange. Equities, commodities, structured products and derivatives such as futures and options are traded on centralized exchanges.
- Via a decentralized market where parties to the transaction transact directly with each other. Bonds, foreign exchange, swaps, direct property and private equity are usually traded in decentralized markets.

The efficiency of a market is closely linked to its:

- Transparency.
- Liquidity.
- Costs of transactions.
- Risks associated with trading on it.

Centralized versus decentralized markets

Transparency

Decentralized markets are less transparent than centralized exchanges. Unlike most exchanges, parties to a transaction in a decentralized market are not obliged to disclose the price at which a deal was struck and there is no central source of information about open positions in particular assets or instruments as there is on centralized exchanges. While information about buy and sell quotes for bonds, swaps, CDS and foreign exchange are usually made available by market data providers such as FactSet, Bloomberg and Reuters, the information given is usually indicative only and may not always reflect the prices at which trades are struck.

Liquidity

Illiquidity can characterize both decentralized markets and centralized exchanges and is more to do with the nature of the instruments themselves than the mode of trading them. Some decentralized markets are extremely liquid most of the time for most securities, such as government bonds, interest rate swaps and foreign exchange; while other decentralized markets are much less liquid – for example, direct property and private equity. While any kind of market can be illiquid, lack of liquidity is more visible on centralized exchanges than on decentralized markets.

Costs of transactions

Transactions costs vary for both centralized and decentralized markets. They include:

- Taxes, which are determined by the jurisdiction in which transactions take place and so can apply to either centralized or decentralized markets. They are typically a small component of overall transactions costs.
- Brokerage and commissions usually apply to transactions on centralized exchanges as well as on many decentralized markets. For property and direct equity, they can be higher than for other assets. Commissions can be negotiated in advance with brokers on a deal-by-deal basis, either as a percentage of the face value of the transactions or as a nominal amount per transaction. Transactions in some markets, notably bonds and foreign exchange, have no explicit commissions. Intermediaries acting as brokers instead make a profit by buying at a slightly lower price than the one they sell at. Commission is thus embedded in the bid-ask spread, and is less transparent than explicit commissions.
- Exchange fees of course apply only to exchange transactions, but tend to be negligible for most transactions.

- Bid-ask spreads are in many markets the largest of all transactions costs. The bid-ask spread on an instrument is a function of its liquidity. Liquidity is affected by, among other things, the number of securities on issue and available for regular sale and purchase, also known as the 'free float', which is not always the same as the size by market capitalization of the issuer or the number of securities on issue.

The Risks

Execution risks include the risk that the trade will not be executed at the anticipated price, which can result from market impact or from opportunity cost. Trades in decentralized markets are in addition subject to counterparty risk.

- **Market impact** can be thought of as the cost of transacting each additional share. For example, if an investor seeks to buy one share; he or she will accept the offer price, which will probably remain unchanged after the transaction. If the same investor buys a thousand of the same shares the price may move slightly after the trade is complete, as each marginal seller in turn has completed his or her order, eliminating the most aggressive sellers and leaving only sellers at higher prices. A buyer of a million of the same shares may find that the sale price (and possibly the bid price) moves even before the trade is complete, as other market participants read the signal that demand for the stock – and therefore perhaps its intrinsic value – has increased.

Electronic trading has arguably contributed to market impact. By reducing the time it takes to execute a trade and thereby increasing the responsiveness of prices to market pressures, modern, electronic, automated trading platforms ironically may have made it more difficult to move large blocks of securities without affecting their prices.

- **Opportunity cost** applies to active investment managers who have discretion about when to trade. It is the cost incurred when an investor sets out to trade a stock at a certain price and fails to complete the trade because the stock price moves beyond the limit set. He or she is then obliged to increase the bid or lower the offer price. If the price is still not high or low enough to attract a seller or buyer for the volume of the trade, this process may need to be repeated several times before the transaction is completed, with the result that the average price transacted is materially less attractive than the initial price. On the other hand, if the investor abandons the transaction, and the price continues to move against him or her, the opportunity cost is increased.

- **Counterparty risk** in the context of implementing trades is the risk that the other party will be unable either to deliver title to the asset or to pay for it. Most exchanges minimize this problem by acting as a central counterparty, acting as both buyer and seller to all transactions. The exchange has no exposure to price movements, and because it has access to information about the beneficial owners of assets transacted on it, it can eliminate the risk that a seller is unable to deliver ownership of the asset. However it is still exposed to settlement risk, the risk that buyers are unable to settle their transactions.

By contrast, traders on decentralized markets must assume the full amount of the risk that the counterparty to their transaction will be unable to perform, either by delivering ownership of the security or settlement.

Exchanges

Exchanges typically are companies, usually regulated by the financial services supervisor within their jurisdiction, that seek to make a profit. They are free to compete with other exchanges for existing business, usually on the basis of their infrastructure and prices. Their purpose is:

- To provide a central forum where buyers and sellers gather to compete for the most attractive prices for assets, securities or contracts.
- To facilitate transactions by providing information about the assets traded on them and the state of supply and demand for them.
- To provide the means for raising investment capital at the most competitive price possible.
- By facilitating capital formation and providing current information about the supply of and demand for risky assets, to help promote investment in risky assets and therefore economic activity and growth.

They are characterized by:

Listing rules – these ensure sufficient initial company reporting so that investors have access to reliable information to support their decisions.

Disclosure rules – these provide minimum standards of on-going company reporting to ensure that investors have access to reliable information to support their decisions.

Information – this allows investors and issuers to remain reliably informed about completed trades and the current state of supply and demand for all securities on issue in order to support investment decisions.

Standardization – this ensures that information furnished by all listed entities is comparable across securities and issuers.

Trading rules – these ensure minimum standards of conduct to ensure fairness and transparency.

Order prioritization – these rules ensure predictable, reliable and fair execution of trades that do not favour some market participants over others.

Central counterparty – this eliminates the risk of non-delivery or settlement failure for buyers and sellers, thereby encouraging confidence and removing a possible source of uncertainty.

Settlement times – these, together with prescribed settlement conditions, ensure predictability and minimize the risk of investors being over or under invested.

Anonymity – the anonymity of buyers and sellers is provided for by most exchanges, although the identity of their brokers is usually made public. Nominal anonymity often cannot conceal the identity of parties to very large trades.

Order driven and quote driven exchanges

There are two main conventions by which exchanges facilitate transactions, order driven and quote driven.

Order driven exchanges work by matching the orders of buyers and sellers, who register the price at which they are willing to sell or buy an asset and the amount they are willing to transact at that price. The exchange matches the buy to the sell orders and records the trade. Most exchanges publish, in real time, the queue of bids and offers, which gives would-be traders the opportunity to adjust their own bids and offers to achieve the best price or to trade an unusually large volume.

Order driven markets can suffer illiquidity if the best buy and sell prices are very different from each other, resulting in no trades in that security or contract.

Quote driven exchanges try to overcome this problem by mandating market makers to ensure liquidity in specified securities, often assigning several market makers to a single security to encourage competition. Market makers are principal traders who use their own funds to buy and sell stock. The market maker is obliged to stand ready both to buy and to sell each of the stocks to which he or she is allocated, usually with a maximum allowable spread between quoted buy and sell prices and a minimum acceptable quantity. Market makers are, in a sense, 'traders of last resort', as investors are always free to trade with other participants.

Off-exchange – dark pools

Dark pools of liquidity, also referred to as 'dark liquidity' or simply 'dark pools' or 'black pools' offer decentralized, electronic trading in securities such as listed equities, that are normally traded on a centralized exchange. Unlike conventional exchanges, dark pools do not publish the queue of bids and offers for the securities traded on them until after the transaction is completed. Dark pools developed in response to the demand by very large investment firms for more anonymity than is offered by conventional exchanges, where transaction information is published in real time. Institutional investors use dark pools to transact large blocks of securities without showing their hand to others and thus avoiding or at least minimizing market impact.

There are three major types of dark pools:

- Independent companies that offer a unique differentiated trading platform.
- Broker-owned dark pools where clients of the broker interact anonymously, most commonly with other clients of the broker, or with the broker itself acting as principal to the transaction.
- Dark pools within conventional exchanges, which can combine the benefits of anonymity and non-display of orders with those of exchange infrastructure and regulation.

Dark pools generally apply similar rules to those imposed by conventional exchanges regarding order types, pricing and prioritization. The difference is that liquidity is deliberately not published. If obliged to make public information about completed trades, dark pools seek to do so with as long a delay as possible in order to reduce their market impact. Liquidity information may not be comparable between competing dark pools because some count both sides of the trade, or even count liquidity that was posted but not filled.

Dark pools transactions are recorded as over-the-counter transactions. In some jurisdictions this means that detailed information about prices, volumes and types of transactions is at the discretion of the dark pool operator, although other jurisdictions demand disclosure.

Dark pools can work both to improve market efficiency and to reduce it. They can work against market efficiency by concealing information about securities that would be visible in a public exchange. For a security that can be traded only publicly, the standard price discovery process is generally assumed to ensure that at any given time the published price is the true price. Where publicly traded securities can be traded off market without publishing the trade, and the proportion of hidden volume increases, the published price can no longer be said to reflect all information about the asset, so it may no longer be the true or 'fair' price.

On the other hand, dark pools can aid efficiency by increasing volume. They can do this because they can facilitate anonymous transactions that may not have taken place in a more transparent environment, since the cost of market impact might have been prohibitive from the point of view of the investor. This increase in efficiency works only if details of the trade are subsequently published.

At the same time, opaque bid and offer queues can expose the investor to the 'winners curse'. As the investor does not know anything about rival bids and offers, he or she risks winning the trade by paying more or selling for less than was necessary to win the bid, and therefore diminishing the profitability of the trade.

While trading on a dark venue can reduce market impact, it is very unlikely to eliminate it altogether. At least some of the liquidity necessary to effect a trade can originate in the public market, as automated broker systems intercept and transact with market-bound orders. This means that one side of the transaction 'disappears' from public view. The fact of the disappearance sends information to the public market that causes impact. Yet limiting trades to other dark pool counterparties can slow down execution by narrowing the universe of prospective counterparties. This leaves the investor with the choice of reducing the speed of execution by crossing only with dark pool counterparties or increasing both speed and market impact by allowing the broader pool of trades on public exchanges to participate.

Block trades

Execution cost and risk can be controlled by means of 'block' or 'basket' trades, which entail buying or selling simultaneously a large number of, usually small, parcels of securities. The benefit to the investor is that an entire portfolio can be implemented instantly, effectively transferring the risk of executing the trade from the investor to the stockbroker. It can also reduce the likelihood of dealing errors and can partially streamline the consequent paper trail.

Baskets can be described by the investment manager to the broker either as a simple list of the securities to be transacted and the volume of each, or in terms of summary statistics, such as beta to the local market, tracking error and the number of stocks.

The disadvantage of disclosing the full list is that it gives away information about the transaction to brokers who competed for and lost the transaction. These brokers therefore know in advance that their competitor now is obliged to trade this basket of securities on market and so can take advantage.

Describing the basket in terms of its summary statistics can avoid this problem, but introduces others in that it can leave the broker with an inventory of illiquid securities. Most brokers build extra margin in to their quotes to compensate for this risk.

Algorithmic trading

Algorithmic trading, also called 'automated trading', 'black-box trading', or 'algo trading', is where computers are programmed to give instructions to trade on the basis of defined prices or price spreads between securities and derivatives contracts, with specified timing and quantity, but without routine human intervention.

Algorithmic trading is used by investment banks, pension funds, trust funds, mutual funds and hedge funds to divide large trades into a number of smaller trades to minimize market impact. Market makers use algorithmic trading to generate trades automatically in order to fulfil their obligations to provide liquidity.

High-frequency trading is a type of algorithmic trading that seeks to benefit from market makers' operations. As well as being used by market makers themselves, it can be used in any investment strategy, including inter-market spread trading, arbitrage or pure speculation, such as trend following strategies.

Front running

Front running is where a broker, having been informed of a large incoming order, trades the security first on his or her own account, subsequently crystalizing a profit by reversing the transaction concerned at a price that is made more attractive by the market impact of the trade itself. This is of course illegal and, for most conventional transactions, fairly easy to police.

Front running can also take place within an investing institution; for example, where managers of conventional portfolios, whose remuneration is only indirectly related to the performance of their portfolios, work in close proximity to hedge fund managers, whose remuneration is linked directly to the returns they achieve. In such situations, the hedge fund manager has both the means and the motivation to front run the conventional manager. Most compliance departments are on the lookout for this kind of front running, but it can be hard to spot if it is well camouflaged.

One way of camouflaging front running is to trade not in identical securities, but in other securities or instruments that are highly correlated with them.

Soft dollars and directed commissions

Soft dollars

Soft dollars are where a broker undertakes to pay some of the expenses of the investment manager in return for a minimum volume of transactions or a minimum nominal amount of commissions over the course of some time horizon, such as a year. This benefits the investment manager by reducing its costs, arguably thereby enabling it to deploy better resources and so offer better service and or performance to its investors. The broker benefits from an assured minimum revenue stream – and consequently denying its competitors some revenues, as well as the kudos that derives from higher reported market share – and denying competitors that quotient of market share.

While investors in the portfolios arguably benefit from possibly better service and performance, the portfolios they manage can incur costs in the form of increased turnover, which in turn incurs not only extra commissions but also market impact, taxes and so on. Where commissions are, in a sense, paid for whether or not they are used, the investment manager has less incentive to scrutinize the benefit to the portfolio of each transaction; especially if the alternative for the investment manager is a cash payment to the broker in order to make up the minimum revenue promised. Even if transactions are justified in terms of better risk and return profiles, pre-paid or pre-committed commissions remove some of the incentive to seek the best execution. Concurrently the broker, knowing that the investment manager is obliged to transact with him or her, may pay less attention to the quality of the execution terms. The result can be less favourable purchase and sale prices and consequently compromised performance.

A grey area of soft dollar services is the provision of research by brokerage houses to investment managers in exchange for a proportion of the transactions they undertake. The practice has been established for decades but recently it has attracted scrutiny from two sources. The first is from regulators who are keen to ensure transparency and fairness for investors. Broker research that is bundled with execution services lacks transparency as its implicit price is not made clear to investors. It can therefore work against their interests in the same way that regular soft dollar agreements can.

The second source of scrutiny comes from some brokerage houses themselves. As their revenues become squeezed, they seek ways to link costs with revenues. A possible solution is priced research, in other words, unbundling research from execution so that the price of each is explicit.

Directed commissions

Directed commissions is where an investor instructs the investment manager to conduct a specified volume of transactions with a nominated broker, usually in exchange for an agreement by the broker to meet some of the investor's expenses.

Directed commissions usually work as a discount or rebate after the transactions are completed, and do not represent a direct obligation on the part of the investment manager, who can still exercise discretion in choosing brokers. But few investment managers are prepared blatantly to refuse to comply with their client's instructions.

If the nominated brokers happen to be those with whom the investment manager normally deals regularly, this arrangement can work quite well. If the investment manager does not usually deal with the nominated broker – for example, because the services provided by the broker are not suitable to the portfolio's requirements – the investor suffers inappropriate service.

In either case, the broker, knowing that the investment manager is either obliged or very likely to transact with him or her, will probably pay less attention to the quality of execution and other services. This will have a real, if hard to quantify, cost to the portfolio, which may well exceed the discounts generated by the agreement.

Portfolio transition

Transition management can control the costs and disruption of transferring assets from one investment manager to another if:

- The existing mandate must be terminated before a new manager is engaged.
- Assets must be transferred from one asset class to another.
- There is significant difference between old and new investment mandates within an asset class.

The process involves engaging a transition manager who is independent of both outgoing and incoming investment managers, whose mandate is to keep the portfolio fully invested and minimize transactions costs, rather than to deliver active investment returns.

The objectives of transition portfolios are to:

- Ensure that the portfolio remains fully invested during the transition.
- Ensure that it is never over invested during the transition.

- Ensure that it complies at all times with the investor's investment policy and constraints.
- Minimize the costs of the transition.

Transition usually entails an *in specie* transfer of portfolio holdings from the outgoing manager to the transition manager, usually with the outgoing manager instructed to carry out no further trades on the portfolio. This minimizes the risk that the outgoing manager, knowing that he or she is on the point of losing the mandate, uses the portfolio as a kind of dumping ground for unwanted securities held in other portfolios.

Stock borrowing and lending

Stock borrowing is where investors borrow the title of securities in order to complete a naked short sale.

To complete a transaction and receive settlement, the seller of a security must deliver title to the security. If the sale is a naked short sale, the seller can do this only by borrowing, or more accurately, renting, title to the securities. Lenders are usually investors who hold the asset as part of a long-term strategy. They can enhance their returns by earning rent from title to the securities that otherwise lies idle.

The benefits of security lending include:

- Increased market liquidity from facilitating short selling.
- Improved returns to long-term investors.

The risk to the lender is counterparty risk, which in this context is the risk that the borrower is unable to deliver title to the security when agreed or on demand.

Security lending agreements usually also specify:

- Which party exercises voting rights during the term of the loan.
- Which party is entitled to dividends during the term of the loan.
- Cost, in effect the rent of security title.
- Margins to be paid by the borrower as a hedge against the lender's counterparty risk.

Summary

Implementation represents a source of risk to an investment portfolio because it can be a source of inefficiency. Sources of inefficiency include lack of transparency of markets, illiquidity and wide bid-ask spreads, market impact, transactions costs and counterparty risk. Centralized exchanges can overcome some sources of implementation risk and inefficiency, or at least ensure that they are visible to the investor. However large transactions can be effectively invisible and other practices, such as front running and indirect subsidization of trades through soft dollars and directed commissions, can compromise the efficiency of portfolio implementation and increase the risk associated with it.

Case Study

This is a transition portfolio using share price index futures contracts to maintain the exposure to domestic equities of a portfolio normally managed actively using only physical equities. The portfolio had recently been restructured, with a large injection of new investment funds. The trustees and managers of the portfolio were engaged in the search for suitable investment managers, which was expected to take three months. In the event it took more than six months.

Because of the recent restructuring and injection of new investment, the portfolio was transferred to the transition investment manager in the form of cash, which was to be invested during the transition using share price index futures. The value of the portfolio was in the vicinity of $50 million. Because of the short-term nature of the assignment, the investor thought it appropriate to have a much shorter than usual reporting cycle. The investment manager agreed to weekly and monthly return reports, because reporting a portfolio of liquid assets and share price index futures is especially simple so could be delivered at minimal cost.

Unlike the manager of a permanent portfolio, the transition manager was given no period of 'grace' before being held accountable for costs and returns. It was expected that the portfolio would be transacted at the futures fair price on the day the cash was transferred. This was not unreasonable, given the relatively small amount to be invested and the liquidity of the futures market. The problem was that, on that day, the futures price traded abnormally above its fair price relative to the underlying physical index. The agreed benchmark was the physical index underlying the futures contract. While this was thought initially to be the obvious point of comparison, it led to serious misunderstandings.

First of all, the investment manager was obliged to buy the derivatives contracts at above fair price. From the outset this compromised the return to the portfolio relative to the asset class, but the investment manager concluded that this known underperformance was preferable to the unknown risk of delaying the purchase of the derivatives until a more favourable price could be achieved. In this he behaved responsibly, avoiding risk many times greater than the relatively small, known performance shortfall implied by the derivatives mispricing.

It is well understood that derivatives contracts are often more volatile than the underlying physical assets because they tend to trade both above and below their fair price; with the width of the band about the fair price determined by – relatively high – transactions costs for the physical asset. Over the following months the derivatives contracts exhibited higher than usual volatility, so that weekly portfolio returns bore little resemblance to the returns of the benchmark. The investor was understandably alarmed by what appeared to be serious a departure from a clearly defined mandate.

Example 17.1 Performance of a transition portfolio

		Period	Portfolio	Benchmark	Difference
		1	-0.22%	4.10%	-4.32%
Interest rate	6.50%	2	-2.73%	-3.23%	0.50%
Dividend yield	1.50%	3	4.01%	3.88%	0.13%
		4	4.03%	3.79%	0.23%
Portfolio size	$50 000 000	5	-3.05%	-2.50%	-0.55%
Number of futures bought	81	5	6.10%	5.44%	0.65%
Point value of futures	$500	Six months	8.02%	11.67%	-3.65%
		annualized tracking error			6.68%
		excluding first month			1.44%

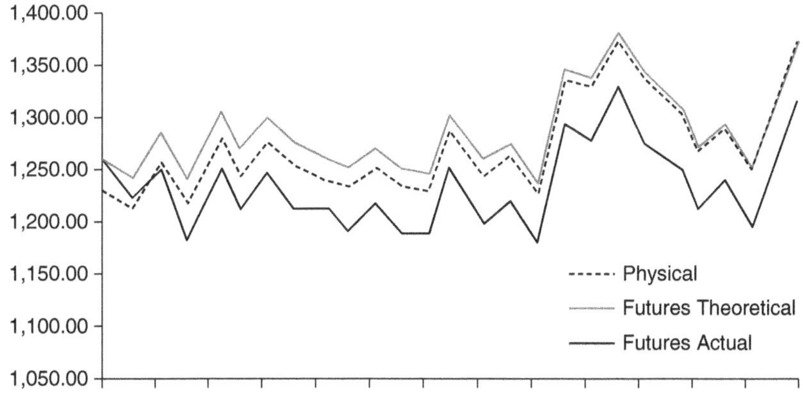

As shown in Example 17.1, futures theoretical is what the investor expected to see, and futures actual is what happened. After a disappointing start, the portfolio performed according to specification, as could be expected in an approximately efficient market.

18 Performance Measurement and Attribution

Prospective investor:	So what has the portfolio's performance been?
Investment manager:	Give me a number, and I'll tell you over what period the portfolio returned that number.

Return measurement is by definition backward looking. It is useful in portfolio selection in the same way that the rear view mirror is useful when driving a car: certainly necessary for decision support, but not as the main tool. It is important because:

- It shows what progress the portfolio is making toward its investment objectives.
- It facilitates comparison with peer group portfolios and benchmarks.
- It can be a factor in how the investment manager is rewarded.

It is generally well recognized that past portfolio returns can be a poor guide to future returns. There are a number of reasons for this, such as:

- The investment manager can change the strategy if the current investment strategy is not working.
- The investment management company's skill base changes from time to time as individual investment managers leave and new investment managers join.
- What worked before may not work in future. Even with consistent strategies and stable investment staff, the range of available investment opportunities fluctuates over time.

Nevertheless, returns are usually regarded as an indication that a strategy is successful or that an investment manager has investment selection skill. In the absence of more robust indicators, past success can signal a potential source of attractive future returns.

Therefore, when evaluating a portfolio, the investor would like to know:

- If the performance is repeatable.
- How much of the result is due to skill and how much is due to chance.
- To what extent the results were achieved at the cost of unacceptable concentrations of risk or vulnerability to nasty surprises.

The purpose of risk-based investment management is to align the sources of risk in a portfolio with sources of expected return. It follows that the aim of portfolio evaluation is to see how each source of risk contributed to the return actually achieved.

Performance measurement, which takes account of the volatility of portfolio returns as well as the returns themselves, adds insight by facilitating comparisons of ratios of return and risk such as information ratios and Sharpe ratios. Risk-based performance measurement and attribution goes further by seeking to identify which sources of risk actually resulted in positive active return. This can help show whether the results were due to intentional risk allocation or chance. This chapter discusses the most commonly used measures of performance and how risk-based performance attribution can improve on them. It discusses:

- Calculating returns.
- Return attribution by portfolio weight.
- Risk-based performance attribution.
- Treatment of cash balances.
- Portfolio turnover.
- Global Investment Performance Standards (GIPS).

Calculating returns

Single period return calculation

The simplest, single period return calculation with no external cash flows, is given as:

$$Rp = PV_{t1}/PV_{to} - 1 \tag{18.1}$$

Where:

Rp = portfolio return

PV_{t1} = portfolio value at the end of the period

PV_{t0} = portfolio value at the start of the period

For example, a portfolio valued at 102.0 at the end of the period and 100.0 at the start of the period has a return of 2 per cent (102.0/100.0 -1).

Example 18.1 adds a cash flow and contrasts the results given by counting the cash flow as having been received arbitrarily at the start, end and in the middle of the period; with the result given by time weighting the return calculation.

Example 18.1 Single period portfolio return with cash flow

Portfolio value at start of period	\$10 000 000
Portfolio value end of period	\$15 000 000
Days in period	30
Cash flow	\$2 500 000
Day of cash flow	10
Portfolio value on day of cash flow	\$12 000 000
Simple return calculation (compounding sub-periods)	20.00%
Simple return calculation (cash flow at end of period)	25.00%
Simple return calculation (cash flow at beginning and end of period)	22.22%
Time weighted return calculation	24.14%

The differences in return from treating the cash flow as having been received at the start, middle and end of the period are too significant to be ignored, so the convention is to use time weighted returns. The time weighted return is calculated by dividing the period into two sub periods, with the first period ending just before the cash flow and the second period beginning with the cash already in the portfolio.

$$Rp = (PV_{cf}/PV_{t0}) \times (PV_{t1}/(PV_{cf} + cf)) - 1 \tag{18.2}$$

Where:
Rp = the return to the portfolio
PV_{t0} = the portfolio value at the start of the period
PV_{t1} = the portfolio value at the start of the period
PV_{cf} = portfolio value immediately prior to the cash flow
cf = the amount of the cash flow

Giving the result:

$$Rp = (\$12\ 000\ 000/\$10\ 000\ 000) \times (\$15\ 000\ 000/(\$12\ 000\ 000 + \$2\ 500\ 000)) - 1$$
$$= 24.14\%$$

In practice, most portfolio returns are calculated daily from aggregate portfolio values, which automatically gives time weighted returns. It has the advantages that:

- It facilitates calculation of returns to subsets of the portfolio, such as by industry classification, for the purpose of holdings based return attribution.
- All changes in the portfolio composition are accounted for, including new funds into the portfolio, redemptions, income in the form of dividends and coupons and portfolio trades.

Multiple period return calculation

Returns for multiple periods are calculated by geometrically linking individual return periods according to the formula:

$$\text{Two period return} = (1 + r_1) \times (1 + r_2) - 1 \qquad (18.3)$$

Where:

r_1 = the return to the first period
r_2 = the return to the second period

Example 18.2 illustrates geometrical linking of a portfolio and benchmark over two periods.

Example 18.2 Geometric linking

	Portfolio return	Benchmark return	Arithmetic difference with geometric linking of periods
Period 1	21.00%	10.00%	11.00%
Period 2	2.00%	2.10%	-0.10%
Two periods	23.42%	12.31%	11.11%

Portfolio and benchmark returns are typically reported for one-, three- and 12-month periods as well as two and five years and since the inception of the fund. Returns for periods longer than a year are annualized to facilitate comparison over time. The formula for annualizing is:

$$(1 + \text{return})^{1/\text{number of years}} - 1 \qquad (18.4)$$

For example, a return over two years of 25 per cent would be quoted as:

Square root of (1 + 25%) – 1 = 11.8034% per annum

The limitations of returns

Returns by themselves tell you surprisingly little about the portfolio, as Example 18.3 shows.

Example 18.3 Monthly portfolio returns

Month	Benchmark	Portfolio	Difference	Month	Benchmark	Portfolio	Difference
Aug-10	-1.2670	-0.9512	-0.3189	Jul-09	2.3247	1.2717	1.0399
Sep-10	1.3724	-0.0517	1.4249	Aug-09	-1.9385	-0.8896	-1.0583
Oct-10	0.4820	0.1496	0.3319	Sep-09	-1.8935	-1.5572	-0.3416
Nov-10	-4.3007	-4.0246	-0.2877	Oct-09	-2.2762	-2.2458	-0.0312
Dec-10	0.2816	-0.0584	0.3403	Nov-09	-2.5996	-2.2466	-0.3611
Jan-11	0.0931	-0.0725	0.1657	Dec-09	-0.8905	-1.1347	0.2470
Feb-11	0.0637	0.6087	-0.5417	Jan-10	2.2392	1.9848	0.2494
Mar-11	4.6329	3.3712	1.2205	Feb-10	2.3731	1.2232	1.1360
Apr-11	1.1505	1.8635	-0.7000	Mar-10	-2.1393	-1.3934	-0.7565
May-11	-1.8511	-1.3861	-0.4716	Apr-10	-0.2819	-0.2319	-0.0502
Jun-11	1.1986	0.9655	0.2308	May-10	0.1232	0.7797	-0.6515
Jul-11	-2.3151	-2.0322	-0.2888	Jun-10	0.1754	0.1699	0.0055
Aug-11	-13.3397	-12.3056	-1.1792	Jul-10	2.0436	1.9196	0.1217

Measured to August 2011 the return of the portfolio in Example 18.3 and its benchmark looks like that shown in Example 18.4.

Example 18.4 Return summary to August 2011

Period	Benchmark	Portfolio	Difference
3 months	-13.98%	-13.88%	-0.09%
6 months	-16.49%	-16.00%	-0.49%
12 months	-0.24%	-2.62%	2.37%
2 years	12.08%	10.44%	1.65%

The same return measurements taken one month earlier look like that shown in Example 18.5.

Example 18.5 Return summary to July 2011

Period	Benchmark	Portfolio	Difference
3 months	1.30%	0.09%	1.21%
6 months	0.19%	-0.76%	0.95%
12 months	16.29%	11.41%	4.88%
2 years	21.43%	18.59%	2.84%

The analysis in Examples 18.3, 18.4 and 18.5 answers the questions about the portfolio's progress toward its long-term return objectives, enables a rudimentary comparison of its returns with its benchmark and peer group portfolios; and could be used in a simple manager remuneration calculation.

But it says nothing about how repeatable the returns are, the roles of skill and chance, what effect risk concentrations had on the result and of course how the sources of risk in the portfolio contributed to the outcome.

For example, was the return variation achieved evenly across asset classes and securities, or concentrated in one or two large imbalances or mismatches relative to the portfolio's benchmark?

Attribution analysis aims to answer questions about what portfolio holdings contributed to return. It works by dividing the portfolio and benchmark into buckets, usually according to country/region or industry/sector or by some other stock classification, measuring the return to each bucket and comparing it to a benchmark corresponding to the classification, such as country indices or industry indices. An example of attribution analysis for a single industry group is given in the section on return attribution.

Return attribution by portfolio weight

The return attributable to a portfolio's weight in, for example, an industry group depends on:

- The difference between the weight of the industry in the portfolio and its weight in the benchmark.
- The difference in composition of the industry group in the portfolio from its composition in the benchmark.
- The return to the industry group.
- The return to the benchmark.

The industry group allocation effect is given as:

$$R = (W_{ip} - W_{ib}) \times (R_{ip} - R_b) \tag{18.5}$$

Where:

R = the relative return attributable to industry i
W_{ip} = the weight of industry i in the portfolio
W_{ib} = the weight of industry i in the benchmark
R_{ip} = the portfolio return to industry i
R_b = the return to the benchmark

In other words, for each industry group, the difference between the portfolio and benchmark weight is multiplied by the difference between the benchmark return to the industry group and the overall benchmark return.

The stock selection effect measures the impact on return variation of the differential composition of the industry group between the portfolio and the benchmark. For each industry group it is calculated as:

$$SS = W_{ib} \times (R_{ib} - R_{ib}) \tag{18.6}$$

Where:

R_{ib} = the benchmark return to industry i

It gives the results of a single period return attribution analysis by industry group.

Example 18.6 shows that the portfolio benefited from being overweight towards banks because this sector delivered a higher return than the benchmark (+9.94 per cent versus –2.35 per cent). Within this sector the portfolio's selection of banks did slightly worse than the benchmark (9.89 versus 9.94 per cent). On the other hand, while the portfolio benefited significantly from being underweight towards gold stocks, it did less well than if it had held more small gold stocks rather than only large ones, since the stock selection effect within the gold industry was –0.05 per cent. The portfolio's overweight position in media also contributed significantly to return variation. Overall, the portfolio benefited from industry allocation, adding 0.25 per cent to overall return, but this was more than off-set by poor security selection within industry groups, which reduced return by 0.31 per cent.

This type of return attribution can be applied to any security classification where individual securities have a unique classification. It can also be extended to the level of individual holdings.

Return attribution adds some information about the sources of portfolio return, but falls into the trap of equating weight with economic exposure; in effect assuming that, for example, the gearing of each asset in the portfolio and the benchmark is exactly 1.0 and that no asset has sensitivity to any asset classification other than the one described by the one it is assigned to.

It also assumes that the asset classifications in the analysis are the factors by which the investment manager selects the portfolio, which may not be the case. For example, an industry-based return decomposition is irrelevant to a portfolio selected according to Fama–French stock characteristics or by stock price or earnings momentum. It can show which holding groups contributed to return but cannot link portfolio returns to the investment selection process that gave rise to them: it gives no information about which investment decisions added value and which didn't. Return attribution by asset weight also gives no information about how much risk was assumed in achieving the results.

Example 18.6 Attribution analysis by industry group

	Average portfolio allocation	Average benchmark allocation	Industry group allocation effect	Portfolio industry group return	Benchmark industry group return	Stock selection within industries effect
Gold	3.62%	5.01%	0.15%	–13.97%	–13.00%	–0.05%
Other metals	6.17%	6.16%	0.00%	1.80%	1.43%	0.02%
Diversified Resources	16.57%	14.18%	–0.02%	–3.14%	–3.04%	–0.01%
Energy	4.23%	4.23%	0.00%	–2.00%	0.61%	–0.11%
Infrastructure and utilities	0.92%	0.99%	0.00%	–9.43%	–9.32%	0.00%
Developers	2.94%	2.93%	0.00%	.25%	.13%	0.00%
Building materials	4.57%	4.23%	–0.01%	–4.53%	–3.96%	–0.02%
Alcohol and tobacco	2.26%	2.17%	0.01%	13.69%	11.57%	0.05%
Food	3.39%	3.21%	–0.01%	–6.94%	–6.81%	0.00%
Chemicals	1.50%	1.60%	0.02%	–16.78%	–16.39%	–0.01%
Engineering	0.32%	1.81%	–0.11%	–1.60%	5.30%	–0.12%
Paper and packaging	2.37%	2.24%	0.00%	–1.25%	–1.19%	0.00%
Retail	3.41%	3.33%	0.00%	–2.34%	–3.13%	0.03%
Transport	3.31%	1.56%	–0.26%	–17.26%	–17.08%	0.00%
Media	9.41%	8.83%	0.06%	7.49%	7.33%	0.01%
Banks	21.94%	18.84%	0.38%	9.89%	9.94%	–0.01%

	Average portfolio allocation	Average benchmark allocation	Industry group allocation effect	Portfolio industry group return	Benchmark industry group return	Stock selection within industries effect
Insurance	2.33%	2.33%	0.00%	–5.50%	–4.55%	–0.02%
Telecommunications	0.00%	0.55%	0.00%	0.00%	–2.84%	0.02%
Investment Services	1.11%	1.77%	–0.03%	6.67%	2.41%	0.08%
Property trust	2.66%	4.49%	–0.05%	–1.66%	0.22%	–0.08%
Misc services	0.26%	1.25%	0.03%	–17.77%	–4.99%	–0.16%
Misc industrials	0.58%	1.44%	0.08%	–9.85%	–12.15%	0.03%
Diversified Industrials	3.82%	4.03%	–0.01%	4.40%	2.47%	0.08%
Tourism	2.32%	2.83%	0.01%	–3.93%	–3.87%	0.00%
Total	100.00%	100.00%	0.25%	–2.46%	–2.35%	–0.31%

For this reason, most performance reports for portfolios of frequently traded securities, such as equities, bonds and exchange traded derivatives, include information about observed return variation over the period. This usually takes the form of portfolio return volatility, tracking error and some measure of exposure to the market in which it invests, such as relative beta to the market or benchmark or relative duration.

More often performance reports give the ratio of return to risk as expressed by the information ratio or the Sharpe ratio, as shown in Example 18.7.

Example 18.7 Return and risk

	Forecast	Observed to July 2011	Observed to August 2011
Annualized relative return two years to:		2.84%	1.65%
Beta	1.11	1.06	1.05
Annualized tracking error	3.41%	3.77%	3.78%
Information ratio		0.75	0.44

Headline risk statistics can indicate how much risk was entailed in achieving portfolio returns, but they do not help understand how the sources of risk in the portfolio contributed to the results achieved. Risk-based performance attribution aims to add this insight.

Jensen's alpha

Jensen's alpha, also referred to as 'Jensen's performance index' and 'ex-post alpha', is the difference between the return of a security or portfolio and the return due to exposure to the benchmark or market in which it invests. It is given as:

$$\alpha_j = r_i - r_f \times [\beta_i \times (r_m - r_f)] \tag{18.7}$$

Where:

α_j = Jensen's alpha
r_i = the return to the asset or portfolio
r_m = the return to the market
r_f = the risk-free rate of return
β_i = beta: the relationship of the asset or portfolio to its benchmark or the market

Risk-based performance analysis

Risk-based performance analysis is conceptually similar to holdings-based return decomposition, with the difference that, instead of asset categories, risk factors are the unit of decomposition. Portfolio exposure, as measured by start of period portfolio beta to the factor for an equities portfolio or duration for a bond portfolio takes the place of portfolio weight.

The factor return effect is given as the return to the factor times the difference between the start of period portfolio and benchmark betas to the factor.

$$R = R_f \times (\beta_p - \beta_b) \qquad (18.8)$$

Where:

R = the factor return effect
R_f = the return to the factor
β_p = the portfolio beta to the factor
β_b = the benchmark beta to the factor

Note that there is one factor level return only. This is because, unlike with stock classifications, the composition of the factor itself is the same for portfolio and benchmark: the only difference is the exposure to the factor of portfolio and benchmark as given by the factor betas. The portion of the portfolio return that is not explained by the sum of all risk factor exposures is attributable to pure stock selection effects.

Example 18.8 Risk-based performance analysis by portfolio risk factor

Factor	Factor risk	Factor return	Portfolio beta to factor	Benchmark beta to factor	Relative factor return
Euro	42.51	0.59	0.63	0.45	0.11
Japanese Yen	14.29	3.26	0.01	-0.02	0.10
Composite value	3.91	-0.44	-0.01	0.02	0.01
Liquidity	13.81	0.59	0.11	0.1	0.01
Emerging Europe	16.23	-0.82	0.03	0.05	0.02
Italy	14.03	-1.36	-0.05	0.01	0.08
Consumer staples	5.91	1.85	0.06	0.1	-0.07
Banking	9.9	-0.5	0.09	0.12	0.02
Other factors					0.44
Stock specific effects					0.49
Total					1.19

Source: R-Squared Risk Management

In Example 18.8 the investment manager's decision to expose the portfolio to the Euro risk factor contributed 0.11 per cent to the portfolio return of 1.19 per cent, while the decision to under-expose the portfolio to the consumer staples factor reduced return by 0.07 per cent. Overall factor related decisions contributed just under half of the return for the period, with more than half coming from selection of individual stocks, independent of common risk factor effects.

The difference between the portfolio level return and the sum of factor based returns is the return due to pure stock selection.

The same method can be used to quantify the return due to the portfolio's exposure to the benchmark, referred to as the benchmark return. This shows how much of the outcome was due to the beta, or duration, of the portfolio to the benchmark and is calculated as the benchmark return times the start of period portfolio relative beta to the benchmark.

The difference between the benchmark related return and the overall portfolio return is referred to as the benchmark alpha. Example 18.9 illustrates that, of the portfolio return of 2.84 per cent, 1.83 per cent was due to the portfolio's exposure to the benchmark. If the benchmark is a standard share price index on which futures and ETFs are traded, the investor could have earned this portion of the portfolio return by buying futures or ETFs, thereby reducing the amount of management fees paid to the investment manager.

Example 18.9 Return attribution by benchmark exposure

	Benchmark risk	**Benchmark return**	**Portfolio beta to benchmark**	**Benchmark return**	**Benchmark alpha**	**Portfolio return**
Benchmark	0.196	1.65	1.11	1.83	1.01	2.84

$$PR_b = R_b \times \beta_b \tag{18.9}$$

Where:

PR_b = portfolio benchmark return
R_b = the return to the factor
β_b = the benchmark beta to the factor

Substituting the values in Example 18.9 gives:

$$1.83 = 1.11 \times 1.65$$

Treatment of cash balances

Most portfolios retain some cash holdings, typically between 5 and 15 per cent of the portfolio value, that result from accumulated revenue from dividends and coupons as well as small increments of new investment in the portfolio. Some cash holding is essential for frictional purposes, such as to smooth transactions and meet expenses.

However, for most single asset class portfolios that are compared to fully invested benchmarks, such as an equity index, the cash holding is a source of relative risk; for example, it is a drag on performance in a rising market. Because cash balances affect both return and risk, they should logically be included in any calculation of performance analysis. Excluding them flatters the return to a portfolio in a rising market and gives a misleading representation of the returns actually received by the investor as well as the risk of the portfolio relative to a fully invested benchmark.

Multi-asset class portfolios typically include some cash allocation in their strategic benchmark, which is usually managed by a specialist cash manager. In addition to the cash asset class, individual asset class portfolios nearly always hold cash in the same way that single asset class portfolios do. There are two ways of treating this cash:

- Include it in the asset class return calculation, which causes a potential drag on the returns of the asset class relative to its fully invested benchmark, but has the advantage that it reflects an active decision by the asset class investment manager to hold uninvested cash.
- Add it to the cash asset class balance, so that it forms part of the asset allocation decision, which has the advantage that it shows the true cash holding of the portfolio across asset classes, facilitating accurate comparison with the benchmark cash allocation and any limits on it.

The effect on the return calculation for the multi-asset class portfolio is the same in each case. The difference is in where the return and risk is attributed.

Portfolio turnover

Extra insight into how a portfolio is managed can be derived by comparing the actual return to a portfolio to what it would have been if the start of period asset weights had been retained, in other words had the investment manager done nothing to the portfolio during the period. The difference between the actual and the buy and hold portfolio is the value added by portfolio turnover, net of transactions costs. Often this analysis shows that the trades subtracted value, but this result should be tempered by the fact that most investment decisions have a horizon longer than one period, so the benefits delivered by the trades may not be evident in a single period analysis. A more meaningful analysis would compare the portfolio's risk profile before and after the trades, which would show how much portfolio turnover improved the alignment of sources of risk with sources of expected return.

Global Investment Performance Standards (GIPS)[1]

GIPS is a performance reporting protocol, developed by the Chartered Financial Analyst Institute since 1980, that aims to facilitate global comparison of investment management firms by setting standards for performance presentations that ensure fair representation and full disclosure of investment performance results.

GIPS is governed by the GIPS executive committee, the objectives of which are:

- To establish investment industry best practices for calculating and presenting investment performance that promote investor interests and instil investor confidence.
- To obtain worldwide acceptance of a single standard for the calculation and presentation of investment performance based on the principles of fair representation and full disclosure.
- To promote the use of accurate and consistent investment performance data.
- To encourage fair, global competition among investment firms without creating barriers to entry.
- To foster the notion of industry 'self regulation' on a global basis.

Key features of GIPS include:

- The GIPS standards are ethical standards to ensure fair representation and full disclosure of investment performance.
- Firms are encouraged to comply with GIPS recommendations in addition to meeting its minimum standards.
- In order to prevent firms from cherry-picking their best performance, GIPS standards demand reporting of at least one composite of actual, discretionary, fee-paying portfolios defined by investment mandate, objective or strategy.
- To ensure the integrity of input data, GIPS requires compliance with specific calculation methodologies and disclosures.
- To be GIPS compliant, firms must meet all requirements of the GIPS standards, including any updates, guidance statements and so on.

The standards cover:

- Historical performance reporting requirements.
- Calculation methodology requirements.
- Composite construction requirements.

- Disclosure requirements.
- Presentation and reporting requirements.

Historical performance reporting requirements

- A minimum of five years of GIPS-compliant annual investment performance or performance since inception.
- Once reported, the performance of a composite must be reported each year to build up a minimum of ten years of GIPS-compliant performance.
- Non-GIPS-compliant performance can be linked to GIPS-compliant performance up to 1 January 2000 provided that the periods of non-compliance are indicated.

Calculation methodology requirements

- Total returns only.
- Returns must be time weighted and adjusted for external cash flows.
- Period and sub-period returns must be geometrically linked.
- External cash flows must be treated according to the firm's established composite-specific policy.

Minimum policy requirements

- Monthly returns from 1 January 2001 must be calculated at least monthly.
- Returns from 1 January 2005 must be adjusted for daily-weighted external cash flows.
- Cash and cash equivalents returns must be included.
- Actual trading expenses or bundled fees must be included.
- Composite returns must be calculated by asset weighting individual portfolio returns using start of period valuations.
- Composite returns from 1 January 2006 must be calculated by asset-weighting individual portfolio returns at least quarterly.
- Composite returns from 1 January 2010 must be calculated by asset-weighting the individual portfolio returns at least monthly.

Composite construction requirements

- Composites must comprise all actual, fee-paying, discretionary portfolios.
- Composites must include only actual assets managed by the firm.

- Simulated performance cannot be linked to actual performance.
- Composites must include all and only comparable portfolio defined according to investment mandate, objective or strategy.
- Retroactive changes to composites are not allowed.
- New portfolios must be added to the relevant composite in a timely and consistent manner.
- Terminated portfolios must be included in the relevant composite up to the last full measurement period that each portfolio was under management.
- Portfolios must not be switched from one composite to another unless necessitated by documented changes to a portfolio's investment mandate, objective or strategy.
- In the event that a portfolio migrates from one composite to another, historical portfolio performance must remain with the original composite.
- From 1 January 2010 carve outs cannot be included in a composite unless the carve out is managed separately with its own cash balance.
- The firm must maintain a consistent policy for removing portfolios from composites.

Disclosure requirements

- Firms must disclose their compliance with GIPS standards using prescribed disclosure statements.
- Firms must disclose their definition of the firm for the purpose of defining firm-wide compliance.
- Firms must disclose the composite description.
- Firms must disclose the benchmark description.
- Firms must disclose what fees have been deducted from performance.
- Firms must disclose what currency is used to report performance.
- Firms must disclose which measure of internal dispersion is presented.
- Firms must disclose the fee schedule appropriate to the compliant presentation.
- Firms must disclose the composite inception date.
- Firms must disclose the presence, use and extent of leverage, derivatives and short positions, if material, including a description of the frequency of use and characteristics of the instruments sufficient to identify risks.

Presentation and reporting requirements

- At least five years of GIPS compliant performance or for the period since the firm's or composite's inception.

- After five years of GIPS compliant performance the firm must present an additional year of performance each year, building up to a minimum of ten years of GIPS compliant performance.
- Composite returns must be clearly identified as gross of fees or net of fees.
- Benchmark total for each annual period. The benchmark must reflect the investment mandate, objective or strategy of the composite.
- The number of portfolios in the composite if more than five.
- Composite asset value as of each annual period end.
- Either total firm assets under management or composite asset value as a percentage of total firm assets under management as of each annual period end.
- A measure of internal dispersion of individual portfolio returns for each annual period if the number of portfolios in the composite is greater than five.
- Observed three-year return standard deviations for the composite and the benchmark, or if this measure is not appropriate an additional three-year observed risk measure.
- The periodicity of the composite and the benchmark must be identical when calculating the EX-POST risk measure.
- From 2000 GIPS compliant performance cannot be linked to non-GIPS compliant performance.
- Returns for less than one year cannot be annualized.

Summary

Portfolio returns are measured with the aim of evaluating investment managers and their strategies, ideally to add insight into how successful a portfolio will be in future. Past returns by themselves add little information and, even combined with portfolio level risk statistics, such as beta to market, beta to benchmark, duration, volatility and tracking error, give only limited true insight. Attributing returns by allocation to subgroups within the portfolio, such as by industry, can help identify some concentrations in return sources, but usually do not relate to any investment decisions and in this sense are arbitrary and do not help distinguish skill from chance or add insight into the likely future performance of the portfolio.

To evaluate the repeatability of successful portfolio outcomes and distinguish the effects of skill and chance, risk-based performance attribution links the portfolio's exposures to the portfolio's risk factors, by which the investment manager selected the portfolio, with the returns that are due to the portfolio's exposure to those factors. Deliberate exposures can then be said to be due to investment selection skill while returns due to incidental or unwanted risk factor exposures can be attributable to unmanaged risk or chance.

Endnote

1. CFA Institute. Global Investment Performance Standards. 2010.

19
Trends in Investment Management

The trend that arguably drives most other trends – the 'mother' of investment management trends – is the democratization of investing, whereby working and middle-class people in both developed and developing countries increasingly invest in equities, bonds, structured products and hedge funds, either directly or via savings in pension schemes.

- In developed economies people are encouraged and, increasingly, expected to take charge of accumulating funds for their retirement as funding for public and company pension schemes thins out.
- In emerging economies in South-East Asia, Latin America and Africa, the number of working and middle-class people with savings to invest and expectations of a comfortable and relatively long retirement continues to grow.

Other things being equal, this trend contributes to a larger pile of savings looking for investment opportunities, itself a significant development.

Arguably more important is the changing ownership profile of assets, which is driving other trends, including:

- Regulation.
- Risk management.
- Transparency.
- Corporate governance.
- The range of tradable instruments.
- The range of investment opportunities.
- Capital formation.
- Specialization of skills in investment management firms.
- Aligning the interests of investors and investment managers.

Regulation

As people own more equities and bonds they become more directly sensitive to what happens in the financial markets[1] with the result that the stability or otherwise of financial markets assumes enhanced political relevance.[2] Governments must therefore be seen to be doing something to protect the current and future welfare of their citizens. From this point of view, the obvious course of action is to regulate investment products and those who deliver them. The other obvious course of action is to see the trend as an opportunity to raise more revenue. Both potentially harm market efficiency through imposing a double tax on the citizens they purport to help and protect.

Another government reaction, which tends to affect emerging economies more than developed ones, is to introduce capital controls. As more money seeks attractive investment opportunities, and as emerging markets with the fastest economic growth represent the best investment opportunities, large and fast flows of capital into and back out of emerging markets can play havoc with economic balances through their effect on the country's currency. Controlling these flows, either by means of capital controls or transactions taxes, can be an attractive – and, from the evidence, reasonably successful – way of protecting an economy against the potentially destabilizing effects of fickle capital flows.

In developed economies, the trend is toward regulation of financial firms and products. In particular, governments seek to ensure greater adherence to fiduciary standards that set, for example, minimum liquidity and maximum gearing ratios, as well as to expand the capture of regulatory controls by broadening the definition of what types of firms count as financial services firms and which therefore should be subject to regulatory and fiduciary obligations.

As products, such as hedge funds, that once attracted only a small number of large investors, increasingly seek investment from a wider population of more modest investors, they attract more attention from regulators.

Regulation of financial instruments seeks, among other things, to increase standardization, in order to help make them easier to understand by a wider group of investors; increase transparency and strengthen risk management.

Risk management

Increased attention to risk management was inevitable following the events of 2007 and 2008. *A priori* this is a welcome development, but it can have unintended effects.

Being largely due to political pressures, the effort is directed mostly at avoiding the consequences of another market meltdown rather than at managing the more salient risks of serial underperformance that causes investment portfolios to fall short of their investment objectives, leaving investors with insufficient retirement income.

Investors, investment management firms and regulators are all focussing on investment risk management.

- Increasingly sophisticated investors seek reassurance from investment managers that the risk in their portfolios is sufficient, but not more than that which is necessary, to achieve the investment returns they expect. They want to see that the investment manager takes only calculated risk and takes sensible steps to eliminate, as far as possible, sources of vulnerability to shocks.
- As often as not, the investor's concern is that there is enough risk in the portfolio to achieve its return objectives, rather than that portfolio risk is too high. While they can, through diversification, manage moderately high levels of risk, bland returns can present a shortfall that can be hard to recover without taking on excessive risk in future periods.
- Some investment management firms increasingly see risk management as a means of adding value to their investment selection processes, as a means of making the most of the portfolio selection skills of their investment managers and as a means of differentiating their services from those of their competitors. Demand for sophisticated risk modelling and measurement systems is increasing, as is demand for professional risk managers to drive them.
- Regulators understandably see risk management as a critical measure to protect investors' interests. Their interest is mainly to ensure that investors have enough reliable and accurate information to make investment decisions with a reasonable expectation that the investment products they choose are what their providers claim them to be. To do this they prescribe risk measures and some procedures that must be applied to the investment products offered to various categories of investors. This can have a number of consequences:
  - Much risk management regulation gives priority to standardization over relevance to the investment portfolio.
  - An increased burden of risk reporting imposes costs on investment firms that are inevitably passed on to investors in the form of increased management fees.
  - Risk management that is driven by regulatory compliance contributes nothing to the investment process and is a drag on both performance and potentially on the investment management firm's

profitability. Because it is largely a fixed cost to the investment management firm, it is particularly burdensome for smaller investment management firms, putting them at a disadvantage to large firms and, at the limit, representing a barrier to entry to the investment management business, thereby reducing investor choice.

- Investment firms, seeing that they are obliged to measure risk according to prescribed measures and methodologies, may conclude that there is no merit in allocating extra resources to carry out their own risk management, thus possibly depriving the portfolios they manage of the benefits of risk management that is more appropriate to the portfolios and their investors – and therefore a more relevant measure of risk that could enable more effective management and control of investment risk.
- Because regulation-oriented risk measures tend to be aimed at the dangers posed by market shocks and crises, they by definition cannot contribute to the, arguably more urgent, task of aligning risks to returns to maximize the probability of reaching investment targets. Concentrating on the risk of losses that would result from a market meltdown necessarily ignores the risks that cause day-to-day volatility that is the main cause of portfolios failing to achieve their return targets. It therefore cannot add value to the investment selection process.
- Ineffective and poorly targeted risk management can be worse than none at all because it engenders a false sense of security.
- As risk management demanded by regulators becomes more onerous, it can encourage box ticking, whereby investment management firms, seeking to contain the cost burden, comply with the letter of the regulation at the expense of constructive and pro-active risk management and risk-based investment management.

Poorly conceived risk management is at best ineffective and at worst can actually exacerbate risk concentrations and therefore vulnerability to shocks by directing portfolio exposures away from their most efficient combinations. An unfortunate effect of another round of large losses in investment funds would be tighter regulation and a further deterioration in market efficiency.

While the overall arguments in favour of regulation of financial services firms and financial products is strong, significant risks can result from poorly designed or poorly implemented regulation of risk management and measurement.

Transparency

Regulators and investors are demanding more transparency of investment products and investment management firms. There is growing awareness that investment products can embed unexpected sources of risk, so requiring minimum levels of disclosure about what they are is logical. The quest for greater transparency of investment products can be even better served by simplification of product documentation to ensure that pertinent risks are communicated effectively rather than, for example, buried in footnotes within excessively lengthy legal documentation.

Some of the most opaque investment products are over-the-counter derivatives such as CDS and CDOs. Despite industry-wide efforts to standardize documentation for these contracts – for example, using standard ISDAs – it can be so complex that even the investment managers and traders who use the documents routinely are not always familiar with all their terms and conditions.

Supervisors and regulators are encouraging further standardization to enable them to be traded on exchanges, which allow much more transparency of prices and the volumes traded as well as the size of open positions, which are not only visible in an exchange traded environment to all participants, but also subject to frequent margin calls, significantly reducing the counterparty risk inherent in the instruments.

Exchange trading lowers the cost and uncertainty for the products' users thereby increasing market efficiency as well as welcoming transparency and predictable settlement schedules.

While exchange trading of derivatives such as CDS may increase their use by investors, it will not eliminate genuine demand for bespoke derivative products, which can be traded only over-the-counter and often necessitate complex documentation. The trend toward standardization and exchange trading can however increase investor choice.

Corporate governance

Enhanced scrutiny by investors of the products they invest in is naturally extending to the firms that deliver and manage investment products. Associated with this growing interest is increased investor activism, where investors see both more reason and more opportunity to influence how the firms they invest in are managed.

While increased scrutiny of the governance of firms of all kinds can bring many benefits, is also runs the risk of rendering long-term planning on the part of firms' managers difficult or impossible. This can happen if small groups of powerful shareholders, whose interests may be short term, veto key longer-term plans.

There is a strong argument for management and owners agreeing a mandate that gives directors and managers discretion about how to achieve defined objectives within clear guidelines, thus effectively harnessing their superior knowledge of the firm and the market within which it operates, while limiting the scope for potentially flawed decision making and outside interference.

Expanded range of tradable investment products

A broader universe of investors stimulates innovation in investment products, especially as the trend toward transparency, standardization of documentation and exchange trading continues, increasing their accessibility and reducing many of the risks inherent in investing in them.

Expanded investment opportunities

Emerging markets such as Latin America and Eastern Europe were once viewed as exotic by investors in developed markets. They are increasingly seen as mainstream as investors become more comfortable with their risks and accustomed to the benefits of the high returns and risk diversification they can bring. As growth in these markets inevitably slows and returns to their assets converge with asset returns in developed markets, investors seek higher returns and more diversification in less mature economies. As these markets emerge, they will present even more investment opportunities, as new firms and industries develop, that will, in turn, seek to tap the expanding pool of savings.

Capital formation

Concurrent demand for capital in new markets and industries, and demand for investment returns on the part of an expanding pool of investors may prompt development of new ways to bring the two together. Crowd funding, which is mainly used to fund development of new online games, could be an early model of an alternative means of raising investment capital for productive enterprises, enabling emerging firms to bypass bank funding and the bond and equities markets.

This trend, if it continues, will present new challenges for regulators and supervisors.

Specialization of investment management skills

As regulation of financial services firms and the services and products they offer increases, it tends to favour large over small and medium sized firms. This trend reinforces the existing tendency toward specialization within the investment industry. For example, investment risk management is now seen as a career path in its own right rather than, as previously, a step toward management of investment portfolios. The result is, for example, risk managers with no first-hand experience of investment management and investment managers with no practical experience of risk management. There are three obvious consequences of this:

- Increased depth of understanding that is possible with greater specialization.
- More mutual incomprehension between different areas of speciality within the investment management firm, for example, between managers of different asset classes, but also between risk analysts and investment managers and between investment managers, risk managers and client services specialists.
- Senior managers of investment management firms with a very narrow set of skills and experiences, which can engender bias in their priorities and decisions; for example, CIOs with experience of managing a single asset class will naturally tend to focus more attention on that asset class, even if it is not justified in terms of expected contribution to overall return and risk – or investor interest. Specialization also affects how senior managers communicate with investors and other interested outsiders to the firm.

Aligning the interests of investors and investment managers

Academics have for some time raised issues to do with the agency effect, where the interests of the investment manager are not the same as those of the investor.[3] This happens because the risks to the investor of severe under performance are in effect capped. Excluding instances of fraud, the worst that can happen to the investment manager is that he or she loses his or her job. He or she will receive severance pay and before long be re-employed, possibly on an even more attractive remuneration package. The investor, by contrast, stands to lose all or most of his or her investment, a position from which he or she may not be able to recover.

The mismatch is even worse if you consider that the investment manager is just as likely, or even more likely, to lose his or her job as a result of events beyond his or her control, such as adverse market events that lead to widespread redundancies. When this happens, the chances of finding another job quickly are in fact much worse because most other investment management firms are likely to be reducing their staff levels too. Being fired for poor performance is therefore not the worst, or even necessarily a bad, thing to happen to an investment manager.

Performance based investment management fees were introduced supposedly to help align the interests of investors and investment managers, but their effect has been more to increase the reward to the investment manager from better than expected performance while still capping his or her potential losses. They therefore arguably increase the incentive for the investment manager to take excessive risks that may result in a higher reward, knowing that the worst outcome for him or her is tolerable.

At the same time, efforts to oblige investment managers to share some of the losses suffered by investors as a result of poor decisions have so far been unsuccessful and in practice would be very difficult to design and implement.

A solution to the agency problem would be a very practical development.

Summary

Some of the trends resulting from the growth in the number and range of investors worldwide are visible in more regulation of investment products and financial services firms, some of which are aimed at prescribing risk management and risk-reporting practices. Increased focus on risk management brings obvious benefits but also some unintended outcomes, one of which is that it imposes extra costs that are inevitably borne by investors.

Other trends are the continued expansion of the range of investment products on offer, and the scope of new underlying investment opportunities as new markets emerge.

Investors may seek new ways to raise capital and invest, possibly bypassing conventional avenues of banks and capital markets, and so posing new challenges for regulators.

An on-going challenge for the investment management industry at large is aligning the interests of investors and investment managers.

Endnotes

1. By contrast, people who do not invest directly in equities and bonds are still exposed to the behaviour of financial markets, but mainly indirectly through the impact it has on employment, interest rates and the price of imported goods.
2. This effect is not limited to democracies: ask Machiavelli how important it is to keep most people more or less happy.
3. According to Woody Allen, an investment manager is someone who invests your money until it is all gone.

Appendix 1
Pricing Interest Rate Securities

Interest rate securities come in two forms, known as discount securities and bonds. The difference between the two is that bonds pay coupons periodically, whereas discount securities pay interest in one payment at maturity. Interest rate securities are nearly always quoted in terms of an interest rate – sometimes referred to as a yield to maturity.

To work out the settlement value of the security from the interest rate, it is necessary to know also the maturity of the instrument and, in the case of bonds, the amount of the coupon and when and how often it is paid. Once these details are at hand, it is a matter of applying the appropriate pricing formula.

The settlement value of a discount security

To work out the settlement value of a discount interest-bearing instrument, one applies the following formula:

$$P = FV/(1 + i \times d/365) \tag{A1.1}$$

Where:

P = the settlement value
FV = the face value
i = the interest rate
d = the term in days of the instrument

Some discount securities are priced using a 360-day year instead of 365. This simplifies the calculation, but before applying the formula, the investor must check which pricing convention is used.

Example A1.1
The face value of a discount security is \$1,000 000, the period is 90 days, with a 360-day calendar year. The security has recently traded at 94.95 – an interest rate of 5.05 per cent (100 – 94.95). The settlement price of the security is thus:

$$\begin{aligned}\text{Settlement Value} &= \$1\,000\,000\,/(1 + ((100 - 94.95)/100) \times 90/360) \\ &= \$987\,532\end{aligned}$$

Thus an investor paying \$987 532 now and receiving \$1,000 000 in 90 days' time will earn an annualized return of 5.05 per cent.

The point value of a discount security

Knowing the settlement value is a big help, but investors are usually also interested to know how the settlement value changes with a given change in the interest rate. This value, often referred to as the point value, is usually derived by calculating the settlement value for interest rates slightly higher and slightly lower than the current rate, then halving the difference to get an average. The point value depends on both the maturity of the security and the current interest rate.

To calculate the point value, the price formula is applied using an interest rate 0.01 per cent higher and lower than the current market. The difference between the settlement values thus obtained is halved to give the point value. The formula can be expressed as:

$$\text{Point Value} = (P_1 - P_2)/2 \qquad \text{(A1.2)}$$

Where:
P_1 = settlement value with interest rate less 0.01%
P_2 = settlement value with interest rate plus 0.01%

Example A1.2
In this case it is:

$$\text{Settlement Value} = \$1\,000\,000 /(1 + ((100 - 94.96)/100) \times 90/360)$$
$$= \$987\,557$$

$$\text{Settlement Value} = \$1\,000\,000 /(1 + ((100 - 94.94)/100) \times 90/360)$$
$$= \$987\,508$$

$$\text{Point Value} = (\$987\,557 - \$987\,508)/2$$

$$= \$24.38$$

The point value will change slightly for short-term instruments, such as this 90-day example, as interest rates go up and down. In general, the longer the maturity of the interest rate security underlying the futures contract, the greater will be the change in point value as absolute interest rates rise and fall.

The settlement value of a bond

The coupons paid during its life complicate the calculation of the bond price. In addition to discounting the face value of the bond, as in the discount security, each coupon payment needs to also be discounted in the same way. The formula that achieves this is as follows:

$$P = c \times (1 + a) + 100 \times v^n \qquad \text{(A1.3)}$$

Where:
$v = 1/(1 - \text{interest rate})$
$a = (1 - v^n)/\text{interest rate}$
n = years to maturity times the number of coupons per year
c = annual coupon income divided by the number of coupons per year

Example A1.3

A bond has a face value of \$1 000 000, a maturity of ten years, a coupon rate of 5 per cent per annum, with two coupon payments per year. The settlement price of the bond, with an interest rate of 5.85 per cent is calculated as follows:

$$\begin{aligned} \text{Price} &= \$\,50\,000/2 \times (\,1 + (1 - 1/(1 + 2.925\,\%)^{20})) \\ &\quad + 100 \times 1/(1 + 2.925\%)^{20} \\ &= \$\,961\,330 \end{aligned}$$

The point value of a bond

As with discount securities, the point value of the bond changes with the interest rate. Estimating the point value is done in exactly the same way for the bond, that is, the bond settlement value is calculated for an interest rate slightly higher and slightly lower, and the difference is halved to give an average.

Example A1.4

Thus the settlement value for this bond with an interest rate of 5.84 per cent is \$962 050, and the settlement value with an interest rate of 5.86 per cent is \$960 611. The difference is \$1 439, so the point value is \$720.

$$\begin{aligned} \text{Point Value} &= (\$962\,050 - \$960\,611)/2 \\ &= \$720 \end{aligned}$$

Appendix 2: Forward Contracts

Theory

Forward contracts are the simplest of all derivative instruments, and can be used in nearly all types of commercial transactions. A forward contract is simply an agreement to buy or sell something at an agreed price at some point in the future. Many goods are bought and sold uniquely by means of forward contracts. For example, if you order a new suit from your tailor, you will expect to pay a fixed sum of money for the suit on the day the suit is finished. Most home purchases link an agreed price to a settlement date. These are examples of forward contracts.

Forward contracts are frequently used by agricultural producers, mining companies and many manufacturers as a means of ensuring that they will receive enough sale proceeds to cover their cost of production for the coming season or production or accounting period. Their customers might wish to buy their products forward to ensure that they have continuity of supply to meet critical secondary production or distribution processes. Thus a producer of raw iron ore might sell production forward to cover extraction costs, while the customer, who is a steel maker, will buy enough iron ore forward to ensure that all blast furnaces are kept busy and there is enough steel to meet expected or contracted demand.

This activity can also be thought of as hedging, because it eliminates the uncertainty that revenues will not cover costs of production (for the primary producer), or that the price of raw materials rises so much that the end product cannot be sold at a profit (for the secondary and subsequent producers).

An important feature of forward contracts is that you can sell forward something you do not currently own, otherwise known as selling short, or shorting. This can be risky of course: the iron ore producer selling forward his or her production runs the risk that the quantity sold forward will not be produced on time. Such an event would necessitate buying the shortfall from another producer, perhaps a competitor. Despite such risks, the ability to sell short can be very useful.

If physical goods can be bought and sold in this way, then why not financial assets? After all both primary and secondary producers can lose if interest rates go up so much that they can no longer comfortably service their debts. Similarly if their customers or suppliers are in a different country, they can lose if the exchange rate moves against them.

This widespread appeal explains why forward contracts, and their descendants – futures, swaps and options – have been used for centuries in everyday commerce; and why they are so extensively used nowadays.

In the context of investment management, forward contracts are nearly always used to hedge some kind of investment risk. The most frequent application is to hedge foreign currency exposure. Forwards may also be used to gain immediate exposure to volatile assets in anticipation of a cash inflow to the portfolio

Pricing

When the settlement date is some distance in the future, the settlement price takes into account the fact that it is not an immediate or 'spot' transaction. The difference between the spot price and the forward price reflects the cost to the seller of not having the use of the proceeds of the sale until the settlement date. It also includes the cost of storage and insurance of physical goods, and is adjusted for any pecuniary benefit of still having possession of the goods, such as rent received. If the goods in question are shares, for example, the buyer expects to be compensated for any dividends paid before he or she actually takes possession.

The difference between today's price, otherwise known as the spot price, and the price actually paid (the settlement price) is known as the forward premium. The formula is:

$$P = s \times (1 + i + h - cf) \tag{A2.1}$$

Where:

P = the settlement value
s = the spot price
h = storage, insurance and other holding costs
cf = cash flows to the asset
i = the interest rate

The interest cost plus other holding costs less income received from holding the physical asset, are collectively known as the 'cost of carry'.

Example A2.1

A farmer is expecting to harvest 100,000 bushels of wheat at the end of August. It is now late February and he has just finished sowing his fields. He notes that, at the current price of \$50 per bushel, he will make a respectable profit, as the direct cost of producing the wheat is expected to be only \$40 per bushel. If the wheat price goes to \$55 he will make an even greater profit, but if it drops to \$40, his end of year celebrations will be more meagre. Note that the farmer's cost of production is the same whether he produces the wheat for sale now or in six months' time. Interest rates are now 5 per cent per annum, so the price he can expect to receive for wheat in six months' time is calculated as:

$$P = \$50 \times (1 + 5\% \times 6/12)$$

$$= \$51.25$$

Another way of looking at this is to say that the farmer is receiving \$51.25 in six months' time instead of \$50.00 now. This equates to an interest rate of 2.50 per cent (51.25/50.00) or 5 per cent annualized.

Example A2.2

A couple nearing retirement want to buy an apartment at the beach. They have found the one they want, and have set their heart on it. The problem is that they won't retire for another year and a half, and until they do, they cannot move away from their present home in the city. The current owner of the beachside apartment is not in a hurry for the cash, but wants to take advantage of this opportunity to sell because he thinks property prices might go down. They agree a current price of \$200,000. Interest rates are currently 6 per cent per annum. The apartment is currently rented out for \$17,000 (8.5 per cent) per year, and regular maintenance is about \$2,000 (1 per cent) per year. The forward price can be calculated as:

$$P = \$200\,000 \times (1 + (6\% - 8.5\% + 1\%) \times 18/12)$$

$$= \$195\,500$$

The vendor thus receives the current price of the apartment, adjusted for related income and expenses, plus an annual rate of interest of 6.0 per cent.

Note that the forward price is less than the current price. This is because the cost of holding the asset, comprising the interest cost plus maintenance – is less than the amount received in rent by the holder of the asset.

An important feature of forward pricing is that it does not take into account any estimation of whether the price of the goods will rise or fall. The forward price is often referred to as the fair price because it is the price at which an investor is indifferent between holding the forward contract or the asset itself.

Foreign exchange forwards

Pricing forward foreign exchange contracts follows the same principle, that is, that the forward premium equates holding the forward and holding the spot. Interest is thus received on the physical currency held, analogous to the cash held in the earlier examples, and it is paid on the currency to be purchased forward, analogous to dividends or rent foregone in the earlier examples. When applied to currencies, these two interest rates are compounded, which means they are divided rather than subtracted. This gives a more exact price, as follows:

$$P = s \times (1 + i_1 \times d/365)/(1 + i_2 \times d/365) \qquad \text{(A2.2)}$$

Where:

s = current or spot exchange rate
i_1 = interest rate in numerator country
i_2 = interest rate in denominator country

Example A2.3

If the current spot exchange rate is £0.65, UK interest rates are 6.5 per cent while US interest rates are 5 per cent per annum. The price of a 90-day forward contract can thus be calculated as follows:

$$\begin{aligned} P &= £0.65 \times (1 + 6.5\% \times 90/365)/(1 + 5\% \times 90/365) \\ &= £0.6524 \end{aligned}$$

Thus the four inputs to the foreign exchange forward price calculation are the spot exchange rate, the expiry of the forward contract and the interest rates in the two currencies for the length of the forward contract. In this case the forward exchange rate implies that sterling is worth more in terms of US Dollars three months hence than it is now. The slightly higher interest rate in the UK is responsible for this.

The pricing of forward exchange rates is based on interest rate parity theory. This theory says that an investor will be indifferent between holding assets in say the UK or the US, providing it is possible to hedge the exchange rate risk for the expected duration of the transaction. Thus holding a three month US Dollar treasury bond will deliver the same result to a US Dollar investor as would buying sterling, investing it in three month UK gilts and selling sterling three months forward.

Hold USD asset		**Create synthetic USD asset**	**Buy/sell GBP**	**GBP asset**
	USD		**USD**	**GBP**
Buy 3 month treasuries	−100	Buy spot sterling @ £0.65	−100	+65.00
		Buy 3 month gilts		−65.00
		Sell 3 month gilts		+66.04
Value of 3 month instrument	+101.23	Sell 3 month sterling @ £0.6524	+101.23	−66.04

Interest rate forwards

Interest bearing securities, including fixed interest assets such as bonds, represent an important application of forward agreements. The price at which forward interest rates are agreed is determined by how much it would cost to create the forward synthetically. In other words, at what price would the investor be indifferent between holding the forward and some equivalent physical asset? For example, the price of a forward three month security – starting in two months' time – is based on the difference between the current yield for two and five month securities. The two-month security can be thought of as the spot, analogous to the physical security in the previous examples, while the five-month security is analogous to the physical. The three-month forward that connects them is analogous to the forward premium. This means that the investor should have exactly the same outcome from investing for two months compounded with a three-month forward agreement as for a simple five-month investment.

Obviously both the short and long instruments should have the same credit quality. In practice, these agreements are usually based on securities guaranteed by a government or major bank. Example A2.4 provides an illustration.

Example A2.4

Interest Rate Forward: Physical 2 Month Investment + 3 Month Forward versus 5 Month Physical Investment

Physical 2 month + 3 month forward	Annual rated	Days	Settlement amount
Invest 2 months	4.50%	61	9 744 702
Redeem 2months			-9 817 988
Invest 3 months	7.36%	92	9 817 988
Redeem 3 months			-10 000 000
5 month interest			2.62%
Annualized			6.25%

5 month physical	Annual rate	Days	Settlement amount
Invest 5 months	6.25%	153	9 744 702
Redeem 5 months			-10 000 000
5 month interest			2.62%
Annualized			6.25%

This example uses discount securities. Thus an annualized interest rate of 7.36 per cent for the three-month forward contract fills the gap between the end of the two-month physical security with an annualized interest rate of 4.50 per cent and the five-month security with an annualized interest rate of 6.25 per cent. The formula is given as:

$$i_2 = [(1 + i_3 \times d_3 / 365)/(1 + i_1 \times d_1 / 365) - 1] \times 365/(d_3 - d_1) \qquad \text{(A2.3)}$$

Where:

i_2 = interest on the intermediate security
i_3 = interest on the distant security
d_3 = number of days to maturity of the distant security
i_1 = interest on the near security
d_1 = number of days to maturity of the near security

Applying this formula, we have:

$$\begin{aligned} P &= [(1 + 6.25\% \times 153/365)/(1 + 4.50\% \times 61/365) - 1] \times 365/(153 - 61) \\ &= (1.0261/1.0075 - 1) \times 365/92 \\ &= 7.36\% \end{aligned}$$

Working backwards, the near month and intermediate month interest rates compound to give the distant month interest rate:

$$\begin{aligned} i_3 &= [(1 + i_1 \times d_1/365) \times (1 + i_2 \times d_1/365) - 1] \times 365/(d_1 + d_2) \qquad \text{(A2.4)} \\ &= (1 + 4.50\% \times 61/365) \times (1 + 7.36\% \times 92/365)] \times 365/(61 + 92) \\ &= (1.0075 \times 1.0185 - 1) \times 365/153 \\ &= 6.25\% \end{aligned}$$

The same principle holds for forward bond contracts. The short dated bond compounded with the forward agreement should deliver the same outcome as the long dated bond. The difference is that the formula for pricing bonds takes into consideration the amount and timing of coupon payments as well as the interest rate yielded by the investment. A bond forward is an agreement to deliver a specific bond at an agreed price and date. This means that each agreement must specify such details as the issuer, maturity date, coupon and yield of the bond. The requirement for such details, together with the more complex bond price formula, means that bond forward agreements are usually more complex than forward agreements for discount securities.

Implementation

Forward contracts are most often used in investment management for buying and selling foreign exchange and some bond and swap instruments. The time to expiry can be as little as a few days, or it can be several months, but it is not often very much longer than that.

Entering into a forward foreign exchange contract, for example, is not very different from entering a spot foreign exchange contract. When placing the order with the broker, the investor nominates the amount to be either bought or sold, the currency, or currencies required and the required settlement date. Foreign exchange dealers nearly always have computer systems that give the exact settlement amount within a few seconds.

When dealing in well-established forward markets, such as foreign exchange, contracts have become standardized by the financial institutions and brokers that deal frequently in these instruments. This means there is usually little legal ambiguity in these transactions, although the documentation may vary slightly depending on which broker or institution the trade is with.

One important aspect of the forward contract that is usually standardized by the broker or institution, if not by the nature of the underlying asset and current practice pertaining to its relevant forward market, is whether the forward contract is for delivery or cash settlement. This can be important. The couple buying the apartment want the apartment at the agreed price on the agreed date and have a delivery contract. A bank buying foreign exchange for forward delivery is quite happy to be paid (or to pay) in cash the difference between the agreed forward rate and the spot exchange rate prevailing at the expiry of the contract.

If the contract is for a cash settlement, the contract must stipulate how the market price for the underlying asset is to be determined. For financial instruments that are not traded on an exchange, a panel often determines this price. A panel usually consists of five or six professional dealers or investors in the market. Each is asked to quote a price to buy and/or sell the agreed amount of the underlying instrument, usually within a fixed time interval, such as a half-hour. The settlement price is then derived as some kind of average of the prices thus obtained. Another way is to nominate a reference price. This is a price quoted by some independent organization, such as a data service or news provider. An example reference price might be the exchange rate quoted by the *Financial Times* at a given hour and day.

Complications can arise when dealing in forward contracts for thinly traded or exotic currencies or instruments. The unfortunate outcome is sometimes that a reasonable price cannot be obtained, and sometimes, no price at all – although this is unusual. The reason for the difficulty is that the banks that deal in such currencies usually buy and sell them as principal, meaning that they use their own money. This means they bear all gains and losses associated with that currency until they can find another trader to sell it to, or buy it from. The longer the bank thinks it will take to balance the position, the higher will be the 'spread' – the difference between buying and selling prices required to compensate the risk of holding an illiquid investment.

Complicating the problems posed by thinly traded currencies and instruments, is the fact that forward contracts, once set in place, are generally destined to stay there until the expiry or settlement date. This can pose a problem if the investor wishes to terminate, or unwind the position. The solution is usually to enter into an equal, opposite transaction with the same expiry or settlement date. Thus two forward agreements are in place concurrently. These will cancel each other out at the time of their mutual expiry.

Forward transactions do not usually attract visible commissions and other transactions costs. The cost is in the difference between the price at which the broker buys and sells the same contract, that is, the spread. The spread reflects the ease with which the broker will find another party to take the other side of the transaction, and the number and competitiveness of other brokers and intermediaries dealing in similar instruments. Transactions costs for forwards are therefore difficult to quantify, but on average, they are less than those of dealing in the underlying physical asset, although this generalization should be read with caution, as spreads can vary enormously, particularly in volatile markets and illiquid assets.

On-going management

Once in place, the forward contract is usually very easy to maintain. Naturally, as the settlement date approaches, the investor must be ready to either pay or receive the required funds. Most custodians provide the necessary reminders as part of their service. Investment managers usually have administration systems in place to perform the same function, so there is usually at least one fail-safe mechanism in place. The penalties for failing to meet a settlement can be very high, usually taking the form of punitive interest and administration charges by the other party and the custodian. If the investor is unable or unwilling to settle his or her part of the transaction, the other party can institute legal proceedings to recover the sum involved.

Thus one of the most important aspects of forward contracts is that they can carry significant counterparty risk. This is the risk that the investor taking the other side of the forward contract will be unable to meet his or her obligations when the settlement date arrives.

To deal with this risk, investors employ systems, formal or informal, of ensuring that they avoid having too much exposure to any one counterparty. Usually these systems rely on the notion of credit limits, which are fixed amounts that can be exposed to each bank or other financial institutions against which a credit exposure might be required. The amounts nominated take into account the total credit exposure of the investor and the credit quality, usually indicated by some rating given by a recognized credit rating agency, such as Moody's or Standard & Poor's. Investment managers generally establish credit limits against each counterparty on behalf of each of their client funds and a collective one for all the funds they manage. The former is, of course, to protect each of their clients against the consequences of default on the part of a counterparty. The latter is to protect the investment management company: even though their own equity is not at risk, their business would suffer enormously if the default of a financial institution were to affect a large number of their clients.

Unlike transactions in physical assets, forward transactions require no initial payment. Settlement occurs at the end of the agreement – the settlement date. This means that the portfolio needs to hold enough short-term, liquid instruments (cash) at least equal to the face value of the futures contract. If this sum is not maintained then the fund is in danger of being over invested, or 'geared'. Economically, this is the same as being in debt, so the portfolio could conceivably lose more money than it owns. If the portfolio has entered into a contract to buy $1,000 000 at £0.6524 in three months' time, then the portfolio should have at least £652,400 in cash at all times throughout the life of the contract. This sum is often referred to as the collateral.

Administration

The three administrative issues posed by forward contracts within investment portfolios are maintaining sufficient cash collateral, the danger of missing a settlement date and revaluation. Most investment managers have some kind of capture system to make sure that there is enough collateral to ensure that the portfolio is never over invested. These are not complicated systems, involving only very simple arithmetic. Managing settlement dates is achieved by streamlining, as far as possible, the procedures surrounding cash flows. Usually this means ensuring that the people nominated as authorized signatories are competent, with adequate understanding of the instruments being used and the strategy they form part of. They need to be generally available to sign relevant documents at short notice. And the number of different signatures required for each transaction type need to be sufficient to protect against mistakes while not so numerous that transactions take hours to prepare.

The question of valuation can be tricky, especially if there is not an active market in the forward contract. With major currencies, this is not usually a problem, as the relevant forward markets are very liquid. Minor currencies and some bond contracts may be less liquid. In such cases the value of the forward contract needs to be estimated from the current spot price of similar instruments. Obviously, if these are known with certainty, setting up pricing systems is relatively easy. Where the inputs to the forward price calculation need to be estimated, such as maintenance costs on real property, the basis for estimating these should be formalized. If the pricing system fails to make clear exactly how the price is estimated, then the forward valuation can be manipulated, with the possible consequence of inaccurate portfolio valuation and return calculations.

Some accounting systems also have a problem with forward contracts. They get confused because there is no cash transaction at the outset. It can thus appear that there is no 'asset' to revalue. These systems need to be modified so that they are able to allocate collateral correctly to reflect the economic exposure of the forward.

The distinction between cash-settled and delivery contracts matters for administrative purposes as well. If the forward contract is for physical delivery, then it is a good idea to ensure that the asset to be received (for a purchase contract) or to be delivered (for a sale contract) can actually be received or delivered on the delivery date. If it is not, then the investor faces the cost of either a forced purchase or sale of the asset, or compensating the other party to the transaction. There is also the risk of legal action. Similarly, for cash-settled contracts, the fund must have enough cash to settle any unrealized losses on the contract or face having to liquidate other assets quickly to meet the shortfall. Urgent cash demands like this can be quite costly, not to mention embarrassing!

Appendix 3: Futures Contracts

Theory

The difference between futures contracts and forwards is that forward contracts are usually traded party to party (over-the-counter), while futures contracts are traded on exchanges (exchange-traded), where the exchange is a legal party to each contract traded. The advantage of exchange-traded instruments is that the exchange brings together many buyers and sellers, allowing competition to ensure the best prices for both buyers and sellers. The exchange also acts as a kind of central counterparty, ensuring that the obligations under all contracts are met. Exchange traded instruments must be standardized so they are less flexible than forwards. The theoretical economic implications are identical for the two instruments, but the practical differences are significant, relating to trading and administrative procedures, costs, ongoing management and risk management, and performance attribution and analysis.

Pricing

The theoretical premium or discount to the spot, physical asset price is identical for futures and forward contracts. That is, it is the current price of the underlying security, adjusted for holding costs and cash flows that occur during the life of the contract. As with forwards, futures contracts can be cash settlement or delivery.

Applications

Futures contracts are used by investment managers mainly in conjunction with equities, bonds and short-term interest bearing investments. The most frequent application is to manage liquidity and to effect short-term asset allocation decisions. They can also be used to create much more complex investment structures such as synthetic swaps, market neutral funds and commodity funds.

As with forward contracts, the main attractions of futures contracts are the ability to sell short at little or no cost and the ability to defer settlement.

The denomination and other characteristics of a futures contract are determined by the exchange on which it is traded. For example, a contract could be on a kilo of gold, in which case the exchange will nominate the precise grade of gold, the source of the reference price for valuing the contract at its expiry, the expiry dates (and the time of day at which expiry takes place), and whether the contract is cash settlement or delivery. When the futures contract expires, delivery contracts will mandate that the buyer receives and the seller delivers the specified quantity of the underlying goods or securities. For cash settled contracts, the buyer will receive and the seller must pay a sum of money equal to the difference between the price of the underlying asset and the price at which it was bought (if the price has gone down the buyer must pay).

The next most important defining feature of a futures contract is its face value. Also determined by the exchange, this is the measure of the size of the contract: the amount of the underlying asset that is represented by each futures contract. The face value indicates how many contracts are required for a specific investment objective. It is usually expressed as a multiple of the futures price, indicating how much money is gained or lost with a given change in the futures price.

Futures on share price indices

Example A3.1

The face value of an S&P500 futures contract is 500 times the traded price of the contract. So an S&P500 price of 850 indicates a face value per contract of $425 000 ($500 x 850). This means that for each contract purchased a rise of one point in the price of the S&P500 brings an unrealized profit of $500. $500 is thus known as the point value of the contract. If one were seeking to gain exposure to $4 000 000 of US equities, one could buy ten contracts and get $4 250 000 worth, or nine contracts and get $3 825 000 worth. The formula is given as:

$$\text{Number of contracts} = FV/(pv \times pf) \tag{A3.1}$$

Where:

FV = face value of investment
pv = point value of futures contract
pf = price of futures contract

Which gives:

$$\text{Number of contracts} = \$4\ 000\ 000\ /\ (\$500 \times 850) = 9.41$$

When the investor is ready to invest physical cash, the futures contract is sold and physical shares are bought. If the market has appreciated in the meantime, the 'opportunity costs' of having delayed purchase of shares is offset by gains in the futures position.

Conversely, if the investment manager needs to divest shares, futures can be used to effectively reduce exposure. While leaving in place the physical shares, futures contracts are sold. To the extent that the sold futures position off-sets the holding of physical shares it is said to be a position in 'synthetic cash'. Economically this is the same as holding short-term interest-bearing instruments.

Futures on discount interest bearing securities

Futures contracts on discount securities and bonds follow the same principle as share price index futures, but the actual calculation is slightly different. This is because in these markets, it is interest rates that are being traded. Interest rates have the annoying characteristic that when they rise the economic benefit to the investor who has bought them goes down, and vice versa. To accommodate this, futures contracts on bonds and discount securities are quoted as 100 minus the interest rate. So an interest rate of 8 per cent is quoted as 92, while 6.5 per cent becomes 93.5, and so on.

Example A3.2

The exchange tells you that the face value of the futures contract on a discount security is $1,000 000, the period is 90 days, with a 360-day calendar year. You learn that the contract has recently traded at 94.95 – an interest rate of 5.05 per cent (100 – 94.95). The settlement price of the futures contract is calculated using the formula for a discount security:

$$P = \$1\,000\,000 /(1 + ((100 - 94.95)/100) \times 90/360)$$
$$= \$987\,532$$

Thus an investor paying $987,532 now and receiving $1,000 000 in 90 days' time will earn an annualized return of 5.05 per cent.

There is no cost of carry for a future on a discount security. Instead, the interest rate implied by the future should be consistent, when compounded with a security maturing on the day of the future's expiry, with the interest rate for a security maturing on the same day as the security for which the future is exchangeable. For example, a future on a 92-day security, expiring in 61 days, should compound with a 61-day security to give exactly the same outcome as a security maturing in 153 (92 + 61) days.

Example A3.3

Interest rate forward: physical 2 month investment + 3 month forward versus 5 month physical investment

Physical 2 month + 3 month forward	Annual rate	Days	Settlement amount
Invest 2 months	4.50%	61	9 744 702
Redeem 2months			–9 817 988
Invest 3 months	7.36%	92	9 817 988
Redeem 3 months			–10 000 000
5 month interest			2.62%
Annualized			6.25%

5 month physical	Annual rate	Days	Settlement amount
Invest 5 months	6.25%	153	9 744 702
Redeem 5 months			-10 000 000
5 month interest			2.62%
Annualized			6.25%

Thus an annualized interest rate of 7.36 per cent for the three-month future contract fills the gap between the end of the two-month physical security with an annualized interest rate of 4.50 per cent and the five-month security with an annualized interest rate of 6.25 per cent is 7.36 per cent.

Futures on bonds

The principle of compounding also applies to bond futures, with the difference that the price must take into account coupons paid on the bonds. Thus a three-year bond future expiring in two months' time must compound with a two-month security to give a yield equal to a bond maturing in three years and two months, as Example A3.4 illustrates.

Example A3.4

Pricing a bond future

Physical 2 month + 3 month forward	Annual rate	Days	Settlement amount
Bond coupon rate	5%		
Coupons per year	2		
Invest 2 months	4.50%	61	-9 826 800
Redeem 2 months			-9,900 703
Invest 3 years	6.2959%	1095	9 900 703
Redeem 3 years			10 000 000
5 month physical			
Bond coupon rate	5%		
Coupons per year	2		
Invest 3 years and 2 months	6.50%	1156	9 826 802
Redeem 3 years and 2 months			-10,000,000

The fair price for the bond future is the interest rate that equates the initial investment and the redemption value for a two-month investment compounded with a three-year bond and a bond with a maturity of three years and two months.

Implementation

Because they are traded on exchanges, futures contracts are standardized. Thus the contract is defined by the underlying asset and the date on which the futures contract expires. The investor entering into such a contract has no knowledge of who takes the other side of the contract, as every contract is purchased from, or sold to, the futures exchange in question.

Unlike forward contracts, where no money is exchanged between parties at the outset, futures exchanges require an initial margin, usually on the day of the transaction, or by the start of the next business day. The size of the initial margin is determined by the relevant futures exchange, and usually takes into account the face value of the contract, and the volatility of the underlying asset or security. The amount can range from about 10 per cent of the face value of the contract to over 50 per cent. Some exchanges pay interest on the initial margin, while some do not. Some exchanges allow the broker to collect and manage the initial margin, in which case the payment of interest is a matter of negotiation between broker and client (the investor). If interest is paid on margins, it is usually at below market rates.

Once a futures contract has been bought or sold, the investor is liable for variation margins, whereby an adverse price move must be matched by a 'top-up' to the initial margin, equal to the value of the adverse price fluctuation. A drop in price of two points for a bought contract with a point value of $500 requires a 'top-up' of $1000. This money is refunded if the price subsequently moves in the investor's favour. The purpose of variation margins is to ensure that all transactions are honoured.

Trading futures contracts is usually not a complicated business. Because most futures markets are a good deal more liquid than markets for physical assets, execution usually takes place quickly. The investment manager is normally advised within a few moments at what price the contract has been struck. The worst danger in dealing futures contracts is that the order, which is usually conveyed by telephone from investor to broker, might be misunderstood. Because many prices are quoted as the last one or two digits, rather than the whole figure, there is a danger that an incorrect assumption is made about the 'big number'. Thus it can happen that someone pays 2753.4 instead of 2743.4 in a volatile market where the price was indicated simply as '3.4'. If the face value of the contract is, say $100 per point, and the order is for 200 contracts, the cost would be $20 000. Occasionally a buy order is confused for a sell order and vice versa. For this reason, nearly all futures brokers and many investment managers have installed call monitoring and recording systems, which typically use audiotapes to record all telephone conversations. When a mistake occurs, the tapes can be retrieved, the fault, if any, assigned and compensation for losses effected.

The cost of transacting futures contracts is usually both very small and visible. The exchange attracts a fee per transaction, usually no more than a few dollars per contract. Since contracts can have face values in the hundreds of thousands of dollars, this fee as a percentage of face value is negligible. The broker will generally take a commission, usually also a few dollars per contract. The real cost of dealing in futures comes from interest income foregone on sums paid as initial and variation margins.

When buying or selling a futures contract, the investor is wise to stipulate whether it is an opening or a closing transaction, as this has the potential to reduce the cost of variation margins. An open bought position can be off-set by an open sold position in which case the two will simply cancel each other out at the expiry of the contract. But while they are both open, the investor must pay variation margins on them both, unless arrangements have been made with the broker and the exchange to calculate margins on the net open position.

Most investment managers do this by executing closing trades with the same broker with whom the trade was opened. In this way the broker can see immediately where bought and sold positions can be off-set.

Once in place, it is usually the job of the investment manager to ensure that futures positions that are due to expire are rolled to the next expiry month at an opportune moment. Rolling the position is a fairly straightforward exercise; involving simply closing the existing position and replacing it with another one in a later expiry month. Because the number of futures held has been calculated using the price of the underlying physical, not the futures price, the number of contracts sold and bought (or bought and sold) is identical from one futures expiry month to the next, and the order is placed as a spread (the price differential between the two expiry months). This leaves only the job of working out what is a good spread. Like the difference in price between the physical and the future, so the price between two futures expiry months depends on the cost of carry. In practice, this means treating the near month as spot, physical instrument.

Example A3.5

Pricing a futures roll

Underlying physical market:	2 725.0
Days to near month expiry:	53
Near month interest rate:	4.50%
Near month dividend yield:	1.20%
Days to distant month expiry:	143
Near distant interest rate:	4.75%
Near distant dividend yield:	1.50%
Near month futures price:	2738.06
Distant month futures price:	2759.70
The fair price of roll = 2759.70 – 2738.06	
= 21.64	

If the position to be rolled is long (bought) then the trade is to sell the near month and buy the next month (a short roll). In this case the investor will be willing to trade the spread for less than 21.64. The opposite is true for a short position (long roll). In practice the spread rarely trades at exactly the fair premium, but usually it is within a band of plus or minus 1 or 2 per cent, reflecting the cost of transacting the basket of physical stock that makes up the index. It is, after all, the ability to substitute futures for physical and vice versa that drives the relative prices of the two instruments, so the spread reflects the cost of doing this.

In practice, most investment managers take various other things into consideration when planning their roll tactics. Most avoid trading too close to the expiry of the contract, especially if it is a delivery contract. It is unfortunate but true that, despite the best efforts of exchanges and regulators, many markets (futures and underlying) can be subject to manipulation by large traders during the last days of the contract. This short-term volatility makes trading very hazardous for the investor taking care of long-term investment positions. If the investor has information leading him or her to believe there are some large positions to be closed by a certain date that might push the spread in one direction or another, then it might be worth the risk to wait and profit from these. But in general the direction of last minute volatility is hard to predict, and the costs of getting it wrong can be high.

Ongoing management

The main issue here is paying variation margins. Some margining systems are more complicated than others, but all are intended to ensure that all parties to futures contracts are able to meet their obligations at the end of the contract. Margins can be payable for both delivery and cash settlement futures contracts. Having placed the initial margin, which covers some adverse movements in the futures price, the investor may see the price move even further against him or her. Each day, at the close of trading, the exchange calculates the amount of unrealized profit and loss for each and every open contract, and aggregates this for each account. If the amount of unrealized loss is greater than the deposit already held, the investor is asked to put more money in.

Example A3.6

Calculation of simple variation margins

200 share price index futures contracts are purchased at an index level of 2743.4. The contract has a point value of \$100, so the face value is \$54 868 000. The initial margin is \$3000 per contract, so the investor deposits \$600 000. On the first day of closing, the contract closes at 2802.0, giving an unrealized profit of \$1 172 000 (2802.0 – 2743.4) x 100 x 200. The following day, the contract closes lower, at 2725.5. The unrealized loss on the position is now –\$358 000 (2725.5.0 – 2743.4) x 100 x 200. No variation margin need be called at his point because the loss is still covered by the initial margin. On the third day, the contract falls to 2705.0, and the investor is called for the appropriate margin. In practice, the investor

would probably have paid a larger sum to begin with, say $1 000 000, because this is obviously a very volatile contract and it is intended to hold the position for some weeks or months. Paying more than the minimum required margin avoids frequent top ups, which can be costly in management time. This cost must be weighed up against the interest forgone on the excess margins paid.

If on the fourth day the contract rises again to 2750.0, and the investor has surplus funds deposited with the exchange or the broker of $132 000, the amount already paid in variation margins. Because the position is now showing a paper profit (unrealized gain), the investor has the right to withdraw these, leaving just the $600 000 initial margin.

Profits realized from closing, or terminating a position could be held by the broker to meet future variation margins, or withdrawn by the investor.

If the investor fails to meet the demand for variation margins by the stipulated time (usually mid-morning the following business day), the exchange will close out the position without delay. Closing out the position means that bought contracts are sold 'at market' (whatever price is bid, no matter how low), and sold contracts are bought back at market. The exchange then demands any losses to be made good. If they are not, the exchange is entitled to treat them as a bad debt, seeking appropriate legal redress. The investor taking the other side of the transaction will, unless the futures exchange is particularly inept, remain blissfully unaware of all this: the exchange will have ensured that this side of the transaction is honoured.

Administration

The two administrative issues are managing margins and ensuring that suitable assets are available for delivery if required.[1] Managing margins is theoretically quite straightforward, but in practice can be quite tricky.

The need to manage margins carefully stems from the fact that not all margins attract interest income, and those that do often attract rates of interest that are substantially less than the going market rate. This is how most futures brokers remain profitable, since commissions are very low. The job of the investment manager therefore is to negotiate the best terms possible for earning interest on initial and variation margins, and then to ensure that the balance of margins left with brokers is minimized.

In practice it is almost impossible to maintain a zero or near zero variation margin. To do so would require frequent transfers of small sums, with attendant administrative headaches.

If the exchange rather than the broker were to levy variation margins, the investor can then often arrange for net payments of variation margins. This means that off-setting positions dealt with by different brokers do not each attract their own variation margins, but that the investor's overall position is evaluated at the end of each closing day and margins levied accordingly. This is known as net margining. Net margining can simplify administration enormously, especially if the investor is dealing frequently with several different brokers, and in several different instruments.

Net margining becomes more interesting when several currencies are involved. Most large futures brokers are able to meet the foreign currency demands for initial and variation margins, so long as the investor is able to maintain a sufficient balance in the base currency account. The broker may require consideration for this service in the form of a buy-sell spread on the foreign currency involved. For the investor, the saving in administrative effort and the consequent reduction in the risk of falling short of the right currency to meet each margin call can be well worth the extra cost.

Nearly all futures exchanges insist that separate accounts be maintained for each client. This ensures that the interests of clients cannot be confounded. Nor can they be confused with positions taken on the broker's own account. Brokers, in other words, cannot net settle with the exchange by aggregating their clients' accounts. Most investment managers apply the same principle to their clients' investments, maintaining separate accounts with each broker for each client mandate and investment type. In general this is accepted as the soundest way of administering large numbers of potentially complex transactions. Sometimes this safety precaution occurs at the expense of confidentiality when the investment manager needs to tell the broker to which account the transaction must be attributed.[2] Some managers get around this problem by ascribing code names to their clients. This generally works well for investment managers with a small number of clients, but errors can creep in and, worse, remain undetected if code names get confused and trades attributed to the wrong client.

Performance measurement and attribution

Performance measurement and attribution issues are almost identical for futures as they are for forward contracts. The primary difference is that, for futures, some cash does change hands before the settlement or expiry date of the contract. Portfolio valuation and performance attribution systems must be capable therefore of recognizing the difference between the payment of an initial margin and settlement for a physical asset. Similarly, the distinction should be clear between variation margins and dividend income, or capital calls on physical assets.

Many systems treat the initial margin as settlement for the future, thus implying that this reflects the portfolio's exposure to the instrument.

Another frequent mistake is to use the futures price in this valuation instead of the price of the underlying physical. For the purpose of calculating the economic exposure of the portfolio to the physical asset underlying the futures contract, one multiplies the price of the underlying physical by the point value and the number of contracts.

Some managers use the futures price for simplicity, since it can be derived from the same documents as margin information. But this choice can have unfortunate consequences, for several reasons. The first is that the price of the futures contract does not always trade at or near its fair price relative to the underlying physical. So if the futures price is too low the portfolio will appear to be underinvested, and geared if the futures trades above its fair value relative to the physical. This is no trivial difference. Futures markets and their underlying physical market can often respond quite differently to similar events, with the result that the futures price can move significantly even though the physical market is stable, with the consequence that the portfolio will show an apparent change in asset allocation with no corresponding investment decision or underlying asset price movement.

Example A3.7

Performance measurement and attribution analysis for a bought futures contract

This example shows three ways of valuing a portfolio containing the share price index futures position set out earlier in this appendix. It also illustrates some of the implications of each method on performance attribution. The important details of the transaction are:

Point value of contract:	$100
Initial margin per contract:	$3,000
Number of contracts bought:	200
Number of contracts sold:	0
Price at which futures traded:	2743.4
Current futures price:	2750.0
Current physical index:	2693.9
Interest rate for cash:	4.50%
Current portfolio value:	$100,000 000

The valuation statement	The right way	The wrong way	The wrong way
	1	2	3
Initial margin	$600 000	$600 000	$600 000
Variation margin	$132 000	$132 000	$132 000
Interest accrued on collateral	$2 288 584	$2 336 900	$0
Cash collateral	$53 146 000	$54 268 000	$0
Equities	$53 878 000	$55 000 000	$732 000
Interest accrued	$1 986 115	$1 937 799	$4 274 699
Cash	$46 122 000	$45 000 000	$99 268 000
Total	$100 000 000	$100 000 000	$100 000 000

Method 1 allocates cash collateral according to the current physical share price index. Method 2 uses the futures price instead, while method 3 does not allocate collateral at all, but treats the margin payments as full settlement of the contracts.

Attribution analysis using method 1	**Profit/ loss**	**Sum employed**	**Return on transaction**	**Contribution to fund return**
Profit/loss on Futures	$132 000			
Interest on Collateral	$2 288 584			
Return on equities	$2 420 584	$53 878 000	4.4927%	2.4206%
Return on cash	$1 986 115	$46 122 000	4.5000%	1.9861%
Total return	$4 406 699	$100 000 000	4.4067%	4.4067%

The attribution results for methods 2 and 3 would be as follows:

Summary attribution analysis for three methods	**1**	**2**	**3**
Return on equities	2.4206%	2.4689%	0.1320%
Return on cash	1.9861%	1.9378%	4.2747%
Total return	4.4067%	4.4067%	4.4067%

Note that the three methods give quite different impressions of how the portfolio is invested.

Endnotes

1. The story is frequently told of a speculator who bought a contract of live beef on the Sydney Futures Exchange in the 1960s. Having congratulated himself on a comfortable profit at the expiry of the contract, he was perturbed when, the following day, 10,000 cows were herded into the street in front of his office in the financial district of Sydney.
2. Preferably at the time the order is placed, not after execution is complete.

Appendix 4: Swaps

Theory

Swaps are, economically speaking, no different from a forward or a futures contract. They are agreements to pay the change in value of a security or good, and receive the change in value of some other good or security. Thus two investors holding two different assets, but desiring the return on the other, agree to swap the change in value and possibly the income streams of their respective assets. Forward agreements and futures contracts are essentially special cases of swap agreements: the investor receives the change in value of the security underlying the forward or futures contract, and gives up the change in value of the cash collateral.

Swaps are transacted over-the-counter, as are forwards. Nearly all swaps are arranged by intermediaries who draw up the agreements, help negotiate prices and arrange settlements.

The main benefit of swaps is that they are almost infinitely flexible, allowing any number of risky assets to be transacted in any combination. Investors entering into swap contracts often swap the returns to quite exotic baskets of securities which might be very expensive and risky to transact in physical form, and for which no viable futures markets exist. Unsurprisingly, the more complicated the swap, the more expensive it is to implement, while swaps that are not much more complicated than futures cost about the same to put in place.

Most swaps take place for liabilities, currency exposures, or both at once. A borrower who can borrow cheaply in US Dollars, but needs to borrow in GB Pounds might initiate a typical swap, agreeing to exchange interest rate liabilities with a GB Pound borrower who needs to borrow in US Dollars, but cannot do so cheaply. Both parties can reduce their borrowing costs and hedge their currency exposures in one go by arranging a swap.

Asset swaps are literally custom-made for investment portfolios and are becoming widely used, especially in emerging markets portfolios. The resemblance of asset swaps to futures and forwards is not hard to spot, although they are no different in principle to liability swaps.

Example A4.1

Asset Swap

Investor A		Investor B
+ return on market A	Earned on index portfolio of physical assets held	+ return on market B
– return to market A	Swapped asset returns	– return to market B
+ return to market B	Swapped asset returns	+ return to market A

Investor A		Investor B
+ imputation tax credits A	Earned on index portfolio of physical assets held	+ imputation tax credits A
– margin		– margin
+ return to market B + imputation tax credits A – margin	Net outcome	+ return to market A + imputation tax credits B – margin

Imagine a US Dollar investment fund, with normal US tax liabilities. The fund would benefit from holding a portfolio of Japanese Yen-denominated stocks benchmarked to the Topix index. At the same time, a Japanese investment fund seeks exposure to the US equity market. The two investors agree to swap the total returns in US Dollars to their respective portfolios. The outcome would look like this:

	USD investor	JPY investor
Physical asset held	S&P500	Topix
Asset start price	1229.23	1086.99
Asset end price	1388.91	1641.53
Currency start price	1.00	112.80
Currency end price	1.00	102.19
Asset return	12.99%	51.02%
Dividend yield	2.50%	0.25%
Tax credit	30.0%	35.0%
Total return in local currency	15.49%	51.27%
Return in USD to physical assets	15.49%	37.04%
Amount paid	-15.49%	-37.04%
Amount paid or received	37.04%	15.49%
Tax credit	0.75%	0.09%
Net outcome	37.79%	15.58%

The US Dollar investor has the best nominal outcome because the Topix performed so well over the period, especially in US Dollar terms. He or she also did well out of the dividend tax credit, whereas the Japanese Yen investor's tax credit is low because the dividend yield to Japanese assets was very low during the period. A swap like this one usually occurs in the context of a much larger portfolio, in which case the overall outcome for the Japanese investor, who would have significant other fairly high-yielding (at least in JPY terms) investments, was probably higher than for the US Dollar investor.

In this example the investors have agreed to swap total returns. This means that they will swap not only the change in the price of the two equity holdings, but also the dividends accrued to them during the period. Many asset swaps differ from this example in that they are designed to swap only the price change, leaving the dividends to the holder of the physical asset. This can greatly simplify administration and revaluation.

Bond index swaps work in much the same way. Bond indices ignore coupon payments, so they are a much simpler way to swap bond exposures than by swapping returns to physical bonds.

The main limitation of swaps is that they can be cumbersome to implement and administer. Because the cost and time taken by both the investor and the intermediary can be significant, and the intermediary's remuneration is normally a fixed percentage of the face value of the swap, small swaps are rarely worth the cost. This often excludes small funds from benefiting from swaps (although standardization of documentation has gone some way to minimizing this problem).

Pricing

Swaps are priced according to how much it costs to construct a hedge, or a replicating portfolio. For a simple asset swap, the intermediary would simply use the closest futures contract available. If this is trading close to its fair price relative to the underlying physical contract, then it provides an obvious solution, as set out in Example A4.2. In other cases there may be no price quotes, or the futures contract does not provide a close enough proxy. This can occur when the required end date of the swap is in the distant future, beyond the date of actively traded futures contracts. It can also lack a proxy when the swap does not expire near a futures expiry date, or if the asset to be swapped does not resemble an existing, actively traded futures contract. In such cases the intermediary might estimate the forward price for each side of the swap directly from the physical, taking into account the value of the dividend tax credit available to each party when estimating the swap spread. The intermediary's commission is then deducted from this.

Example A4.2

Pricing an asset swap

	Investor A	**Investor B**
Asset	S&P500	Topix
Date now	31 December 1998	31 December 1998
End date of swap	30 November 1999	30 November 1999
Asset price now	1229.23	1086.99
Interest rate	4.50%	1.50%
Dividend yield	2.50%	0.25%

	Investor A	Investor B
Tax credits	30.00%	35.00%
Spot exchange rate	1.00	112.80
Forward exchange rate	1.00	109.83
Futures price	1251.73	1099.42
Return in local currency	1.83%	1.14%
Return in USD	1.83%	−1.52%
Value of tax credit	0.75%	0.09%
Swap price (+ve = receive, −ve = pay)	3.35%	−3.35%

Implementation

From the investor's point of view, the main considerations are how well the swap agreement fits the investment strategy and price. Swaps are usually customized to meet investors' precise needs, but sometimes a small amount of flexibility on the part of the investor can lead to a big saving. For example, if both investors were happy with S&P500 and Nikkei 225 instead of needing say MSCI for their foreign exposure, the basis risk to the intermediary would be eliminated (because futures contracts can be used to hedge it). This would allow the intermediary to significantly reduce the fee required for arranging the swap.

Like forward contracts, investors engaging in swaps need to bear in mind that swaps carry counterparty risk that needs to be managed.

The documentation of swap agreements has become much simpler in the last decade or so with the widespread acceptance of International Swap Dealers' Agreement (ISDA) documents. ISDA sets out a standard wording for swap agreements, with additions to accommodate any unusual features. For most swaps, ISDA has cut weeks off the negotiation and implementation, increasing the potential benefit to investors of this very useful instrument.

Currency management is fairly simple for most asset swaps. If the investor requires foreign currency to be hedged, this can be incorporated into the swap agreement, such that the reference prices are based on hedged rather than unhedged returns. Example A4.3 is an example of a hedged asset swap.

Administration

Because of counterparty risk, and because swap agreements tend to last at least a year, swaps usually have several settlement dates within their lifetime. The most popular arrangement is for quarterly settlement dates and resets. Thus, all unrealized profits and losses are paid after three months, leaving no amounts outstanding, helping to guard against credit risk becoming unmanageable.

Normally the intermediary calculates the amount of the settlement and sends the draft calculation to the investor who then checks it. The custodian and trustees are then informed of the impending cash flow. The unrealized profit or loss will then become part of the fund's liquid holdings.

At the same time the face value of the swap is reset to reflect the changes in the values of the assets underlying the swaps.

Revaluation of swaps between resets can be a headache, especially if the assets and liabilities being swapped are not traded on recognized markets. Example A4.3 shows how to revalue a simple equity swap.

Example A4.3

Revaluation and reset of an asset swap

Revaluation Date	15 December 1999			
Last reset date	30 November 1999			
Face value of swap	$100 000 000			
Investor pays	S&P500	Total return	in USD	
Investor receives	FT100	Total return	in USD	
Return on	S&P500	Total return	in USD	1.8132%
Return on	FT100	Total return	in USD	-0.2305%
Investor pays	$1 813 213			
Investor receives	-$230,479			
Investor pays	$2 043 692			
Swap reset value	$97 956 308			

Performance attribution

Once the revaluation problem has been solved, performance attribution should fall into place. The problems are very similar to those posed by forward contracts. In short, the impact on the fund's performance of an asset swap will be no different from that of holding the underlying assets minus fees paid for arranging it.

Synthetic swaps

Sometimes it is not necessary to arrange a swap through an intermediary because all of the required components of the swap exist in the form of traded markets. A strategy that uses exclusively exchange-traded instruments, but whose composition resembles a swap is often called a synthetic swap, as in Example A4.4.

Example A4.4

Synthetic Swap

Swap details	Revaluation date	15 December 1999
	Last reset date	30 November 1999
Face value of swap	$100 000 000	
Investor pays	S&P500	Price only in USD
Investor receives	FT100	Price only in USD

Contract details	S&P500	FT100
Point value	$500	£25
Initial margin	$18 750	£3 000

Market information	30 11 1999		15 12 1999	
	S&P 500	FTSE 100	S&P 500	FTSE 100
Price only index	1 388.91	6 597.17	1 413.19	6742.17
Total return index	4 373.03	346.19	4 452.32	353.97
Dec futures	1 392.38	6 617.00	1 416.72	6 762.44
Short-term interest Rate	4.50%	4.75%	4.50%	4.75%
Dividend yield	1.56%	1.21%	1.56%	1.21%
Exchange rate $1=	$1.00	£0.6279	$1.00	£0.6435

	30 11 1999			15 12 1999		
Portfolio Structure	**Face value**	**Percentage of portfolio**	**Number of contracts**	**Face value**	**Percentage of portfolio**	**Number of contracts**
Physical Shares Indexed to S&P500	$90 000 000	90.00%		$91 631 891	89.65%	
Short S&P500 Futures	–$90 279 150	–90.28%	–130	–$92 084 876	–92.33%	–130
Long FT100 Futures	$100 076 516	100.08%	381	$100 095 439	100.36%	381
Short-term securities	$5 742 146	5.74%		$5 752 765	5.77%	
Initial margins S&P500	$2 437 500	2.44%		$2 437 500	2.44%	

	30 11 1999			15 12 1999		
Portfolio Structure	**Face value**	**Percentage of portfolio**	**Number of contracts**	**Face value**	**Percentage of portfolio**	**Number of contracts**
Initial margins FT100	$1 820 354	1.82%		$1 776 224	1.78%	
Variation margins S&P500				-$1 582 109	-1.59%	
Variation margins FT100				-$280 665	-0.28%	
Total cash	$10 000 000	10.00%		$8 103 715	8.13%	
Total	$100 000 000	100.00%		$99 735, 07	100.00%	

As with a standard asset swap, the physical assets are held in domestic securities where the investor has some comparative advantage, in this case the right to domestic dividend tax credits. The essential components of the swap are effected by selling short futures on domestic stocks and buying futures in the required foreign market, in this case the UK market. The physical share portfolio will nearly always be indexed to the share price index with the most liquid futures contract, for example, S&P500 in the USA.

The synthetic swap is structured and managed slightly differently from a regular swap because of the need to allocate cash to initial and variation margins relating to the futures positions. The starting proportion will usually be about 90 per cent shares and 10 per cent liquids, although if one share-market is a lot more volatile than the other, a higher proportion in cash might be necessary. Liquidity management is fairly straightforward most of the time, at least while equity markets move in the same direction from day to day. As long as this is the case, variation margins on the short domestic futures position will largely off-set those on long offshore futures positions. If the futures broker is happy to call variation margins on a net basis for the whole portfolio, the problem is greatly simplified.

Example A4.5

Profit and loss		
Physical shares indexed to S&P500	$1 631 891	1.63%
Short S&P500 futures	–$1 582 109	-1.58%
Long FT100 futures	–$280 665	-0.28%
Short-term securities	$10 619	0.01%
Variation margins S&P500	–$1 582 109	-1.58%
Variation margins FT100	–$280 665	-0.28%
Total cash	–$1 896 285	-1.90%
Total portfolio	–$264 393	-0.26%

This simple asset swap structure approximates a hedged international portfolio because all physical assets are held in domestic currency. This is fine if the investor wants the risk and return of the foreign stock-markets, but not the associated currency risk and return. For a fully hedged return, the investment manager must ensure that futures profits on offshore markets are repatriated at regular intervals to minimize unwanted currency exposure. If the investor requires an unhedged return, then the manager must unhedge the face value of the foreign futures contracts by buying forward foreign exchange to give the appropriate currency exposure on the face value of assets held in each country.

Example A4.5 illustrates the effect of currency risk on the unrealized profit on the FT100 position. It is this currency effect that accounts for the difference in outcome between the synthetic swap and its standard counterpart. Had the investor unhedged the swap position by selling forward contracts in Pounds equivalent to the face value of the FT100 position, the return to the swap would have been 2.48 per cent less because the investor would have bought Pounds at a forward rate of £0.6279 on 30 November, rather than at £0.6435 on 15 December.

The main benefit of the synthetic swap is that, because physical assets are invested in the domestic equity market, it can entitle the investor to dividend tax credits on 90 per cent of the international portfolio, which can amount to about 25 per cent of the dividend yield. Because it comprises only of exchange-traded instruments, the synthetic swap is easy to revalue, with no fee payable to an intermediary, making it quite cost-efficient. There are drawbacks of course. Implementation and ongoing management can be tricky.

Liquidity management is critical. The manager needs to ensure that there is always enough ready cash to meet variation margins. At the same time too much available cash means that the physical portfolio will be underinvested, foregoing some of the benefits of the dividend tax credit. Most of the time liquidity of about 10 per cent is sufficient as equity markets tend to move up and down together, and the net short and long futures positions approximately off-set each other. Occasionally, though, the domestic market might move sharply up while most other markets move sharply down, or vice-versa, straining the 10 per cent cash allowance.

Advantages and disadvantages of swaps over futures and forwards

The overwhelming advantage of swaps is their flexibility. Investors can construct any combination of assets and liabilities to fine-tune their exposure to return and risk to exactly match their requirements. Swaps enable investors to venture beyond the limitations of recognized markets while largely avoiding the risk of illiquidity and settlement headaches that usually deter from such exotic investment destinations. Moreover this can be achieved within virtually any time frame imaginable. Settlement and reset dates need not coincide with traditional quarter-ends or month-ends, but can comply with the exact time horizon of the investor.

Currency hedging can be automated by stipulating the currency in the swap agreement, largely obviating the need to establish and manage forward foreign exchange positions.

Asset swaps provide a very effective way of maximizing the benefit of dividend tax credits by allowing the investor to hold physical assets in domestic equities while still enjoying the superior return and risk combinations afforded by holding international assets.

The main disadvantage is that the cost of setting up can be prohibitively expensive if the face value of the swap is small or the nature of the swap complex. Similarly, for complex swaps, finding enough suitable intermediaries to ensure competitive bids can be hard, and ongoing valuation can be troublesome, particularly for some 'total return' (as opposed to price only) equity swaps.

Counterparty risk needs to be managed. While swaps rarely constitute such a large proportion of an investment portfolio to pose a serious threat to the quality of the overall investment, swap counterparty risk needs to be incorporated at the portfolio level with bond, money market and foreign exchange counterparty risks. This is particularly true where the fund employs a number of different asset managers.

Appendix 5: Options

Forwards, futures and swaps oblige buyers and sellers to trade at fixed prices regardless of how unattractive the prices at expiry relative to the going market rate. Options, on the other hand, allow the investor to walk away from the deal if the contracted price does not compare favourably to what is currently offered by the market at the time of the contract's expiry. This is the essential feature that sets options apart from forwards, futures and swaps.

Options come in two flavours: call options and put options. The buyer of a call option benefits if the underlying asset appreciates, while the call seller loses. A put buyer benefits from price decreases, while the seller of puts loses.

To obtain the benefit of the right to walk away from a deal that has become unattractive, the option buyer must pay a premium. This can be thought of an insurance premium.

Think of an individual who has learned that he is about to receive a significant sum of money in about three months' time. He is keen to invest this money in the stock-market, where he intends to leave it to appreciate for several years. He would like to effect this investment as soon as possible but has reservations about the market's likely behaviour between now and when the cash is actually available. He could do nothing and wait until the cash materializes. If the market appreciates in the meantime, he will have missed this opportunity. Alternatively he could buy futures. This covers the danger of the market going up, but what if it falls sharply? He would lose money. The other solution would be to buy options on the stock-market. That way, if the market goes up, he can exercise his option to buy shares at a pre-agreed price (the exercise price). If the market falls, as he fears it might, he instead buys shares at the lower market price, abandoning his option. In this case he will have forfeited the premium paid at the outset, but has nevertheless insured himself against the market appreciating too much before he can get his investment in place.

Pricing

The primary determinant of how much an option is worth is the underlying asset. The option cannot be worth more than this asset. The second element is the price at which it is exercisable, the exercise price. The call option cannot be worth less than the difference between the current price of the underlying asset and the exercise price of the option. These two prices serve as the upper and lower bounds for calculating the option price and determining the intrinsic value of the option, the value of immediate exercise. To narrow it down further, we need to know:

- The time to expiry of the option.
- The interest rate.
- The volatility of the underlying asset.

These elements determine the time value of the option, which, together with the intrinsic value, make up the option price. The most frequently used method of estimating option prices is known as the Black-Scholes option pricing formula. For a call option on a physical asset, this is:

$$pc = s \times N(d1) - pe \times N(d2)/e^{iy} \tag{A5.1}$$

Where:

pc = the price of the call option
s = the current price of the asset
pe = the exercise price of the option
i = the risk-free interest rate
vol = the volatility of the underlying asset
y = the time to expiry in years
e^{iy} = the interest rate continuously compounded

N(d1) and N(d2) are terms describing the probability of the share price being sufficiently volatile that the option expires in-the-money. They are calculated as:

$$N(d1) = [\ln (pa/pe) + (i + vol^2/2) \times y]/vol \times y^{0.5} \tag{A5.2}$$

$$N(d2) = N(d1) - vol \times y^{0.5} \tag{A5.3}$$

The option premium reflects the likelihood that the option will expire in-the-money. An option is in-the-money if the asset price is greater than the exercise price for a call option, and less than the exercise price for a put option. An option on a volatile asset is more likely to expire in-the-money than a fairly stable one, so other things being equal, a volatile asset will have a higher option premium. Similarly, the more time to expiry the option has, the more time there is for it to move into-the-money. The interest rate serves a similar purpose in options prices as in forward and futures prices: it adjusts for the fact that most of the settlement occurs at the expiry of the option, even though the holder has gained exposure to movements in the price of the underlying asset.

Some options can be exercised at any time up to the exercise or expiry date, while others can only be exercised on the last day. American options can be exercised before the exercise, while European options cannot. In practice there is little distinction: most options traded on recognized markets are American, but early exercise does not happen often, for reasons that are explained here. So, though American, most options are priced as European.

By exercising an option early, the holder is forfeiting the time value of the option. This is rarely a rational thing to do. If the option holder wishes to cash in the gains made on the option, it makes more sense to sell it – by which action the remaining time value is received as part of the sale price of the option. Sometimes options are exercised early; most often when the option is on a physical share that is close to its ex-dividend date. As the option holder is not entitled to receive dividends and the owner of the share is, it is entirely possible that the value to the investor of the dividend (including tax credits) is greater than the remaining time value, in which case the investor happily forfeits the time value of the option in exchange for entitlement to the dividend.

Options on futures

Many futures contracts have options traded on them, and these instruments offer an important source of flexibility for implementing short-term asset allocation shifts. Conceptually, options on futures are no different from options on physical assets, but they are priced slightly differently, as the delayed settlement aspect is already taken into account in the futures premium. The formula for pricing a call option on a futures contract is:

$$pc = [s \times N(d1) - pe \times N(d2)] / e^{iy} \tag{A5.4}$$

Where:

$$N(d1) = [\ln (s/pe) + vol^2/2 \times y]/vol \times t^{0.5} \tag{A5.5}$$

$$N(d2) = N(d1) - vol \times y^{0.5} \tag{A5.6}$$

Figure A5.1 shows the structure of a call option price. The value of the underlying asset is shown as the diagonal line starting at zero. Note that a fully paid share can be thought of as an option with an exercise price of zero. (The share price cannot go below zero, so the buyer cannot lose more than what he paid for it.) The other diagonal line shows the intrinsic value of the option. This represents the relationship between the price of the option and the underlying asset at the option's expiry. It is zero at the exercise price, then appreciates one-for-one with the underlying asset. The curved line between the asset price and the intrinsic value is the value of the call option. An option with a very long time to expiry behaves very much like the underlying asset. As the option approaches its expiry date, the time value decays and the price of the option converges to its intrinsic value. Note that the option time value is always greatest when the option is at-the-money, that is, when the asset price is about the same as the exercise price, reflecting the fact that this is the price where uncertainty about the option's final value is greatest.

The potential gains to the buyer of an actual option are theoretically unlimited, at least for a call option. While losses are limited to the premium paid for the option. For the seller of an option, the outcome is the reverse: a predefined maximum gain and potentially unlimited losses, especially for call options.

Figure A5.2 shows the payoff to the holder of a call option when it expires. If the price of the underlying asset goes up, potential profit is unlimited. If it goes down, the option buyer loses no more than the premium paid. The point of indifference of the option holder in this case is when the asset price is equal to the exercise price less the premium paid. In this case \$16.29 (\$20.00 – \$3.71).

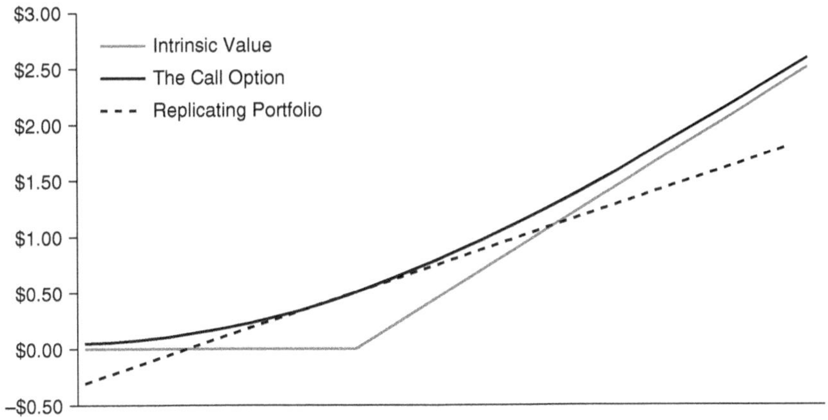

Figure A5.1 The call option premium

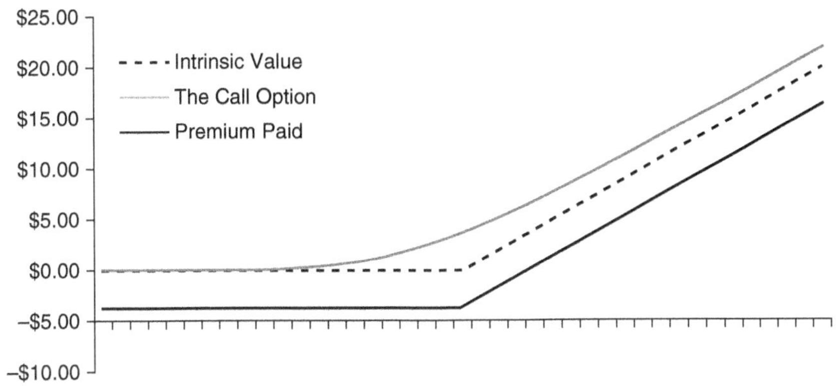

Figure A5.2 The option premium

The call option buyer will generally be happy if the underlying asset appreciates, as the gains will be those of the asset less the option premium paid. If the asset price goes down, the call option holder will lose the premium paid, but will avoid potentially larger losses from holding physical assets. But what happens if the asset price stays at the same level? The option buyer has lost the option premium, seemingly for nothing. All options suffer time decay because the time value of the option dwindles to nothing as the option nears expiry. Time decay is most obvious when the asset price is stable.

As with forward, futures and swap prices, option prices take no account of the likely direction of the price of the underlying security.

Assumptions

The formula for pricing an option relies on a number of simplifying assumptions about the behaviour of the price of the underlying asset. The most important of these is that the asset returns are approximately normally distributed (lognormally to be precise, the difference is that lognormal prices cannot go below zero, while normal prices can, meaning that positive and negative price fluctuations are equally likely); and that the price moves incrementally, not in large jumps.

Other assumptions implicit in option price theory are that the interest rate and the volatility of the underlying asset remain stable for the life of the option, that markets are perfectly liquid and that there are no transactions costs. Of these, the most troublesome is the assumption of stable volatility. Volatility is a measure of how quickly and how far the price of the asset moves about, regardless of direction, in a given time frame. Asset price volatility often remains stable for extended periods, and then changes significantly without warning. The effect on the option price of changing volatility is most acute for at-the-money options with plenty of time left to expiry.

Put-call parity

Put-call parity is one of the most endearing features of options. It says that call options can be constructed using put options and vice versa.

Figure A5.3 shows that combining a short put and a long call option with the same exercise price gives the same outcome as a forward or futures contract on the underlying asset. The relationship is expressed arithmetically as:

$$pc - pp = pf - pe \qquad \text{(A5.7)}$$

An investor holding a risky asset might believe that the asset is going to depreciate in the short term, although its long-term prospects are bright. Rather than incurring the costs of selling the asset and buying a call option, the exact same outcome can be achieved by buying a put option and continuing to hold the physical asset.

In Table A5.1, the investor wishes to temporarily reduce his exposure to one particular asset in his portfolio. The stock is currently trading at \$11.50. He can either sell the shares and buy call options or he can hold the stock and buy put options. Both option series have an exercise price of \$10.00 and time to expiry of 90 days. The calls are trading at \$1.66 and the puts are trading at \$0.04.

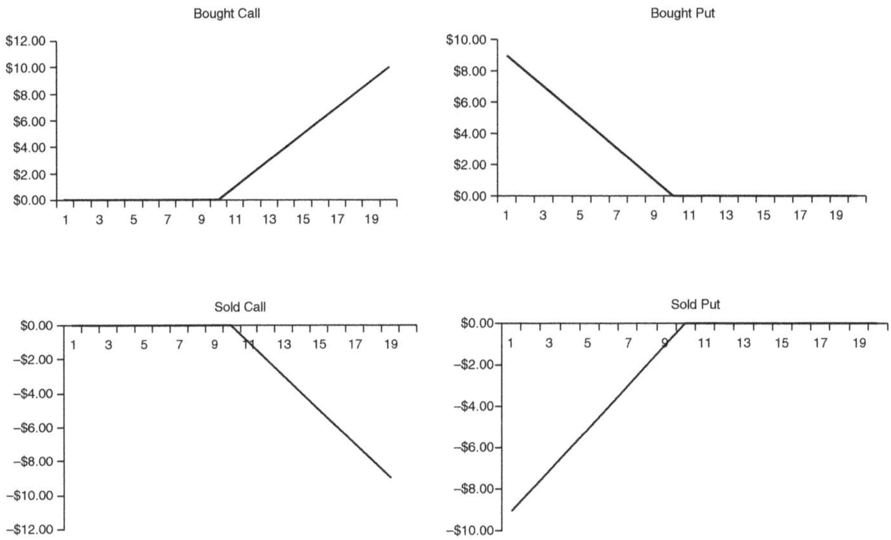

Figure A5.3 Put-call parity

Table A5.1

Share price	$11.50	x	1000
Exercise price	$10.00	x	1000
Call premium	$1.66	x	1000
Put premium	$0.04	x	1000
Interest rate	5%		
Volatility	22%		
Time to expiry	90 days		
Transactions costs	0.50%		
	Strategy 1: Sell stock, buy call		strategy 2: Hold stock, buy put
Sell 1000 shares	$11 500.00		
Buy 1000 calls	–$1 660.00		
Buy 1000 puts			–$40.00
Interest on proceeds of share sale	$121.32		
Transactions costs	–$65.80		–$0.20

Outcome A: share price =	**$15.00**	
Profit/loss on shares	–$3 500.00	
Exercise options	$5 000.00	$0.00
Option premium	–$1 660.00	–$40.00
Interest income	$121.32	
Transactions costs	–$65.80	–$0.20
Net outcome	–$104.48	–$40.20

Outcome B: share price =	**$8.00**	
Profit/loss on shares	$3 500.00	
Exercise options	$0.00	$2,000.00
Option premium	–$1 660.00	–$40.00
Interest income	$121.32	
Transactions costs	–$65.80	–$0.20
Net outcome	$1 895.52	$1,959.80

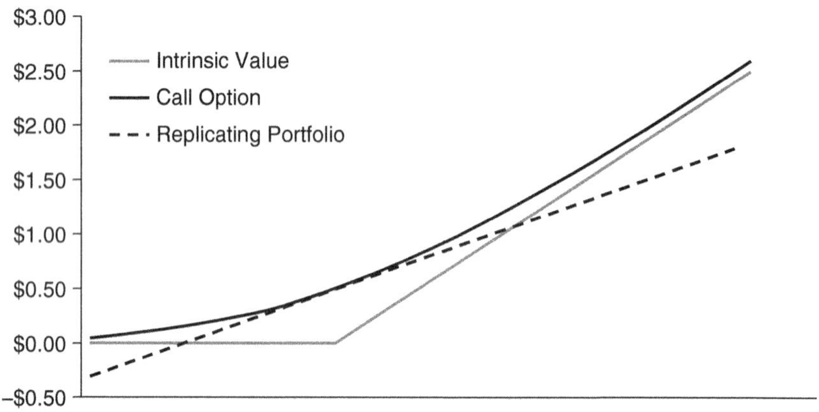

Figure A5.4 Replicating options

In strategy 1 (Table A5.1) the investor benefits from share price appreciation by exercising the options. The put buyer is protected against the fall in the share price because by exercising the puts he is able to effectively sell shares at $10.00, so he only suffers the loss of $1.50 from the starting position. The difference in outcome for the two strategies is always $64.28, which is the difference in transactions costs between the two strategies.

Combining call options and the underlying asset to create a put is often referred to as creating a synthetic put option. The limitation of synthetic options is that bought options can only be replicated using other bought options, and vice versa.

Example A5.1

Replicating call options

Initial asset price:	$20.00
Exercise price:	$20.00
Time to expiry:	1 month
Interest rate:	5%
Implied volatility:	20%
Option delta:	0.5395

	Constant Hedge				Dynamic Hedge				
Day	Share Price	Value of Call	Value of Replicating Call	Difference	Option Delta	Change in Option Delta (Shares Bought & Sold)	Funds Employed	Value of Portfolio	Cumulative Cost of Dynamic Hedge
Col	1	2	3	4	5	6	7	8	9
1	$20.00	$0.50	$0.50	$0.00	0.5395	0.5395	$10.79	$10.79	$0.00
2	$22.30	$2.39	$1.74	–$0.65	0.9780	0.4385	$20.57	$21.81	$1.24
3	$21.50	$1.62	$1.31	–$0.31	0.9180	–0.0600	$19.28	$19.74	$0.46
4	$19.00	$0.11	–$0.04	–$0.15	0.2000	–0.7180	$5.64	$3.80	–$1.84
5	$23.40	$3.47	$2.34	–$1.14	0.9987	0.7987	$24.33	$23.37	–$0.96
6	$25.60	$5.67	$3.52	–$2.15	1.0000	0.0013	$24.36	$25.60	$1.24
7	$22.00	$2.08	$1.58	–$0.50	0.9733	–0.0267	$23.77	$21.41	–$2.36
8	$18.00	$0.01	–$0.58	–$0.59	0.0231	–0.9501	$6.67	$0.42	–$6.25
9	$19.50	$0.21	$0.23	$0.02	0.3352	0.3121	$12.75	$6.54	–$6.22
10	$21.50	$1.58	$1.31	–$0.27	0.9425	0.6073	$25.81	$20.26	–$5.55
11	$23.00	$3.05	$2.12	–$0.93	0.9988	0.0563	$27.11	$22.97	–$4.13
12	$22.00	$2.06	$1.58	–$0.48	0.9840	–0.0148	$26.78	$21.65	–$5.13

Options can also be created by combining cash and the underlying asset. This is known as a replicating option. Figure A5.4 illustrates this, showing the relationship between the change in the price of the option and that of the underlying asset. The x-axis shows the underlying asset and the curved line shows the price of a call option. The change in direction of the intrinsic value of the option shows where the exercise price is. When the asset price is equal to the exercise price, a movement in the price of the asset of 1 causes the call option to move by 0.5 in the same direction. Thus the option is said to have a delta of 0.5. When the asset price is very low, the call option is very unresponsive to movements in the asset price, so the delta is close to zero. On the other hand, when the asset price is much greater than the exercise price, the delta of the option converges to 1, and the option behaves like the underlying asset. Mathematically speaking, the delta is the slope of the tangent to the curved line describing the price of the option.

This relationship can be used to construct a replicating option. To do this the investor simply holds a portfolio of cash and the underlying risky asset such that the percentage of the risky asset held corresponds to the delta of the option to be replicated. To replicate a long call position, the investor progressively buys the asset as its price increases and sells it as it goes down.

If all the assumptions applied in option pricing hold true, the outcome would be identical for the replicating and the actual option. Unfortunately, prices move in erratic ways, jumping this way and that. Because the replicating option is always following price movements, it will be buying too high and selling too low. (The replicating portfolio moves along the straight tangent, while the actual option moves along the curved option price line.) This shortcoming is compounded when the underlying asset price zigzags, causing losses to the replicating position to accumulate. Similarly if the asset turns out to be more volatile than originally estimated, the outcome to the replicating option will deteriorate further. This effect is exacerbated by transactions costs incurred along the way by the replicating option, resulting in a further difference between the outcomes of the replicating and actual options.

The table in this example illustrates this effect. If the replicating portfolio is left unchanged, then as the share price moves, the value of the actual option diverges from the value of the replicating option. This is seen in column 4 of the table. On the other hand, the cost of adjusting the hedge can be punitive when the price of the underlying asset is very volatile. This is demonstrated in columns 7, 8 and 9 of the table.

Just as replicating bought options using dynamic hedging can be costly if markets are volatile, the same volatility can work to the advantage the investor who has bought options and hedges them dynamically using the underlying asset.

The practice of constructing a replicating portfolio is also known as delta hedging. The risk of the replicating portfolio under-performing the actual option because of large, discrete price movements in the underlying asset is known as jump risk.

Option volatility – gamma

The risks associated with decay of time value and of losses due to underestimating the volatility of the underlying asset are indicated by the option's gamma.

Example A5.2

Delta and gamma of an option portfolio

Initial asset price:	$20.00
Exercise price:	$20.00
Time to expiry:	1 month
Interest rate:	5%
Implied volatility:	20%
Option delta:	0.5395

Number bought and sold	Exercise price	Exercise date	Call/put	Option price	Option delta	Weighted delta	Option gamma	Weighted gamma
310 000	$20.00	31 03 00	Call	$1.73	0.5632	174 578.90	0.0557	17 252.33
–40 000	$25.00	31 03 00	Call	$0.05	0.0507	–2 026.25	0.1760	–7 040.82
200 000	$22.50	31 03 00	Call	$0.29	0.2148	42 964.15	0.1124	22 473.91
–150 000	$27.50	31 03/00	Call	$0.01	0.0081	–1 208.69	0.2417	–36 261.06
180 000	$21.50	30 06 00	Call	$1.00	0.4265	76 766.36	0.0522	9 398.82
500 000	$27.50	30 06 00	Call	$0.08	0.0567	28 330.30	0.1188	59 387.86
1 000 000.00					0.3194	319 404.76	0.0652	65 211.04

Gamma is the rate of change in the option delta for a small change in the underlying asset price.

Gamma is positive for all bought options, call or put, and is negative for all sold options. A high absolute (ignore the sign) option gamma says that time decay is happening quite fast, and that the delta of the option is likely to move about very quickly. A positive gamma means that the portfolio can do quite well in a volatile market, but will suffer in static one. A negative gamma indicates the opposite.

The options in this example are all on a single underlying asset, with a share price of $20.00 and an estimated volatility of 25 per cent. The delta is 0.3194 and the gamma of this portfolio is 0.06. A 10 per cent increase in the price of the underlying asset brings the delta to 0.5275, making the option considerably more sensitive to changes in the price of the underlying asset.

When the share price goes up by 25 per cent to $25, the aggregate delta increases to 0.7505, but the gamma reduces to 0.0198. This is because the large position in March $20 call has moved further in-the-money, with a consequent reduction in its gamma, which, because of the size of the holding relative to the overall portfolio, has a strong impact on the portfolio's aggregate delta and gamma. The effect is even more dramatic with a further 25 per cent shift in the price of the underlying asset, after which the aggregate delta is 0.9089 and the gamma 0.0076.

When analysing the gamma of a portfolio, most managers do not generally try to aggregate options on different assets, although they may look at collective gamma measures in assets that are highly correlated.

Implied volatility

Accurate or effective estimations of option prices, volatilities and gammas depend on correctly forecasting the volatility of the underlying asset. This can be difficult, as asset volatilities can shift quite suddenly, changing the risk profile of the entire options portfolio. Investors with negative gamma (having sold more options than they have bought) can lose from an upward shift in volatility, while a downward shift will hurt investors who have bought options, in the expectation of plenty of volatility in the underlying asset.

Of all the things that determine the price of an option, only the volatility cannot be determined in advance. This means that, given the price of an option, the volatility of the underlying asset implied by that option price can be deduced easily and precisely. So when comparing prices options and the physical asset, or those of different options series, many investment managers calculate the volatility that is implied by the option price. Computing the implied volatility of an option is a matter of trying different volatility estimates in the option price formula until the price calculated matches the one quoted.

Implementation

Buying and selling options follow much the same principles for other derivatives. Exchange traded options are transacted in the same way as futures contracts, while over-the-counter options resemble forwards or swaps.

Exchange-traded options are available on most major share price index futures, futures on interest rate instruments such as bonds and bills, currency and commodities futures as well as on individual stocks. Option premia are normally quoted in the same units as the underlying asset or derivative contract, with exercise dates corresponding to the futures expiry dates. Exercise prices for exchange-traded options are usually set so that there is at least one option series that is in-the-money and one that is out-of-the-money. As the futures price moves up and down, new exercise price series are added to ensure enough choices. Not all are always liquid enough to trade; as most trading takes place in those series that are near-the-money.

Like futures contracts, options can be traded as spreads, in which case the order is given as the difference between the prices of the two option series. In addition to the spread between two expiry months, investors can also trade the spread between two exercise prices within the same expiry month.

Options on physical securities

Trading options on physical stock is not very different from options on futures, with the main difference that most markets for options on physical stocks are not as liquid as options on futures contracts, particularly for put options. This is because hedging put options requires the ability to sell short the underlying asset, which, for physical securities is expensive on some markets, and impossible on others.

Over-the-counter

Implementing over-the-counter options is similar to implementing swap contracts. With similar limitations: they can be expensive to document and implement, especially for small face values, and once set in place, they can be expensive to reverse. Most over-the-counter option agreements are for at least one year, often using ISDA standardized contracts for swaps.

The premium applying to over-the-counter options is theoretically identical to the exchange-traded kind. Because the option price is driven by the cost of hedging, an option agreement is relatively standard, the price quoted will be close to that for comparable exchange-traded options. If the option has some unusual features, the price quoted will be higher.

Other things being equal, standard features that will keep the price of the over-the-counter option down include:

- An easily traded underlying asset.
- An exercise date that is near the expiry date of a futures contract on a similar asset.
- Denomination in a major currency.
- Reasonably standard exercise provisions.

As a rule, any option that is difficult to hedge is likely to be expensive.

Like swaps, the main advantage of over-the-counter options is flexibility. The investor can implement the precise asset exposure required to meet the particular investment objective, perhaps applying exotic options. Exotic options are options with non-standard exercise provisions, such as the exercise prices that are specified at the option expiry rather than at the outset. The exotic exercise price might be specified as the average price of the underlying asset over a given period (which may or may not be the period of the option itself) or it might be exercisable against the maximum, or the minimum price of a given asset.

The main disadvantages of exotic and other over-the-counter options are that, once in place, the option agreement can be difficult to terminate, and the price of the option is not transparent: it is hard to be sure that the price quoted is fair. This problem is much worse for highly customized options agreements because fewer intermediaries have the resources to quote prices for difficult to hedge options and exotic options.

Ongoing management

Once in place the requirements for managing options vary enormously according to whether the options are exchange-traded or over-the-counter and whether they are bought or sold. Exchange-traded options have the same administrative requirements as futures contracts with the exception that variation margins for bought options are limited to the amount of the option premium. Some exchanges demand that this amount is paid when the option is purchased; others apply margining procedures until the full premium is paid.

Most brokers remind their clients of in-the-money options nearing expiry, to avoid forfeiting a valuable asset, but ultimately it is the responsibility of the investor to notify the exchange or the seller of the option that he or she intends to exercise.

Over-the-counter options are managed in very much the same way as swaps, again with the exception that, once the option premium has been paid, quarterly settlements, if they are due, are only paid to the buyer of the option.

Administration

Administration of options need not be too complicated, for exchange-traded options at least. Premiums are usually paid at the time of the purchase, although some exchanges have introduced systems of margined premiums, by which the premium is applied in the same way that variation margins are. Sellers of options on futures contracts usually pay variation margins, as for a futures position. Sellers of options on physical shares usually are required to pledge or deposit the shares with the exchange to ensure delivery.

Over-the-counter options are more complex, mainly because they are much more difficult to value. Valuation is achieved by applying some estimate of the implied volatility of the option, which in turn can be derived from some asset or basket of exchange-traded assets that resemble the underlying asset.

Once the valuation problem has been solved, administration follows the same principles as for swap agreements.

Performance measurement and attribution

Effective attribution depends on the correct treatment of cash collateral. The issues are similar to those for futures, with the extra consideration of the option delta, as set out in Tables A5.2 and A5.3.

Table A5.2 Performance measurement and attribution analysis for a bought call option on a futures contract

Point value of futures contract	$100
Initial margin per futures contract	$3 000
Number of contracts bought	200
Number of contracts sold	0
Call option purchase premium	311.0
Call option current premium	302.5
Exercise price of option	2 500.0
Option delta at purchase	0.74
Current option delta	0.77
Futures price at option purchase	2 743.4
Current futures price	2 750.0
Current physical index	2 693.9
Interest rate for cash	4.50%
Current portfolio value	$100 000 000

Table A5.3 The valuation statement

	The right way	The wrong way	The wrong way	The wrong way
	1	2	3	4
Option premium	$6 220 000	$6 220 000	$6 220 000	$6 220 000
Variation margin (sold options only)	$0	$0	$0	$0
Interest accrued on collateral	$1 518 634	$1 555 837	$0	$2 052 258
Cash collateral	$35 266 060	$36 130 000	$0	$47 658 000
Equities	$41 486 060	$42 350 000	$6 220 000	$53 878 000
Interest accrued	$2 519 739	$2 482 536	$4 038 373	$1 986 115
Cash	$58 513 940	$57 650 000	$93 780 000	$46 122 000
Total	$100 000 000	$100 000 000	$100 000 000	$100 000 000

The correct allocation to equities takes into account, as with futures, the value of the underlying physical – not the futures price. This is then adjusted by the current delta of the option to reflect the extent to which the option is behaving like the underlying asset class.

The error with method 2 is that the futures price is used instead of the underlying physical to estimate the equivalent equities exposure. Method 3 makes the mistake of only allocating the amount of the premium to equities. Method 4 goes to the other extreme, neglecting the adjustment for the delta, and so treating the option as if it were a futures position.

Performance attribution is dealt with as shown in Table A5.4.

Table A5.4 Attribution analysis

	Profit/ loss	**Sum employed**	**Return on transaction**	**Contribution to fund return**
Profit/loss on futures	–$170 000			
Interest on collateral	$1 518 634			
Return on equities	$1 348 634	$41 486 060	3.2508%	1.3486%
Return on cash	$2 519 739	$58 513 940	4.5000%	2.5197%
Total return	$3 868 373	$100 000 000	3.8684%	3.8684%

The attribution results for methods 2, 3 and 4 would be as shown in Table A5.5.

Table A5.5 Attribution results

Attribution analysis	1	2	3	4
Return on equities	1.3486%	1.3858%	–0.1700%	1.8823%
Return on cash	2.5197%	2.4825%	4.0384%	1.9861%
Total return	3.8684%	3.8684%	3.8684%	3.8684%

If, on the other hand, the objective of the option trades is simply to enhance the return to the investment portfolio, independent of the portfolio's exposure to other asset classes; then the best approach is to compare the total outcome of the options activity with a position invested only in short-term liquid assets.

Appendix 6: Convertible Notes

These are also called hybrids. Usually issued by listed companies, they comprise a bond and one or more options. The simplest kind of convertible note is a bond with a maturity of five to ten years, paying coupons once or twice annually. In addition to the bond, the investor has the right to convert the bond, at specified dates, to common equity in the company.

They are called hybrids because they do not fit neatly into the categories of either bonds or equity. Companies issue them when the equity market is trading at a low price to earnings ratio. In such conditions, issuing common equity can be expensive. Similarly the market may be demanding too high a yield on the company's bonds to make a simple bond issue attractive. Convertible notes can seem to do the trick nicely.

Theory

In theory convertibles are a bond with some option agreement added on. The simplest is a European call option exercisable at or near the maturity date of the bond. If the company's common equity is greater than the face value of the bond, then the investor will exercise the option and either hold the equity in the portfolio, or sell it at market to realize the profit. If the equity is trading below the face value of the bond, then the investor will simply redeem the bond.

Many convertible notes have more complicating modifications. The most common is substitution of a forward agreement for the option. In such cases the investor is obliged to take equity at the maturity of the bond, whether or not this is an attractive proposition. These securities are more accurately called converting bonds.

Pricing

As the pricing of any hybrid depends on the precise terms of the security, only simple convertible notes and converting bonds will be dealt with in detail here. For more complex securities, estimating the fair price depends on correctly identifying all the components of the instrument. Sometimes this is much easier said than done, and careful scrutiny of the issue documentation is required. It is not uncommon to find, or worse – to overlook, some imbedded short put provision secreted away on a back page somewhere. The good news here is that sometimes these securities with obscure provisions that are not clearly documented can trade above or below their fair price and so represent opportunities for risk free profits for the investor. If there is an imbedded short put position, then the right to convert the debt instrument to equity becomes an obligation, with quite different implications for asset allocation and risk management.

A **convertible note** is a bond plus an option. The bond component is priced using the standard bond price formula:

$$\text{Price} = \text{Coupon} \times (1 + a) + 100 \times v^n \qquad \text{(A6.1)}$$

Where:

Coupon = annual coupon rate/coupons per year
n = number of coupons to maturity
$v = 1/(1 + \text{yield})$
$a = (1 - v^{20})/\text{yield}$

The option component is priced using the formula for a call option on physical shares with one or two modifications:

$$\text{Call} = Pa \times d1 - Pe \times d2 / e^{rt} \qquad \text{(A6.2)}$$

Where:

Pa = the current price of the asset
Pe = the exercise price of the option
r = the risk-free interest rate
t = the time to expiry in years
e^{rt} = the interest rate continuously compounded

N(d1) and N(d2) are terms describing the probability of the share price being sufficiently volatile that the option expires in-the-money. They are calculated as:

$$d1 = [\ln (Pa/Pe) + (r + \text{sigma}^2/2) \times t)/\text{sigma} \times t^{0.5} \qquad \text{(A6.3)}$$

$$d2 = d1 - \text{sigma} \times t^{0.5} \qquad \text{(A6.4)}$$

The modifications stem from the fact that it is the company issuing the options, not some stock, futures or options exchange external to the company. This is important because it means that when and if the options are exercised, some of the company's debt will be replaced with equity, thus diluting the interests of the existing equity holders and altering the debt to equity ratio.

In this example, the bond is valued as a normal bond with maturity and coupon patterns the same as for the note itself. The yield input to the bond valuation is the current risk-free interest rate for a similar maturity plus the margin over the risk-free rate that the firm's bonds would normally trade.

The option pricing is a little more complicated, but the most straightforward way of doing it is to use the Black-Scholes formula with some adjustments. The first adjustment to be made is to discount the current share price for dividends to which holders of common stock would be entitled (because the convertible note does not participate in common stock dividends). To do this, the present value of the dividend stream is calculated and deducted from the current share price.

Then the share price needs to be adjusted for the dilution factor. This reflects the fact that, if the options are exercised (the convertible notes are converted into

Example A6.1

A simple convertible note

Date now	01/01/00	
Interest rate	5.00%	
Convertible bond details		
Face value of each note	$1,000.00	
Conversion rate: 1 bond	20	Shares
Maturity date of bond	31/12/09	
Annual coupon rate of bond	8.50%	
Coupons per year	2	
Next coupon date	01/03/00	
Number of notes on issue	50,000	
Conversion periods	One month prior to each coupon date plus one month prior to bond maturity	
Equity details		
Current share price	$35.00	
Annual dividend yield	2.50%	
Dividends per year	2	
Next dividend date	01/02/00	
Bond rating: LIBOR plus:	3.75%	
Share price volatility	28%	
Number of shares on issue	500,000,000	

equity), then the value of the firm's equity is increased. The dilution factor is easy to estimate. It is:

The face value of the convertible notes at maturity

The face value of the convertible notes + The current value of Equity
Which is calculated as:

$$50{,}000 \times \$1000 \,/\, (50{,}000 \times \$1000 + 500\,000\,000 \times \$35) = 0.2849\%$$

Thus the share price is adjusted as follows:

(Current Share Price – Present Value of Dividends) / (1 + Dilution Factor)

Calculated as:

($35.00 – $7.02) / (1.002849) = $27.90

The exercise price of the option is the value of each note converted into equity at the maturity of the note. This is the face value of each note ($1,000) divided by the number of shares to which it is convertible (20), giving an exercise price of $50.

The expiry date of the option is the maturity date of the note because to exercise it early would be to forfeit the remaining time value of the option.

To give a price for the convertible note that is comparable to its face value, the option value is adjusted to reflect the number of shares received on exercise.

Example A6.2

A simple convertible note

Value of bond	$1011.68
Present value of equity dividends	$7.02
Dilution factor	0.2849%
Value of call option	$8.68
Value of convertible note	$1185.29

A converting bond is a bond plus a forward contract. Sometimes the forward contract is explicit, but more often it comes in the form of a sold put option. (See the section on synthetic options in Appendix 4.) To complicate things further, the put option sometimes has an effective exercise price and/or date that is different from the call. This can make pricing and risk analysis very labour intensive and error-prone.

Example A6.3 shows a simple converting bond. The bond details are identical to those in this example. The price at which the bond is converted to equity is the same but conversion in this case is mandatory, whereas in Example A6.3 it was optional. As the implied short put option is very much in-the-money, it is quite valuable, so its inclusion significantly changes the value of the instrument.

Example A6.3

A simple converting bond

Value of bond	$1,011.68
Present value of equity Dividends	$7.02
Dilution factor	0.2849%
Value of forward	–$37.16
Value of convertible note	$268.39

In this case the value of the equity forward is calculated as:

the current share price adjusted for the dilution factor
less the present value of the conversion price
less the present value of common stock dividends

The value of the converting bond is the sum of the value of the bond and the value of all forwards, taking into account the number of shares for which the bonds are redeemed.

Applications

Convertible and converting instruments are usually issued by firms wishing to issue debt without borrowing from banks. By incorporating an equity component in the bond, they hope to reduce their cost of borrowing by offering a slightly lower coupon than would otherwise be necessary. The only problem with this approach is that markets frequently undervalue the equity component, so while the firm is reducing its apparent cost of borrowing, it is doing so at the cost of giving away equity cheaply.

Investors buy hybrid instruments for a number of reasons:

- They find the yield on the instrument attractive, and are not averse to converting it to equity in due course.
- They find the yield on the instrument attractive, and will sell the security when the yield drops sufficiently.
- They see the instrument as a way of buying the equity cheaply.
- They intend to strip the bond from the equity component, selling both separately for a short-term gain.

Most transactions in hybrids are on the part of the last group. Typically their transactions take place during or near a conversion period. This activity can be very lucrative if the required trades can be effected at low cost. One error frequently committed is to sell on market a short-dated option against a long-dated call option embedded in the hybrid. This strategy runs the risk that the short option is exercised, forcing the investor to either convert the hybrid to meet the option obligation, or purchase the common stock in the market. The cost of doing the latter can eat into the profits expected from the hybrid strategy. Selling longer-dated options can reduce this risk and allow the investor to benefit from a greater amount of time decay.

Implementation

Hybrids are traded on most stock-markets alongside common equity issues, and so follow the same trading rules applying to equities.

The limitation with nearly all hybrid instruments is liquidity. Trading activity in hybrids is often patchy, except when an interest payment or conversion period is imminent. Along with patchy trading activity, hybrids frequently suffer from wide bid-ask spreads. This can pose a number of problems, mainly for valuation.

Ongoing management

For the investment fund holding hybrids as a long-term investment, ongoing management is not much different from holding shares. The most important issue is valuation of the instruments, and assessing their contribution to the riskiness of the portfolio.

Long-term holders of hybrids usually have the choice once or twice each year of converting their fixed interest investment to equity. Few do so, except at the final conversion date. This is because early conversion is exactly the same as early exercise of an option: it forfeits the remaining time value of the option and so fails to derive the full economic benefit of the instrument.

Administration

Along with over-the-counter derivatives such as forwards, swaps and over-the-counter option agreements, valuation is a significant administrative hurdle. As hybrid instruments are traded on recognized exchanges, this might seem surprising at first. But the lack of liquidity in these instruments often means that the price quoted by the exchange is quite different from either its economic value or the price at which it actually could be sold.

Once the valuation is solved, or at least recognized, administration of hybrid instruments follows very much the same procedures as common equity holdings. Except that, if and when the bond is converted into equity, there will be a change in asset allocation for the fund, which will occur without an apparent decision prompting it. The holding will disappear from one part of the asset listing report and miraculously reappear somewhere else. It will not appear in the related transaction report, save perhaps as a miscellaneous entry.

Performance measurement and attribution

Hybrids pose some interesting questions for performance measurement and attribution analysis because they straddle the divide between fixed interest and equities. The most common approach is to treat them as pure equity. After all, they are traded on equity exchanges. This approach is sensible enough for converting instruments (bond plus forward). But the economic value represented by convertible (bond plus option) is primarily a bond, especially if the option is out-of-the-money.

Identifying and separating the value of the bond and the equity component of hybrids is important not just for attribution analysis. It also makes asset allocation easier by quantifying the changing value of both with changes in equity prices, credit ratings and interest rates. Thus if the price of the underlying equity goes into serious decline, the equity component will converge to zero, while the bond component will decline to reflect the company's altered credit rating. When the final conversion period arrives, the instrument will already be recognized as virtually all bond, so no noticeable adjustment needs to take place. Alternately, if the instrument has always been treated as an equity, and conversion does not take place, then a sudden shift will occur for no reason that is apparent to the asset allocation committee or the fund's trustees.

One approach to the asset allocation problem is to put hybrids in an asset class of their own. This idea has the appeal of simplicity, but it clouds over some fairly important considerations. Treating them as a separate asset class implies that they are essentially different from other asset classes. The problem is that they are not: they are combinations of bonds and equities. Measuring their real impact on portfolio performance and risk means assessing the contribution to portfolio bond and equity performance of each component of the instrument. This includes treating coupons received as interest received, and when the fixed interest is converted to equity, dividends are equity dividends.

In practice this can be tiresome. Because the components of the instrument do not have traded prices, they must be valued as if they were over-the-counter instruments. To carry out a thorough revaluation and performance appraisal therefore means finding an objective measure of the volatility of the underlying equity and applying it to the option components of the instrument.

Example A6.4

Performance measurement and attribution analysis for a simple convertible note

Date now	01-Jan-00
Interest rate	5.00%
Convertible bond details	
Number of notes held	8,000
Conversion rate	20
Current price	$1,185.00
Purchase price	$1,084.22
Purchase date	01/07/99
Bond details	
Value of bond	$1,011.68
Value of bond at purchase	$968.82
Option details	
Current share price	$35.00
Share price on purchase date	$28.00
Option value	$8.68
Option value on purchase date	$5.77
Current option delta	0.63

The valuation statement	The right way	The wrong way	The wrong way
	1	2	3
Option premium	$1,388,900	$1,388,900	$1,388,900
Interest Accrued on collateral	$54,096	$0	$106,143
Cash collateral	$2,146,196	$0	$4,211,100
Equities	$3,589,192	$1,388,900	$5,706,143
Bonds	$8,673,760	$8,673,760	$8,673,760
Cash	$87,737,048	$89,937,340	$85,620,097
Total	$100,000,000	$100,000,000	$100,000,000

In method 1, the exposure to equities resulting from a holding in convertible notes is calculated as the number of convertible notes held times the conversion rate, times the current share price, times the current option delta:

$$8000 \times 20 \times \$35 \times 0.63 = \$1\ 388\ 900$$

The exposure to bonds is the number of convertible notes held times the current bond value:

$$8000 \times \$1011.68$$

Method 2 makes the mistake of only allocating the amount of the premium to equities. Method 3 goes to the other extreme, neglecting the adjustment for the delta, and so treating the option as if it were a futures position.

Performance attribution is dealt with as shown in Table A6.1.

The attribution results for methods 2, 3 and 4 would be as shown in Table A6.2.

Table A6.1 Performance attribution

Attribution analysis	Profit/ loss	Sum employed	Return on transaction	Contribution to fund return
Profit/loss on options	$465,700			
Interest on collateral	$54,096			
Return on equities	$519,796	$3,589,192	14.4823%	0.5198%
Return on bonds	$342,879	$8,673,760	3.9531%	0.3429%
Return on convertible notes	$806,240	$12,262,952	6.5746%	0.8062%
Return on cash	$2,157,084	$87,737,048	2.4586%	2.1571%
Total return	$3,825,999	$100,000,000	3.8260%	3.8260%

Table A6.2 Attribution results

Attribution analysis	1	2	3
Return on equities	0.5198%	0.4657%	0.5718%
Return on bonds	0.3429%	0.3429%	0.3429%
Return on cash	2.1571%	2.2112%	2.1050%
Total return	3.8260%	3.8260%	3.8260%

Bibliography

Ackler, D. and Duck, N., Reference Day Risk and the Use of Monthly Returns: A Warning Note, Discussion Paper 04/557, revised April 2006. Bristol: University of Bristol.

Arnott, Robert D., Bernstein, Peter L., What Risk Premium is 'Normal'?, *AIMR*, 2002.

Barker, M.D., *Forecasting the Long Term Return on Equities*, Institute of Actuaries of Australia, 2003.

Black, F., Universal Hedging: Optimizing Currency Risk and Reward in International Equity Portfolios, *Financial Analysts Journal*, July–August 1989, p. 16.

Black F., Litterman R., Global Portfolio Optimization, *Financial Analysts Journal*, vol 48 n.5, 1992, pp. 28–43.

Bodie, Z., Kane, A., Marcus, A.J., *Investments*, Burr Ridge Irwin, 1993.

Braudel, F., *Civilisation and Capitalism 15th–18th Centuries*, N.Y.: Harper & Row 1981–84.

CFA Institute *Global Investment Performance Standards*, 2010.

Chiang, A.C., *Fundamental Methods of Mathematical Economics*, New York: McGraw Hill. 1974.

EDHEC Risk Institute *What are the Risks of European ETFs?* January 2012.

Dimson, Elroy, Marsh, Paul, Staunton, Mike, *Rethinking the Equity Risk Premium*, Research Foundations Publications, 2011, pp. 32–52.

Grinold, R.G., Kahn, R.N., *Active Portfolio Management: A Quantitative Approach for Producing Superior Returns and Selecting Superior Returns and Controlling Risk*, London: McGraw Hill Professional, 1999.

Keynes, J.M., *The General Theory of Employment Interest and Money*, N.Y.: Harcourt, Brace and Company, 1936.

Kohli, J., *An Empirical Analysis of Resampled Efficiency*, Worcester: Worcester Polytechnic Institute, 2005.

Kritzman, Mark, *The Portable Financial Analyst*, Chicago: Ill, Probus, 1995.

Lakonishok, Josef, Schleifer, Andre and Vishny, Robert W., *Study of the US Equity Money Manager Performance*, Washington DC: Brookings Institute, 1992.

Mackay, C., *Extraordinary Popular Delusions and the Madness of Crowds*, 1841.

MacKenzie, D., Spears, T. *The Formula that Killed Wall Street? The Gaussian Copula and the Material Cultures of Modeling*, Edinburgh: University of Edinburgh, June 2012.

MacQueen, Jason, *To Optimise or Not to Optimise? The Case Against Optimization*, London: Quant, May 2010.

Markowitz, H.M., *Portfolio Selection: Efficient Diversification of Investment*, Cowles Foundation Monograph 16, New Haven, CT: Yale University Press, 1959.

Michaud, R., and Michaud, R. *Efficient Asset Management: A Practical Guide to Stock Portfolio Optimization and Asset Allocation*, Boston, MA: Harvard Business School Press. 2nd edn., 2008.

Minsky, H.P., The Modeling of Financial Instability: An introduction, in *Modeling and Simulation*. Proceedings of the Fifth Annual Pittsburgh Conference, 1974.

Nassim, Taleb, *The Black Swan: The Impact of the Highly Improbable*, New York: Random House and Penguin, 2007.

Ohana, Steve, *Financial Rogue Waves*, CFA UK Society, 2010.

PRMIA-SunGard APT Buy-side Market Risk Management Trends, 2013.

Rachev, Z., Menn, C., Fabozzi, F.J. *Fat-tailed and Skewed Asset Return Distributions - Implications for Risk Management, Portfolio Selection and Option Pricing*, Hoboken: John Wiley & Sons, 2005.

Rosenberg, B., Extra Market Components of Covariance in Security Returns, *Journal of Financial and Quantitative Analysis*, vol 9, March 1974, pp. 263–74.

Rudd, A., Optimal Selection of Passive Portfolios, *Financial Management*, vol 9, n.1, Spring 1980, pp. 57–65.

Rudd, A., Clasing, Henry K. Jr., *Modern Portfolio Theory, Second Edition*. Orinda, CA: Andrew Rudd, 1988.

Sadka, Ronnie, Momentum and Post-Earnings-Announcement Drift Anomalies: The Role of liquidity Risk, *Journal of Financial Economics*, vol 80, 2006, pp. 309–49.

Satchell, S., Allen, D., *I/N Investing*, London: Quant, 2012.

Scarth, Neil, The Extinction of sell-side research: what it means for asset managers, CFA UK Society, 2013

Sharpe, William F., *Budgeting and Monitoring the Risk of Defined Benefit Pension Funds*, Stanford: Stanford University, 2001.

Sharpe, William F., Capital Asset Prices: A Theory of Market Equilibrium Under Conditions of Risk, *Journal of Finance*, vol 19 n. 3, September 1970, pp. 425–42.

Sharpe, William F., *Portfolio Theory and Capital Markets*, New York: McGraw Hill, 1970.

Glossary

130–30	A hybrid conventional and long short portfolio whereby bought positions represent 130 per cent of the portfolio's investment, 30 per cent is 'funded' by selling short stocks worth 30 per cent, giving a net exposure of 100 per cent.
16.00 GMT (Greenwich Mean Time)	Widely used time of day to revalue foreign currencies.
Accrual	An accounting entry to recognize an impending transaction settlement.
Accumulation Index	A share price index contract that incorporates reinvested dividends. See also Price Index, Total Return Index.
Active weight	The portfolio weight less the benchmark weight for a security or category of securities.
ADR	American Depository Receipt - an instrument listed on a US exchange, backed by shares in a non-US exchange. See also SDR.
Agency trading	The practice of purchase and sale of securities on behalf of another party.
Aggressive portfolio	A portfolio whose composition can be very different from its benchmark. See also Conservative portfolio.
AIMA	Alternative Investments Management Association.
AIMR	Association for Investment Management Research.
Algo trading	A practice whereby computers are programmed to give instructions to trade on the basis of defined prices or price spreads between securities and derivatives contracts, with specified timing and quantity, but without routine human intervention.
Algorithmic trading	A practice whereby computers are programmed to give instructions to trade on the basis of defined prices or price spreads between securities and derivatives contracts, with specified timing and quantity, but without routine human intervention.

Alpha	The component of the return to an asset or portfolio that is due to mispricing of the asset. True alpha represents riskless returns.
Alternative Investments	Assets or asset classes with unusual return characteristics.
American Option	An option that can be exercised before the exercise date. See also European Option.
Arbitrage	The purchase and simultaneous sale of two economically identical instruments or assets to yield a risk-free profit.
Arbitrage pricing theory	Stock valuation theory equating the value of an asset with the sum of market valuations of its subsidiaries.
Arithmetic link	Adding returns for consecutive investment periods. See also Geometric link.
Asset liability management	The practice of matching or optimizing the investment portfolio according to the projected liabilities of a fund.
Asset swap	Transaction whereby two investors exchange the variation in value of nominated assets.
At-the-money	Asset price equals exercise price. An option with zero intrinsic value.
Attribution Analysis	The analysis of investment returns over a single investment period to determine where and by how much investment returns varied from benchmark returns.
Automated trading	A practice whereby computers are programmed to give instructions to trade on the basis of defined prices or price spreads between securities and derivatives contracts, with specified timing and quantity, but without routine human intervention.
Balanced Portfolios	A portfolio which invests in several asset classes simultaneously. Balanced portfolios combine asset allocation and security selection within asset classes.
Basis Risk	The risk that a derivative position will not exactly offset the physical asset that it is intended to hedge.
Basket or block trade	The aggregation of a number of individual purchases or sales to a single transaction.

Bear funds	Portfolios designed to profit from falling markets. Most bear funds invest in equities markets, although theoretically they can operate in any liquid market that allows short selling or where liquid derivatives markets facilitate short exposures.
Benchmark	A reference portfolio or asset for the purpose of comparing investment portfolios.
Benchmark alpha	The difference between the benchmark related return and the overall portfolio return.
Benchmark-hugging	An active portfolio with insufficient active risk to meet return objectives.
Beta	The sensitivity of an asset or a portfolio to another asset or benchmark portfolio.
Bid-ask spread	The concurrent difference in the buy and sell price of a security or contract.
Black Box	A quantitative asset allocation or stock selection model which does not permit the user to check intermediate calculations or carry out reasonableness checks.
Black pools	Decentralized, electronic trading platforms in securities such as listed equities, that are normally traded on a centralized exchange. Unlike conventional exchanges, black pools do not publish the queue of bids and offers for the securities traded on them until after the transaction is completed.
Black-Scholes	Fisher Black and Myron Scholes were the authors of the widely used eponymous technique of pricing options on assets and portfolios.
Bond Volatility	The change in settlement value of a bond corresponding to a change in the interest rate of 0.01 per cent. See also Dollar Value of One Point, Volatility of Bonds.
Bonus Issue	The practice of replacing existing shares with a larger number of new ones. See also Stock Split.
Bottom-up Management	Stock picking based on detailed knowledge of individual companies, regardless of sector exposures.
Boutique Managers	Investment management firms specializing in a particular asset class or investment strategy.
Business risk	The risk that their business loses money or fails to make a profit.

Call option	The right, but not the obligation, to buy an asset or futures contract at an agreed price at an agreed time. See also Put Option.
CALPERS	California Public Employees Retirement Service.
Capital Asset Pricing Model (CAPM)	A framework for valuing equities and modelling equity risk, based on single market factor.
Capital Guarantee	An assurance by an investment manager that the return to the portfolio will not be below zero in nominal terms in a given period.
Capitalization weighted index	Index of share or other asset prices, the composition of which is determined by the market value of component assets. See also Price weighted index.
Cash	Short term low yield liquid instruments, usually issued by government or a bank. See also Liquid Assets, Risk-free Asset.
Cash Settled Contract	A derivative contract which ends with a cash payment of the difference between the traded price and the final price of the contract.
CFA	Chartered Financial Analyst.
Charting	The practice of scrutinizing charts of historical prices to identify visible, repeating patterns in price movements. See also Technical Analysis.
Chief Financial Officer (CFO)	The Head Accountant.
Chief Operating Officer (COO)	Responsible for non-trading activities in an investment management firm.
CIO	Chief Investment Officer.
Clearer	A bank or other financial institution, or a consortium that stands between parties trading assets or other instruments on an exchange. By taking part in exchange transactions, the Clearer ensures performance of transactions taking place on the exchange. Also known as a Clearing House.
Clearing House	A firm that guarantees performance of transactions by participating in each. See also Clearer.
Close Trade	The transaction to sell (buy) a bought (sold) derivative contract.

Closed Funds	Closed Pooled Funds are subscribed at the outset with no new units issued subsequently. Investors wishing to exit the fund must seek a buyer for their units. Closed Funds are often traded on stock exchanges, and may or may not have a pre-set termination date.
Closet Index	The sum of the various portfolios within a fund effectively form an index fund because the risks in each component portfolio are offset by other portfolios in the fund.
Collateral	An asset held or pledged to support performance of the terms of a transaction.
Collateralized Debt Obligation (CDO)	An investment instrument constructed by the bundling of many small loans into securitized instruments for re-sale on the secondary market.
Comingled	A portfolio with multiple owners. Each investor purchases a share of the portfolio. Each share, or unit, participates in capital gains and losses and income to the portfolio. See also Unitized, Pooled.
Commodities Trading Funds (CTF)	Funds that exploit mispricing and trends in commodities, usually transacting in commodity futures contracts.
Commodity-linked notes and deposits	A type of Exchange Traded Note that invests in commodities and commodity derivatives.
Compound Interest	Interest calculated for each period on both principal and interest accrued in previous periods. See also Compounding, Continuously Compounded Interest, Simple Interest.
Compounding	The procedure of calculating interest payable on interest. See also Compound Interest, Continuously Compounded Interest, Simple Interest.
Conditional value-at-risk (CVaR)	A measure of extreme loss that describes the shape of the loss distribution in the tail, to the left of VaR, thus indicating how long the tail could be, rather than simply a point outcome. See also Expected Tail Loss (ETL), Expected Shortfall (ES).
Conservative Portfolio	A multi-asset class portfolio that resembles the strategic benchmark. See also Aggressive Portfolio.
Constant proportion debt obligations (CPDO)	A structured product that is designed to deliver long term exposure to corporate bond returns in a highly rated debt security.

Constraints	Limitations on the allowable allocations or transactions in a portfolio.
Consultant	Person or firm providing independent advice to investors on investment strategy, structure and management.
Continuously Compounded Interest	Interest calculated continuously on interest accrued in previous periods. See also Compounding, Compound Interest, Simple Interest.
Contribution Holiday	A period during which members pay lower contributions than normal, or even none at all.
Convertible Hedge	An investment strategy combining convertible instruments and derivatives or other instruments, designed to eliminate unwanted risk.
Convertible Notes	Instruments combining a bond and a call option on an equity. See also Converting Bonds, Hybrids.
Converting Bonds	Instruments combining a bond, a call option and a put option on an equity. Sometimes combines a bond and a forward agreement. See also Convertible Notes, Hybrids.
Convexity	The change in duration of a bond or portfolio of bonds for a small change in the interest rate.
Core Portfolio	A low-risk portfolio complemented within a fund by high-risk satellite portfolios.
Core-satellite	Portfolio structure comprising low risk core portfolios and high risk, specialist satellite portfolios.
Corporate Action	An activity by a listed company that changes its capital base or structure in some way.
Corporate Governance	Exercising shareholder rights, such as casting votes at General Meetings and voicing opinions on management policies of companies in which the fund has a significant holding.
Correlation	The degree to which the returns to assets or portfolios resemble each other. Correlations range from -1 (perfectly offsetting returns) through zero (no relationship at all) to +1 (perfectly similar returns). See also Covariance.
Cost of Carry	Ancillary costs associated with holding an investment, including interest cost, insurance, income foregone.

Counter-cyclical Stocks	Stocks which outperform other stocks in a period of economic slowdown or recession. Usually include basic foods, tobacco and discount retailers.
Counterparty Risk	The risk that a person or entity participating in a transaction will be unable to perform his, her or its obligations under the terms of the transaction.
Coupon	Regular payments to holders of bonds.
Covariance	The degree to which the returns to assets or portfolios resemble each other. Covariances can be negative (offsetting returns), zero (no relationship at all) or positive (similar returns). See also Correlation.
CPPI	Constant Proportions Portfolio Insurance. An alternative technique to Black-Scholes for constructing portfolio protection programmes.
Credit Default Swaps (CDS)	Over-the-counter derivatives instruments linked to the default on a debt instrument.
Credit-linked notes and deposits	A type of Exchange Traded Note that invests in commodities and commodity derivatives.
Credit Risk	The risk that a borrower will be unable to honour the terms of a loan or that the loan will be downgraded.
Credit Spread	The difference in yield between interest rate securities with different risks of default.
Cum Dividend	After the dividend has been declared but before the date of entitlement. See also Ex Dividend.
Cum Interest	Bond that is about to make an interest or coupon payment. See also Ex Interest.
Currency Hedge	Derivative contracts designed to modify or cancel the risk of holding physical assets in a foreign currency.
Currency Neutral	An asset or portfolio with no excess currency exposure because the foreign currency held exactly equals the value of the asset or portfolio.
Cut in Rate of Return	The amount of portfolio return given up in return for portfolio protection.
Dark liquidity	Decentralized, electronic trading platforms in securities, such as listed equities, that are normally traded on a centralized exchange. Unlike conventional exchanges, black pools do not publish the queue of bids and offers for the securities traded on them until after the transaction is completed.

Dark pools	Decentralized, electronic trading platforms in securities such as listed equities, which are normally traded on a centralized exchange. Unlike conventional exchanges, dark pools do not publish the queue of bids and offers for the securities traded on them until after the transaction is completed.
Data-mining	The practice of using historical data to test and validate investment models.
Deadweight	The benchmark weight equivalent of a portfolio holding.
Deal Arbitrage	An investment strategy designed to exploit price changes associated with corporate actions.
Debentures	Bonds issued by firms.
Debt to Equity	The ratio of total debt to the market value of total equity. It can be expressed as D/E.
Defined Benefits Funds	Contributors pay in an amount determined by the administrator, and receive a pre-set amount or annuity, usually a multiple of final salary at a given date, usually retirement.
Defined Contributions Funds	Contributors pay into the fund, and receive the sum of what they have paid in plus investment returns, less administration and other costs.
Delivery Contract	A derivative contract which ends with delivery of physical assets from the seller to the buyer.
Delta	The change in value of an option relative to a small change in the price of the underlying asset or portfolio.
Delta Hedging	On-going management of replicating options. Continuous readjustment of portfolio weightings according to estimated delta of replicated option. See also Dynamic Hedging, Replicating Options.
Derivative	An instrument that derives its value from other securities or contracts, with forward settlement provisions.
Derivatives overlay	A portfolio of derivatives designed to alter the asset allocation of a physical multi-asset class portfolio.
Dilution Factor	The amount by which the share price is affected by a new share issue.
Directed Brokerage	A fund manager or sponsor stipulates to an investment manager that a given proportion of the portfolio trades must be assigned to brokers nominated by the fund manager. See also Directed Commissions.

Directed Commissions	A fund manager or sponsor stipulates to an investment manager that a given proportion of the portfolio trades must be assigned to brokers nominated by the fund manager. See also Directed Brokerage.
Discount Brokers	Brokers offering execution-only services.
Discount factor	The interest rate that comprises the denominator in a discounted cash flow calculation.
Discount Security	A debt instrument paying no coupons, where interest is subtracted (discounted) from the purchase price and the face value is paid at maturity.
Discounted Cash Flow	A procedure designed to adjust the value of future cash flows to reflect their timing. See also Dividend Discounting and Net Present Value.
Discounting	The procedure for imputing interest payable in the price of a fixed interest security.
Distressed debt	Securities of companies or government entities that are either already in default, under bankruptcy protection, or in distress and heading toward such a condition.
Dividend	Sum paid by a firm to its shareholders.
Dividend discounting	A procedure designed to adjust the value of future dividends to reflect their timing. See also Discounted Cash Flow and Net Present Value.
Dividend stripping	A trading strategy where the investor buys a share immediately before the ex-dividend date and sells it immediately after, or ex-dividend.
Dividend Yield	The ratio of dividends paid annually to the market price of the share.
Dollar Value of One Point (DV01)	The change in settlement value of a bond corresponding to a change in the interest rate of 0.01 per cent. See also Bond Volatility, Volatility of Bonds.
Duration	A measure of the maturity and timing of cash flows of a fixed interest instrument.
Dynamic Hedge	The technique of constantly adjusting the hedge ratio of an asset or portfolio. Most often used in replicating option positions and portfolio protection programmes.
Dynamic Hedging	On-going management of replicating options. Continuous readjustment of portfolio weightings according to estimated delta of replicated option. See also Delta Hedging, Replicating Options.
Earnings Yield	The ratio of annual earnings per share to the market price of the share.

EBIT	Earnings Before Interest and Taxes.
Efficient Frontier	The line described by all assets or portfolios that have the best possible mix of expected returns and risk.
Efficient Markets Hypothesis (EMH)	Theory of asset prices that says that the price of an asset incorporates all information currently known about it.
Efficient Portfolio	A portfolio with the lowest possible risk for a given expected return, or the highest expected return for a given level of risk.
Employee Stock Options	Options granted to employees of the company, usually to help align the interests of the employees with those of the company's shareholders.
Equilibrium	The point at which supply and demand are matched. See also Fair Price.
Equitize	Convert exposure of a non-equity asset to an equity exposure, usually using share price index futures contracts.
Equity Dilution	Change in share price resulting from a new issue of shares. See also Dilution Factor.
Equity Risk Premium	The difference in return between equities and long-term bonds that reflects the difference in risk.
Equity-linked notes and deposits	A type of Exchange Traded Note that invests in commodities and commodity derivatives.
European Option	An option that cannot be exercised before the exercise date. See also American Option.
Event Driven	An investment strategy designed to exploit changes in strategy and structure of selected firms, or the markets in which they are traded.
Ex -ante	Predicted or forecast.
Ex Dividend	After the entitlement date of the dividend, but before the dividend is paid. See also Cum Dividend.
Exchange-traded	Transactions taking place within recognized stock or futures exchanges. See also Over-the-Counter.
Exchange-traded notes	A debt security with a maturity date, which is backed by the credit of the issuer. When held to maturity, the investor receives a cash payment that is linked to the return of a physical asset or index or a portfolio of physical assets, less management fees.
Exchange-Traded Fund (ETF)	A portfolio of investments listed on a stock exchange.

Exercise Date	The date on which an option is exercisable, and after which it lapses.
Exercise Price	The amount payable (receivable) by a call (put) option holder to purchase (sell) the underlying asset on the exercise date.
Ex-interest	A bond that has just made and interest or coupon payment. See also Cum-interest.
Expected shortfall	A measure of extreme loss that describes the shape of the loss distribution in the tail, to the left of VaR, thus indicating how long the tail could be, rather than simply a point outcome. See also Expected Tail Loss (ETL), Conditional Value at Risk (CVaR).
Exponential Weighting	Incremental weighting returns where increments increase exponentially. See also Linear Weighting.
Expected Tail Loss (ETL)	A measure of extreme loss that describes the shape of the loss distribution in the tail, to the left of VaR, thus indicating how long the tail could be, rather than simply a point outcome. See also Conditional Value at Risk (CVaR), Expected Shortfall (ES).
Ex-post	Observed.
Extreme Risk	Asset price and factor volatility in extreme or stressed market conditions. See also Normal Risk.
Extreme tail loss	A measure of extreme loss that describes the shape of the loss distribution in the tail, to the left of VaR, thus indicating how long the tail could be, rather than simply a point outcome. See also Conditional Value at Risk (CVaR), Expected Shortfall (ES).
Face Value	The value against which interest is calculated. See also Par Value.
Facilitation portfolio	A portfolio of physical assets and derivatives instruments held by a broker in order quickly to meet big sell and buy orders from wholesale clients.
Factor Models	Tools to assist in portfolio construction and risk analysis using pre-defined factors to compute covariance matrices.
Factors	Influences on the price of an asset or portfolio.
Fair Price	The price at which the expected return to an asset exactly reflects its expected riskiness.
Fama–French three factor model	A framework for valuing equities and modelling equity risk, similar to CAPM, but with three factors instead of the single market factor.

Financial assets	Bonds.
Fitch	A credit ratings agency. See also Moody's, Standard & Poor's.
Fitted Curve	A yield curve model derived from observed bond yields with different maturities.
Fixed Interest	Instruments that earn a fixed interest rate until they mature.
Floor	The minimum yield in a Constant Proportions Portfolio Insurance portfolio.
Forward Contract	An agreement to buy or sell a fixed asset or security at a fixed date in the future.
Forward Foreign Exchange	A foreign exchange transaction with a settlement date more than two days after the transaction date.
Free float	The proportion of the company that trades regularly.
Frictional Liquidity	Cash held in a portfolio as a result of income received, awaiting investment or required to meet small redemptions and other requirements for cash, such as rights issues.
Front Office / Front End	The transactions and implementation functions of an investment management firm.
Front running	A practice whereby a broker, having been informed of a large incoming order, trades the security first on his or her own account, subsequently crystallizing a profit by transacting the securities concerned at a price that is made more attractive by the market impact of the trade itself.
FTA	Financial Times Actuaries - a provider of international equity indices.
Fund Manager	A person or firm charged with overseeing the investments of a pension fund, mutual fund or other jointly owned investment.
Fund of Funds	An investment fund that buys units in other investment funds. See also Manager of Managers.
FX -linked notes and deposits	A type of Exchange Traded Note that invests in commodities and commodity derivatives.
Gamma	A measure of the change in the option delta relative to the change in the value of the underlying asset or portfolio.
Gapping	A significant discrete change in the market value of an asset or portfolio.

Gearing	The sum of the face value of all assets and derivatives contracts exceeds the value of the physical assets in the fund. Alternately, where the fund has borrowed.
Gearing Ratio	The ratio of total debt to the market value of the company (measured as total debt plus market value of total equity). It can be expressed as D/(D+E).
General Level of Interest Rates	The average risk free interest rate over all maturities. See also Yield Curve.
Geometric Link	Compounding the returns for consecutive investment periods. See also Arithmetic Link.
GIGO	Garbage in, garbage out.
GIPS	Global Investment Performance Standards.
Government curve	The yields of bonds issued by governments over different maturities.
Growth capital	The purchase of a, usually minority, equity investment in relatively mature companies aimed at expanding or restructuring operations, entering new markets or financing a major acquisition.
Growth Stocks	Stocks with a high Price to Book ratio.
Herstatt Risk	Foreign exchange settlement risk due to time zone disparities, in particular that a counter-party will fail after having settled one side of a foreign exchange transaction but before settling the other side.
HML	High Minus Low, one of the three Fama–French factors.
Home bias	The tendency of investors to hold more of their assets in the home country than can be justified on the basis of economic efficiency.
Hybrids	Instruments combining a bond and a call option, a bond, a call and a put option, or a bond and a forward agreement on an equity. See also Convertible Notes, Converting Bonds, Hybrids.
Implied Volatility	The standard deviation of the movement of the price of an asset that is indicated by the price of an option on that asset.
In Specie	Transferring assets from one investment management firm to another in the form of physical assets such as equities or bonds.
Incidental Risk	Risk that is not intended by the investment manager. See also Intentional Risk.

Index credit default swaps	Exchange-traded derivatives instruments linked to the default on an index of basket of debt instruments.
Inflation linked bonds	Bonds where the principal is linked to a defined index of inflation.
Information Ratio	Return variation from the risk free rate of return divided by return volatility.
Initial Margin	A sum paid on opening a derivative position to provide collateral for adverse price movements in the contract.
Intentional Risk	Active risk, for the investment manager expects to earn active return. See also Incidental Risk.
Interest Cover	The ratio of total earnings (usually EBIT) to interest payable over the same period.
Interest Rate Parity	Theory of exchange rate equilibrium that equates the difference between forward and spot foreign exchange rates with the difference between interest rates with same maturity as the forward settlement.
Interest rate-linked notes and deposits	A type of Exchange Traded Note that invests in commodities and commodity derivatives.
In-the-money	An option with positive intrinsic value.
Intrinsic Value	Asset price less exercise price for a call option. Exercise price less asset price for a put option. Total option price less time value.
Investment Manager	The person within the investment management firm who carries out investment decisions.
Investment risk	The risk of failing to meet investment objectives.
Investment Universe	The set of assets from which portfolios and benchmarks are selected.
Investor	The owner of the money invested.
ISDA	International Swap Dealers' Association.
Jump Risk	The risk of significant, discrete changes in the market value of an asset or portfolio.
Kurtosis	A measure of the fatness of the tails of a distribution.
Lambda	A measure of the increase in return associated with a small increase in risk.
Leverage	The value of a firm's total debt divided by the value of its total equity. See also Gearing.
Leveraged buyouts	The purchase of a firm using debt capital.

LIBOR	London Inter-Bank Offered Rate.
LIBOR curve	The yields payable by banks to other banks over different maturities.
Linear Weighting	Incremental weighting returns where increments are equal. See also Exponential Weighting.
Liquid Assets	Short term low yield instruments.
Liquidity	A description of the volume of transactions in an asset or market. Very liquid indicates many or frequent transactions, illiquid indicates few transactions.
Liquidity spread	Theory of interest rates that says that longer maturities entail greater risks for investors who demand a risk premium to compensate for the fact that at longer durations there is more uncertainty and a greater chance of a rise in inflation or an extreme event that causes the value of the bond to fall.
Long	Net Bought. See also Short.
Long-term Benchmark	Asset mix designed to deliver required return over the life of a fund. Used as a comparison for short term tactical asset allocation.
Low volatility anomaly	The apparent anomaly that low-beta stocks perform better than would be predicted by CAPM.
Manager of Managers	An investment management firm that specializes in investment strategies that engage other investment managers. See also Fund of Funds.
Manager Risk	The risk to an investor that an investment manager fails to meet expected performance criteria.
Margin Trading	The practice of borrowing money to invest whereby the investments form the collateral for the loan.
Market Efficiency	Asset prices that reflect all information available about the asset.
Market Impact	The change in the price of an asset due to the market's reaction to a transaction or the expectation of a transaction.
Market linked investments	A type of Exchange Traded Note that invests in commodities and commodity derivatives.
Market Makers	Individuals or firms designated by stock and derivatives exchanges to provide liquidity in nominated instruments by quoting buy and sell prices.
Market Neutral	An investment strategy whereby the net exposure to the market is zero.

Market segmentation hypothesis	Theory of interest rates that says that financial instruments of different terms are not substitutable.
Market Timing	The practice of timing purchases and sales to exploit very short term fluctuations in asset prices.
Maximum drawdown	The magnitude of the decline from an historical peak to a trough in the value of the fund.
Mean	Average.
Mean Reversion	The tendency of values in series of data to converge to their long term average.
Mean-variance Efficiency	The optimal combination of expected return and risk. Lying on the Efficient Frontier.
Mean-variance Optimization	The technique of using expected returns and covariances to choose portfolio weightings giving the highest portfolio return for a given level of risk; or the lowest risk for a given portfolio expected return. See also Optimization.
Mezzanine capital	Subordinated debt or preferred equity securities that typically are junior to other debt obligations but senior to the company's equity.
Moody's	A credit ratings agency. See also Fitch, Standard & Poor's.
Moving Average	The average share price over a rolling period of a given length, such as the most recent 3, 30 or 900 days.
MSCI	Morgan Stanley Capital International, a provider of international equity indices.
Multiple expansion	A trading profit that results from selling a company for a higher multiple of earnings than was paid at acquisition.
Multi-strategy	A portfolio of portfolios or a fund of funds that invests in a range of asset classes.
Net Margins	The practice of calculating margins for derivatives positions on the basis of overall holdings instead of on individual holdings.
Net Present Value	A procedure designed to adjust the value of future cash flows to reflect their timing. See also Dividend Discounting and Discounted Cash Flow.
Nominal Returns	The increase or decrease in the face value of an asset or portfolio over of an investment period divided by the face value of the asset or portfolio at the start of the investment period. See also Real Returns.

Normal risk	Asset price and factor volatility in normal, stable market conditions. See also Extreme Risk.
Off the Shelf	Products developed commercially. Usually refers to software products.
Open Funds	Open Pooled Funds allow new funds to be invested, and withdrawals at any time. Open Funds do not generally have a termination date.
Open Outcry	System for transacting securities or instruments on an exchange whereby brokers deal face to face with each other.
Open Trade	The starting or initial transaction to buy or sell a derivative contract.
Opportunity Cost	The return foregone.
Optimal Portfolio	The portfolio weightings giving the highest portfolio return for a given level of risk; or the lowest risk for a given portfolio expected return.
Optimization	The technique of using expected returns and covariances to choose portfolio weightings giving the highest portfolio return for a given level of risk; or the lowest risk for a given portfolio expected return. See also Mean-variance Optimization.
Option Delta	The change in the value of an option relative to the change in the market value of the underlying asset or portfolio.
Option Gamma	The ratio of the movement in the delta of an option to a corresponding move in the price of the option. See also Option Volatility, Option Delta.
Option Time Decay	The attrition of the time value of an option as the expiry date approaches. Sometimes referred to as Theta.
Option Volatility	The movement in the price of the option corresponding to a movement in the price of the underlying asset or contract. See also Option Delta, Option Gamma.
Order-driven	An exchange trading system that relies on prices from intending buyers and sellers. See also Quote Driven.
Orthogonal	Correlations equal to zero. Changes in asset prices that are unconnected with each other. See also Statistically Independent.
Out-of-sample	Historical data from a period different from the reference data period.

Out-of-the-money	An option with negative intrinsic value.
Over-the-Counter	Transactions taking place outside recognized stock or futures exchanges. See also Exchange traded.
Par Value	The value against which interest is calculated. See also Face Value.
Parametric	Defined by parameters.
Participation Rate	The ratio, in the context of portfolio protection, of option face value to risky assets in the underlying portfolio.
Passive Investment	An investment strategy which uses no judgement at all, but relies solely on predefined decision rules for all on-going investment decisions.
Path Dependency	The relationship, for an asset or portfolio, between future returns and past returns.
Payout Ratio	The ratio of the dividend paid per share and the earnings per share for the same period.
Performance Analysis	The analysis of compound periods of attribution analysis to identify patterns of strengths and weaknesses in an investment strategy.
Point Value	The local currency value of a one point move in the price of a futures contract.
Pooled	A portfolio with multiple owners. Each investor purchases a share of the portfolio. Each share, or unit, participates in capital gains and losses and income to the portfolio. See also Unitized, Comingled.
Portfolio Optimization	The technique of selecting a portfolio with the highest expected return for a given level of expected risk or the lowest expected risk for a given expected return.
Premium	The price payable for an option.
Price Index	A share price index contract that does not incorporate reinvested dividends. See also Accumulation Index.
Price Momentum	A measure of recent return history of an asset.
Price to Book	The ratio of the market price of the share to its book value (usually the price at which it was issued, adjusted for stock splits and other relevant corporate actions).
Price to Book Ratio	The market price of an asset divided by its book, or accounting value.
Price-weighted Index	Index of share or other asset prices, the composition of which is determined by the market price of component assets. See also Capitalization weighted index.

Prime broker	A provider of multiple services to a hedge fund.
Principal Components	The technique of applying regression analysis to quantify factors relating to historical returns to an asset or portfolio. The factors are identified subsequently by inspection.
Principal Trading	The practice of purchase and sale of securities for the benefit of the person or entity carrying out the trade.
Principle Components Analysis	Statistical analysis that assigns undetermined factors to historical return data to explain as much as possible of the estimated portfolio variance.
Private equity	Investment in unlisted equity assets.
Protection Strategies	Investments which are designed to limit the extent of adverse outcomes in a given investment period.
Pull to Par	Convergence to par or face value of fixed interest security prices as the instrument approaches maturity.
Purchasing Power Parity	Theory of exchange rate equilibrium that equates the real price of goods in different currencies after adjusting from transport costs and taxes.
Pure Alpha	An investment strategy with non-zero relative returns but zero exposure to the market.
Put option	The right, but not the obligation, to sell an asset or futures contract at an agreed price at an agreed time. See also Call Option.
Quote-driven	An exchange trading system that relies on prices quoted by designated market makers. See also Order Driven.
Ratings triggers	A clause in a loan or bond contract that makes the loan due in full if the companies' credit rating is lowered beyond a certain point, usually to a 'speculative' or 'junk bond' rating.
Real assets	Assets that are not bonds.
Real Estate Investment Trust (REIT)	Listed securities that invest in physical property assets, conform to defined regulatory conditions and embed tax concessions to domestic investors.
Real Returns	The increase or decrease in the face value of an asset or portfolio over an investment period, adjusted for inflation, divided by the face value of the asset or portfolio at the start of the investment period. See also Nominal Returns.

Real Time	Continuously. Usually refers to transmission of market information.
Recovery Rate	The percentage of the value of a loan that can be repaid following default or partial default by a borrower.
Reference Price	An asset or commodity price quoted by an independent, official or semi-official source.
Reinvestment Risk	The risk of interest rates changing between bond coupon payments and following the maturity of a bond.
Relative Value	The market or fair value of a security relative to the market or fair value of another security.
Relative value	A hedge fund strategy that, in theory, carries no net exposure to the market in which it invests.
Replicating Options	Options created using a combination of liquid securities and the underlying asset or contract. See also Delta Hedging.
Reserves	A sum of money held as a 'cushion' to allow a fund to meet its liabilities during periods of lower-than-expected investment returns or higher-than-expected liquidity demands on the fund.
Residual Risk	The risk of an asset or portfolio that is not 'explained' by factor analysis or market exposure. The square root of Residual Variance.
Residual Variance	The risk of an asset or portfolio that is not 'explained' by factor analysis or market exposure. The square of Residual Risk.
Return to Equity	A firm's total profits divided by the total value of its equity.
Return Variation	Portfolio returns minus benchmark returns.
Reverse Optimization	The technique of computing the expected returns to individual assets implied by a particular portfolio composition.
Rights	Options-like instruments issued by a company to its existing shareholders, entitling them to subscribe to new shares at below market prices.
Risk Model	A collection of stock betas to risk factors and the factor covariance matrix.
Risk Preference	Appetite for risk, or tolerance of losses.

Risk-adjusted Return	Portfolio return minus the product of the benchmark return and the portfolio beta to benchmark.
Risk-free Asset	Short-term low yield liquid instruments, usually guaranteed by a major bank. See also Risky Assets.
Risky Assets	Assets more risky than short-term low yield liquid instruments. See also Risk-free Assets.
Roll	A special case of a spread trade, where a derivatives position in a near settlement month is exchanged for an identical position in a more distant month.
Roll down	The effect observed in a positively sloped yield curve, where lenders profit from the passage of time since yields decrease as bonds get closer to maturity.
Satellite Portfolio	A high risk portfolio which complements a low risk, 'core' portfolio.
Scenario Analysis	See also Stress Test. Calculations of portfolio returns resulting from different sets of asset returns.
Scrip Lending	See also Stock Lending. Lending share certificates, or access to the entitlements of share certificates by long term investors to other investors for short periods in return for rent paid on the face value of the shares in question.
SDR	Statutory Depository Receipts - an instrument listed on a US exchange, backed by securities listed on a non-US exchange. See also ADR.
Secondary directs	The sale of portfolios of direct investments in operating companies, rather than limited partnership interests in investment funds.
Sector neutral	A hedge fund strategy that carries no net exposure to sectors or industries.
Sensitivity analysis	A measure of the impact on a portfolio of small changes from one period to the next in the values of assets and factors to which it is exposed.
Serial correlation	Correlations between return in consecutive periods.
Settlement Date	The date on which payment is made for and the purchase of an asset or security.
Settlement Price	The price actually paid for an asset or security.
Share Buy-Backs	The practice of a company buying its own shares in the marketplace.

Sharpe Ratio	The difference between the portfolio return and the benchmark return divided by the tracking error. See also Information Ratio.
Shock factor	The variable to be tested as part of a Stress Test.
Short	Net Sold. See also Long.
Short Selling	Selling securities or instruments that are not currently owned.
Short Squeeze	The necessity to repurchase quickly, in an appreciating market, securities that have been sold short.
Short-term Asset Allocation	Asset allocation that exploits the investment manager's insights into near term macro-economic conditions. See also Tactical Asset Allocation.
Simple Interest	Interest payable as for a single period. See also Compound Interest, Compounding, Continuously Compounded Interest.
Simulation	An analysis methodology that works by computing, from given information and a sample of historical returns, a large number of possible outcomes from which aggregate information is derived.
Skew	A measure of the asymmetry of a distribution, defined as the difference between the mean and the median.
SMB	Small Minus Big, one of the three Fama–French factors.
Soft Dollar	A broker 'pays' for a service, such as on-line security prices or security research, to be delivered to an investment manager in return for a pre-defined amount of the investment manager's share purchase and sale business in a given period.
Special purpose entity	A legal entity, separate from its parent firm with its own assets, which issues bonds in its own name.
Spot Foreign Exchange	A foreign exchange transaction that is settled within two days of the transaction date.
Spot Price	The current price for an asset or security.
Spread Trade	A transaction comprising the simultaneous buying and selling of very similar instruments, such as futures which vary only in their settlement month.
Standard & Poor's	A credit ratings agency. See also Fitch and Moody's.

Standard Deviation	The distance from average describing 32 per cent probability. One standard deviation either side of the mean captures 68 per cent of all eventualities. Two standard deviations either side captures 95 per cent.
Statistically Independent	Correlations equal to zero. Changes in asset prices that are unconnected with each other. See also Orthogonal.
Stock Lending	See also Scrip Lending. Lending share certificates, or access to the entitlements of share certificates by long term investors to other investors for short periods in return for rent paid on the face value of the shares in question.
Stock Split	The practice of replacing existing shares with a larger number of new ones. See also Bonus Issue.
Strategic Benchmark	The long term asset allocation designed to ensure that investment returns meet the investors' requirements.
Strategy asset allocation	The long term asset allocation designed to ensure that investment returns meet the investors' requirements.
Stress Test	See also Scenario analysis. Testing the effect of a defined and economic shock to quantify what impact it would have.
Stressed investments	Investment in securities of companies or government entities that are either already in default, under bankruptcy protection, or in distress and heading toward such a condition.
Strike Price	The price at which an option is exercised. See also Exercise Price.
Style	A collective term for Fama–French factors.
Style Managers	Investment managers who manage to a Style index, such as Growth or Value.
Survivorship bias	A bias sometimes found in time series analyses, which stems from the omission of stocks that failed at some time between the start of the data sample and the time of the analysis. It biases results because the errors thus introduced cannot be assumed to average out over large sample sizes.
Swap curve	The yields of bonds issued by corporate borrowers of a given credit quality over different maturities.
Swap Reset	Re-designation of the face value of a swap contract, usually coinciding with periodical settlement of amounts due on the swap.

Synthetic Cash	The economic position resulting from simultaneously buying a physical asset and selling its exact face value in futures, forward contracts or swaps.
Synthetic Options	Options created using a combination of options and the underlying asset or contract.
Synthetic secondaries	The sale of portfolios of direct investments in operating companies, rather than limited partnership interests in investment funds.
Synthetic swap	A swap that is replicated by a suite of bought and sold physical securities and futures.
Systems theory	A theory describing naturally-occurring processes, which are either self-correcting or self-perpetuating.
T Plus Two	Two days after the transaction date.
Tactical Asset Allocation	Short term asset allocation which exploits the investor's insights into near term macro-economic conditions.
Takeover Premium	The amount by which the price paid for a dominant shareholding exceeds the traded price for normal parcels of the same shares.
Technical Analysis	The practice of scrutinizing charts of historical prices to identify visible, repeating patterns in price movements. See also Charting.
Thin Market	A very illiquid market.
Time Value	That part of the option price that is a function of the asset volatility, time to maturity and interest rate. Total option price less intrinsic value.
Time Weighted Cash Flow	Treatment of mid-period cash flows whereby the period is divided into sub-periods to reflect the timing of cash flows.
Time-series analysis	The analysis of past returns.
Top Down Management	Stock picking in the context of overall sector management.
Total Return Index	A share price index contract that incorporates reinvested dividends. See also Price Index, Accumulation Index.
Tracking Error	A measure of the amount by which a portfolio's performance is likely to differ from some known benchmark portfolio. The standard deviation of the sum of differences between portfolio and benchmark returns. Also the square root of the Variance.

Trend Analysis	The analysis of the direction of asset price movements to assist forecasting future prices.
Undertakings for Collective Investment in Transferable Securities (UCITS)	A type of fund subject to European regulation that permits it to marketed to retail investors throughout the EU.
Unintentional Risk	Risk for which no return is expected.
Unitized	A portfolio with multiple owners. Each investor purchases a share of the portfolio. Each share, or unit, participates in capital gains and losses and income to the portfolio. See also Pooled, Comingled.
Unwind	To reverse or close a position that comprises multiple transactions.
Value Stocks	Stocks with a low Price to Book ratio.
Value at Risk (VaR)	A measure of extreme loss that gives the outcome for a given probability.
Variance	A measure of the amount by which a portfolio's performance is likely to differ from some known benchmark portfolio. The sum of differences between portfolio and benchmark returns over a defined period. Also the square of the Standard Deviation.
Variation Margin	A sum paid subsequent to opening a derivative position to cover existing unrealized losses and to provide collateral for adverse price movements in the contract.
Venture capital	An investment in equity that helps finance less mature companies.
Volatility	The standard deviation of returns. The range within which returns are expected to occur 68 per cent of the time.
Volatility of Bonds	The change in settlement value of a bond corresponding to a change in the interest rate of 0.01 per cent. See also Dollar Value of One Point and Bond Volatility.
Volatility trading	A trading strategy designed to benefit from forecast rises and falls in option implied volatility.
Whipsawing	Losses incurred in a zigzagging market.
Wrong way risk	Concentrations of credit exposures that exacerbate counterparty risk.

Yield Curve	The relationship between interest rates and time to maturity for bonds of a given credit quality.
Yield to Maturity	The interest rate implied by the settlement price of a bond.
Zero Coupon Curve	A theoretical yield curve describing pure interest rates for a range of maturities, excluding the effects of coupon payments.

Index

Printed and bound by CPI Group (UK) Ltd, Croydon, CR0 4YY